DOCUMENTARY HISTORY of the STATE of MAINE

CONTAINING THE BAXTER MANUSCRIPTS

VOLUME V

(1692-1729)

EDITED BY
JAMES PHINNEY BAXTER, A.M., LITT. D.

HERITAGE BOOKS
2010

HERITAGE BOOKS
AN IMPRINT OF HERITAGE BOOKS, INC.

Books, CDs, and more—Worldwide

For our listing of thousands of titles see our website
at
www.HeritageBooks.com

A Facsimile Reprint
Published 2010 by
HERITAGE BOOKS, INC.
Publishing Division
100 Railroad Ave. #104
Westminster, Maryland 21157

Originally published
Portland, Maine
1897

— Publisher's Notice —
In reprints such as this, it is often not possible to remove blemishes from the original. We feel the contents of this book warrant its reissue despite these blemishes and hope you will agree and read it with pleasure.

International Standard Book Numbers
Paperbound: 978-0-7884-1556-2
Clothbound: 978-0-7884-8517-6

PREFACE

THE documents in this volume fall within a period of great interest and importance to students of Maine history, and have been selected to largely embrace Indian affairs and questions of ownership of lands, which agitated those who were struggling to establish themselves along the outposts of civilization. This volume closes the present series, and the next will begin a new one.

JAMES PHINNEY BAXTER.

MACKWORTH ISLAND,
July 31, 1907.

CHRONOLOGICAL TABLE OF CONTENTS

			PAGE
1962-3	Feb.	Coll. Ledgels Memor.ll touching trade with the Indians, &c.,	1
1692	Oct.	12 Sir William Phipps to Earl of Nottingham,	2
1692-3	Feb.	21 Sir William Phipps to Earl of Nottingham,	4
1693	Aug.	11 The Submission and Agreements of the Eastern Indians,	7
		French Designs in New England,	12
1697	Dec. 2-12	Letter from John Nelson from Paris relating to the Designs of the French,	13
	Apr.	12 John Nelson's Memorial relating to Nova Scotia,	18
	Apr.	13 Petition of John Nelson,	16
	July	2 Extract of a Memorial from M.r Nelson,	20
	Nov.	2 John Nelson's Memorial relating to the Fishery on the Coast of Nova Scotia &c,	21
1697-8	Jan.	4 Mr. Crowne's Acct of the Engl: Title to Penobscot,	25
1698	Sept.	15 Letter from M. Villebon to Mr. Stoughton,	30
	Oct.	18 Affidavit of John Swasey and Wm. Jeggels,	32
	Oct.	24 Letter from Mr. Stoughton to ye Board,	34
	Nov.	4 Letter from John Nelson relating to the French pretentions to the sole Right of fishing upon the Coast of Accadie,	37
	Nov.	11 Letter from Benjamin Jackson concerning the Claims of the French to St. George's River,	40
1699	Nov.	10 Letter from Wolfgang Will.m Römer,	42
1700	Mar.	27 Letter from Jos. Storer, John Wheelwright & Jonathan Hamond relating to ye Indians,	43
	Apr.	11 Letter from Wolfgang W.m Römer,	45
	Apr.	13 William Rayment's Memorial relateing to the Indians,	52
		Address of Governor & als of New Hampshire,	54
		Petition of Earl of Limerick concerning Pemaquid,	56
	May	10 Answer to Earl of Limerick's Petition concerning Pemaquid,	57
1700	June	13 Capt John Alden's Relation to the Earl of Bellomont,	57
	June	17 Letter from J. Laborie,	59
	June	19 Capt. John Alden's Second Relation to the Earl of Bellomont,	60

CHRONOLOGICAL TABLE

				PAGE
	June	21	Colossians Discovery,	63
	June	22	Letter from Earl of Bellomont to Mr. Sec̞ry Vernon,	65
	July	9	Letter from Earl of Bellomont to Mr. Sec. Vernon,	67
			Letter from Earl of Bellomont,	68
	July	16	Letter from Earl of Bellomont,	71
	Sept.	3	Letter from Isa Addington,	73
	Nov.	20	Mem! from Mr Crown relating to his Title to Penobscot in New England,	74
			Mr. Crown's Petition relating to his Title to Penobscot in America,	82
			The bounds of Nova Scotia and Penobscot, with the lands belonging to it, as they are exprest in Cromwells Patent, and ye deede of partition,	83
	Dec.	20	Letter from Wm. Stoughton,	84
1700-1	Jan.	22	Report on John Crown's Petition,	86
1701	June	3	Memorial of Propositions made with the Eastern Indians,	87
	Aug.	8	Letter from Mr Brouillan, Govr of Accadie,	96
	Aug.	9	A Memorial of the Council & Representatives of the Massachusetts Bay,	98
	Aug.	22	Isaac Addington to Govr of Accadie,	103
1718	Mar.	14	Letter from Mr. Carkesse,	114
1719	Feb.	17	Letter from Samll. Shute to Wm Popple Esq.,	104
			An Answer to the First Query Propos'd by the Rt Honble the Lords of Trade &c referring to the Province of the Massachusetts Bay,	106
	Mar.	14	Letter from Cha Carkesse to Wm. Popple Esq.,	114
	May	26	Letter from Edward Southwell,	116
	June	4	Answer to Several Queries relating to the State of the Province of the Massachusetts Bay,	117
	June	26	Letter from J. Bridger,	119
	July	9	Letter from J. Bridger,	125
	July	17	Letter from J. Bridger to Hon. Wm. Popple,	126
	July	23	Letter from J. Bridger,	128
			Several Affidavits & other Papers relating to the Difference between Mr. Bridger & Mr. Elisha Cooke,	130
1720	Apr.	8	Letter from E. J. Bridger,	134
	Aug.	20	Mr. Blechyden to the Lords Commissioners for Trade and Plantations,	142
	Oct.	11	Letter from J. Dummer to Wm. Popple,	143
1721-22	Feb.	2	Letter from Mr Newman,	145
1722-23	Mar.	23	Letter Col. Thos. Westbrook to Lt. Gov. Dummer,	146
1722	Apr.	10	Letter from Gov. Shute,	148

OF CONTENTS ix

				PAGE
	Apr.	10	Votes of the House of Representatives (at the Session of the General Assembly held at Boston March 15, 1722),	148
	June	27	Elisha Cook Esq. per Order of the Committee on the Petition of John Smith,	149
	July	4	Letter from John Penhallow to Gov. Shute,	150
	July	6	Letter from John Wheelwright to Gov. Shute,	151
	July	8	Journal of the House of Representatives,	152
	Sept.	23	Letter from Thos. Westbrook to Gov. Shute,	153
	Oct.	1	Letter from Zach Trescott to Judge Dudley,	156
	Nov.	16	Letter from Mr. Sharpe to the Lords Commissioners for Trade and Plantations,	157
1723	Dec.	16	Letter Thos. Westbrook to Lt Gov. Dummer,	159
1723-24	Jan.	28	Letter Thos. Westbrook to Lt. Gov. Dummer,	160
1723	Apr.	6	Letter Thos. Westbrook to Lt. Gov. Dummer,	161
	June	25	Memorial & Petition of James Woodside,	163
	May	22	Letter from Mr. Dummer to the Lords Comiss^{rs} for Trade and Plantations,	165
1724	Jan.	6	Defence of Robert Armstrong,	166
	Jan.	19	Letter Lt Gov. Dummer to Mons. Vaudreuil,	175
1724-25	Jan.	25	Letter Capt. Saml Hinckes to Lt Gov. Dummer,	179
1724	Feb.	4	Letter Lt. Gov. Dummer to Lt Kennedy,	180
1724-25	Feb.	8	Letter from Col. T. Westbrook to Lt Gov. Dummer,	181
1724-25	Feb.	16	Letter Col. Westbrook to Lt Gov. Dummer,	182
1724	Mar.	23	Letter Allison Brown to Col. T. Westbrook,	182
	Mar.	24	Letter from Thos. Westbrook,	183
	Mar.	29	Letter Col. T. Westbrook to Lt Gov. Dummer,	183
			Letter Richard Davenport to Col. T. Westbrook,	184
	Apr.	1	Col. T. Westbrook to Lt Gov. Dummer,	184
	Apr.	2	Letter Col. T. Westbrook to Lt Gov. Dummer,	185
	Apr.	6	Letter Col. T. Westbrook to Lt Gov. Dummer,	187
	Apr.	8	Letter Capt. Johnson Harmon to Col. Westbrook,	188
	Apr.	11	Col. T. Westbrook to Lt Gov. Dummer,	188
	Apr.	13	Col. T. Westbrook to Lt Gov. Dummer,	189
	Apr.	16	Col. T. Westbrook to Lt. Gov. Dummer,	190
	Apr.	19	Letter from Nathan Knight,	193
	Apr.	20	Letter Wm. Peperell & others to Col. T. Westbrook,	190
	Apr.	21	Col. T. Westbrook to Lt Gov. Dummer,	191
			Col. T. Westbrook to Lt Gov. Dummer,	192
	Apr.	26	Col. Thos. Westbrook to L. Gov. Dummer,	193
	Apr.	27	Capt. Jos. Heath to Lt Gov. Wm. Dummer,	194
	Apr.	28	Letter Col. Thos. Westbrook to Lt Gov. Dummer,	195
	Apr.	29	Capt. John Penhallow to Lt Gov. Dummer,	196
	May	1	Col. T. Westbrook to Lt Gov. Dummer,	197

CHRONOLOGICAL TABLE

			PAGE
May	6	Jeremiah Moulton to Lt Gov. Dummer,	198
May	16	Col. T. Westbrook to Lt Gov. Dummer,	199
May	18	Capt. John Penhallow to Lt Gov. Dummer,	199
May	20	Col. Thos. Westbrook to Lt Gov. Dummer,	201
May	21	Letter Lt. Gov. Dummer to Col. Thos. Westbrook,	201
June	2	Col. T. Westbrook to Lt Gov. Dummer,	202
		Col. T. Westbrook to Lt Gov. Dummer,	202
June	5	Col. T. Westbrook to Lt Gov. Dummer,	203
June	6	Col. T. Westbrook to Lt Gov. Dummer,	204
June	9	Letter Lt Gov. Dummer to Gov. Saltonstall,	209
June	13	Col. T. Westbrook to Lt Gov. Dummer,	205
June	24	Capt. Jos. Heath & Col. T. Westbrook to Lt Gov. Dummer,	206
June	29	Zach Trescott to Edw. Hutchinson,	207
July	13	John Wainwright to Lt Gov. Dummer,	213
July	16	John Minot to Lt Gov. Dummer,	208
July	19	Samuel Hinckes to Lt Gov. Dummer,	212
		Letter to Capt. Durrell,	214
Aug.	18	Col. T. Westbrook to Lt Gov. Dummer,	215
		Col. T. Westbrook to Lt Gov. Dummer,	216
Sept.	1	Letter Lt. Gov. Dummer to Secretary Willard,	218
Sept.	8	Letter John Gray to Lt Gov. Dummer,	219
		Letter Col. T. Westbrook to Lt Gov. Dummer,	220
Sept.	12	Lt Govr Wentworth to the Lords Commissrs for Trade and Plantations,	221
Sept.	15	Lt Govr Dummer to Mons. Vaudreuil,	223
Sept.	16	Letter John Penhallow to Lt Gov. Dummer,	224
Sept.	18	Letter Lt Gov. Dummer to Colo Wheelwright,	225
		Letter "Lt Gov. Dummer to Col. Westbrook,	225
Sept.	28	Letter from Thos. Westbrook,	226
		Letter to Mass. Agents in London,	227
Oct.	7	Letter Joseph Heath to Lt Gov. Dummer,	229
Oct.	9	Letter Saml Hincks to Lt Gov. Dummer,	231
Oct.	15	Letter James Parker to Lt Gov. Dummer,	230
Nov.	17	Letter Lt Gov. Dummer to Capt Wheelwright,	232
Nov.	21	Letter John Schuyler to Lt Gov. Dummer,	233
Dec.	16	Letter Gov. Wm. Burnet to Lt Gov. Dummer,	234
Dec.	22	Letter Hez. Wyllys Secy of Conn. to Lt Gov. Dummer,	235
Dec.	29	Letter Col. T. Westbrook to Lt Col. Johnson Harmon,	238
1725	Feb. 18	Thomas Sanders to Lt Gov. Dummer,	238
1725-6	Feb. 18	Letter Edmund Mountfort to Lt Gov. Dummer,	239
	Mar. 3	Letter from William Canedy,	240
1725	Mar. 22	Letter from John Schuyler to Hon. Wm. Dummer,	240
	Mar. 26	Letter S. Thaxter & W. Dudley to Lt Gov. Dummer,	241

			PAGE
Mar.	30	Letter John & Hannah Hunt to Lt Gov. Dummer,	243
Apr.	4	Letter Col. Westbrook to Lt Gov. Dummer,	243
Apr.	5	Letter Lt Gov. Dummer to Col. Westbrook,	244
Apr.	14	Letter John Gyles to Col. Westbrook,	245
		Letter Lt Gov. Dummer to Col. T. Westbrook,	246
Apr.	15	Letter John Gyles to Lt Gov. Dummer,	246
Apr.	16	Letter from Thos. Westbrook,	248
Apr.	17	Letter Lt Gov. Dummer to Capt. Bane,	249
Apr.	20	Letter John Minot to Lt Gov. Dummer,	250
		Letter John Gray to Col. T. Westbrook,	255
Apr.	21	Letter from Col. J. Wentworth,	255
Apr.	27	Letter Lt Gov. Dummer to Capt. J. Gyles,	256
		Warrant,	257
		Letter Lt Gov. Dummer to Col. T. Westbrook,	257
Apr.	28	Letter Nathan Knight to John Gray,	259
		Letter Col. T. Westbrook to Lt Gov. Wm. Dummer,	259
Apr.	30	Letter from Arch^d Cuming et als,	260
May	4	Letter Capt. John Gray to Lt Gov. Wm. Dummer,	265
		Letter Col. T. Westbrook to Lt Gov. Wm. Dummer,	266
May	11	Letter Gov. Dummer to Capt. Bourn,	267
		Letter Corp. Benj. Hassell to Lt Gov. Dummer,	268
May	12	Letter Eleazer Tyng to Lt Gov. Dummer,	268
May	13	Letter Lt Gov. Dummer to Col. Wentworth,	270
		Letter Lt Gov. Dummer to Col. Eleazer Tyng,	270
May	14	Letter Eleazer Tyng to Lt Gov. Wm. Dummer,	271
		Letter Lt Gov. Dummer to Col. Eleazer Tyng,	272
May	17	Letter Col. T. Westbrook to Lt Gov. Wm. Dummer,	273
		Letter Col. T. Westbrook to Lt Gov. Dummer,	274
May	18	Letter Lt Gov. Dummer to Capt. Bourn,	275
		Letter Lt Gov. Dummer to Col. Otis,	276
May	19	Letter Col. Eleazar Tyng to Lt Gov. Dummer,	277
May	21	Letter Col. T. Westbrook to Lt Gov. Dummer,	277
May	23	Letter Lt Gov. J. Wentworth to Lt Gov. Dummer,	278
May	24	Letter from Richard Davis,	279
		Letter Lt Gov. to Capt. Cornwall,	280
May	25	Letter Capt Saml Hincks to Lt Gov. Dummer,	281
May	26	Col. Johnson Harmon to Lt Gov. Dummer,	282
May	28	Letter from Lt Gov. J. Wentworth,	283
June		Instructions to Capt. Sanders,	284
June	4	Letter Lt Gov. Wm. Dummer to Col. Johnson Harmon,	285
		Letter Lt Gov. Wm. Dummer to Col. T. Westbrook,	285

CHRONOLGICAL TABLE

			PAGE
June	21	Letter Lt Gov. Wm. Dummer to Lt Gov. J. Wentworth, ...	287
		Instructions to Col^s Noyes & Appleton, .	287
June	22	Letter Col. T. Westbrook to Lt Gov. Wm. Dummer, ...	288
		Letter Col. T. Westbrook to Lt Gov. Dummer,	289
June	23	Letter Col. John Appleton to Lt Gov. Dummer,	290
		A. Cumings Esqre to Mr. Secy. Popple, . .	291
		Letter Lt Gov. Dummer to Col. Johnson Harman,	292
June	24	Letter Col. T. Westbrook to Lt Gov. Dummer,	292
June	25	Letter from Mr. Delafaye, ...	292
June	26	Letter Col. T. Westbrook to Lt Gov. Dummer,	296
		Letter Lt Gov. Wm. Dummer to Col. T. Westbrook, ...	297
June	28	Letter J. Stoddard & J. Wainwright to Lt Gov. Wm. Dummer, ...	298
		Letter John Stoddard & John Wainwright to Lt Gov. Wm. Dummer, ...	298
July	3	Thos. Westbrook to Hon. Wm. Dummer, . .	299
		Col. T. Westbrook to Lt Gov. Wm. Dummer,	300
		Col. T. Westbrook to Lt Gov. Dummer, .	301
July	4	Col. T. Westbrook to L^t Wm. Dummer, . .	302
July	6	Petition of Robert Armstrong, . . .	302
		Affidavit, ...	303
July	7	Col. T. Westbrook to Lt Gov. Wm. Dummer,	304
July	8	Col. T. Westbrook to Lt Gov. Wm. Dummer,	304
July	9	Lt Gov. Wm. Dummer to Gov. J. Wentworth,	305
July	9	Lt Gov. Wm. Dummer to John Stoddard & John Wainwright, ...	305
		Lt Gov. Wm. Dummer to Col. T. Westbrook,	306
		Lt Gov. Wm. Dummer to Col. T. Westbrook,	307
		Lt Gov. Wm. Dummer to Capt Sanders, . .	308
July	10	J. Stoddard, Sha Walton & Jno Wainwright. Comm^{rs} to Wenemonet & other chiefs, .	308
July	12	Capt. Joseph Heath to Lt Gov. Wm. Dummer,	309
		Col. T. Westbrook to Lt Gov. Wm. Dummer,	310
July	14	Josiah Willard to Col. T. Westbrook, . . .	311
July	21	Col. T. Westbrook to Lt Gov. Wm. Dummer,	312
July	23	J. D de St. Castin to Lt Gov. Wm. Dummer,	313
July	26	Capt. S. Wheelwright to Lt Gov. Wm. Dummer,	315
		Capt. S. Wheelwright to Col. T. Westbrook, .	315
July	28	Col. T. Westbrook to Lt Gov. Wm. Dummer,	316
July	31	R. Waldron to Lt Gov. J. Wentworth, . .	317
		Lt Gov. Wm. Dummer to Col. T. Westbrook,	317
Aug.	7	Orders to Capt White & Wyman, . . .	318
		Capt. James Grant to Lt Gov. Wm. Dummer, .	318
Aug.	12	Col. T. Westbrook to Lt Gov. Wm. Dummer,	320
		Col. T. Westbrook to Lt Col. J. Harmon, .	320

OF CONTENT xiii

		PAGE
Aug. 16	Lt Gov. Wm. Dummer to Col. Armstrong,	321
Aug. 18	John Bacon to Lt Gov. Wm. Dummer,	324
	Lt John Pritchard to Lt Gov. Wm. Dummer,	326
Aug. 22	Lt Col. Johnson Harmon to Col. T. Westbrook,	327
Aug. 23	Saml Jordan to Lt Gov. Dummer,	328
Aug. 25	Saml Cranston to Lt Gov. Wm. Dummer,	328
Aug. 27	Dr. Bacon liberty to wait on Lt Gov.,	329
	Orders to Capt. Smith,	329
	Letter Col. T. Westbrook to Lt Gov. Wm. Dummer,	331
Sept. 1	Col. T. Westbrook to Lt Gov. Wm. Dummer,	331
Sept. 2	Capt. Thos. Smith to Lt Gov. Dummer,	332
Sept. 5	Johnson Harmon to Lt Gov. Dummer,	333
	Col. T. Westbrook to Lt Gov. Dummer,	333
Sept. 6	Letter H. Holland & others,	333
Sept. 9	Col. Thos. Westbrook to Lt Gov. Dummer,	334
	Orders to Col. Harmon & Capt Moulton,	335
	Lt Gov. Dummer to Col. Westbrook,	335
Sept. 10	H. Holland & others to Lt Gov. Dummer,	336
	H. Holland & others to Cols Partridge & Stoddard,	337
	Col. T. Westbrook to Lt Gov. Dummer,	337
Sept. 13	Josiah Willard to Henry Hollard & others,	338
Sept. 16	Col. T. Westbrook to Lt Gov. Dummer,	338
Sept. 24	Lt Gov. Dummer to Col. Westbrook,	339
Sept. 25	Ch: Delafaye to the Lords Commissioners,	340
Sept. 29	Col. Wm Pepperrell to Lt Gov. Dummer,	340
Oct. 1	Col. T. Westbrook to Lt Gov. Dummer,	341
Oct. 4	John Minot to Col. Stephen Minot,	342
	Josiah Willard to Col. Westbrook,	347
	Josiah Willard to Capt Thos Smith,	347
	Josiah Willard to Col. Wm Pepperrell,	348
	J. Willard to Capt. Grant & Lt Bragdon,	349
Oct. 7	Col. T. Westbrook to Lt Gov. Wm Dummer,	349
Oct. 14	Saml Willard to Lt Gov. Dummer,	350
	Lt Gov. Dummer to Gov. Armstrong,	351
Nov. 5	Letter from James Stevenson,	352
Nov. 15	Samll Stacy to Lt Gov. Dummer,	352
Dec. 21	Lt Gov. Dummer to Col. T. Westbrook,	353
1726 Jan. 4	Resolve,	354
Jan. 13	Rev. Christopher Toppan to Lt Gov. Dummer,	354
Jan. 28	Col. T. Westbrook to Lt Gov. Dummer,	357
Mar. 25	Lt Gov. Dummer to the Lords of Trade, &c,	368
Oct. 4	Wenungenit to Lt Gov. Dummer,	365
Dec. 15	Capt. Joseph Heath to Lt Gov. Dummer,	366
1726-7 Feb. 27	Capt. John Gyles to Lt Gov. Dummer,	355
Mar. 6	Capt Thos Smith to Lt Gov. Dummer,	357

CHRONOLOGICAL TABLE

			PAGE
	Mar. 14	Lt Gov. Dummer to Wenungennet,	358
		Lt Gov. Dummer to Col^s Stoddard & Partridge,	359
	Mar. 17	Capt. John Gyles to Lt Gov. Dummer,	359
		Capt. Thos Smith to Lt Gov. Dummer,	360
	Mar. 21	Lt Gov. Dummer to Capt. John Giles,	362
	Mar. 22	Col. Saml Partridge to the Commissioners at Albany,	364
1727	Mar. 24	Capt. Jos. Heath to Lt Gov. Dummer,	367
	Mar. 27	Capt. John Gyles to Lt Gov. Dummer,	370
		Ph. Livingston & others Comm^{rs} to Col^s Stoddard & Partridge,	371
	Mar. 31	Wm Woodside to Lt Gov. Dummer,	373
	Apr. 3	Col. Partridge to Lt Gov. Dummer,	374
		Capt Thos Smith to Lt Gov. Dummer,	374
		Capt. John Gyles to Lt Gov. Dummer,	375
	Apr. 8	Capt. John Gyles to Lt Gov. Dummer,	376
		Capt. John Gyles to Lt Gov. Dummer,	379
	Apr. 13	Capt. Joseph Heath to Lt Gov. Dummer,	379
		Secretary Willard to Comm^{rs} for Ind. Affairs,	381
	Apr. 25	Secry^s Letters to Capt Heath & Gyles,	381
		Capt. John Gyles to Lt Gov. Dummer,	383
		Cpt. Gyles Conference,	385
	Apr. 28	Capt. John Giles to Lt Gov. Dummer,	385
	May 4	Memorial of Capt. John Gyles to Lt Gov. Dummer,	387
	May 15	Capt. Thos Smith to Lt Gov. Wm Dummer,	388
	May 15-16	Capt. John Gyles to Lt Gov. Dummer,	389
	May 16	Capt. John Gyles to acquaint Wennogenet,	391
	May 19	John Gyles Enterpet,	391
		James Blaggdon or Braggdon inlisted into service,	392
	May 20	Wm Vaughan to Hon. Wm Dummer Esqr	390
	May 23	Letter L. Gov. Dummer,	393
		Letter L. Gov. Dummer to Col. Wheelwright,	397
	May 26	John Gyles Enter^r,	398
	May 27	John Gyles Enter^r,	398
		L. Gov. Dummer to Capt. John Gyles,	399
	May 29	Wm Dummer to Capt. John Gyles,	392
		L. Gov. Dummer to Capt. Heath & Capt. Gyles,	393
	June 8	Letter Samuel Jordan to Lt Gov. Dummer,	400
	June 12	Letter Chiefs of Norridgewock Woweenock & Arressegontoogook to Lt Gov. Dummer,	400
	June 12	Letter Capt. Joseph Heath to Lt Gov. Dummer,	401
	June 14	Letter Capt. John Gyles to Lieut. Gov. Dummer,	403
	June 17	Letter Lt Gov. Dummer to the Penobscot Sachem,	405
		Letter Lt Gov. Dummer to Capt. John Gyles,	406
		Letter Lt Gov. Dummer to Lieut. Clark,	406
		Letter Lt Gov. Dummer to Indians at Richmond,	407

OF CONTENTS xv

			PAGE
	June	17 Letter Lt Gov. Dummer to Capt. Jordan,	407
	June	22 John Gyles, Enterp^r,	408
	June	26 Capt. John Gyles to Lt Gov. Dummer,	409
		Wenogent to Lt Gov. Dummer,	409
	June	27 Governor's Message,	411
	June	30 Letter from Joseph Heath,	410
	Aug.	7 Letter from John Wentworth,	411
	Aug.	24 Letter from John Wentworth,	415
	Oct.	10 Message from the House,	416
		Message from Lieut. Govr,	417
	Oct.	11 Vote,	417
		Message from the Lt Govr,	418
		Petition of Samuel Jones,	418
	Oct.	14 Message from the Governor,	420
1728		Petition of Domini Jordan et als,	420
		Falmouth Petition relative to Claims of Old Proprietors,	421
		Petition of Heirs &c. of Ancient Proprietors &c. of Falmouth,	423
	Oct.	2 Letter from Mr. Ralph Gulston,	428
	Nov.	2 Capt. John Gyles to Gov. Wm Burnett,	430
	Nov.	18 Letter Saml Wainwright to Gov. Burnett,	430
1729	Mar.	26 Colonel Dummer to David Dunbar,	431
		Grant of land to John Beauchamp & Thos. Leverett,	434
	Sept.	1 Petition of Robert Boyes & David Cargill,	439
	Oct.	9 Colonel Dunbar to the Lords Commissioners,	440
		The Claims of Christopher Toppan,	445
	Nov.	14 John Gyles to Colonel Dunbar,	445
		Chiefs of the Indians of Penobscot to Col. Dunbar,	446
	Nov.	15 Lieut. Gov. Wentworth to the Lords Commissioners,	448
	Nov.	28 Thomas Coram Esqr.,	436
	Dec.	3 Lieutenant Govr Dummer to Colonel Dunbar,	450
	Dec.	4 Colonel Dunbar to Govr Dummer,	451
	Dec.	10 Colonel Dunbar to Mr Secretary Popple,	453
		Colonel Dunbar to the Duke of Newcastle,	458
	Dec.	26 Lieu^t Govr Dummer to the Duke of Newcastle,	468

DOCUMENTARY HISTORY

OF THE

STATE OF MAINE

Coll. Ledgels Memor^{ll}. touching Trade wth. the Indians &c.

The Northern parts of America called New England very much distressed by a warr with ye natives assisted by ye French is greatly added to if not wholy continued by some practises amongst themselves openly done without restraint. The Peltry of y^t Countrey is generally & more espetialy in ye Eastern parts taken by ye Indian natives, & from them purchased by ye English with severall commodities viz Blanketing & linnen for cloathing, corne, kettles, Iron, steel, liquors, powder, lead, shot & gunns &c at very great rates which turns to ye great advantage of ye concerned but is of fatall consequence to ye publick by supplying their enemys with ye necessaryes of their own destruction as may apear by ye vast depredations made on many but most immediately those parts where it hath been so done. In ye year 1688 when ye Indians first broke with ye English ye Government then took such care y^t no person upon what p^{r}tence soever should trade or be concernd with either French or Indian by which means ye Indians were so distressed for want of fire-arms powder & lead y^t they scarcely did subsist & ye Cheifs of them came to make supplication for a Peace in ye moneth of Aprill 1689 a few dayes before ye revolution there hapened

& ye Indians not finding whom they expected to apply to returned in few dayes & continue a warr to this time wch they have been & are enabled to do by ye English themselves. In ye begining of ye year 1689 a Briganteen of which one Hunt was Ma^r brought into Boston much Peltry purchased as above at her going out upon y^t voyage gave out to be bound to Bermudas & so cleard at ye respective offices but disposed ye goods then aboard to ye Indians or French or both who then were in ye greatest want for powder &c with which they were then supplyd in great plenty. Since then many have used ye same trade & continue so to do without any contradiction.

End: *Coll Ledgel's Mem^ll touching trade with the Indians & French in New England.*

Rec^d feb. 1692/3

Sir William Phipps to Earl of Nottingham.

My Lord

my duty obliges mee to Give their Maj^ties and Your Lordship an account of the state of their Maj^ties affaires here, I have in two letters Since my arivall informed your Lordship of what had then occurred and now to avoyd giveing your Lordship the trouble of reading a long letter I have given the particulars of what occurs att present in a letter to Mr Blathwayt which I have intreated may be laid before your Lordship, onely I beg leave once more to represent of how great advantage the Conquest of Canada will bee, not only to their Maj^ties and to the English Nation but alsoe to your Lordship as it may bee mannaged, if his Maj^tie will be pleased to give mee his instructions therein and a Sufficient Supply of Ships and stores of warr among which some Morters and bombs will be necessary & to be ready here to attaque that place in the Spring I doubt not but heaven will give Successe and the people of this Province are inclined to goe with mee and declare if his Maj^tie is pleased for to order it and to appoynt me to Comand in that Expedition there shall bee noe need to presse men. My Lord Your Noble and Generous disposition inclines you to favour all designes that tend to promote Such good effects wch makes multiplicity of arguments needlesse I will onely beg that if this be ordered by their Maj^ties I may by your Lordships Comand have an oppertunity to expresse my forwardnesse in any particular service to your Lordship I have with Six hundred men beaten our french and Indian Enemys and gave the plunder and Captives to the Soldiers wch hath much encouraged them many of the Enemy were killed and but two of our men I have caused a new Fort to be built att Pemaquid and have put the Gonns sent by their Maj^ties into it and have put it into a Condition to secure our easterne parts which much satisfyes their Maj^ties Subjects in this Province it being the first check given to the Enemy for severall yeares past. I have alsoe caused the inhabitants of Port Royall to renew their oath of alegiance to their Maj^ties there are some few persons here that two much Idolize the old Charter and others who envy the favours conferred on mee by their Maj^ties that seeks my prejudice, I beg the favour of your Lordship that I may have liberty to defend my selfe in what relates to their Maj^ties Service if any of my Enemys attempt to lessen their Maj^ties favourable oppinion of mee That their Maj^ties may have a longe and happy

reigne, and your Lordships happinesse may be beyond Expression Encreased is the harty and earnest desire of
Your Lordships most faithfull
humble Servant
William Phips

E:)   *Sr Wm Phipps*
Boston Octob 12. 1692.

Ad:)   To
the Right Honble the Earle of Nottingham
att Whitehall
in England

Sir William Phipps to Earl of Nottingham.

Boston in New England Feb: 21st 169$\frac{2}{3}$
May it Please your Lordship
By the Captain of the Samuell & Henry, I gave ye account, that at my arrivall here, I found the prisons full of people, Comitted upon suspition of witchcraft; and that Complaints were Continually made to me, that many persons were grieveousely tormented, by witches, and that they cryed out vpon severall persons by name, as the Cause of their Torments. The number of those Complaints increasing every day, by advice of the Liev.^t Govern.^r and the Councill, I gave a Commission of Oyer and Terminer to try som of the suspected witches, and at that time the generallity of people, represented the matter to me as Reall witchcraft, and gave very strange instances of the same ; The first in ye Comission was the Liev.^t Governour, and the rest were persons of the best prudence and ffigure that could then be pitched upon, and I depended vpon the Court for a right method of pro-

ceeding in cases of witchcraft; att that time I went to Command the Army at the Eastern part of the Province, for ye ffrench, and Indians, had made an attacque vpon som of the frontier Towns, I continued there some time, but when I returned I found people much dissattisfyed, at ye proceedings of the Court, for about twenty persons, were Condemned, and Executed, of wich number some were thought by many persons to be inocent, the Court still proceeded in the same method of trying them, which was by the Evidence of the afflicted persons, who when they were brought into the Court, as soone as the suspected witches, looked on them, instantly fell to the ground, in strange agonies, and grieveouse torment; but when touched by them vpon the arme, or some other part of their flesh, they imediately revived, and came to themselves, vpon which they made oath that the prison^r at the Barr, did afflict them, and that they saw theire shape or Spectre, com from their bodyes, which put them to such paines, and torments; when Inquired into the matter, I was Informed by the Judges, that they began with this, but had humaine Testimony, against such as were Condemned, and undoubted proof of their being witches; But at length I found that the Devill, did take vpon him the shape of inocent persons, and some were accused, of whose Inocency I was well assured, and many Considerable persons, of vublamable life, and conversations were cryed out vpon as witches, and wizzards: The Deputy Govern^r notwithstanding persisted vigorousely in the same method, to ye great dissatisfaction, and disturbance of the people, vntill I put an end to ye Court, and stopped the proceedings; which I did because I saw many inocent persons, might otherwise perrish, and at that time I thought it my duty to give an account thereof, that their Maj^{ties} pleasure conferming this pplexed affaire might be signifyed, hopeing that for the better ordering thereof, the Judges learned in the Law in England, might give such rules, and directions, as have been practiced in England, for proceeding in soe difficult and nice a point: when I putt an end to ye Court, there was at least fifty persons in prison, in great misery by reason of the extream Cold, and their poverty, most of them haveing onely spectre Evidence, against them, and their mittimus's being defective, I caused some of them to be lett out vpon Baile, and put the Judges vpon Considering of a way to relieve others, and prevent their perishing in prison, vpon which some of them were Convinced, and acknowled that their former proceedings were too violent, and not grounded vpon a right foundation, but that if they might sitt againe they vould proceed after another method; and whereas Mr. Increase Mather, and severall other Divines, did give it as their Judgement, that the Devill might afflict in the shape of an Inocent person, and that the look, and the touch of the suspected persons, was not sufficient proof against them, these things had not the same stress laid vpon them as before; And vpon this Consideration, I pmitted a Speciall superior Court to be held at Salem, in the County of Essex, on the third day of January, the Liev^t Govern^r being Chief Judge, Their method of proceeding being altered, all that were brought to tryall to the number of fifty two were cleared saveing three, and I was informed by the Kings Attorney Gen^ll that some of the Cleared, and the Condemned, were vnder the same Circumstances, or that there was the same reason, to Clear, the three Condemned, as the rest according to his Judgem^t The Deputy Govern^r signed a varrant for their Speedy Execution, and allso of five others, who were Condemned at the former Court of Oyer and Terminer, but Considering how the matter had been managed, I sent a reprieve whereby the Execution was stopped vntill their Maj^ties pleasure were signifyed, and declared; The Liev^t Govern^r vpon this occasion, was enraged and filled with passionate anger, and refused to sitt vpon the Bench at a Superior Court at that time held at Charles towne; and indeed hath from the begining hurryed on these matters with great precipitancy; and by his warrant hath caused the Estates, goods and chatles, of the Executed, to be seized and disposed of, vithout my knowledge, or Consent; the stop put to the first method of proceeding, hath dissipated the black Cloud that threatened this province, with destruction, For whereas this delusion of ye Devill, did spread, and its Dismall effects, touched the lives and Estates, of many of their Maj^{ties} subjects, and the reputation of some of the principall persons here, and indeed vnhapply clogged, and interupted their Maj^{ties} affairs, which hath been a great vexation to me.

I have no new Complaints, but peoples mindes before divided, and distracted, by different opinions, concerning this matter, are now well Composed.

My Lord
I am yor Lordships most faithfull humble servant
William Phips

$E:$) *Feby 21 1693*

To The Right Honble
The Earle of Nottingham
att Whitehall London.

The Submission and Agreements of the Eastern Indians.

Province of the
Massachusetts Bay
in New England

At Fort William Henry in Pemaquid the Eleventh day of Augt In the Fifth Yeare of the Reign of our Soveraign Lord and Lady

William and Mary by the Grace of
God of England Scotland France
and Ireland King and Queen
Defend.^{rs} of the Faith &c^a 1693.

WHEREAS a bloody war has for some yeares now past been made and carried on by the Indians within ye Eastern parts of the s^d Province against their Maj^{ties} Subjects the English through the instigation and Influences of the French. And being sensible of the miseries which we and our People are reduced unto by adhering unto their ill Counsells. Wee whose names are hereto subscribed being Sagamores and Chief Captaines of all the Indians belonging unto the Several Rivers of Penobscot, Kenebeck, Amarascogin and Saco, parts of the s^d Province of the Massachusetts Bay within their s^d Maj^{ties} Soveraignty, having made application unto his Excellency Sr William Phips K^{nt} Cap^n General and Governour in Chief in and over ye s^d Province that the War may be put to an end Doe lay down our Arms and cast our selves upon their said Maj^{ties} Grace and Favour And each of us respectively for our selves, and in the name and with the free consent of all the Indians belonging unto the several Rivers afores^d and of all other Indians within the s^d Province of and from Merrimack River unto the most Easterly bounds of s^d Province hereby acknowledging our hearty subjection and obedience unto the Crown of England Do solemnly covenant, promise and agree to and with the said Sr William Phips and his Successors in the place of Cap^n General and Governo^r in Chief of the afores^d Province or Territory on their s^d Maj^{ties} behalfe in manner following Viz^t

That at all time and times for ever from and after the date of these presents We will cease and forbear all acts of hostility towards the Subjects of the Crown of England, and not offer the least hurt or violence to them or any of them in their persons or Estate, but will henceforward hold and maintain a firm and constant amity and friendship with all the English.

Item We do abandon and forsake the French Interest and will not in any wise adhere to, aid or assist them in their Wars or designes against the English, nor countenance, succor or conceale any of the Enemy Indians of Canada, or other place that shall happen to come to any of our Plantations within y̆ English Territory, but secure them if in our power and deliver them up to the English.

That all English Captives in the hands or power of any of the Indians within the Limits afores^d shall with all possible speed be set at liberty and returned home without any Ransom or Payment to be made or given for them or any of them.

That their Maj^{ties} Subjects the English shall and may peaceably and quietly enter upon improve and for ever enjoy all and singular their Rights of Land and former Settlem^{ts} and Possessions within the Eastern parts of the s^d Province of the Massachusetts Bay without any pretentions or claimes by us or any other Indians, and be in no wayes molested, interrupted or disturbed therein.

That all Trade and Commerce which hereafter may be allowed betwixt the English and Indians shall be under such management and Regulations as may be Stated by an Act of the General Assembly, or as the Governour of s^d Province for the time being with the advice and consent of the Council shall see cause to direct and limit.

If any controversy or difference at any time hereafter happen to arise betwixt any of the English and Indians for any real or supposed wrong or injury done on one side or the other, no private Revenge shall be taken by the Indians for the same, but proper application be made to their Maj^{ties} Government upon the place for remedy thereof in a due course of Justice. We hereby submitting ourselves to be Ruled and Governed by their Maj^ties Laws and desire to have the benefit of the same.

For the more full manifestation of our sincerity and Integrity in all that which we have herein before covenanted and promised. Wee do deliver unto Sr William Phips their Maj^ties Governour afores^d Ahasombamet Brother to Edgeremet Wenongahewet Cousin to Modochawando and Edgeremet and Ragatewawongan alias Sheepscot John to abide and remain in the custody of the English, where the Governour shall direct as Hostages or Pledges for our fidelity and true performance of all and every the aforegoing Articles reserving liberty to exchange them in some reasonable time for a like number, to the acceptance of the Governo^r and Council of s^d Province so as they be persons of as good account and Esteeme amongst the Indians as those which are to be exchanged IN TESTIMONY whereof we have hereunto set our several marks and Seales the day and yeare first above written

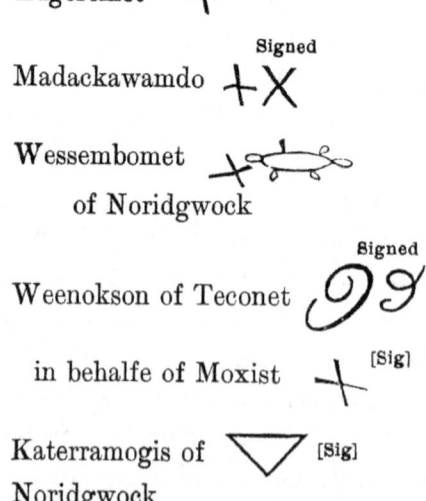

The above written Instrument was deliberately read over and the serveral Articles and Clauses thereof interpreted unto the Indians who said they well understood and consented thereto, and was then signed, Sealed and Delivered in presence of us

OF THE STATE OF MAINE 11

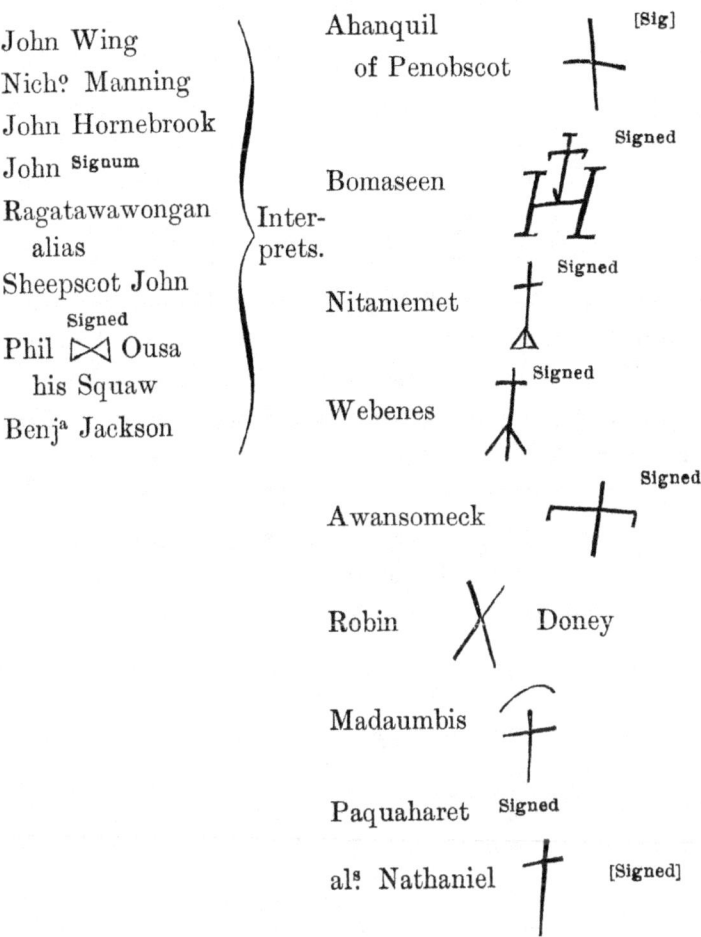

John Wing
Nich? Manning
John Hornebrook
John Signum
Ragatawawongan
  alias
Sheepscot John
  Signed
Phil ⋈ Ousa
  his Squaw
Benj^a Jackson

} Interprets.

Ahanquil
of Penobscot   [Sig]
                   Signed

Bomaseen
                   Signed

Nitamemet
                   Signed

Webenes
                   Signed

Awansomeck
                   Signed

Robin ✕ Doney

Madaumbis

Paquaharet Signed

al^s Nathaniel   [Signed]

A true Copy
E^{xe} by Is^a Addington Secr̃y

E:)   *Articles of Agreement of the Eastern
        Indians in Massachu^{ts} Colony
              Aug. 11. 1693.*

x x x x x x

The generall State of the Province we observe both from your aforesaid Letter, and from the Representation you have made of it in conjunction with the Councill and Assembly together with other Papers that now lye before us; Your proceedings upon the News of the Discovery of the late conspiracy here, appeare to have been suitable to the occasion; Your diligence also in the defence of Piscataqua, and otherways for the Annoyance of the Enemy, upon their taking of Pemaquid is answerable to the Trust reposed in you, Thô the easy surrender of that Fort by those that were in it is not so but on the contrary a reproachfull Action unworthy of English men; And we shall therefore expect a further Account of Your proceedings against the Governor of that Fort, whom you say, you have put under confinement, and as we are however upon this occasion to assure you that his Majesty will always have a particular regard to the security of New England, and the adjacent provinces, so we must needs exhort you in the meane while (and doubt not of your readinesse in it) to continue your utmost care and vigilance in putting things into such order, and giving such timely assistance to Your neighbours as may hinder any new irruptions of the French, and the Northerne Indians into those Provinces, the preservation of which will be your best security.

This we are so much more obliged to presse you in, because the fresh News we have received from Newfoundland gives us also fresh apprehensions of danger threatned to you; Monsieur D'iberville he that commanded the French Forces and Indians the last Summer at Pemaquid has now in like manner taken St John's in Newfoundland, sent away all the English Inhabitants (whereof above 200 are already arrived at Dartmouth) and made himself Master of the whole Countrey; threatning, as those that are arriv'd from thence report, so soon as the Season permits, to fall upon New England. This therefore we say, lays an obligation upon you, to exert an extraordinary vigour in preparing for the defence of that Countrey. Thô his Majesty will certainly be mindfull of it, yet he may well expect that the Inhabitants of that Colony should also Act their part in repairing their Forts, and putting all places that are most exposed (Saccoe particularly) into a condition of making a firm resistance. But more especially we must also needs minde you of the importance of resetling a Fort at Pemaquid, or rather at some convenient place that may be pitched upon thereabouts, a little more remote from the Sea; By which means we conceive, it being freed from the Attacks, which the former Fort was exposed to by Ships, it will the more easily be depended against any Attempts that can be made upon it by Land.

x   x   x   x   x   x

(No Endorsement)

Paris, Decembr $\frac{2}{12}$ 1697.

May it please Your Lordships.

That having sometime before my coming from England to this place laid before Your Honours a certain Memorial relating to the 8th Article in the Treaty of Peace concluded between his Majesty and the French King which as you then did approve of, soe likewise were pleased to lay your Commands for further information of anything that might occur or come to my Knowledge by my being in France, and by my acquaintance and frequenting those here who are more particularly interested in those Countries, wherein I have not been wanting to sound their intentions as far as opportunity has permitted and am thereby ye more confirmed of the necessity of maintaining our Rights and having them especially inserted by Articles conformable to my Memoire as aforesaid. But what I have now further to ad for Your Lordships Information is, That the French will endeavour and accordingly Instructions will be given unto their Commissioners to extend their limitts unto the River of Kenebeck, designing to make that the boundarie between us and them on the Eastern parts of New England, under the plausible pretence that that River being most noted and of the largest extent of any in those parts. Crossing through the Land almost unto the Great River of Canada, they thereby shall be able to withhold their Indians under such a noted boundarie from any future Excursions upon us on the Westerne side, but presuming that it will not be disagreeable unto your Lordships that I give my sentiments herein which I the rather doe to prevent any surprize or mistake which may arise from any their specious pretences. I shall therefore expose before your Honours the nature consequence and value of such a concession wch in time to come may be as fatall and irreparable unto the Interest of the Crown and the prosperity of those Countryes as the late surrender of Nova Scotia (by the Treaty of Breda) has proved, at first I cannot see any further security concerning the Indians but on the Contrary those of that River being now our greatest Enimies will rather be incouraged then otherwise, seing their country delivered up to the French, which those barbarous Nations will rather interprett to be for want of Power to keep, then any voluntary resignation, so that we shall thereby become the object of their scorne and contempt, which will sooner incourage then restrain them in their insolencies and enterprizes upon us.

Whereas if the French will bonafide endeavour to maintain and promote the Publique Peace and tranquility nothing is more easy then to restrain them under the limitts they were formerly bounded in which is the River St George about 5 leagues to the Eastward of Pemaquid and was alwayes the ancient Boundarie in my late Uncle Sr Thomas Temple's Patent further then which they have no manner of pretence or claime, But the consequence to us on the Contraie will be of utmost moment, at first we hereby shall deprive our selves of 4 or 5 of our best fishing Islands and Harbours, Secondly the said River being of much larger extent then Pesquataqua will be a perpetuall supply of Masts, Timber, Deal boards &c when the other will fail many parts of it being almost exhausted by the Continuall Exportation that has been made

3dly the goodness of the land and its convenient situation renders it advantagious to be re established, by which and a prudent management with the Natives which I do not hold it impossible to regain them to their ancient amity with us, for that it will manifestly be their interest soe to doe, by reason of their being amongst us, and that we can and alwayes do supply them cheaper and give better prizes for their peltry then the French, for it was not thrô hatred to us, but by the mismanagement of some amongst us of which the French took advantage to insinuate and influence them to break out into a War as at present; I say that notwithstanding all which they are to be regained, being a people that love and studdy their own interest as much as others &c

As to our Fisheries on the coast of the Cape Sables I find they will obstruct us if they can, and that nothing but a vigorous asserting of our uninterrupted right and Custome (ever since those Countries have been inhabited) will preserve us, But having in my former Memorial, said what is requisite on this and other subjects, I shall not further detain your Lordships, hoping about 3 weeks hence I may be in London, where if in anything I may be Serviceable to the publique interest I shall allwayes be most ready to obey Your Lordships Commands, being Your Lordships

Most humble and most obedient Ser.^t

J.º Nelson.

Endorsed.

Copy of Mr Nelson's Letter from Paris relating to the Designs of the French for extending their Boundaries on the Eastern parts of New England Decemb.^r $\frac{2}{12}$ 1697

To their Excellencies the Lords
Justices of England.

The Petition of John Nelson, Nephew and Executor to Sr Thomas Temple Bar.^{nt} late Governor of Nova Scotia &c

humbly Sheweth.

That the said Sr Thomas Temple long since did purchase from one Monsr Charles de la Tour, tho inheritance of Nova Scotia, and part of the Country called L'Accadie and all the Forts, plantations and trade thereof to him and his heires &c., which said Countries were first discovered and planted by Sr William Alexander, afterwards Earl of Sterling, and others of the Scotish Nation in the time of King James the First, and by the Authority of that Crown the Government and proprietie thereof was granted unto the said Earl and his heires &c. and by him afterwards conveighed unto the aforesaid Mr Charles de la Tour, to hold under the Crown of Scotland, and by him quietly enjoyed untill the then Common Wealth of England, did in the year 1654 possess themselves of it, It being in the hands of a Frenchman, who thereupon Comeing to England, and makeing out his Title from under the said Earl of Sterling, and the Crown of Scotland, his right was allowed and he restored, and thereon conveighed his said right unto Sr Thomas Temple as aforesaid, who enjoyed the same, untill the Treatie of Breda, did build divers Forts for the Defence thereof and made other Improvements, which cost above 16,000£ notwithstanding which upon some false Sugestions of the French Ministers, that it did formerly belong unto the Crown of France, his late Majesty King Charles the Second did without any Examination or Notice given unto the parties concern'd at the aforesaid Treatie, article to restore the same unto France, and by severall Orders of Councill required the delivery thereof unto Mon^{sr} de la Grand Fountaine a person sent by the French King & which was accordingly complyed with That the said Sr Thomas Temple dying did by his last will devise all his right and title of the premises unto your petitioner, who during this present war with France hath hazarded both his person and Estate in the recoverie thereof where through misfortune falling into their hands, has been kept a Prisoner in France for this five years last past, and does yet so continue under Caution &c. and in the mean time the said Country being for the most part regained by the English, the same hath been by surprise included in the Patent of the Government of the Massachusetts Bay in New England & this being the true state of the Case and your Petitioner being informed of a Treatie now on foot between England and France, and fearing that his Majesty for want of information should be surprized in this Affaire, by neglecting or quitting so considerable a part of his Dominion and Trade, as well as the proprietie of your Petitioner & Therefore Your Petitioner humbly prayes that Your Excellencys will be pleased to make a timely representation of this affair unto his Majesty that such due care

and Consideration may be had thereof as to his Majesty in his great Wisdome– shall seem Just and Expedient &c.
And your Petitioner shall ever pray.

Endorsed ——— *N° 6.* ————————
Copy of M.ʳ Nelson's Petition relating to his Title to Nova Scotia as Nephew to S.ʳ Thomas Temple deceased / April the 13.ᵗʰ 1697.———

To the Honourable the Lords Commissioners for Trade &c

Conformable unto your Lordships desires some times since signified unto me, I have here annexed a Breif and Summarie Account of the Originall right and title the Crown of England hath unto the Countries of Nova Scotia, and L'Accadie, which memoire or paper tho' long since delivered in unto M.ʳ Vernon may have need of your Lordships revivall, and perticular instance in this Conjuncture, and for as much that the French doe yet retaine some parts on the North side of the Bay of Fundie, in those Countries it is not improbable, but that they will yet continue their pretentions unto the whole. Where as setting aside, all other our antient and just Titles thereunto, we have a present and actuall right by Conquest made upon them of Port Royall, The Mines and Siganectoe which are in the bottom of the said Bay of Fundie (or the Bay Francois, as the French call it) and so all along the Coast of Cape Sables, unto a place called Merleguash about 60 leagues beyond the said Cape Eastward, which said Countries are very considerable from the fisherie, whereon depends the chiefest of the Trade of New England, New Hampshire &c which if well assured unto us, might in a manner Equall and be of as much advantage as Newfoundland therefore I presume it may be thought worth our Insisting upon, Especially since it hath cost so much charge in the reduction of it by Sr William Phips in the year 1690, and since by the yearly attendance and gard by his Majestys Frigatts given unto the French Inhabitants of those parts, who have all of them, that is to say the Inhabitants of Port Royall the Mines and Siganectoe divers times renewed their Submission and alleadgeances unto the Crown of England, by oaths administred unto them, and by contracts in writing &c one of which being an Originall Signed by the most Notable of the principall Inhabitants of Siganectoe, unto myself in the year 1691. I here produce unto your Lordships, and I am informed that since my restraint in France, the Government of the Massachusetts and the Commanders of his Majestys Ships residing in those Countries have allmost every year received the English pretentions of right by Conquest and have accordingly received the like acknowledgments from the French who remain upon the place. This being all I am able to informe your Lordships, what improvement may be made thereon, is not for me to determine. But am very sure that it is greatly the Interest of the Crown to maintain our right herein, which may the more Evidently appear from the great mischiefs which has befallen us ever since that precipitant and unadvised rendition of the said Countries unto the French by the Treaty of Breda, whereby we have not only lost the greatest and best part of our Fishing Coast, but also it has been the reason of all our differences with the Indians, which has been so fatall, as to lay wast and desolate near 50 leagues of the most flourishing parts in those Countries and will for ever be of the same consequence if his Majesty should forego, or give up unto the Enemy what does belong and is soe necessarie unto us &c

This is all att present what does offer in this affair from your Lordships most humble and most obedient servant

J? Nelson.

Aprill the 12th 1697.

Postscript.

Your Lordships may please further to take notice, that the said Inhabitants of Port Royall &c have accepted as Majestrates such whom the Government of Boston did from time to time place over them, who for their greather ease and Incouragement did allways put in place such of their people as were most agreeable unto them &c

Endorsed.

No. 7.

Copy of M! Nelson's Memorial relating to Nova Scotia and parts adjacent   April the 13th 1697.—

Extract of a Memorial from M! Nelson dated the 2nd July 1697.

You may please to take notice that after the surrender of Accadie unto the French, in the year 1670 by S! Thomas Temple the successive Governours of New Yorke did (by virtue of orders from England as I suppose) make claime unto a part of said Countries, that is to say from Pemtagoet to the River S! Croix as having of it inserted in the Duke of York's Patent. But the French still kept Possession until S! Edmund Andros made an attempt upon it by summoning in one M! S! Costeine to acknowledge his Dependance on the Crown of England upon whose refusal he went with a Friggat to Pemtagoet pillaged his house of what he found in it, but himself escaped on which arose (by the said

Costeins instigation) the Indian War, with which we have ever since been infested.

Endorsed.   —N? 8.—
 Extract of a Memorial from Mr Nelson relating to the Country Westward of the River St Croix annexed to the Government of New Yorke.
July the 2^d 1697.

To the Right Honourable the
Lords Commissioners of the Council
for Trade and Plantations &c.

May it please Your Honours &c

That having some time since received from Mr Secretary Popple your Lordships commands whereby I am required to lay before your Honorable Board what does appear to me in this present Conjuncture of peace with the ffrench to occur and be conducive to his Majestys and this kingdomes interest in the northern parts of America &c. Having from my Experiences in those Countries of Accadie, Nova Scotia, Canada, and New England, made some reflections upon the 8th Article of the Treaty now concluded with the ffrench King, wherein I finde that Commissioners are to be appointed for the settling of Limits or Exchange of Lands, as also to determine all differences that may arrise &c. Now to the intent that those who shall be so appointed on our part, may not be under surprise or mistake or want of information, I make bold to prefer unto your Lordships consideration this following Memoriall &c.

1. That whereas one of the greatest interests of this Nation, both for riches and strength, does consist in the maintenance and incouragement of our Navigation and Maritime imployments great care is to be taken that the ffrench

do not by virtue of the 7th Article (wherein restitution is to be made them of Port Royall and the Coast of Accadie) exclude us from our Fishery on the said Coasts upon the High Seas, which they formerly have endeavoured to do, and on which pretext they have committed divers depredations and surprisalls of our vessels in time of Peace, the original and ground of their pretentions took its rise from what had been acted under the Government of my late Uncle Sr Thomas Temple (before the Surrender of that Country to them in the year 1670) who being at a great charge in the building of Forts and otherwise for protection of our Fishery from the neighbouring ffrench and Indians, did levy and receive from every vessell so ffishing (that is to say making or drying of their Fish on the shoares) the summe of five pounds whereon the ffrench at first contented themselves with the said summes for those that made use of their Coasts not pretending or exacting anything for such as made their voyages on the High Seas, or that wooded or watered in their Harbours &c. But in process of time according to the capriciousness of their Governours, they have often Extended their pretensions unto any and every part of the said High Seas, which tho we never did conceede to them, yet they have often taken and made prize of our vessells so ffishing, untill at length some provision and redress was made by the Treaty of Neutrality concluded on in the yeare of 1686 (as I best remember) between My Lord Chancellor Jeffery and other Commissioners then appointed and the French Ambassador Barillen, referrence thereunto ought to be had for a more perfect information in this affaire, but such is the consequence hereof, that in case no permission or settlement be made in express manner and forme, it will be a perpetual cause of disturbance in those parts and will be the obstruction and hindrance of the imployment of above one thousand fishermen, to the impoverishment of those Colonies, the

Destruction of Trade, and Diminution of His Majestys revenues, herein likewise is to be considered, that whatever by our fishery is taken out of the Seas, is so much ready money or Bullion imported into the Realm, from foreigne Nations, and as we have justice on our side, so have we had an uninterrupted usage and Custom, from the first settlement in those parts untill of late Yeares, and thô fisheries upon the High Seas have sometimes been the dispute of Nations, yet we finde all to claime an equall right of possessing what they can get in that unstable Element if without use of their neighbours shoares &c. Now to cut off and prevent all ground of dispute it will be of the utmost importance and consequence not only to assert and maintain our liberty and right upon the High Seas as aforesaid, but to renue and Establish that mutuall permission of admitting each other unto the Priviledge of refreshing themselves with all Necessaries, as Wood Water &c for their money on the Coastes and in the Harbours of each others Territories &c.

2^d There are other things of deep weight and moment, concerning the Boundaries and Limitations in those vast territories and Trade with the Indians— especially between New York and Canada, wherein the French have and will continually incroach upon us by the advantage they have from the Rivers and Lakes running on the backside of all our Plantations and Colonies, which thô they have no wayes Established, nor have any settlements upon them, yet pretend to appropriate to themselves the sole right of Trafick with the Natives, whereby we shall be confined unto the narrow bounds of our settlements, whereas formerly this Limitation and pretention was unknowne unto us and our people without interruption were free in theire Voyages and Trafick with divers Nations— situate on the Lakes and Rivers aforesaid which priviledge I presume ought to be asserted and continue unto us &c

3ᵈ It will be most necessary that such provision and regulation be made for the mutual peace and safety of each other, in regard of the Indians, that neither party shall abett, incourage or supply the Natives in their Wars, or attempts, which they may at any time undertake to the disturbance of either; but on the contrary upon the complaints of the party so suffering, the other shall consult and agree unto such methods, as may be thought fitting to reduce them unto Peace and quiet, for which intent for more safety and assurance, and to remove all suspicions and jealousies, of secret coniving and underhand dealing, it shall be permitted unto the Governours of either party for their own satisfaction as they may think fitting, or the occasion may require, to send or cause to reside with each other such person or persons as they shall see meet, whereby not only to consult and advise what is to be done for prevention of such mischiefs, but likewise to be Eye witnesses of the faithfulness of each others intentions and proceedings, and for Detection and bringing to due punishment all such particular persons, who for their private advantage, shall at any time infringe the Regulations that may be concluded on this subject &c.

The three foregoing heads as I humbly conceive them to be of utmost importance both for His Majestys interest and honour, the peace and prosperity of his subjects; soe doubt not but that your Lordships after due reflection will see cause to make such Reports hereon unto his Majesty or those appointed by him for the settlement of the Plantation affaires that effectuall care may be taken for the securing and establishing the tranquillity of those parts and the Trade and Interest of the Nations &c.

This being what I have to offer I hope that Your Lordships will favourably overlook the defects you may finde herein, and which is the rather to be excused since it proceeds from the earnest desire I have of contributing what I can unto the

publique good, as also in obedience unto your Lordships commands, being with all possible respect your Lordships most humble
     and most obedient servant
       J° Nelson.

Endorsed— No. 9. Copy of Mr Nelson's Memorial relating to the Fishery on the Coast of Nova Scotia and other things proper to be had in consideration in treating with the French Commissioners pursuant to the Treaty of Reiswisck.
Novemb.^r the 2nd 1697.

A Memorial concerning the English title to Penobscot, and other lands adjacent, to be presented to ye right hon^{ble}, the Lords Commissioners, of the Councill of trade, and plantations. /

King James the first by his Letters Patents, under the great seale of Scotland, bearing date the 10th of September 1621, granted to Sr William Alexander Lord of Menstrue, and to his heires for ever, all those lands lying in America, called Nova Scotia. The said Sr William Alexander, by his deed, bearing date the 30th of Aprill 1630, made over all his right, and title, in the aforesaid lands, to Sr Claud de St Estienne, Lord of La Tour, and of Vuarre; and to his son, Sr Charles de St Estienne, Lord of St Deniscourt, and to their heires for ever. The said Sr Claud and Sr Charles de St Estienne, were french protestants, who for the liberty of their religion had many yeares before left France; and for their good services done, in promoting the said Plantation, they were both created Baronets of Nova Scotia.

About the yeare 1631, King Charles the first consented to

give up the Aforesaid country of Nova Scotia to France; for what reason is not knowne, the French having not ye least pretence of any kind to it. For it was both discovered and planted, by the English, and subjects of England and named Nova Scotia by King James the first.

Before the delivery of the said country, King Charles the first articled wth the French, that the said Sir Claud and Sr Charles de St Estienne, should enjoy their rights, in the said Nova Scotia, his Majesty thinking himselfe, bound in honor to take care of 'em: as appeares by an originall letter, from the said Sr William Alexander, to the said Sr Claud de St Estienne.

By vertue of this Article, the said Sr Claud and Sr Charles de St Estienne, did enjoy their lands in Nova Scotia; though wth much molestation from the French Governors Sr Claud dying, Sr Charles became proprietor of all Nova Scotia.

Many yeares before this, some inhabitants of Plimouth, in New England, discovered Penobscot and began to seale themselves there a place many leagues westward of Nova Scotia. But being much distourbed, by ye French Governours of Nova Scotia, they began to neglect ye plantation; and when the said Charles de St Estienne was proprietor of all Nova Scotia, he built a fort at Penobscot, and tooke all the lands, extending from Penobscot to Musconcus bordering on Pemaquid.

About ye yeare 1654, Cromwell having a Fleete at New England, under the command of one Major Sedgewicke, he ordered 'em to saile to Nova Scotia, and require the French Governor to deliver it; it being antiently a part of the English dominion, to which the French had no just title. Major Sedgewicke saild thether, and found the said Sr Charles de St Estienne, in possession both of Nova Scotia, and Penobscot; both which, together with all the lands belonging to 'em, the said Sr Charles de St Estienne quietly resigned.

For having suffer'd great oppression under ye French Governours, he desir'd to live under the English protection.

Not long after, he came over to England, and petition'd Cromwell, that he might enjoy his lands, which was granted. Then the said Charles de St Estienne, by his deed, bearing date the 20th of September 1656, made over all his right, and title, in all the afore said lands, both Nova Scotia and Penobscot, to Thomas Temple, and William Crowne, Esquiers, and their Heires for ever; for the summe of three thousand three hundred and odde pounds. The said Charles also reserved to himselfe, and his heires for ever, considerable Annuall profitts from the aforesaid lands.

Then all the three aforesaid proprietors, went over to take possession of their lands; Thomas Temple going Governor by Cromwells commission. Not long after their arrivall, the said Thomas Temple, and William Crowne divided their lands.

And William Crowne by a deed under his hand and seale, made over to ye said Thomas Temple and his heires for ever, all Nova Scotia, as it is limited, in the said deed and the said Thomas Temple, by his deed, bearing date ye twelfe of September 1657, made over to ye said William Crowne, and his heires for ever, all his right and title in Penobscot, and in all the lands and Islands, lying without ye bounds of Nova Scotia; from the river Machias in ye East, to the said Masconcus bordering on Pemaquid. They also signed, and sealed interchangeably bonds of twenty thousand, to bind each other to performance of Articles.

For sometime the said William Crowne possessed Penobscot, and his other lands quietly. He also built a trading house, far up ye river of Penobscot, at a place called Negue; to which he gave his owne name, and called it Crowne's point.

But the said Thomas Temple, hearing there was a great

beavor trade at Negue pretended the said William Crowne, had broke some article or another, and by violence tooke from him, his fort at Penobscot, his trading house at Negue, and all his lands. And the courts of justice in New England were so partiall to the said Thomas Temple, that William Crowne cou'd have no justice from them.

Thus it continued, till the restauration of King Charles the second. Then the said Thomas Temple and William Crowne, came over, and proving their titles to the aforesaid lands, before the King, and the Lords, and others, of his Majestyes Privy Council, they were adjudged to be right full proprietors, and were permitted to returne, and repossesse their lands. Then the said William Crowne, threatning to complaine to his Majesty, and the Privy Council, of the heavy wrongs he had suffer'd; The said Thomas Temple desir'd him to forbeare promising him, not only the restitution of his lands, but any reasonable satisfaction. And the said William Crowne being desirous to returne to New England The said Thomas Temple gave him letters, to his Agents in New England, requiring 'em to restore to him his fort of Penobscot, & all his lands. But when the said William Crowne arrived in New England, he found contradictory letters, written from the said Thomas Temple, to his Agents; strictly charging them to keepe him out.

The said Thomas Temple, was created a Baronet of Nova Scotia by King Charles the second and got a commission from his Majesty to be Governour of Nova Scotia and Penobscot; upon his arrivall in New England, the said William Crowne complained to him, of his unjust and shamefull proceedings, which Sr Thomas cou'd not vindicate; and to end differences, he prevaild wth ye said William Crowne, to grant him a short lease of Penobscot; and the rest of his lands; and severall New England merchants were bound for payment of rent.

But the said Sr Thomas Temple kept the lands, and never payd any rent. Nor wou'd the courts of New England intermedle wth the case, for they said, it was a debate about lands, that lay out of their Jurisdiction.

Thus it continued till ye yeare 1668, when at ye treaty at Bredah, ye French prevailed wth King Charles to surrender up Nova Scotia. And accordingly, a commission was sent under the great seale of England to Sr Thomas Temple, empowring, and requiring him to deliver it.

Sr Thomas Temple knew very well that Penobscot, and the aforesaid lands belonging to it, were no part of Nova Scotia but they being the said William Crownes estate, he out of envy and hatred to William Crowne, and to impoverish, and totally disable him, from taking his advantages at law against him, when he was out of his Governement, for all the notorious wrongs he had done him, whilst he was in it; the said Sir Thomas Temple, presum'd to go beyond his commission, and deliver up Penobscot to the French.

When King Charles was inform'd of what Sr Thomas Temple had done, he was extremely displeas'd with it; and wou'd not consent to it,— Not long after a war broke out betweene France and Holland. And the Dutch tooke the fort at Penobscot from ye French, levell'd it wth ye ground, and then entirely quitted it.

Not long after, King Charles, commission'd the Governour of New Yorke, to take Penobscot, and the lands belonging to it, under his jurisdiction. And the Governor of New Yorke, did accordingly and put a garrison in ye said trading house at Negue, alias Crownes point. William Crowne being deceased, his eldest son John Crowne, having information, that his Royall Highnes ye Duke of Yorke, had begg'd Penobscot of ye King, the said John Crowne petition'd his Highnes to restore him ye inheritance, which his Father had purchas'd; and his Highnes referrd him to ye Commissioners of his revenew. And the cause lay before 'em undetermin'd, during ye latter end of King Charles's reigne, and all ye reigne of ye late King James.

By what has beene said, it is apparent the French have no pretence to Penobscot, for the English first discovered it; the English, and subjects of England possest it almost forty yeares. The French had it in King Charles's reign for a short while, and got it, not by vertue of any treaty, but beyond their expectation, it was put into their hands by the treachery of Sr Thomas Temple ye Governor.

And they lost it in a short time to ye Dutch, and the Dutch quitting, both the last Kings quietly possessd it, to ye end of their reignes.

End :)   *New England*
M^r. Crowne's Acc^t. of the Engl:
Title to Penobscot.

Recd. the 4th Jan^ry }
Read   }   *1697/98*

M. Villebon to M. Stoughton
Translation.

Sir,

I write to you by Mr David Bassett whom I have detained here ever since the last Year, and whom His Majesty is pleased to pardon for whatever he has done against his Interest upon condition of his settling in this country, as he has engaged to do; So that I am confident you will be willing (as I should be in the like occasion) to suffer him to return, and let him to make an end of his Affairs without any wrong or hindrance.

I am much surpris'd, after what I writt to you about those Indians of Ours that are in prison, that you have return'd no answer to what I desird of you, and that you persist in keeping them. I will say nothing more to you of it, referring you to what I writt in my last of 27th June 1698.

I am informed that you have many that Fish upon our Coasts, and that you suffer your People to trade in the French Habitations. You must expect, Sir, that I will seize on whatsoever English shall be found fishing or trading, the rather for that you cannot but know that it is absolutely forbidden by the Treaty betwixt the two Crowns, which you yourself sent me; And that M^r De Bonaventure Commander of the Kings ship L'Envieux confirm'd it to you, sending back at his arrival on these Coasts some of your Fishing Vessels which he had taken, & giving you to understand by the King's Order that if any more came either to Fish or Trade they should be made Prize of.

I am Order'd by the King my Master to conform my selfe to the Treaty of Neutrality concluded at London the 16th of Nov^{br} 1686 with King James as to the Affairs of America.

I have also express Orders from his Majesty to maintain the Bounds between New England and Us, which are from the head of the River of Kennebeck to the Mouth of it, leaving the Channel free to both Nations. Therefore I make no question, Sir, but you will act accordingly and give over pretending to treat the Indians that are settled there as your Subjects, thereby to prevent all those unhappy consequences which may happen by reason of their neighborhood to you. I have not else, but to assure you that I will do all that lyes

in my power towards the execution of the Orders which I
have received from his Majesty.
   I am with all sincerity, Sir,
     Your most humble servant
       Le Chevalier de Villebon
From the mouth of St John's River
  Septemb.^{r} the 15th 1698.

End:)   *New England.*

*L̃re from ye French Govr of Nova Scotia to Mr Stoughton
relating to their pretentions to ye fishing &c in those parts.
Referred to in Mr Stoughton's L̃re of ye 24th Octr 1698.
Rec.^{d} Decr 19th 1698.*

The Testimony of John Swasey Master of the Sloop
Dolphin and William Jeggels master of the Sloop
Sparrow, of full age testifieth and Saith.
That on or about the Twenty second day of September last,
as we were on the Coast of Cape Sables, bound homeward,
We were forced by stormy weather to go into Chebucta, and
as we were going in we saw a ship in the said Harbour upon
which we tack'd and stood off and presently we saw a Boat
come off from said ship and came to us with about twenty
Men, many of them had Armes and came and boarded our
Vessels, and commanded us to go into the Harbour, which
we did, and we were carried on board the Man of War, and
the Captain by his Interpreter examined us what our business
was there, We told him we were poor Fishermen that fished
on the Banks, They ask'd how we dare to be so bold as to
come on their Coast a fishing it being their Land and Coast
and Banks were their priviledge, and in some short time we

were sent aboard our Sloops and brought in under the Ships Stern, and they took away our Sails and carried them on board the Ships, and kept us there till the twenty fourth day of said September, and then the Captain sent for us aboard and he told us that he had given warning by David Hilliard that the English were not to fish there, and that he had power to take us for our fishing there, it being our priviledge, and he said that he would dismiss us for this time, but said he would take all he could and had power so to do, for they did forfeit their vessels by fishing there.

The Ship was about foure or five hundred Tuns and had about Twenty Guns mounted, The Interpreters name was Perot who as he told us, had formerly lived with Mr John Nelson of Boston.

John Swasey

Salem 18th October 1698.   William Jeggels.

John Swasey and William Jeggels of Salem personally appeared before us the Subscribers two of his Majestys Justices of the Peace for the County of Essex in his Majestys Province of the Massachusetts Bay in New England, and made Oath to the Truth of the above written Testimony at Salem

this 24th October 1698

Copy   Benj^a Browne

Examined   p   Is^a Addington   John Higginson

                                    Secr̃y

Endorsed. No. 4. Copy of the Affidavit of John Swasey and W^m. Jeggels relating to the Pretentions of the French to the sole Right of Fishing on the Coast of Nova Scotia.

Octob^r the 24th 1698.

Letter from Mr Stoughton Lt Govr of the Mass: Bay to ye Board

R.^t Honble

In mine of the 25th of July past directed unto Sr Henry Ashhurst and Mr Phips, Agents for this his Ma.^{tys} Province, I advised them of the Information I then had of the pretensions made by the French unto the Fishing ground or Banks lying in the high Seas off & about the Coast of Accadie or Nova Scotia, and that Eastern Country, which have all along, even from the discovery and first Settlement of this Countrey, been used and improved for Fishing as the just right and priviledge of his Ma.^{tys} Subjects until this time, when a Captain of a French Ship of War, meeting with some of our Fishermen ab.^t their Imployment near that Coast, signified unto them that he had orders from the French King to guard that Coast, and to seize & make prize of all English Vessels that he should find fishing in those Seas. And our s.^d Agents were instructed to make your Lordp.^s acquainted therewith, and humbly to move that due care might be taken to secure unto his Ma.^{tys} Subjects the benefit of the Fishery as heretofore, and to prevent any thing that might in the least infringe or deprive them of that liberty & advantage wherein I presume they have applied themselves unto yor L.^d ships accordingly.

Since which I have received some further Information about that matter, and the peremptory challenge of the French unto the Sole right of Fishing on those Grounds, As also to extend the bounds of their Dominion through the Main Land, as far as the River of Kennebeck, and from the head thereof unto the mouth of the same as by a Letter of the 5th of September past from Mr Villebon Governor for the French King in L'Accadie or Nova Scotia, on behalfe of his Master directed unto my selfe, which original Letter with the other Information is here inclosed.

It's advised by the Council, as necessary for the Kings Service, that this matter, of so great import unto his Maj^tys^ Interests, be forthwith laid before your Lord^ps^ that it may be reported unto his Ma^ty^ Apprehending there may be a proper Season for asserting and establishing of the ancient Boundaries of these Countreys, and the ancient usage, right and priviledge of his Ma^tys^ Subjects for fishing in these Seas, At the meeting of ye Comission^rs^ to be appointed on both sides, conforme to the 8th Article of the Treaty of peace for examining and determining the rights and pretensions of either of the Crowns to the places situated in Hudson Bay.

Mr John Nelson a Gent^m^ well knowing and experienced in the State of the Country of Accadie or Nova Scotia, and all circumstances attending the overtures and changes that have hapned there of long time past, and of the utmost bounds Westward ever pretended unto by the French, has acquainted the Governm^t^ here with some memorials, which, in obedience to your Lordp^s^ Commands, he has lately laid before your Lordp^s^ relating unto his Ma^tys^ Interests in these Northern parts of America and particularly representing and setting forth the utmost bounds of the Countrey of Accadie or Nova Scotia to the Westward ever pretended unto by the French, extending no farther than the Eastern side of the River of St Georges, and that only by virtue of the Treaty of Breda before which all that Countrey was intirely in the possession of the English and also setting forth the free and ancient usage, right and priviledge of his Ma^tys^ Subjects of fishing on that Coast: Copys of which Memorials are herewith inclosed; whereto I humbly pray your Lord^ps^ to be referred, particularly that Dated from Paris January 26th 1698, wherein is humbly insinuated the fatal and irreparable hurt and damage unto the Interest of the Crown & the prosperity of his Ma^tys^ Territories in these parts that will be consequent of making any concession to the French in their unjust & unreasonable pretentions now made. And the Argum^ts therein offered against any concession thereto (which to repeat would be to give your Lord^ps a needless trouble) seem to be very demonstrative and of great weight; Besides what might be added, that if so large a part of this Province, as is now claimed by the s^d Pretensions of the French, should come into their possession, many of his Ma^tys Subjects would be excluded from their ancient rights and Settlements acquired as well by Grants and Confirmation derived from ye Crown of England, as by purchase from the Natives, and having by their hard labour and great cost and charge, cleared and improved that part of the Countrey, and planted several Towns therein And there are so many large, comodious and safe harbours on that shore, that, upon any eruption with France, and War hapning betwixt the two Crowns, the French would have such advantage by them, as greatly to annoy, if not wholy ruine, the navigation of this countrey; It would also utterly deprive his Ma^tys Subjects of a chief part of their Fishery, whereon they have so great dependance.

Our Agents are Instructed to wait upon your Lord^ps about this important affair.

His Ex^cy the Earle of Bellomont still remaining at New Yorke (his Ma^tys Service there not dispenseing with his Lord^ps yet leaving of that Province) is made acquainted with this application unto your Lord^ps upon this Subject of so great consequence, and is humbly requested to Second and enforce the same by fresh application from his Lord^p which time would not allow of by this Conveyance by reason of the distance, but I hope will be forwarded by ye next. I pray your Lord^ps that such early and effectual care and provision may be had and taken in this important and momentous affair, as to prevent the evil and fatal consequences attending the groundless and unreasonable pretensions of the French as afores.^d And that the ancient known Boundaries of these his Ma^{tys} Territories, & rights and priviledges of his Subjects as afores.^d may be asserted and established that so they may reasonably hope to enjoy peace and quiet, which is not probable, whilst the French in so neare a neighbourhood persist in their unjust pretexts before mentioned.

Having nothing further at present of moment for his Ma^{tys} Service to observe unto your Lord.^{ps} With my hearty wishes for your Lord.^{ps} happiness, I am with all possible respect

R.^t Honble   Your Lord.^{ps}
Boston in N: England   Most humble faithful Servant
October 24th 1698.

W^m. Houghton

Lords Comiss^{rs} of the Council
for Trade and Plantations./

Boston New England
Novr 4th 1698

May it please Your Lordships.

While I was in England and also in France I then in obedience unto your Commands did prefer unto your hon^{ble} Board divers Memoires relating unto the French in those parts. It is to be hoped (that if the Commissioners on both sides have entred into Treaty, as is stipulated in the 7th and 8th Articles of the Peace concluded at Riswick that due reflections and improvements have been made of the said Memorials, so that his Majesties Colonies and Subjects in these parts may be protected from the Innovations and violences with which they are not only menaced, but have actually been put in Execution by the French upon them, under pretence of the late Treaty of Neutrality made in London in the year 1686, between the late Lord Chancellor Jefferies and the Ambassador Barrillon; Whereby the Fishing on each others Coasts seems to be debarr'd, but under collour of which they are now endeavouring to extend their pretentions something like as they have formerly done in Flanders, where their claime unto dependances did exceed the very concessions made unto them so here much of the same nature, under the Title of their Coasts, they now Endeavour to exclude us from the priviledge of Fishing upon the High Seas, Whereas according unto all Civillians who have wrote of this matter, they do determine that fishing on a neighbours Coast is naturally to be understood, when it is within the Rivers, Harbours, Bays Inletts or Creeks, or that use be made of the shoares &c^a. but that the bankes upon the high Seas are and allwayes have been the univ'ersall right and consequently free to all nations. The drift and design of the French by these pretensions is very obvious, as the increase of their Navigation both in Ships and Seamen Trade and Riches, so on the contrarie in the same proportion our decrease herein is our weakening in all these. I doubt not but whenever any calculation shall be made it will be found that more Men are Imployed more Riches Money and Bullion imported into Our Nation by this Trade then by any other produce or Commerce that the Nation does afford, so that from these reasons doubtless but that your Lordship^s will see cause soe to represent the Matter to the King and Councill as may put some reasonable limitt unto the French pretensions and secure his subjects in so antient and Uninterruped a right and priviledges, I humbly Conceive that the matter, cannot admitt much dispute, since that they themselves do dayly and of necessity take most of their Fish that supplies France on our Coasts of England, so that the distance, observed there by them, may serve here for a very good direction and Example for their Coasts of Nova Scotia also Accaddie as they now call them, Your Lordships having formerly admitted both my discourse and writing to you on this subject, what is now with so much importunity represented unto your honours by the Lieutenant Governour and Councill of this Province. I the rather presume to second, for that having lately, made a voyage unto those parts, and by reason of my affaires, being conversant with them, am fully convinced that unless some vigorous and resolute measures be taken in this matter not only the welfare of these Countries but the Interest and Trade of the whole Nation will in a short time come to nothing in these parts.

Upon Your Lordships perusal of my Memorialls formerly given, you will readily perceive that at the time of my Informations on this and other things, they were something more then conjecturall, so that my apprehensions now being Joyned with the Generall Consternations of this Countrey, and wherein his Majesties honour and Interest has so great a part I trust may have weight enough to induce your Lordships strenous and Effectual working in our behalfs. The liberty I have taken in representing this and other matters before your honours I hope will be favourably interpretted as an effect of my zeal for the Publick good, and in observance of your Commands &c. being as I am in all humble Duty.

Your Lordships most humble and
most obedient Servant
Jo.^h Nelson.

Endorsed. —*N°. 11.*—

Copy of Mr Nelson's Letter from Boston in New England relating to the French pretentions to the sole Right of Fishing upon the Coast of Accadie.

Novemb^r the 4th. 1698.

May it please your Lordships

This is to acquaint your Lordships, that Monsr Vilbone The French Governour of St John's, Bordering upon this Province Eastward, has lately by his Letters to this Government, Laid Claime to all that Tract of Land, lyeing between the Rivers of Kenebeck, and St Georges, pretending it belongs to the French Government, And has alsoe Forbid the English Fishery, upon that Coast. Threatning to make Prize, of such as Fish there for the Future.

As this Claime is unjust, being an Incroachment upon the English Dominions, soe it is likewise very Prejudiciall to the Interest of his Majestie, and the English Nation, for that Tract of Land (as I am informed by many persons that have lived there formerly before the Destruction of the English Settlements by the Indians) Abounds with Masts, and Excellent Timber, For building his Maj^{ties} Ships of War, and is accounted the best part of all this countrey, for the Plentifull Production of all sorts of Navall Stores. And if the French get the same into their Hands, it will not onely Defeat his Maj^{ties} designe, of being Supply'd from thence with Navall Stores, and Destroy the Rights & Propertyes of his Subjects to their Lands, and Fishery there, but will be a vast advantage to the French, & make way for their further Incroachments.

The bounds of the French Government, before the Treaty at Breda, reach't noe Further (as we are here informed) Then the River of St Croix, But because Sr Thomas Temple, Pattent for Nova Scotia, Extended as far West as St Georges River, the French obtained a Surrender of all that Pattent to them, by the Treaty at Breda, which was more by Ten Leagues on the Sea Coast, then what belonged to them. And now they claime to Kenebeck River, which is yet Ten Leagues Further West, It is not knowne upon what pretence they make this Claime, Unlesse upon Acco.^t of the Indians, who Inhabit there, and have Joyned with them in the War, whom they call their Masters Subjects. And some designe they have formed among themselves, to supply the French King with Masts, and Navall Stores, from thence.

Being Employed as one of the four persons sent hither by his Maj^{tie} to inspect and send from hence Navall Stores, for The Use of his Maj^{ties} Royall Navy, I thought my selfe bound in duty to his Maj^{tie}, to give your Lordships an Acco^t, of this matter. That the Claime of the French may be Opposed, by the Commissioners of his Maj^{tie}, when they meet those of the French King, to settle the Bounds, according to the Article of Peace, which I am informed is to be this Winter. Most Humbly Praying that this may find acceptance with your Lordships, I beg leave to Subscribe my Selfe

My Lords

Boston in New England Your Lordships
 November 11th 1698./ Most Faithfull Obedient
            Humble Servant
            Benjamin Jackson

End:) For His Maj^{ties} Service
 To The R^t. Honble the Lords of the Councill
  of Trade at Whitehall./

<u>New England.</u>

L̃re from M^r. Jackson Com^r. for inspection of Naval Stores concerning the Claim of the French to S^t. George's River dated 11th Nov. 1698.
 Rec^d. Decr. 19th. 1698. Read the 23th Decr. 1698.

Considerations upon the Iconographical Draught and Profiel of Pemaquid and Piscataqua (both to be new) Forts, marked A & B.

I am of opinion That Pemaquid new Fort (marked in the Draught with black prickt Lines) ought in part to be made and erected, as it is represented in the Draught A & B afores.^d

First I premise that instead of filling all the Wall Walkes & Breast workes (excepting 4 feet in the Breast worke above the Stone wall which should be of good Earth) they ought to be vaulted, which will render it an ever lasting work and afford to the Souldiers Lodgeings &c must be built by themselves, wch will augment the cost & entail a charge of continual repair –

Secondly, Piscataqua New Fort (represented in the Draught with red prickt Lines) ought to be built almost in conformity to the above mentioned Profiel of Pemaquid, only that it be considered (That as the Great Island on the Superficies near & about the Fort is altogether very rocky and no earth to be got near it) 'tis necessary that the Wall Walks be singly vaulted in as much as the charge of bringing Earth to fill it would much exceed that of the other.

Thirdly, It is not to be understood That all the Walls of Pemaquid and Piscataqua Forts must be altogether precisely alike built and vaulted (as is laid down in the afores.^d Profiel) but only a part of them, and for the rest a skilful Architect may governe himselfe therein (by the Situation and ground) so as to improve all advantages and good husbandry.

Fourthly & Lastly, To anticipate an objection that may be raised touching the Draughts & Profiels of the Forts of Orange and Schenegtade in the County of Albany in the Province of New Yorke and Castle Island in the County of Suffolke in the Massachusetts Province, Why they are not proposed in their construction, cannon proofe &c. It may be added that only such Guns as are portable on horses which is not well to be done through a Wilderness but with much difficulty, can be improved against the two first, and the last being a mile and some three quarters of a mile distant from the nearest of the adjacent Islands, is only exposed to an Attack by Sea, which will be both difficult and dangerous to Ships that shall approach against a Fort and Batterys regularly and advantagiously raised by the Seaside: Under these considerations I conceive an extraordinary charge may be well Saved.

    Wolfgang Willm Römer

Boston
  November 10th 1699.

May it please your Lord^p.

We the Inhabitants of this Town of Wells have rec^d a sutable supply of Souldiers for our present support, for the which as our Duty we return to your Lord^p as our acknowledgements your great prudence Love and fatherly care extended to us in this releife has much Incourag'd and Cheared our hearts. Your Lord^{ps} Quickness in sending such a supply unto us has prevented our Address for the same. We do give our most humble thanks to your Lord^p and honoured Councill therefore. We would crave leave to lay our present wants in your Lord^{ps} view Armes and Amunition are of absolute necessity for defence if war should arise, and we are but single arm'd at the best and if any of them should faile here is no Recruits to be had. Our store of Ammunition is too little, and that little is not good, we humbly pray your Excellency to consider this want and if it may be to Grant a Supply. We would also give your Lord^p a short Informacon of some ill designs of the Indians lately discovered by an Indian man of some account amongst them: he coming to an English house, asked what made the English go to Garrison there being some Remote families removed, we told him it was not for any harm Intended to them but upon some suspition of the Westward Indians. We asked him if he knew any Reason why so many Indians came from so many parts to Winnebessehkick and there about he owned that there was many Indians there but what their designe was he knew not. Two days after he came again to the same house, and three English men with him, there being one at that house could discourse with him in his own Language then he did say that last Summer there was a great plot among the Indians at Pennycook and Winnebessehkick and other Indians to make war with the English and had brought their design to an head about our Indian Harvest and was in Arms ready to set out upon the design and had it not been for Kahton Bamet the Sagamoor of Pegnohket they had strok the blow upon us before Winter We asked him if he thought that that Sagamoor could prevent them now he said he could not tell but he had done it then but there was now many Indians at the forementioned places and some of them came from Canada, some of the Indians have told this Winter that the peace that is now is no good peace for it was but Two proud Rascally Fellows that made it, and their Sagamoor did never consent to it. We have Inform'd upwards of 40 of our Indians among us this Winter to their perfect understanding of ye falsnesse of the Report raised that the English designed their destruction, and told them it was raised by Evill minded men and upon their faithfullness and Truth the King and your Lord^p would protect and Love them and that the English would do them no harm: but we find some of them very hard to believe it. We humbly pray your Lord^p to admit Capt James Gooch to

give a further acc.ᵗ particulars and of our State and Condicõn
We subscribe our selves in behalfe of the Inhabitants
Your Lord.ᵖˢ most humble Serv.ᵗˢ

Joseph Storer
John Wheelwight
Jonathan Hamond

27.ᵗʰ March 1700.

End:) *Copy of a L̃re from M.ʳ Storer, M.ʳ Wheelwright & M.ʳ Hammond to y.ᵉ E of Bellomont, relating to y.ᵉ Indians.*

Dated 27.ᵗʰ March 1700. Referred to in y.ᵉ E. of Bellomont's L̃re of y.ᵉ 20.ᵗʰ of April 1700

Rec.ᵈ June 27 } 1700
Read July 2.ᵈ

To the R.ᵗ Hon.ᵇˡᵉ the Earl of Bellomont, Capt.ⁿ General and Governour in chief of his Ma.ᵗʸˢ Provinces of the Massachusetts Bay, New Yorke & New Hampshire.

The Memorial of Col.º Wolfgang William Romer his Ma.ᵗʸˢ Chief Engineer in America —
Touching the five Rivers.

In obedience to your Lordp.ˢ Order I embarqued at Boston the 28ᵗʰ of last July on board the Province Gally & arrived in Piscataqua river the next day, where I had the honour of meeting your Lord.ᵖ and receiving your Order to take the Plan of the great Island and Fort thereon, and also of the entrance into that river, and to sound the s.ᵈ river from the mouth thereof as far as New Castle which accordingly I performed with all the exactness I could, as your Lord.ᵖ will see in the Chart more at large.

I find the Fortification on the s.ᵈ Island extream bad and uncapeable of defending the entrance into that noble & important River not being sufficient to endure three or four days attack of an Enemy. The place where the s.^d Fort stands is very proper if there were Workes built that were defensible. The importance of that river, and the growing Trade of that place and Countrey requiring it. But, besides that, a good Strong Tower on the point of Fryers Island, a Battery on Wood Island, and another single Battery on Clarks Island would be very necessary.

As for the Great Island on which New Castle stands, a good redoubt near to the horse Ferry would be very convenient for maintaining a correspondence between the s.^d Great Island and the Main Land because that, upon occasion, Succours might be conveyed thence to the Great Island Fort, and also because an Enemy would be thereby hindred from passing through little harbour in small Vessels up to Portsmouth.

The 30th of August, Capt Southack Comander of the Gally brought me your Lord^{ps} Order to go and visit St Georges river. We accordingly sailed out of Piscataqua river the 1st of September, and arrived in St Georges river the 7th of the same month. I took the plan of the s^d River which I found difficult of entrance, not only because of several Islands, but also rocks wch lye under water. Yet when we were once within those Islands and rocks we found fair large Bays where Ships of a 150 Tun could ride. About those Bays we perceived good store of rich Land fit for habitation and Improvement but which was never inhabited by other than Indians. On the out side of the largest of the Islands there are several Plantacons or Farmes, which by means of the late War were deserted by ye Inhabit^{ts} There is little Timber there about fit for building Ships, that which there is being only fit for building houses & for Fuell

The Coast adjoyning to St Georges River is reckoned extraordinary good for Fishing, the French have taken the best part of it, which is from the river of Penobscott to that of S:te Croix which s:d River of S:te Croix is said to have been formerly the Boundary between N England & Nova Scotia before that Nova Scotia and Accadie were del:d to the French by S:r Thomas Temple ⸺

Pemaquid River and Fort

This River is nine Leagues to the Westward of S:t Georges the mouth or entrance whereof is spacious and noble and without any difficulty or danger Ships go imediately into safe harbour from the main Sea there being but two Leagues from thence to a Point called the Barbekin which is close by the Fort. The Chart will shew the Situation of the Fort and depth of the River.

The Land of Pemaquid is much better than that about S:t Georges there was there formerly a Village of 36 well built houses on a neck of Land, where stood the Fort, the Inhabitants had their Farmes in the neighbouring country where there were a great many Farmers besides who had not houses in Pemaquid yet were forced to retire thither in the Wartime, and 'tis supposed that had the peace continued till this time Pemaquid would have been a place of importance because of its Fishery, its Trade with the Indians and the Trade which would have arisen from the productions of the Countrey. Besides, this place is considerable because of its Frontier which covers and Shuts in the rivers of Damarascot, Sheepscott and Kennebeck

The French have intirely demolished the Fort of Pemaquid which appears to have been extreamly ill built & not defensible your Lord:p may observe by the Profil of the s:d Fort in the Chart, that there was no order or proportion observed in building it, its Walls were made of clay mixed with Sand brought from the Sea shore instead of Lime. Insomuch that (as I have been informed) when the French besieged it the Commander having ordered two great Guns to be fired at the

Enemy the Wall of the Fort was so very much shaken that he was forced to have it supported with great Beams of Timber which was partly the cause that the place was shamefully Surrendred to the French. This was the Fort that made such a noise and which the Countrey were made to believe was impregnable the loss of which disheartned them extremely and made the Inhabitants desert the whole Eastern Country. For the better Security of this Frontier and its port or harbour, I am of opinion there ought to be a good Fort built much about the same place where the former Fort stood & care taken for conveying in fresh water to furnish the Garrison in case of a Seige. And that the defence toward the Sea ought to be lower down or more horizontal than formerly: Besides, for its better defence in case of a Seige by Sea, I am of opinion there should be a good Battery guarded by a Redoubt, or by a round Tower on Johns Island, and another Battery of Six pieces of canon 18 pounders, on Cuckolds point. This being done that Bay would then be Secure.

Kennebeck River

This River is a fine one and convenient for great Ships when they are once got two Leagues within ye Islands that are before its mouth which Islands lye to the Main Sea they are then safe from all danger and afterward the river is navigable for great Ships up as far as Newtown And thô it be navigable higher up yet 'tis somewhat hazardous by reason of the little Islands and rocks which lye in the middle of ye river whose rapid course makes it stil more hazardous for ships.

As to the Soil, that of Rowsick Island, on which Newtown formerly stood is very good, and so is the Land that lies towards the West and South West along the s^d river. There are also several excellent Meadows thereabout, Your Lord^p will see in the Chart the course and depth of the s^d river.

There was never any other Fortification but that at Newtown, which was a small square Fort palisado'd, Therefore I have marked on the Chart the places which ought to be fortified not only for the defence of the mouth of the river but also for that of the river itself within the countrey, and this last I hold very necessary because the Savages have two Forts at the head of the River which are cald Naridgewack and Comeso quantick. They have two Jesuits in each Fort which do great hurt to the Kings interest, and that of the Publick because they instil into those people an aversion & hatred for his Ma$^\text{ty}$ & his Subjects. Before the War there was a palisado'd Fort on Damarascove Island for defence of the Fishermen & a little higher there was another place cald Cape Newagin where the people cur'd their Fish, and two harbours where they secured their Vessels from Storms. And thô those harbours lye open to the Sea yet in case of necessity they serve turn, when the Fishermen cannot get into Kennebeck river.

Casco Bay.

I find Casco bay the noblest, as I do the Countrey about it the fertilest thats in all New England. There are in this Bay a great many Inlets from the Sea those that lye on the North East and South by West sides are the deepest, and are 15 miles from each other. The s$^\text{d}$ Bay is cover'd from the storms that come from the Sea, by a multitude of Islands, great and small there being (if one may believe report) as many Islands as days in the year. Your Lord$^\text{p}$ may observe the Situation of this Bay in the Chart and of part of the Islands, and also its Soundings, wherein I was particularly careful, as I was in all other places, where I thought it necessary.

The Plan of the Fort in great as I have taken it will give your Lord$^\text{p}$ an intire view of its Situation, and of its strength formerly. The French and Indians burnt it during the late War it was built of Wood & very ill contrived being so seated on a neck of Land, that it could not be relieved. And as it was ill built so was it as ill kept in repair Yet in confidence of this Fort people were encouraged to build a pretty large Village called Falmouth, consisting of 46 houses and a good church but all lys now in ruines There are stil to be seen the remains of houses of two stories high with stone walls and Chimneys, and there are 180 Farmes, besides a great many Fishermens houses.

'Tis great pity that so fine a country should be deserted, And in case it were to be resetled I could advise a much more comodious place for building a Town which without doubt would thrive and grow a pace and it would be much more capeable of being relieved and defended than the former Town was. I have marked the place for this new Town on the Chart with red lines where your Lord? will see my projection thereof.

Saco River

From Casco Bay I came to Winter harbour, four miles from the mouth of Saco river, and went up in the pinnace as high as the first Falls or Cascades where I found a small Fort, ill seated and worse built it was made of clay and sand instead of Lime and the most considerable part of it, which is a small Tower in forme of an irregular Pentagone, is ready to fall, and in a word useless. The Fall or Cascade makes so great a noise that one can scarce hear ones selfe speak. This place is not so much a Frontier as a place of defence for the Salmon Fishing.

That which I shall observe (because this River is only deep enough for sloops) is,

(1) That in my opinion there must be a good redoubt made a mile and halfe from the Cascade or Fall, and a Boom cross the river to hinder the Indians in their Canoes from coming round about the s^d Falls, and so to the Sea for which reasons we ought to be Masters of the river. At the head

whereof the Indians have a Fort cald Narracomecock, where they have also two Jesuits. The redoubt and boome I have mark't on the Chart with red lines.

(2) Since the people of New England have enriched themselves by their Fishing which is their principal Trade, it would be proper in my Judgement to make a good Battery guarded by a redoubt at Winter harbour or Stage gut point to secure their Sloops and other Fishing boats; which, indeed, ought to be done in several places on the Eastern Coast where at present have no Sort of refuge to the Eastward of Saco, to shelter them from Pirates or other Enemies. The Land along this river is very good & fertile & well stor'd wth woods for Ship building & for houses.

What remains to be observed is, That at the head of this River above the first and greatest Falls, it takes its course N. N. E. where the last mentioned Indian Fort which is built at some distance from the s^d River, and the two former Indian Forts (which I mentioned in the Article of Kennebeck river) do center all three within two or three days Journy of each other by wch means the Savages can conveniently correspond. And upon occasion draw together in a body as often as they please, which is a thing well worth reflection especially against another War do happen.

It is likewise observable That all these Indians I have been mentioning were our cruellest Enemies all the late War which they made appear on all occasions, They took & burnt Falmouth and besieged Wells, a Village to the Westward of Saco, consisting only in 10 or 12 houses which were fortified & well provided with provision & Ammunition who (thô they were besieged by 500 French and Indians) so well defended themselves that the Enemy were beaten and forced to retire with considerable loss. Among others, three of their best Captains were killed one whereof (& he the most regretted) was a Kinsman of ye Count de Frontenac, and as a token of their revenge, having taken an old Englishman they roasted him alive on a spit in sight of the English in Garrison This is one mark, among many others, of the horrible cruelty of French Papists and Indian Infidels

    All which is humbly submitted to your Lord^{ps} consideration by

        Your Lordships
        Humble and obedient Servant

Boston   Wolfgang Willm Römer
the 11th April 1700.

    To his Excellency the Earle of Bellomont
Province of the Massachusetts Bay
in New England

    The Memoriall of William Rayment Lievtenant of the New Detached Company Posted in his Ma^{tys} Service within the County of York in the Province aforesaid.

Sheweth

    That within the space of three weeks last past at sundry times divers of the Eastern Indians to the number of Twenty or thereabouts of men and women have first and last showen themselves at and about the Town of Wells where this Narrator with a party of the said company are posted, and discoursed with some of the Inhabitants of said Town, professing themselves for peace, particularly on Saturday the 6th of April Instant Twelve Indians came into the Town of Wells (who for some days before had shown themselves to some of the Inhabitants but seem'd shye, avoiding to be spoken with) of which number there was one named Tom, who bears the title of Capt and is said to have been very active in Comitting of murder and rapine dureing the time of the late Rebellion, who at first pretended not to understand nor speak English, but afterwards having discovered that he could do both, he then began to be free of discourse, and Inquired of this Narrator the reason why there was so many souldiers posted there and the Inhabitants went to Garrison, I replyed because the Indians threatned to make war and burn the English houses. he said there was no such thing Intended, the English and they were as Brothers. the Narrator then demanded of him why the Indians were gathered together in bodys at severall places, he replyed that the English Governour meaning Governour Winthrop had seized the Natick Sagamore, and said he would kill the Indians, and fifteen of Natick Indians had come to Pennicook to stir up the Indians there to make war, and also to Uncas another Sagamore to the Westward, and the Pennycooks had sent unto the Kennebeck Indians to acquaint them therewith and to excite them to Joyn them in making of war but they utterly refused. Then this Narrator demanded of him what the Pennycooks would do, seing the Eastern Indians would not Joyn them he replyed the Pennycooks were but a few and could do nothing were (as he expressed himselfe) no more than all one a Papoos or Child. The Narrator laboured to disabuse him and Confute the falsehood of such a Report that the Governor had seized upon any Indian, or Intended any harm to the Indians, and read your Excellencys Proclamacõn unto him and the other Indians who seem'd to be well satisfied and say very good Governor, and professes the Indians have no designe for war they have hunted much this Winter and taken but little Game are very poor and pinch't for want of provisions and further saith they are now going out a hunting for the space of Two moons as he term'd it, and then would return back againe

Wm Rayment

Boston
  April 13th 1700/
signat. Cor. Is^a Addington Secr̃y.

End:) *N? 9. Massachusets Mem^l. of Lieu^t. Rayment to ye E of Bellemont, about the Indians. Dated April y^e. 13th 1700 Referred to in ye E of Bellemont's Lre of the 20th April 1700*

    Rec^d. June 27 } 1700
    Read July 2^d.

Liev^t. William Rayment's Memorial relateing to the Indians – Ap^r. 13th 1700.   a True Copy

Bellemont

    To the King's Most Excellent Majesty
    The humble addresse of the Governor Councel and Representatives of your Majesty's Province of New Hampshire in America Conven'd in Generall Assembly

May it Please your Maj^{ty}

    Wee your Majesty's most dutifull and Loyall Subjects having a deep Sense of the many blessings we Injoy by means of your most auspicious Reign and Just administration, the happy Influences whereof reach and effect us that live in one of your remotest Provinces in America. We blesse God with all the powers of our souls y^t yor Maj^{ty} has by his Divine assistance accomplish'd those great and glorious atchievments whereby you have rescu'd the Liberties of

England and of all Europe from Popish Tyranny and oppression. The present peace which under God we owe to your Majesty's matchless bravery and Conduct must be acknowledged a wellcome Relaxation to us that are but a handfull of people in this province and have had to do all the Late war with a barbarous and Treacherous Enemy the Eastern Indians, whose bloody Nature and perfidy have been much aggravated and Improv'd of late years by Popish Emissaries from ffrance who have taught 'em that breaking faith with, and murdering us is the Sure way to gain paradise; and so far have they deluded their Indian Disciples with their Inchantments and vile Superstition, that they are taught to Spare neither age nor Sexe, having kill'd and Scalp'd all (Except a very few) both old and young that came within their power during the whole Course of the war, and we know not how Long these bloody Indians will forbear their hostilities. The ffrench Missionaries continuing among them as they do, and poysoning them with their Hellish doctrines to the withdrawing them from their former Obedience and Subjection to yor Maj^{ty}

We have great reason to Blesse God for your Majesties uniting the province of New York to that of Massachusetts Bay and this province under the Governm^t of the Earle of Bellomont, it being the happiest Step your Maj^{ty} could have made for our protection, Inasmuch as it is the likelyest way to subdue or exterminate these Eastern Indians that Infest us, to Ingage the five Nations of Indians in the province of New Yorke (who have always been a terror to 'em) to make war upon them.

That your Maj$^{ty s}$ unwearied Care and vigilance for the Interest and happinesse of your people may raise in all our hearts and affections that Just veneration and respect that's due to the Lustre of your glorious name and actions: and that your Maj^{ty} may after a long and prosperous Reign over

us receive an Immortal Crown of glory as a reward of the unspeakable blessings and advantages you have brought to all your Subjects is the most earnest and Incessant prayer of
May it please your Majesty
Your Majesty's most devoted most
humble and most faithfull Subjects and Servants
Bellomont

John Hinckes Nath Fryor Peter Coffin W^m. Partridge Sam^{ll} Penhallow, Speaker Robert Elliot John Gerrish Richd Waldrom Moses Lewis John Pirkerin James Render Joseph Gruett Henry Dow Nath Hill John Fuller John Woodman John Smith Theodore Attkinson

Petition of Earl of Limerick concerning Pemaquid.

To the Kings most Excell^t Majesty.
The humble Petition of Thomas Earle of Limericke.
Sheweth

That your Petitioner being desireous to retire to and pass the Remainder of his life in your Majesties Dominions in America; And there being a Tract of Land Called Pemaquid, which was formerly the private Estate of the late King James, and Yields little or no benefit to your Majesty.

Your Petitioner most humbly prays that your Majesty will be graciously pleased to grant him the said Tract of Land, with such Franchises and Priviledges & under such an Acknowledgement Regulations and Reservations of all Legall Rights to any former Grants there made by the Kings Governors of New York or New England as to your Majesty shall seem meet

And your Petition^r shall ever Pray &c.

(No endorsement)

Answer to Earl of Limerick's Petition concerning Pemaquid.

L.ᵈ Stamford & others to the Earl of Jersey.

To the R.ᵗ hon.ᵇˡᵉ y. Earle of Jersey
My Lord.

In answer to your Lordships Letter of the 27th Aprill signifying To Us his Majesties pleasure that we should consider of the Earl of Lymerick's Petition to his Majesty for a Grant of some Lands in America called Pemaquid, We desire you would please to inform his Majesty that the whole Country between Nova Scotia and the Province of Main, in which Pemaquid is included, has already by his Majesties Royal Charter to the Inhabitants of the Province of the Massachusets Bay, been granted to them with pow.ʳ to make and pass Grants of particular Tracts of Lands within the whole Boundaries of that Province, but with a Reservation nevertheless that no Grants of any Lands between the River of Sagadehock and the Gulph of S.ᵗ Lawrence (in which Pemaquid is also included) should be of any force untill his Majesty his heirs or Successors shall have signifyed his or their approbation of the same; By which it appears that his Majesty cannot gratify the Petitioner in the Matt.ʳ of his request, untill a Grant of such Lands be first obtained from the Corporation of the Massachusets Bay. We are:

     Signed
       Stamford
    Ph. Meadows Wm. Blathwayt
    John Pollexfew Abr. Hill
Whitehall May } Geo. Stepney.
the 10.ᵗʰ 1700 }

Cap.ᵗ John Alden's Relation to the Earl of Bellomont.

Capt.ᵗ John Alden was with me the 13.ᵗʰ of this Instant June, and told me he was newly returned from Penobscot

River to ye Eastward where he saw and discoursed with Monsr de Saint Castin a French Gentleman that lives there, and with whom the s.^d Alden has traded Several years. Monsr de St Castin told him he hop'd he should Shortly come under the King of England's Government, for that he had much rather be a Subject of England than a Slave to France; he likewise said that the true Boundary between England and France to the Eastward was the River of Ste Croix and said the English would do well to insist on it vigorously, otherwise the French Court would try to cozen 'em out of it. Capt Alden desired him the s.^d Castin to write by him to the Governour of N. England what he had then related about the Boundary but he said he could not venture to do such a thing least his Letter should be carried to Quebec. he, Viz.^t St.^t Castin told Capt Alden That the Jesuits had taken indefatigable pains to stir up the Indians everywhere to make War upon the English and said they were very wicked in so doing. I desir'd Capt Alden to put what he told me in writing by way of Memorial, and set his name to it but he desir'd to be excused, Saying, That St Castin was his Friend and Correspondent, and he, viz: Alden, could not do anything that would expose Monsr de St Castin This I immediately writ down after Capt Alden had left me.

Monsr de St Castin is said to be a Gentleman of a good Family who leaving France on Some disgust in his Youth, came & settled on Penobscot River married the chief Sagamore's Daughter, Speaks the Indian tongue, lives after the Indian manner, and is become Chief or Sagamore of the Penobscot Indians consisting in about 130 Families, being grown rich by Trade. 'Tis said the French Governours of Canada & St Johns have sent several times to him to go to them, but he would not go near 'em He professes great kindness to the English and Speaks English. He gave advice to some of the late Governours here, of the designes of the French against this Countrey, and the return he had was the sending a Frigat & some souldiers, who ravag'd his Country and burnt the Wigwams or houses of him and his Indians, Which faithless action he complains of to this day.

E: Capt. John Aldens Relation to the Earl of Bellomont, of what passed between him & Monsr. de S^t. Castin, about the Eastern bounds between us & the French.
13 June 1700 –

A New Oxford ce 17 Juin 1700

Monseigneur

Lors que Jeus lhonneur d'écrire a vôtre Excellence Je ne luy enuoyay pas le certificat de nos habitents sur le sujet de Monsr. Bondet, parce qu'ils n'êtoient pas tous Icy : Je l'ay en fin retiré et l'envoye a vôtre Excellence. au sujet de nos Indiens Je me sens obligé D'avertir Vôtre Excellence, que les quatre qui etoient revenus non, obstant toutes les protestations qu'ils me firent a leur arrivée leur retour n'a eu d'autre but que d'engager ceux qui avoient été fidelles a sen aller avec eux, de sorte qu'ils en ont gagné la plus part, et partent Aujourd huy pour Penikook au nombre de vint cinq hommes femmes et enfans ; Je leur préchay hier en leur propre Langue et les exhortay Aussy fortement qu'il me fût possible a rester ; mais Inutillen. Ils me dirent pour raison que les habitans de New roxbury Les troubloient Incessament, que tout le monde les trompoit, mais ces raisons ne me satisfaisant pas, Je voulus en avoir quelque autre, Ils me dirent ensuite, que la religion des Indiens de Penikook etoit plus belle que la nôtre que les françois leur donnoient des croix d'argent a metre au col. Je fis tout ce que je peus pour leur faire voir le contraire. Ils ajouterent qu'on leur faisoit de grandes promesses dans ce pays la, au lieu qu' Icy ils avoient au Roy qui les maltraitoit, les ayant fait coucher tout lhiver sur la dure sans aucun secours, la dessus je leur ay representé, que la on ils alloient ils servient tous esclaves, que quand on auroit besoin de soldats on les fair oient marcher par force, au lieu qu' Icy ils joüissent d'une entiere Libertié, et que le Roy n'a D'autre dessein que de les proteger, &c enfin Ils m'ont asseuré qu'il y avoit une autre forte raison qu'ils ne pouvoient pas dire mais qu'on la sauroit bientôt, ils sont encore Icy pour tout ce jour, et Il m' aperçois qu'l y en a plusieurs qui commencent a changer de dessein Je ne per dray point de moment pour les retenir s'il m'est possible etant secouru de ceux qui restent, si j'avois sceu plustot leur dessein, j'aurois mieux reüssi; dans tout ce qu'ils disent je voy que les pretres agissent vigoureusement et qu'ils couvent quelque entre prise qu'ils fairont Eclore quand Ils en trouveront loccasion favorable, voila Monseigneur ce que mon devoir m'obligeoit a faire sçavoir a vôtre Excellence J'ajouteray seulement que Je feray gloire dans quelque occasion que ce soit de faire connoitre a vôtre Excellence que Je tacheray de ne me rendre J'amais Indigne des graces que l'ay receües, et de temoigner toute ma vie que Je suis.

  Monseigneur
   De Votre Excellence
    Le tres humble tres obeissant
    et tres soumis Serviteur
    signé   J Laborie

Capt. John Alden's Second Relation to the Earl of Bellomont.

on Tuesday morning the 1st of aug: 99. Coll Allen Came to my Lodging at Mr Waldron's house at Pescattaway and desir'd I would Let him have a Tryall for the Lands of the province of N. Hampshire, and that if I would favour his Cause he would make me a handsome recompense, but I told him I would keep Clean hands and that I never had taken nor ever would take a bribe.

on Tuesday evening the 8th of aug. 99. Coll Allen came to me at Mr Waldron's house at Pescattaway, and offer'd me if I would favour his Cause ag^t the people of N. Hampshire, he would match a younger daughter of his to my younger son and would make her worth 10000£ in mony, and that he would divide the province with me besides but I told him that I would not sell Justice, if I might have all the world, and that both my sons were children, and not fit to marry. he desir'd I would be there, but I told him I would not do such a thing for the world, because it would be very unfair so to do. he still press'd my marrying my younger son to his daughter, and told me a third part of ye people of ye province had already turn'd tenants to him at a Quit rent of 3^d p acre: that the woods and timber of the province would be of a vast value; and there had been and still is an extravagant wast Committed in his woods by men who had made estates out of 'em.

on Saturday morning the 12th of Aug: 99. Coll Allen walking with me before Mr Waldron's door, renew^d his offer of a match between my son & his daughter, and told me his pretension in N. Hampshire & other parts of N. England was worth 22000£ p an. at 3^d p acre Quit rent, that the Lands were 1700000 acres, and that his patent gave him a right as far as Cape Ann and to Salem in the Boston Government.

on Tuesday morning the 15th of Aug: 99. Coll. Allen Came to my Chamber in Mr. Waldron's house and shew'd me some writings relating to his title to the Lands afores^d and then renew'd his offer of 10000£ wth his daughter to my younger son, if I would favour his Cause, and he told me again that he valu'd his Interest at 22000£ p an. besides the woods.

on the 17th of aug. 99. I left Pescataway to Come tow^{ds} Boston, and Coll. Allen conducting me as far as Hampshire (where I din'd at Mr Cotton the Minister's house) where walking on the green before Mr Cotton's house, he again urg'd me upon the former proposition of a match between my son and his daughter, and that I would favour his Cause against the Inhabitants of N. Hampshire. I made answer I would do him Justice but no favour.

ab^t the Latter end of this Last feb: or beginning of March Coll. Allen was here at Boston, and press'd me wth more earnestnesse than ever, to accept of his former proposition of a match between my son and his daughter, and that upon the terms afores^d viz: 10000£ in mony and half his pretension to the Lands and woods afores^d but because it was the same proposition he had made me so often before I did not write it down in my table book as I had done at all the foregoing times.

I have severall Letters from Coll Allen, some whereof do plainly hint the foremention'd offer to me, and more particularly and plainly the match between my son and his daughter.

all which premisses I am ready to declare upon oath when thereunto required

Bellomont

Boston the 19th of June 1700 –

Memorandum. That Coll. Allen told me twice or thrice he was very sure the Inhabitants of N. Hampshire upon my Countenancing his title were ready to turn tenants to him Imediately, and that severall of them had told him so, and that in a week's time he Could raise 20000£ on the s^d. Inabitants by way of fines half of which sum he would pay me as his daughter's fortune.

Bellomont

E:)   *An Account of Coll. Allen's*
                  Offer to the E. of Bellomont &c.

Colossians Discovery June 21: 1700.

Colossians drawing off, because he is assur'd of war this Sumer and that peace can't be continued, neglects to hill his corne on that Accompt, thô he now and then doth a little, that the English may not suspect his Resolutions.

The reason of his not being gone Nenequabbens brother's being Scalded, but upon his being well and able to travail he and all the rest must be gone Woodstock must be clear'd of Indians within three weeks because there must be no Indians about the Towns in the heart of the Countrey.

The Indians now publickly own their intentions of drawing off bid Neighbour Farewell, and cunningly to blind them tell them they have no ill designe intend no hurt would not have them frighted nor go into Garrisons, Yet tell John Sabin privately that this is only to blind the people whom thô they promise to return again after a while viz six weeks yet also to him aver they never will they know they must not

June 23d at night.

Colossians came and told John Sabin It might be he might never see him more As for the War he could not tell which side might prove strongest yet as to his concernes if the Indians prevail'd he should not be endamaged. On his reply concerning the Governours improving other methods than ever yet were taken he rejoyn'd, some say the Governr intends to use dogs against the Indians but if they would have such as would do any service they must be doggs that bullets would not enter they would carry a Quiver of Arrows they valued little what could be done against them We have had Wars with the English so long that we see what they can do. Upon proposing to him the unlikelyhood of their being supplied with Amunition he replied they should never want, for, divers French had married Indian Squaws, and they had promised to supply them and others had promised to do the same privately thô they must not be seen in it unless a War commence between Engl: & France & <u>another way</u> Towns will be taken by surprize either by lesser or greater numbers as we shall judge needful There's Mendon, such a Town we can take in two hours, and in every Town we heare there is a barrel of powder & private men have some a pound, some more, and they won't have opportunity to shoot much of it away before we take them.

His projections about ruining the Countrey built upon their designe to kill all Cattle Swine &c. destroying fields by which means he concludes men will be soon starv'd out particularly Woodstock. he reckons himselfe and another can starve that Town out by such methods in a years time and then when people are so starv'd out they will apace draw off for Europe, Ships would walke very fast

As to the Maqua's

He is assur'd (else he would not go) that they would stand by the Indians, and that they would find quarrel one way or another with my Lord when he should treat them for Maqua's so bigg cunning they have sent great quantitys of moneys to the M to the value of one hundred pounds, and one told him for his part he had sent 20^s Solomon tells him that the Macqua's love John Sabins name on the score of his service to the Pennecook Indians at Woodstock.

Nenequabben on 24th instant.

He is sorry for trouble arising in a streight what to do his Family gon to Pennecook already yet unresolv'd w^t to do, thinks best for him to be English side, the Indians disgusted at him English and Indians all say Governour very cunning man but Indians can, for all that, and will blind his Eyes, for he can't see they'l speak him fair and he little thinks how near trouble is

To his Cousin Eben: Sabin Menequabben with tears in his Eyes said he was in a great Streight his Family was gone to Pennecook to the other side, and he thought he must go too, And if he did he must fight against the English and that lookt hard.

Some Indians drawn off, before they went away, a man who had lett Land to them complained (when they told him they were going) that they had promised him pay for his Land, to which they replied they freely gave him all their Labour and so drew off.

Keensotuk (who is Grand Child to the late King Philip Sachem of Mount hope) informed John Sabin that the Pennecooks would certainly this Sum̄er make war upon Owaneco the Sachem of the Mohegin Indians for their discovery of the Plott to the English and added that if the English helpt them then it would draw ye Warr upon them if not it was likely the Mohegins would privately kill John Sabin or some other English man and then lay it on the Pennecooks, and that would occasion a War betwixt them and the English so that a War would certainly commence.

Colossians informed John Sabin that the Macqua's are every week some or other of them at Pennecook and some of other Indians from Canada & ye Eastward, that the Pennecooks do labour to prejudice the Macqua's against the Mohegins, laying the blame of ye discovery upon them and belying them, to incense the Macqua's, tell them that the Mohegins out of scorn hung up the Present of Wampum in the smoke and made a derision of it.

The Earl of Bellomont to Mr Sec^{ry} Vernon

Boston the 22th June 1700

Sir

if you have patience to read my Long letter to the Co. of Trade wch I now send you, it will give you I hope an

Idea of the rise that might be made of these Plantations, for therein I have writ for the Last time ab.^{t} Naval stores and Masts and Ship timber. The papers I send Inclosed wth this Letter will surprize, especially that wch discovers Blathwait's bargain wth Coll. Allen for half his pretended Interest in N. Hampshire and a great part of this province. I have now sent the same papers to my Lord Chancellor, and my Lord Jersey, and I hope among you, he I mean Mr Blathwait will be Crossebit by this bargain of his wth Allen 'tis plain who sold the Lands in the province of N. York to ffletcher. if it could be Lawfully done, the seizing Coll Allen's papers would discover this villanous bargain of Blathwait's wth him wch would a thousand times more deserve an Inquisition of the H. of Comons than that they bestow'd 9 hours debate on the 6.th of Last Decr I hope those two Lords and yourselfe will with vigor oppose Mr Blathwait's treacherous sale of these plantations from England. The Management of them has been hitherto most ridiculous, and all by that man's means who has made a milch Cow of 'em for many years together we have a fresh account of the Indians wch is bad enough but the hasty departure of this Ship will not permit me to relate it to you. I have not had any Letter from the Co: of Trade since that of the 21.st of Last aug: wch is very discouraging I wish you Ministers would set a right value on these Plantations, and then we Governors would be more regarded and should hear from you oftener.

one Robinson the Master of a Ship belonging to this Town arriv'd here a moneth ago from London, and tells me he met Mr. Weaver at the Sun Coffy house behind the Royal Exchange a week before he left London, and Mr Weaver having a packet of Letters in his hand for me, Robinson desir'd he might bring it to me, but Mr Weaver told him he had positive orders to send the packet to N. York; and Mr Weaver deliver'd the packet before his face to one Jeffers

Master of a ship bound to N. York, and Robinson says Jeffers deliver'd it to the Master of the Coffy house, and desir'd him to keep it for him. now this Jeffers was the Master that petition'd the Council of Trade against me. This was about 13 weeks ago, and Jeffers pretended to be ready to sail the next day; yet he is not heard of at N. York, and I suspect some foul play is done to the Letters sent me. There ought to have been duplicates of the packets from the Ministers: for 'tis a terrible Thing to be us'd as I am.

I am wth respect
Sir Your most faithfull humble Servant
Bellomont

Cap. Alden's second relation to me of the Eastern bounds between us & ye ffrench I now Inclose to you as a thing worth your observation 'Twere worth while to Inquire who order'd Mr Weaver to send ye packet to N. York and if there be a Trick in it, that will discover it.

E:)   *Earl of Bellomont 22 June R 9 Aug. 1700*

The Earl of Bellomont to Mr Sec^{ry} Vernon

Boston the 9th July 1700

Sir
I write now in the anguish of my soul, being quite dispirited for want of orders from you Ministers to support the King's and Nation's Interest in these Plantations. you will see that I have writ by this Conveyance to the Council of Trade, and I will trouble you no more on that subject, referring you to a Copy of my Letter to them, wch I send you.

There Came hither two ships from London, the Last week in May, wch brought me not a Letter from any of the

Ministers, and another ship four days ago, but not a Letter by that neither, what must the people here and in N. York thinke, but that either the King and his Ministers have no sort of Care or value for these Plantations, not minding whether they fall into ffrench hands or no: or else that I am in disgrace wth the King, and that all this neglect proceeds from a personall Slight to me. I never in all my life was so vex'd and asham'd as now; I put the best face I can on it, but I find other people take the liberty to Judge of the present Conduct of affairs in England.

it had been kindly done of the Ministers to have rebuk'd M^r. Weaver's Impertinence in staying all this while in England from the duty of his Imployment, where he has no just pretence of businesse, unlesse taking his pleasure may be Call'd so; In my opinion, he should be order'd peremptorily to Come away with the first ship, or be turn'd out, and another Capable man sent in his place.

I am with respect Sir
Your most faithfull humble servant
Bellomont

E:)   *Ea of Bellomont 9 July R 16 Aug 1700*

Boston the 9th July 1700

My Lords

The reason of my troubling your Lo^ps again so soon after my Letter of the 22th of last moneth, is to acquaint you wth some things that have occurr'd since then, wch I think deserve being Transmitted to your Lo^ps

A   The Indians about the Towns of Woodstock and New Oxford (consisting in ab^t 40 families) have lately deserted their houses and corn and are gone to live wth the Penicook Indians, wch has much allarm'd the English thereabout, and some of the English have forsaken their houses and farms and remov'd to towns for their better security. that the Jesuits have seduc'd those 40 families of Indians is plain from severall accounts I have receiv'd; some whereof I now send viz: Mons.ʳ Labourie's Letter to me, w.ᶜʰ is a very plain evidence of the French Jesuits debauching those Indians. Mons.ʳ Labourie is a French Minister plac'd at New Oxford by M.ʳ Houghton the Lieu.ᵗ Governor and my selfe at a yearly stipend of 30.ˡⁱ out of the Corporation Mony, there are 8 or 10 French families there that have farms, and he preaches to them, and at the same time Instructed those Indians having for that purpose learnt the Indian tongue to enable him to preach therein.

I also send some Memoranda deliver'd me by M.ʳ Rawson a Minister, who writ 'em down from M.ʳ Sabin's mouth; M.ʳ Sabin's the person I formerly nam'd to your Lo.ᵖˢ that gave me severall advices concerning the Indians. M.ʳ Sabin is so terrified at the Indians of Woodstock and N. Oxford's quitting their houses and corn, that he has thought fit to forsake his dwelling, and is gone to live in a Town. All the thinking people here believe the Eastern Indians will break out against the English in a little time.

B Mons.ʳ d'Iberville is lately come to N. York from building Forts at Mechisipi in the bay of Mexico and manning them, I shall not animadvert on his coming to York, but refer your Lo.ᵖˢ to the Lieu.ᵗ Gov.ʳ of N. York's letter to me, a Copy whereof I now send your Lo.ᵖˢ Mons.ʳ d'Iberville came in a 50 gun ship call'd La Renomée.

C The Assembly is still sitting here, but will break up this week, and I must be gone to N. York, to keep touch w.ᵗʰ the 5 Nations of Indians whom I have promis'd to meet at Albany the 10.ᵗʰ of next moneth thô to litle purpose I fear, for having not yet receiv'd orders from your Lo.ᵖˢ or any of the Ministers about those Indians or any of the things I writ to you of, I am quite in the dark, and know not wch way to move. if I could have had orders this spring, I would by this time have had a good sod Fort at Onondage's Castle, wch would have cover'd that and the rest of the 5 Nations from the French, and have Incourag'd those nations above all the things that can be thought of, and that for about 1200^li but the sumer is now almost gone, and I am in great fear our Sloath and neglect of those Indians all this time, will be the losse of them. I thanke God I shall be no way accountable for the mismanagement that will probably loose us the Indians, and our plantations on this whole Continent, having given frequent advices home of the condition of the Indians, and what I thought would secure their affection to us.

D I have rec^d no letter from your Lo^ps since that of the 21st of last Aug: wch is almost a year, except 3 or 4 lines wch serv'd for a cover to the King's Lett^r of the 10th of last Novr they write me word from N. York that a pink was newly arriv'd there from London in 8 weeks, who assures 'em that Jeffers to whom Mr Weaver deliver'd your Lo^ps packet ab^t the 15th of March was in the River of Thames on the 23rd of April. 'Tis wonderfull to me that Mr Weaver could find no body to send the packet with but Jeffers who had complain'd against me to your Lo^ps as I have been Inform'd, a crosse ill condition'd fellow, and who hates me. I sent yesterday for Capt Robinson the Ma^r of a ship belonging to this town, who arriv'd here from London the last week in May, he repeated to me what he had told me before, that a week before he sail'd he met Mr Weaver at the Sun Coffy house behind the old Exchange, and seeing a packet wth him, he desired he might have the bringing it to me, Mr. Weaver refus'd, saying he was positively order'd to send it by Capt Jeffers to N. York, and Capt Robinson saw Mr Weaver deliver the packet to Jeffers and Jeffers deliver it to the master of the Coffy house to keep till he should call for it.

and Capt Robinson sail'd out of the River the 21st of March every body believes Jeffers has plaid the Rogue.

E   it were to be wish'd in such a Conjuncture as this, that your Lo^{ps} would write often and that your secretary would take care that all your packets be deliver'd into honest hands, and receits taken for them. and I desire it may be hereafter observ'd that ships coming to Boston are accounted among the seafaring men to have the advantage of those bound to N. York at least a 3^d part of the way, thô in point of distance N. York is but a 100 leagues further from England than this place is.

F   I hope your Lo^{ps} will not suffer Mr Brenton and Mr Weaver to loyter any longer in England from their duty here. their ramble is most unaccountable, and so far from being reasonable, that 'tis not honest: and they make very bold wth the Ministers at home

G   I had bespoke 400 wheelbarrows and other Tools to be provided for building a Fort for the Indians, but to my great amazement and discomfort, I am not directed in that or any thing else.

I am sorry there was not a duplicate of your Lo^{ps} packet by Jeffers, sent by another ship.

I am wth respect My Lords
Your Lords^{ps} most humble and obedient servant
Bellomont

Boston the 16th July 1700/

Sir

I am now in the hurry of leaving this place, being to imbark to morrow for N. York

My letter to your board will Inform you among other things, of the addresse of my selfe and the Gen.^{ll} Assembly to the King, wherein we complain of the Incroachments of the French on the fishing and Eastern bounds of this province, and supplicate his Ma:ty for his Royall Charter of Incorporation for Harvard – Colledge. I make it my earnest request you will favour and promote the Charter w:th your board, and that you will please to advise and assist S:r Hen: Ashhurst in carrying it on, and managing his solicitations rightly.

I had news yesterday by the Captain of the Galley whom I sent w:th goods and provisions to the Indians on Kenebeck River, that there is some mischief hatching between the Jesuits and those Indians, that there was a generall meeting of the Indians at one of their Castles call'd Naridgewack on that River, and that upon the last day of June, where all the Indians took the sacrament at the hands of those Jesuits.

Moxes the chief Sagamore told the Captain he had lately receiv'd an angry Letter from the Governor of Canada, chiding him severely for holding any sort of Correspondence w:th me and threatning him what the King his master would do to punish him and his Indians if they held any intercourse w:th me. he likewise told the Cap:t that the Jesuits had Insinuated to 'em that the King their Master was resolv'd to maintain all the country eastw:d of Kenebeck River against the English and that they viz: the Indians were great fools if they suffer'd the English to enjoy any lands to the Westward of the s:d River. he told the Captain the Penicook Indians would fall on the Monheags very soon. Cap:t Southack deliver'd me a memorial containing these and severall other matters, but I have not time to get it transcrib'd. you may please to tell the lords of the Council of Trade of this, if you think it worth the telling.

I am unfeignedly Sir
Your humble and faithfull servant
Bellomont

I find I forgot in a late Letter of mine to your board (wherein I desir'd some tools if we were to fortifie our frontiers) to bespeak 10 or 12 dousen of pick axes, w.ch I desire may be sent, if y.e rest of y.e tools be sent.

Boston Sept.r 3.d 1700

Hon.ble S.r

Inclosed herewith are the Minutes of Council begining the 28.th of March 1700 and continued down to the 17.th of July following inclusive, And the Journal of the General Assembly at their Session begun and held the 29.th day of May last past; As also the Acts and Laws then made and passed, all which are made up in one packet and committed to the care of M.r David Robinson Commander of the Ship Elizabeth; whose receipt I have taken for the same, and wish them safe to your Honours hand. The last I sent was by Henry Lowder Master of the Ship Sea Flower of this place; who sayled for London something more than a fortnight since.

This Province is in present quiet; but the Government are not without just fears and Jealousies of an Eruption and general Insurrection of the Indians; who seemed to be fastned to the Interests of our ill neighbours the French, being debauched by the Priests and Jesuits that are sent among them. his Excell.cy has lately sumoned the Sachems and principal Indians of the five nations to attend his Lord.p at Albany in order to recover or prevent their defection; the Issue whereof is not yet known here; It would greatly endanger his Ma.tys Interests in these Territory's, if the Indians should enter into a general Combination, our Frontiers are of so large extent, that it would be impracticable to secure our Towns from their Inroads; And it's no less difficult to have access to the Indian Settlements; which are far remote in a dismal wilderness and their manner of liveing far different from the English.

This Government have ordered the Erecting of a Fort and Trading house at Casco Bay; which is now in doing and may probably prove of some advantage to engage the Indians by makeing reasonable supplies to them, and to check their Insults, if they should breake forth into rebellion.

I have not farther at present, onely to pray your Hono.^{rs} acceptance of the tenders of my humble service and to believe that I am, with much Respect

Honble S.^{r}

Yo.^{r} Hono^{rs} Very humble & obedient servant

Is^a Addington

Cap.^{n} Robinson will be going for N : Engl^d about Feby next: And may be heard of at the Sun Coffee-house behind the Exchange

rec.^{d} Novr the 4th 1700

Mr. Crowne's title to Penobscot; and other lands adjacent.

King James the first, by his Letters Patents under the Great Seale of Scotland, bearing date the tenth of September, 1621; graunted to Sr William Alexander, Lord of Menstrue, principall Secretary of State, of the Kingdome of Scotland, and to his heires for ever, all that country in America, call'd Nova Scotia.

King Charles the first, confirmed this graunt, in the yeare 1625.

The said Sr Wiiliam Alexander, by his deede, bearing date, the thirtyeth of Aprill 1630, made over all his right, and title, in the greatest part of the said Nova Scotia; to Sr Claud de St Estienne Lord of La Tour, and of Vuarre, and to his son Charles de St Estienne, Esqr Lord of St Denis court, and to their heires for ever.

The said S.r Claud, and Charles de S.t Estienne were French Protestants; who for the good service they did, in discovering the said lands to the English; and assisting, and promoting the plantation, both with their persons, and fortunes, were naturaliz'd, and created Baronets of Nova Scotia.

The said S.r William Alexander, by authority of the aforesaid Letters Patents, erected two Baronyes in Nova Scotia; one he call'd La Tour, and the other S.t Denis Court. And in the afore mention'd deede, he graunted to the said S.r Claud, and his son Charles de S.t Estienne, and to their heires for ever, all jurisdictions, and priviledges in those countryes that a scotch Marquesse, Earle, or Baron, has in Scotland and the titles of Baron La Tour, and Baron S.t Deniscourt.

About the yeare 1630; the French put in their claymes to Nova Scotia, pretending it to be a part of Canada; and not long after prevaild with the King to surrender it.

They also earnestly sollicited the King, to abandon the interests of the said S.r Claud, and S.r Charles de S.t Estienne, but that his Majesty absolutely refusd; it being against his honor so to do; as appeares by an originall letter, written from the said Sir William Alexander, to the said S.r Claud de S.t Estienne, dated the 16.th of Aprill, 1631: which letter can at any time be produced. Accordingly when his Mat.y delivered Nova Scotia to the French, he articled that the said S.r Claud and S.r Charles de S.t Estienne shou'd enjoy their lands.

Penobscot, was first discovered by some inhabitants of New Plimouth, in New England. They sent one Cap.t Willet, with a vessell and some men, to take possession of it, and build and plant there, for their advantage; which he did, and possesst it quietly, till Nova Scotia was delivered to the French; and one Mounsieur D'Aulney seut Governour of it.

Then y.e said Mons.r D'Aulney sail'd from Nova Scotia, towards Penobscot: and hearing that Cap.t Willet was designing to saile to Boston; Monr. D'Aulney way layd him: and meeting with him at sea, he invited him aboard his vessell, pretending he was desirous to entertaine him as a friend. Capt. Willet was aboard; but when Monsr. D'Aulney had him there, he told him if he wou'd peaceably deliver Penobscot to him, he would at a certaine time he nam'd, give him the full value of it in beavour, and other furres: but if he refus'd he let him know he was his prisoner, and he wou'd carry him to Nova Scotia.

Capt. Willet finding himselfe in a dangerous snare, thought it was his safest way to accept of Monsr. d'Aulneys proposall, for the price, and time of payment, and in the meane while to gain his liberty, he surrenderd Penobscot to D'Aulney; and then saild to Boston, and acquainted his owners, and employers, what a tricke D'Aulney had put upon him.

When the time of payment was come; his owners sent him to receive the beavours and furres, D'Aulney had promisd. when he arrived at Penobscot, he found D'Aulney there. D'Aulney hearing Capt. Willet was in the harbour, went with some men aboard him, and pretended his beavours and furres were ready, and he shou'd have 'em next day, if he pleas'd. Meane while he desired to make him welcome and treate him aboard his owne vessell, which he did very liberally. The treate lasted till midnight then D'Aulney cuts Capt. Willets cable, turnes him a drift; goes with his owne men aboard his own boates, and then call'd out to Capt. Willet, and let him know, he had payd him for Penobscot, as much as ever he intended, and bad him begone.

Capt. Willet then saild to Boston, and once more acquainted his owners, how he had beene abus'd by D'Aulney, and what litle hopes there was of payment; then they acquiesc'd, and never troubled themselves about Penobscot more.

By this treachery Penobscot was gotten by D'Aulney and the French.

D'Aulney's next endeavour was to get S! Claud and
S! Charles de S! Estienne out of their estates.
They resided in Nova Scotia, in a large fort they had built
upon S! John's river, and calld it S! Johns fort; and mannd
it w^h Scotts. D'Aulney beseiged the fort, and forc'd
S! Charles to fly to New England for succour, where he borrowed five hundred pound of one Major Gibbons; and with
that money, mannd a vessell, for the reliefe of his Fort; but
when he came thether he found his fort taken, most of the
scots put to ye sword his lady dead; poysond as he was
inform'd by her enemyes the Fryers.

Then S! Charles went to France and complaind. The
French King abhorr'd D'Aulneys wickedness, and gave
S! Charles commission to be Governo^r of Nova Scotia,
authority to resume all the lands Mons! D'Aulney had taken
from him, and orders to send the said D'Aulney a prisoner
to France, to answer for all his villanyes.

And to make the said S! Charles de S! Estienne farther
satisfaction, for all the dammages he had suffered by the
tyranny of D'Aulney, which were upwards of thirty thousand
pounds the French King gave the s^d S! Charles Port Royall,
and Penobscot.

Then the said Sir Charles saild to Nova Scotia; but before
he arrived, D'Aulney had by his insolence and tyranny, made
himselfe so hate full to his owne people; that crossing a
river in a canoe, one of his servants that went wth him, overset the canoo, and drownd his master— When S! Charles
arriv'd the Fryers having lost their friend, made peace with
S! Charles and S! Charles marryed D'Aulneys widow.
Then the Fryers delivered up to him, not only his owne
lands, but all that D'Aulney had possest.

In the year 1654, some English men o'war were at Manahadas, then a Dutch colony, now call'd New Yorke; in order
to beseige it, for then there was a war between England, and

Holland. But newes arriving of a peace, before they had taken the Towne, and the Souldiers loath to returne without plunder, they saild to Nova Scotia, and found S.᷊ Charles de S.᷊ Estienne, in possession of all Nova Scotia and Penobscot, both as governour, and proprietour, his father S.᷊ Claud being dead.

Then though at that time there was great amity betweene England & France, the English Fleete landed men upon S.᷊ Charles tooke severall of his houses, plunderd 'em, and then burnt 'em, and at length made him yeild up all Nova Scotia, Penobscot, and all the lands belonging to it, and then they carryed him with them to England. When S.᷊ Charles was in England; he complained to some Members of one of Cromwells Parliaments, which was then sitting of ye violence, and injustice done him, at a time when there was full peace betweene England & France. Cromwell, to stop complaints in Parliament against him let S.᷊ Charles know after he had petition'd him that if he wou'd compound for his lands, as other subjects of England did, he shou'd enjoy 'em, otherwise not S.᷊ Charles consented, then Cromwell enjoynd him to pay of all the English souldiers that were in Nova Scotia, and that cost S.᷊ Charles above two thousand pound.

Then the said S.᷊ Charles, by his deed, bearing date, ye twentyeth of September 1656, made over all his right & title to Nova Scotia, to Penobscot, and all the lands belonging to it, from the river S.᷊ Croix, to the river Musconcus, bordring on Pemaquid, to Thomas Temple, and William Crowne Esquiers, and their heires forever for the summe of three thousand, three hundred and seventy odde pounds. The said S.᷊ Charles also reserv'd to himselfe, and his heires forever, the twentyeth skin of all kinds of Peltry, of equall value, with the rest; as also the twentyeth part of all the fruits and productions of the earth, of what kind soever.

Then the aforesaid three proprietours, went over, and tooke possession of their lands; the said Thomas Temple going governour by Cromwells Commission.

Not long after their arrivall there, the said Thomas Temple, and William Crowne divided their lands, And the said Thomas Temple by his deede, bearing date the twelfe of September 1657, made over all his right and title to Penobscot, and all the lands from the river Machias, on ye East, to the river Musconcus on the west, bordring on Pemaquid, in New England to the said William Crowne, and his heires for ever. And the said William Crowne, made over all his right and title to Nova Scotia, to the said Thomas Temple and his heires for ever.

Then the said William Crowne, tooke possession of Penobscot, dwelt in it, and built a considerable trading house, some leagues up the river, at a place antiently call'd Negue; but by himselfe Crownes point.

In the yeare 1662, the said Thomas Temple, and William Crowne came over to England: and had a hearing before King Charles the second, and the Lords and others, of his Majestyes most hon^{ble} Privy Councell then in being. And by the Lord Chancellour Hide, and the major part of the Privy councell, their titles to the aforesaid lands were adjudged to be good, and they permitted to returne, and repossess 'em, which they did. The said Thomas Temple was created by the King a Baronet of Nova Scotia, and commissiond to be Governour. Sr Thomas Temple, being once more Governour, oppress'd the said William Crowne; and forc'd from him a lease, of Penobscot, and all the lands belonging to it; for a rent far short of the value; and two considerable rich New England merchants, were bound for the payment of ye rent and for very good reason, for they farm'd, all the said lands of Sr Thomas Temple: but neither they nor S.˙ Thomas payd the said William Crowne a farthing rent.

Then the said William Crowne sued 'em before the Governours of New England, but the Governours, and merchants being all brethren of one Independent congregation in Boston in New England, y˙ᵉ Governours protected their brethren in their dishonesty; and pretending the dispute was, about a title of lands, which lay out of their jurisdiction, they refus'd to give y˙ᵉ said William Crowne judgement, upon a bond made by their owne brethren, in their owne towne of Boston, nay they rejected a verdict given by one of their owne juryes, at the tryall, in behalfe of the said William Crowne; By vertue of the aforesaid partiall and corrupt judgement; S.˙ Thomas Temple, and the said merchants, enjoyd the said William Crowne estate, and payd him nothing for it.

Thus it continued, till the yeare 1668; when King Charles consented to deliver Nova Scotia, to the French; and sent a commission under the great seale, to S.˙ Thomas Temple to deliver it.

S.˙ Thomas being at that time, in possession of Penobscot, and all the lands belonging to it, by vertue of the aforesaid lease, presum'd to deliver 'em all to the French, pretending they were a part of Nova Scotia; which he knew to be false, but they were the estate of the said William Crowne. Therefore to impoverish, and totally disable the said William Crowne, from following him to England, and sueing him there, for the many hundred pounds he owed him, for nonpayment of rent, he gave up Penobscot, and all the lands belonging to it, to the French; for which when he came to England, King Charles sent him to yᵉ Tower.

Before S.˙ Thomas deliverd Nova Scotia, he demolished all the Forts there, and brought away yᵉ gunnes, because they were his owne: but Penobscot he delivered entire, with all the gunnes, and ammunition in it; because they belonged to the said William Crowne. Therefore if he had brought them to Boston, the said William Crowne, might have seiz'd and sold them.

To conclude; Penobscot, with all the lands belonging to it, was originally an English Plantation; discovered by some inhabitants of New Plymouth, in New England; and they were the first of any Christian nation that settled there. The French got it, by an impudent cheate, put upon the English, by Mounsieur D'Aulney, the French Governour of Nova Scotia.

Some yeares after, it came againe into English hands; and the French got it, a second time, not by any right or title they had to it, but by the falsehood, and corruption, of S[r.] Thomas Temple, the English Governour, for which he was punish'd, but not so much as he deserv'd.

Not many yeares after S[r.] Thomas Temple deliver'd it; a war broke out betweene France, and Holland. Then y[e] Dutch sent a man of war or two, to Penobscot, who beate downe the Fort there, carried away all the French they found there prisoners, brought all the great gunnes, and ammunition that were there to Boston, in New England, and sold 'em to y[e] Governours and people of Boston, for almost six hundred pounds; and they put 'em in the Castle, which guards their harbour. When the Dutch had done this, they tooke no care of Penobscot, but entirely abandond it. Then King Charles once more tooke possession of it; and put it under the command of the Governour of New Yorke; who made considerable benefit of it; suffring none to trade there without his leave. And an order was issued out, by the Governour and councell of New Yorke, bearing date the 28th of November 1683, for the disposing and planting, Penobscot, and all the lands belonging to it, lying betweene Nova Scotia, and Kennebecke river.

And no opposition was made to the said order, by ye French, notwithstanding the great interest they had at that time in the English court.

Penobscot was under the dominion of England & ye command of the Governour of New Yorke, all the latter end of the reigne of King Charles the second; and all the reigne of the late King James, By consequence his present Majesty, has beene in possession of it all his reigne; and the French have not the least pretence to it.

By the death of the aforementioned William Crowne, all his right and title, to Penobscot, and all the lands from the river Machias, on the East, to the river Musconcus on ye west, bordering on Pemaquid, is descended to his eldest son, and heire John Crowne who now humbly petitions for restauration or compensation.

End: *New England*
  Mem^l. from M^r. Crown relating to his Title to Penobscot in New England.
Rec^d. } *Novr. 20th 1700.*
Read

The Peticõn of John Crowne Gent.

To the Right Hono^ble the Lords Com^rs for Trade and Plantations.
  The humble Peticõn of John Crowne Gentleman.
Sheweth

That your Pet^r. is rightfull Proprietor of Penobscot, and other Lands in America, lying westward of Nova Scotia; from the River Machias on the East, to the River Musconcus on the West, bordering on Pemaquid. The said Lands were purchased by your Pet^rs. Father; and possest by him, till

1668; when Sr Thomas Temple, Governour of Nova Scotia, being in Possession of them, by virtue of a Lease from your Pet^{rs} Father, presum'd to give em up to the French, for his own Sinister ends, without any authority from the King. And now your Pet^r is inform'd that the Limmits of his Maj^{ties} Dominions in America, Are to be settled by English and French Comm^{rs}.

Your Pet^r therefore does most humbly Pray your Lord^{pps} that his Claime to the aforesaid Lands may be heard.

And Y^r Pet^r as in Duty bound shall ever pray &c

End :   *New England*
    Mr Crown's Petition relating to his Title to Penobscot in America.

The bounds of Nova Scotia, and Penobscot, with the lands belonging to it, as they are expresst in Cromwells Patent, and ye deede of Partition

In Oliver Cromwells Patent, the bounds of Nova Scotia, are thus mentiond From Mereliquish on the East, to the Port and cape of La Heve, leading along the coast, to Cape Sable, from thence to a Port, now called La Tour, heretofore named L'omery. From thence following the coast, to the cloven cape. From thence to the cape, and river of Ingogen; thence to Port Royall; and from thence following the coast, to the bottome of the bay. From thence along the bayes to St Johns Fort. After this, Oliver Cromwells Patent, mentions no other place, in Nova Scotia by name; only sayes, all along the coast, to Pentagonet, alias Penobscot, thence to St Georges river, and thence to Musconcus.

The true bounds of Nova Scotia, are only to be found, in the originall Patent, graunted by King James the first. But they were alwaies judged, by S.[r] Charles S.[t] Estienne, Thomas Temple, and William Crowne, the Proprietours and possessours to be Merelequish on the East, and the river S.[t] Croix on y[e] west. And beyond the river S.[t] Croix, Nova Scotia extends not westward.

The said Thomas Temple and William Crowne, divided their lands; And Thomas Temple by his deede bearing date the twelfth of September 1657 made over to William Crowne, and his heires for ever, Penobscot, and all the lands lying westward of the river Machias to y[e] river Muscongus, bordring on Pemaquid Machias Penobscot, and Musconcus, are the only remarkeable places, mentiond in the deede of Partition. Machias is a river that runs some few leagues westwards of S.[t] Croix; the utmost westward boundary of Nova Scotia. In S.[r] Charles de S.[t] Estiennes deede to Thomas Temple, and William Crowne, no places are perticularly named, only in generall all New Scotland, as it is bounded, in the originall Patent, graunted by King James the first, to S.[r] William Alexander, and his heires; and as it is mentioned in the said S.[r] William Alexanders deede to S.[r] Claud and the said S.[r] Charles de S.[t] Estienne and their heires: And all New Scotland, with other lands adjoyning, as they are mentioned in Oliver Cromwells Patent, to the said S.[r] Charles de S.[t] Estienne, Thomas Temple, and William Crowne.

R.[t] Hon[ble]

A   In obedience to the Commands of Their Excellencies the Lords Justices in Council by Their Order of the 18th of July last signified in your Lord.[ps] Letter of the 1st of August (a copy of s.[d] order being also inclosed) Directing the respective Governours of his Ma[tys] Plantations in America to transmit an Accompt to your Lord.[ps] in the most particular manner, of the method of proceedings in the several Courts upon Tryal of all Sorts of Causes in the s.^d Courts in those parts respectively; I have taken care (in the absence of our Governour the Earl of Bellomont, who is now within his Government of New Yorke) of the observation of the s.^d Order, and accordingly herewith transmit to your Lord.^{ps} the Accompt thereby required in as particular manner as well can be, hopeing it will answer his Ma.^{tys} and your Lordships expectation and satisfaction.

B I crave leave further to observe to your Lord.^{ps} the present repose and quiet of this his Ma.^{tys} Province after the late Alarm of troubles threatned to arise from the Indians by a fresh Insurrection & breaking forth in open hostility, and how necessary it is in order to ye continuance of this quiet that the French Priests and Missionaries be removed from their residence among them, the Indians taking measures from their evil counsels and suggestions, and are bigotted in their zeal to their pernicious and damnable principles; But the removal of those Incendiaries is rendred difficult whilst the claims and pretensions to the Boundaries of Territory and Dominion betwixt the English and French are depending undetermined, or at least the determination not known in the Plantations.

C This Government have lately erected a Trading house with a Fortification, and setled a Garrison at Casco Bay for accomodating of Trade with the Indians and by kind usage and treatment of them therein hope to oblige them and to divert their conversation & commerce with the French and have likewise made provision for Trade with them at Saco Fort and other places, and by meanes of their drawing thither to gain the advantage for instructing of them in the true Christian Religion, To which end two English Ministers are sent to reside in the Eastern parts, one at the Fort at Saco, and the other at Casco Fort.

I am also credibly informed That the French in Nova Scotia or L'Accadie have slighted their Fortification at the River S! Johns, and are removed to Port Royal where they are fortifying and setling a strong Garrison, having Artillery and souldiers sent from France this year for that purpose, and are likewise about to settle a Garrison at the River S! Georges; and possibly think to make Encroachments further Westward into his Ma^{tys} Territory, even as far as the River of Kennebeck whereto they have lately made pretensions, thô altogether groundless and without any Shew of Reason or Justice; however, hereby they will strengthen and confirm the Indians in their Interests and have the Command over them, and annoy our Fishery unless a stop be put thereto by an adjustment and Settlement of the Boundarys; The which I thought necessary for his Majesties Service to lay before your Lordships.

Having nothing further to give your Lord^{ps} the trouble of at present. I am with all imaginable respect

Right Honble
Your Lordships

Boston   Most humble & obedient Servant
 December ye 20th 1700.   Wm. Stoughton

Lords Commiss^{rs} of the Council for Trade &c.

Report on John Crown's Petition.

To the Kings most Excellent Majesty
May it please Your Majesty.

In obedience to Your Majestys Commands upon a Petition of John Crown Esqr where of a Copy is hereunto Annexed, We have examined his Title to the Lands therein mentioned, and thereupon humbly Report.

That the Country called Penobscot lying South West from the River S.t Croix, (the Ancient Boundary between Nova Scotia and New England) appears unto Us to have formerly belonged to his Father M.r William Crown and to be descended to the Petitioner.

But that in the Execution of the 10.th Article of the Treaty of Breda for the Surrender of Accadie (or Nova Scotia) to the French the said Country of Penobscot was delivered up to them, thô it be not truly Comprehended in the Treaty, as being no part of Accadie) and that they have thereupon claimed a Title to it, which has ever since remain'd in dispute between England and France, Whereby the Petitioner has been deprived of the advantage which he might otherwise have made by his Right to the Propriety of the said Country, without any Compensation from the Crown (that we know of) either to his Father or himself for the loss arrising to them by the Surrender of more than was required by the Treaty.

All which nevertheless is most humbly Submitted.
Signed

		Stamford	Lexington
Whitehall		Ph: Meadows	Blathwayt
January the		J. Pollexfen	Ab: Hill
22.nd $170\frac{0}{1}$		G: Stepney	M.r Prior

(No Endorsement)

Casco Bay June the 3.d 1701

A Memorial of those heads or Propositions on which Col.o John Phillips, Col.o Penn Townsend, Cap.t Nathaniel Byfield & John Nelson, being Commisionated by the Hon.ble William Stoughton Lieu.t Governour and the Hon.ble the Council, for the Province of the Massachusetts Bay in

New England, did treat with the Eastern Indians, and were as followeth viz:

Sometime after that the Commissioners and the Indian Sagamore or Chiefs had taken each their places at a Table set under a Tent spread in the Woods, The Commissioners began and told them, by two English Interpreters and one Indian

Com: We are here sent by his Ma^{ty} to treat with you and renew our Friendship with you.

Ind: We are here also generally met together and are very glad to see you.

Com: 1 Prop: That our great Master King William having been duly informed of that renewal and confirmation of Friendship which you offered unto our late Governour the Earl of Bellomont in that great Assembly of Indians, with whom you did desire to joyne in a mutual & publick League of amity with us he has ordered us to informe you how well he has accepted the same and that he has commanded the Government of the Massachusetts punctually to perform and conforme themselves to all things contained in the s^d Treaty concluded with you at Albany in October 1700.

We know that King William hath power to make peace when he will, and we are glad that he hath accepted us into the League of Friendship & that you are now sent to confirme it.

2 Pro: That since the death of the s^d Earl of Bellomont, there is come new and express Orders from our Comon Father the great King William by which we are commanded to come unto you in this country to renew & keep fresh in memory the afores^d Treaty, and as Brethren & Friends to rejoice with you in the happy fruits of so well a setled peace amongst us, whereby all former mistakes and injuries may be for ever buried and forgot, and at the

same time to shew you our hearts, both in setling the Trade so to yʳ advantage as that for the future you may never want anything and at cheap rates and prices, as also to bring unto you the presents which the King has been pleased to send you.

Ind: Ansʳ We are very glad that the great King William hath so far taken notice of us as to send you amongst us that the friendship between us may be confirmed which we do from out hearts agree to, and from this day forward it shall be for ever talked of amongst us, and we also desire that all former inquiries and Mischiefs that have been committed on either side may be forever buried under ground. We are also thankful for the good Settlement of the Trade for us, and we pray that we may have Goods sold to us at a cheap rate, and that no Rum may be sold the Indians.

3 Pro: That the experience of the benefits of the present peace & quietness is sufficient to convince how it ought inviolably to be maintained and that neither party believe or hearken to any who by false or subtle perswasions shall seek to disturb it, but rather hold them Enemies for so doing. and if unhappily any misunderstanding should arise by any wrong done unto you by our People, upon yoʳ Complaint due punishmᵗ shall be inflicted & satisfaction made which we likewise expect on your parts to be performed to us.

Ind: Ansʳ We promise to observe it and desire the same thing of you.

4ᵗʰ Prop: That in future confirmation of your amity & freindship, we are to offer unto you the protection of our great and mighty Prince King William who under this Covenant of peace looks upon you as his Children, and therefore is ready to defend you against any that shall invade or disturb you

Ind: Ansʳ In case any Nation should make War upon us

we do not desire that our Uncle King William (which Title we esteem equal to Father) should loose any men on our Account until we have tried what we can do for our own defence.

5th Prop: That we are likewise to note unto you our Jealosies concerning the French by whom you have been so often seduced, that through their false reports you may not again be deceived, but rather call to remembrance those times when by a full confidence and love we were useful unto each other, which same Trust you may see we are again endeavouring to restore not only by a free Trade and supplying of you with powder, lead, Armes and all other things you may need at such prices as the French (who cheat you) cannot do whereby you may be the better enabled to keep your promises so lately made unto the E: of Bellomont, in cutting down trees in the path so for ever stopping the way to Quebec since we shall for your safety furnish whatever you want, at your own doors and spare you the labour of going so far.

Ind. Ansr. In case we should stop up our roads to Canada many of our Brethren would be hindred from coming over to us, besides many amongst us care not to be deprived of the liberty of going whither they please, yet we think there will be little necessity of going to the French since we may be so well supplied with what we want from the English.

6 Prop: That from the repeated Treatys made with you whereby you have put your selves under the protection of the Crown of England &c our great King William do's expect the punctual performeance of your promises for the future, and on his part you shall ever receive such favour & protection as is due unto his Children

Ind: Ansr. We do not mind any talk but what we now say, we resolve to stand to it, and it comes from our very hearts.

7 Prop: That altho a Solemn peace had lately been con-

cluded between his Ma^ty and the French King which was to have lasted for ever Yet thrô his perfidious and false dealings therein, our King will be forced to enter into a new War with him, unless satisfaction be made for the prosecution of which he is making greater preparations than ever. We are therefore the rather desirous of making this known unto you, to the intent you may not be surprized at it, nor receive any reports which the French may make of us on y^r regard, since we design nor intend any thing that may break our covenants with you but that in whatever shall happen you may be assured of perfect peace and quiet from us, and unto all those Indians who shall not take any part or assist the French in case the War should break out again with them.

Ind: Ans^r. We thank you that you will give us notice of the likelyhood of a War between the French and the English, and we desire to keep ourselves free, and not to be under the command of any party, and we will endeavour what we can to bring the Indians that live upon the French Ground under the same Obligations with our selves. And if any damage happen to be done upon the English by the Indians that may pretend to belong to any of our three Forts of Norridgawog, Ammassakuntick or Narrakamagog, we desire the English would not believe it till they have sent to us for information, and we promise to make inquiry into the matter and if they belong to us we will endeavour to do you Justice for if we should not, we should all become equally guilty.

8 Prop: That for your further assureance and advantage in abiding in ye Country the Government has thought good to settle with you an Armourer who for the future shall repair or mend any or all of your Guns that may prove defective. and that gratis so that you may have no pretence or occasion of going to Canada or to the French in these parts for want of this or any supply whatsoever.

Ind: Ans^r We are very thankful that we can have Guns mended here for nothing especially because formerly when any of our Guns were but a little broken we lookt upon them as lost, and we promise to bring in no Enemies Guns to be mended. Here the Indians Queried whether the Penobscot Indians might not be included in benefit of having their Guns mended, on which condition they promised to use their best endeavours to engage them as themselves in this same Treaty.

The Answer was that all Indians in friendship with us should have the same priviledge.

9 Prop. That to the intent of perfecting our future & mutual friendship & acquaintance we have thought good to offer and invite your sending of some of your Children to live amongst us whom we shall take care of both for their maintenance and Education & to return them at such times as you shall desire, and that if you are any ways inclineable to have your young men see England and King William, we shall send them whereby you may be better informed of the circumstances of our Nation.

To this ninth Proposition they desired time to consider, and whereon it being near night and bad weather, we broke up until the next day.

June the 4th.

Ind. Ans^r. We conclude not to send any of our Children to England, because Moxus his son when he was sent to France, he died there, And we conclude not to send any of our children to Boston because we formerly had two of our children at Boston, called John & Robin, which we believe have by this time learned to read & write English enough, and they never yet have been returned amongst us

10 Prop; That it is left unto your selves seriously to consider what may yet remain or be most for your ease safety

and advantage which as we earnestly desire, so shall readily hearken unto, and perform anything that may be consistant with his Ma^ty honour and the safety of his Subjects in these countrys &c

Ind: Ans^r   We desire to be informed about the two Children mentioned in our answer to the 9th Paragraph

Comiss^rs Reply   Those two Children were taken in War, and disposed of by those to whom they did belong, and we hear that one of them is dead and the other is now in London where he is well provided for and we believe he hath lost his Language and that he will not incline to return but if he be willing we shall use our Endeavours to procure him

Ind;   You ought to force him to come home for we have a great mind to see him we forced some of your Captives to return home

Com^r   He is out of our Government, and we can't force him but we shall use our utmost endeavour to obtain him.

2^ly   We desire that if you should hereafter have occasion to treat with us we might meet together at Merry Meeting

Reply   The Indians must then be at the Pains to prepare a house for our Accomodation.

Ind;   We are willing to do it, and we desire that always we may have timely notice of the time of meeting by a Letter from this Fort at Casco bay, and we shall not hearken to any other.

3^ly   We desire to have a Trading house erected at Merry Meeting.

11 Prop   That we cannot avoid taking notice of your affecting or wearing a french flagg or Colours, which if you purpose to maintain any setled correspondence or friendship with our nation must for the future be forborne in this or any part of his Ma^tys Dominions, and that you meet and treat with us under English Banners which at your

desire or request we shall take care to supply you with as occasion may require.

Ind: Ans.^r   We thought it necessary to have some flagg or other, and having no other we put up a white one, but if you will please to furnish us with an English flagg, we promise to wear it for the future as a signal between us.

12 Prop: That we are in an especial manner directed to invite you unto an Union with us in the true Christian Religion, separated from those foolish superstitious and plain Idolatries with which the Roman Catholicks and especially the Jesuits and Missionarys have currupted it, to which intent we are to offer you the assistance of Teachers for your Instruction in like manner as is practised amongst those Indians who live amongst us, of whom great numbers have happily received, and live in the faith of our Lord Jesus Christ, in which great undertaking we shall expect nothing more on your parts than your good treatment of those Ministers whom we shall at any time send amongst you.

Ind: Ans.^r   It much surprizeth us that you should propose any thing of Religion to us, for we did not think any thing of that nature would have been mentioned.

Furthermore nothing of that nature was mentioned when the peace was concluded between all Nations, Furthermore the English formerly neglected to instruct us in Religion which if they had then offered it to us, we should have embraced it and detested the Religion which we now profess, but now being instructed by the French we have promised to be true to God in our Religion, and it is this we profess to stand by.

Com: We propose that for a perpetual remembrance of our good agreement, each party should raise a heap of stones.

Ind: We do well agree to it, and we understand it better than signing of a writing.

Two heaps of stones were accordingly raised in the

place of Treaty that is to say, the Commissioners on the English part each of them laid one Foundation stone, and the men then present wth them made up the heap in a square Pyramide. And the Indian Sagamore each of them for their part likewise laid a Foundation stone, and then all the Indians and their children made up their heap in a roundish Pyramide, to west of the English, upon the point formerly called Andrews his point, now mutually agreed forever hereafter be called the two Brothers point, from the two Pillars.

Upon information of some English Captives yet remaining amongst them, a demand was made for their release.

The Indians replied, We know not of any amongst us but if we can possibly see that Child of ours which is in England it will be great encouragem^t & we will endeavour to redeem any captives of yo^{rs} that we can heare of either at Canada or elsewhere.

Concerning the Indians that treated with the Maqua's in October last. The Indians say that those Indians that then treated with the Maqua's went on their own heads.

Com: Shall we then tell the Maqua's that all y^t Treaty goes for nothing.

Ind: After a considerable non plus, they replyed that those Indians were only sent to know the Issue of the Earl of Bellomonts Treaty with the Maqua's.

The names of the Chief Sachems.

Moxus
Dondomhegon } of Narridgawogg

Wasahombomet
Abomhomen al^s } of Amassakantick
Jno Maherimet

Adeawanadon
Madagwunesseak } of Narrackamagog/

John Phillips
Penn Townsend
Natha^l Byfield
J^o Nelson

A true Copy Exam^d
Is^s Addington Sec$\tilde{r}$y.

My Lord

I should think I ill upheld the character of those of my Nation, and the perfect union which we ought to endeavour to preserve with our Neighbours if, at my arrival by order of the King my Master on the Coasts of Accadie, of which his Ma^{ty} has honoured me with the Command, I did not witness to you by the advice I give you of my arrival in this Province, that I desire nothing so much as to imploy all my care and all the knowledge which a long experience in the trade of War ought to give me, in keeping in an exact discipline the Souldiers Inhabitants and Indians of our Colonies, that nothing for the future may interrupt, by any offence on their part towards you the good Sentiments which we have of entertaining a loving & advantagious Correspondence as long as it shall please the King of England yor Master and him whose most faithful & humble Subject I have the honour to be

Having left the Affairs of Europe when I came from thence is a doubtful situation as to war or peace, I thought it my duty, My Lord, to represent to you as far as I can, and the King my Master has left it to my disposal, that it seems to me of consequence for the publick safety of your Inhabitants as well as ours, to find out away to avoid the havock and crueltys of the Indians who breath nothing but blood and all sorts of inhumane and odious torments to us as well as our Enemies, which cannot be hindred but by a particular treaty from you to us, during all the courses and acts of hostility on our Coasts, in not espousing the differences which our Soveraign Princes may issue in Europe by force of armes./

My Lord, I do not propose these sorts of agreements but as far as the consent of the King of England your Master may resolve you, and if, after having well examined our common Interests, you be determined in case of War, to a suspension of Armes on your side as well as ours, till you have informed and have received Orders from his Ma^{ty} of Britain on this Subject we do assure you, that on our side shall be held, till then a firme and sincere peace, expecting a declaration made faithfully on the Resolutions which you shall take, of which we pray you to give us advice with the same fidelity which we promise on our part.

My Lord, If hereafter the proposal which I make you singly for the good of yours and our People do not suit the Interests of both Crowns we will make to you as we expect you will to us, a publick declaration before we enterprize any thing which may break our Treaty of Union and good Correspondence.

My Lord, This is what I dare promise my selfe to have ratified by the King my Master; if yours will do the same, I pray you would let me know it with speed that so I may know what to do.

I cannot omit advising you that I have orders to hinder, conformeable to the Treaty of Ryswick, all English Vessels from coming to fish in sight of the Lands of this Province. I pray you would let it be known in your Ports.

Assuring you nevertheless, My Lords, that in all things, that shall not hinder the Interest of the King my Master, you shall never have a Neighbour more desirous than I shall be to contribute to every thing that may be for the good of our Colonys, and of yours in particular that so I may attract the honour of your esteem and good will being perfectly

   My Lord Your most humble & most obedient Servant
At the Fort at Port Royal   Brouillan
 the 8th August 1701./
Superscribed
   To my Lord Bellomont Govern^{r}. General of New
    England, or, in his absence to him that commands
               at Boston
.Copy Exam^{d} p Is^{a} Addington Sec$\tilde{r}$y.

To the Kings most Exellent Majesty

A Memorial of the Council & Representatives of your Ma^{tys} Province of the Massachusetts Bay in New England.

May it please your Majesty.

Upon perusal of your Ma^{tys} several gracious Letters of the 19th of January and 2^{d} February of $170\frac{0}{1}$ directed to your Ma^{tys} Governour or Commander in chief for the time being of Province, and on mature consideration of your Ma^{tys} Royal this Commands therein signified, We crave leave in all humble and dutiful manner to represent to your sacred Ma^{ty}

As to the Complaints of the Spoil of woods by cutting down & converting to private uses such Trees as are or may be proper for the service of your Ma^{tys} Royal Navy.

We are ignorant of any grounds for complaints of that nature, none having been made to the Government here of any such practice within this Province which had it been we should have endeavoured to restraine and prevent the same.

Your Ma^{ty} having been pleased by Your Royal Commission in ye second year of your Ma^{tys} Reign to grant unto Jahleel Brenton Gent. the office of Surveyer of all and singuler Woods, Fir trees and other Timber trees within these your Territories fit and proper for the use of your Ma^{tys} Royal Navy Impowring him his Deputy or Deputys to view Survey and marke all such Trees and to register the same &c., And the s^{d} Mr Brenton & his Deputys being in the actual Exercise of S^{d} Office: We might reasonably expect, had any obstruction been given them therein or any spoils made, they would have made application to the Government for redress thereof, but they have not offered at any time any such Complaint. And Timber proper for Your Ma^{tys} Service is of so great value and esteem here that no persons who have any such will readily spoile imbezel or convert it to other use because it would be much to their disadvantage.

As to Fortifications.

The last Summer we caused a small Fortification to be erected at Casco Bay, where there is a Garrison posted, upwards of fifty miles to ye Eastward of any present Settlement of the English whereby we design'd to Accomodate the Indians for Trade, and to supply them at easie rates thô with loss to the Publick to prevent their going to the French therefor, and to fix them in the English Interests, as also to encourage the resettlement of that part of the Province. And a Plantation will be speedily set forward there in case a new War do not commence.

The Fort formerly erected at Pemaquid, cost us not less than Twenty Thousand pounds to build and maintain the same, and we are not sensible we had in any measure a proportionable advantage thereby. The Situation thereof was on a Promontary towards the Sea Much out of the ordinary roads of the Indians Yet were we careful to furnish & supply the same with all necessary Stores and provisions & had newly reinforced the Garrison (which with that recruit consisted of more than four score men) and sent them fresh supplies a little before it unhappily fell into the hands of the Enemy. Had the Commander been as well furnished with conduct and Resolution it had probably been defended.

We are humbly of opinion That the building of a Fort at Pemaquid, lying upwards of one hundred miles distant from any part of ye Province at present inhabited by the English, can be no security to our Frontiers, or Bridle to the Indians. The only benefit we conceive might arise thereby would be to shelter a few Boats that may be imployed in fishing towards those parts and at some times put in there. And it would draw such a considerable charge upon your Ma^{tys} Subjects as they cannot possibly support.

We are actually at work in raising New Fortifications on Castle Island near Boston (the place of greatest Import within this your Ma^{ty} Province) under the direction and oversight of Col? Romer, your Ma^{tys} Engineer, which workes will amount to considerable Sums of Money. And 'tis further necessary could we be able to support the charge thereof (which indeed we cannot) that Fortifications should be made in Several other places within this Bay near Boston, as Salem, Marblehead, Glocester, Plymouth and Hull, being so many Avenues by which the Enemy may make Impressions upon us.

Our incapacity for doing what is necessary in this respect where we are more nearly concerned We hope with Submission, will sufficiently excuse us from contributing to the charge of building and maintaining of Forts in the Province of New Hampshire. Their ability to maintain the Fort in that Province is proportionably much greater than that of your Ma^{tys} Subjects in this to do what is necessary as to Fortifications here. This Province was at very great charge to give them assistance during the late War, and must necessarily further assist them if War arise again, thô they have not done any thing towards reimburseing what was before.

As to the Quota of assistance in men or money for New Yorke. We cannot be able to comply therewith without apparent hazard of exposing your Ma^{tys} Interests within this Province. The Line of our Frontier both by Sea and Land is of far larger extent than that of New Yorke and do's necessarily require by far, a greater number of men to guard the same We lye much more open & exposed to an attack by sea than New Yorke do's, and if they be in hazard much more shall we, And if War happen with France we must expect the Indians will break forth again. The Line of our Frontier against them is upwards of two hundred miles in length, and the French Indians in the late War found none, or little Difficulty to come from Canada down the Rivers either in their Canoes or on the Ice in the Winter Season and infest our Northern & Western Towns whereto they can have a more easie access than to Albany, and 'tis not to be thought but that they will again make use of such advantage, The Inland Frontiers of New Yorke are strengthned with some of your Ma^tys Foot Companys being constantly upon duty, and have the five Nations a Barrier to them who will be ready at all times to give them notice of the approach of an Enemy and afford them assistance Also, other of your Ma^tys Colonies lye more contiguous to New Yorke and can more readily afford them Succours than this Province they lying less exposed.

The vast Expence this Province was at in the time of the late War for the preservation of your Ma^tys Interests within the same, and in the Province of New Hampshire (which without assistance from hence would become an easy prey to the Enemy) besides ye devastations then made by the Enemy have reduced your Ma^tys Subjects here to an extream depth of poverty. The Wounds they have received both in their persons & Estates are so recent, that they would labour of insuperable difficulty to be anew embroyled in War, and liable to be transported to Serve in another Province whilst their Families & Estates lye exposed at home.

As to the sending Accessories in Piracy into England for Tryal; We fear the practice thereof will put discouragement on persons to discover any such Accessories they may know or be informed of, lest they themselves be obliged to accompany them into England as Witnesses which may prove ruinous to many to be taken upon a sudden and carried away from their business and Families. And the like may be said as to persons accused or taken up on Suspition who may appear innocent & be acquitted on their Tryal.

By the afore going Representation, In which we have endeavoured truely to set forth the danger your Ma^tys subjects and Interests within this Province will be in, of being exposed by a new War with France .... together with the Indians breaking out again upon us, and our incapacity of doing what is necessary for our defence against so potent an Enemy as the French and to counter worke the crafty designes & surprizes of the barbarous & bloody Salvages, who have such advantages against us; Your Ma^{ty} may be pleased to take a view of the State of our affairs and to judge of our wants especially of Canon, small armes & other Stores of War for the furnishing of your Ma^{tys} Fortifications within this Province as also some ships of War of greater force than those at present assigned to this Station for the better guarding and securing of the Coast in case of War: For which we humbly implore your Ma^{tys} Grace.

We humbly crave leave further to subjoin to the answer made by Sr Henry Ashhurst to the Petition preferred to your Ma^{ty} by the Earl of Lymrick for the grant of a Tract of Land called Pemaquid, That, besides the Grant thereof made in your Ma^{tys} Royal Charter for this Province, the s^d Land with others lying both to the Eastward and Westward thereof was anciently granted by the Council of Devon to particular persons as their own property and by them since allotted out, and a great part thereof actually improved, until the Inhabitants were forced away by the hostility of Indians, and will be again resetled, if peace continue which Lands are also purchased of the Indians.

All which is most humbly submitted by Your Ma^{tys}

Most dutiful, obedient and Loyal Subjects

Boston	John Foster	Ja:Russell
August 9th 1701.	Peter Sergeant	Elisha Cooke
Joseph Lynde	John Hathorne	John Higginson
Penn Townsend	Elisha Hutchinson	Barnabas Lothrop
E^m Hutchinson	Sam Sewall	Natha^l Byfield
Benj^a Browne	Jonathan Convin	Wm Browne
	John Thacher	

In the Name, and by the Order, of the House of
    Representatives./   Nehemiah Jewett Speaker.

Sr.

You having been pleased by your Letter of the 8th of August currant directed to the Earl of Bellomont our late Governour and in his absence to such as have the Command within this Province (which by ye death of the Governour is devolved by his Maty on us his Council upon the place) to informe us of your arrival on the Coast of Accadie, and that the King your Master has honour'd you with the Command thereof, therein also expressing the good sentiments you have of entertaining a friendly and neighborly correspondence with this Government; We assure you of the like on our part in all things not inconsistent with the Interests of the King our Soveraign Lord and Master & shall studiously avoid all occasions to the contrary.

Sr. We approve your generosity in proposing to find out a way to restrain the rapines inhumane and barbarous crueltys practised by the bloody Salvages in time of War towards the people of Your Nation and ours, and shall be ready to agree with you in concerting of such methods as may be effectual to that end.

We also take notice of your other Proposal for a Suspension of Armes within these Territories if it happen that War be declared betwixt the two Crowns until we shall have represented the same unto our King, & have received his Orders on that Subject, which you assure us till then shall be held firm on your side if we so agree, and to have the same ratified by the King your Master.

Concerning which: Being by late Intelligences from England given to Understand the peace do's continue and no Declaration is made of War, and being in daily expectation of the arrival of a General to be sent us by our King, and know not what Instructions he may bring; we cannot at present take any resolutions in that affair; But whilst on your side, all acts of hostility shall be forborn, we shall not be forward to be the Aggressors, or to enterprize any thing to interrupt our mutual quiet and repose.

S.r As to the orders you intimate in yours to have received to hinder, conformeable to the Treaty of Ryswick, all English Vessels from coming to fish in sight of the Lands of Accadie; We must observe to you, that such orders are so far from being conformeable to the Treaty of Ryswick as that they are directly contrary to the V.th Articles of the s.d Treaty it having been the accustomed indubitable right and priviledge of the English to fish in the high Seas on that Coast for time out of mind.

We trust and expect you will not suffer any obstruction to be given to our Fishing Vessels in that their lawful Imploy whereof we shall have a just resentment, and esteem it not only a breach on your part of that good Neighbourhood which you profess to maintain but also to be contrary to Justice; Whereas we shall on our side contribute all that is necessary, not derogatory to the honour and Interests of the King our Master to preserve intire a good understanding betwixt your selfe & us, Praying you to believe that we are

S.r Your most humble Servants

Boston August 22. 1701 By command of y.e Council

Is.a Addington Secry.

Superscribed To M.r Brouillan
 Governour of Accadie at Port Royal

Boston N England Feb: 17th 1719.

Sir,

I hope my Letter that I wrote in Answer to Yours is long before this come safe to your hands.

I send you now Inclosed an Answer to the Queries you transmitted to me by Order of the Lords of Trade and Plantations relating to the Province of the Massachusetts Bay w.ch I desire you will lay before the Hon.ble Board and that you will also acquaint them that I cannot get the Queries relating to New-Hampshire well answered untill I go to that Province which will not be till the latter end of April, by which time I believe the Map of the Province will be finished. So that I shall be able to send the Queries answered with the Map of the Province of New Hampshire by the first Ship that shall Sail in May.

I desire also you will Acquaint their Lordships, that the 73 Article of my Instructions runs as follows

" And for as much as great Inconveniences may arise by
" the liberty of printing within His Majestys said Province
" you are to provide by all necessary Orders, that no Person
" keep any Press for printing nor that any Book, Pamphlet
" or other Matter whatsoever be printed without your espec-
" ial leave and licence first obtained. These His Majestys Instructions have been notifyed to all the Printers, yet notwithstanding due Notice has been given Nathaniel Proone has not only printed a Book without Licence but has even ventured to print what I have absolutely forbiden. Upon which I Summoned the Council and Acquainted them with His Majestys Instructions, who told me they could not find out any method to Punish the Printer because there was no Law against it. I afterwards Applyed my self to the Kings Attorney General who advised me to Acquaint the Lords of Trade & Plantations with this breach of His Majestys Orders and to get further directions from them in this matter.

I desire you will let me have a line in answer as soon as possible to assure me that this Letter came safe to you, I am
    Sir Your hum^{ble} Servt
     Samll Shute
To William Popple Esqr

End:) *Massachusetts*
L^r. from Coll Shute to ye Sec̃ry, dated ye 17 Feb^{ry} 1719/20 with answer to Queries, promising a map, & desiring advice

upon a Case relating to his Instruction against Printing there, without his Licence.

An Answer to the First Query Propos'd by the R^t. Honble the Lords of Trade &c. referring to the Province of the Massachusetts Bay.

By the best Computation That I have been able as yet to make the English Inhabitants within the Province of the Massachusetts Bay may be reckoned at Ninety four thousand Souls ~

Whereof the Regular Militia as they have been returned to me by the Officers of the Several Regiments &c: Amount to Fifteen thousand Six hundred and Eleven Men ~

Besides which within the said Province there are of the Indian Natives who are Civilized, and make some profession of the Christian Religion, and dwell in several parts of the Province in perfect friendship with the English Improving their own Lands &c to the Number of twelve hundred; Including Men Women and Children ~

With respect to Slaves either Negros or Indians (but most Negros) they may be computed at about two Thousand ~

Within this three years last past there have come from Ireland a Considerable Number of Famillys & Persons to settle the Eastern parts of the Province, & Else where to the Number probably of five or Six hundred Men Women and Children ~

As for white Servants Imported and Sold in this Province in the year 1717. there was entered at the Impost Office the Number of One hundred and Twenty Six Viz^t. 113 Males & 13 Females, the most of them from London Dublin & Belfast in Ireland, and the Island of Jersey; of Negro Slaves fifty three Imported the Same year Viz! 37 males 16 Females a particular Account whereof is Annexed; No great difference for seven years last past.

Servants Imported from June 29th 1717 to June 29th 1718. as reported in the Impost Office Boston

In what month	from whence	males	Females
1717 July	Antigua	1	
	London	15	
August	South hampton	4	
	Dublin	14	
	Leverpole	2	
	London		1
September	Dartmouth	26	4
	France	5	
	Belfast	9	
	London	2	
October	Glasgow	1	
November	Newfoundland		1
	Bristol	2	3
	London	1	
	Glasgow	4	
December	London	1	
January none			
February none			
March	Connecticut	1	
1718 April	Topsham	2	
	Ditto	3	
	London		2
June	Jarsey	19	2
	London	1	
		113	13
Negroes Imported in said year of which Several Exported		37	16

At the Enterance of the Harbour of the Town of Boston there is Castle William, a regular Fortification and in good Condition Eighty great Guns Mounted a Captain with other Officers and a Company of thirty Men. There are also in the Town two small Batterys, but of no use, wholly out of repair.

At Salem and Marblehead there are two small Forts both gone to ruine and not supported in a time of Peace.

In the County of York. There's a small stone Fort at Brunswick with fifteen men and an Officer a pretty good defence against the Indians.

At Winter harbour, a small Fort in a poor condition with ten Men and an Officer.

To the 2^d Q

In the Neighbourhood of this Province to the North East or towards Nova Scotia there are two Tribes of Indians one of them known by the name of the Kennibeck Indians One hundred fighting men who live chiefly at a place called Neridgiawack within a Sort of Fort made of Wood and where, is a small Chappel and a Jesuit. There are two or three other small Settlements of Indians that may make out in all fifty fighting men at Pennicook Amarascogin and Pegwoket. One other Tribe called the Penobscot Indians lying up the River of that name One hundred and fifty fighting Men, both Tribes too much inclined to the French Interest thro the Influence of the Jesuits who have allways one among them, and during the late Warrs between England and France they have been bloody Enemys to the English; At present they are pretty Quiet; but there is no depending on them ~

To the Westward near Albany there are several Nations or great Tribes of Indians that are in Alliance and Friendship with the English Government of New Yorke, but are so far distant, that we have Scarse any thing to do with them ~

Northwest and towards Canada there are some Tribes of Indians, but their Situation is so near the French Settlements that we call them the French Indians and they are perfectly under their Governm^ts and at three or four hundred Miles distance from us; their Numbers not very great .~

To the 3^d Q.

At Canada the French have Considerable Settlements, the principal are Quebec & Monreal ~

Quebec is not very populous, but well Fortifyed, There lives the Governour, the Intendant and a Bishop and there are some Religious Houses. The City and the Governours House have several Batterys and Platforms of great Guns~ To Quebec the Ships from France goe once a year Viz^t in the Summer, and carry Merchandize from France for the Trading part, pay, and Supply for the Soldiers; There may be about two hundred Soldiers at Quebec, the Countrey thereabout not much Peopled; Upon the Isle of Orleans a little below the City are good Farmers that raise good Wheat and Beef. Up the River two hundred Miles near Southwest is Monreal, an Island, a pretty Strong place, There lives the Liev^t Governour and two Companys; near Mon real live also the French Indians & thither they resort for the most part, from thence they Trade and Correspond with Albany and the Indian Nations thereabouts from Mon real the French also carry on their Trade to Missasippe. There is also a small Settlement of the French at Trois Rivieres & at Chamblay still nearer to Albany but not very considerable ~

From Canada it is That in a time of Warr between England and France, the French Influence and Actually Imploy their Indians to Annoy and Destroy the English Settlements both of this Province and the Colony of Connecticut and some times the Province of New York. This Province have had two fair Towns destroyed in two years Successively in the last Warr by a party of two hundred Indians headed by French Officers from Canada And it is difficult, considering the Vastness of the Frontiers to know how to prevent such

Incursions in a time of War, unless the two Crowns should Agree never to Imploy the Indians on either side against each other even in Case of a Warr ~

As to Cape Breton,
The Province of Nova Scotia lyes between us and the French Settlement there, and without doubt Governour Phillips will transmitt your Lordships a particular Account of the Circumstances of the French there; they have yet no regular Fortification in that place. But in Case of a War between the two Crowns the French would certainly be very troublesome to all the English Plantations in North America. It is generally thought that it might be of Service to His Majesty and a Security of the Trade of his Subjects if there were a small Fort built at the Isle of Canso which is near Cape Breton, and so another between that & Annapolis Royal. But of these things the Governour of that Province will be the best Judge.

It hath been of the last Mischief to His Majestys Government and People of these Countreys to suffer the French Jesuits to reside among the Indians that are under the English protection & particularly at Kennebec & Penobscut both which are within His Majestys Territory. This is what I have had the honour to represent once and again to your Lordships.

To the 4th Q.

The Trade of the Province has been of late years under great discouragements occasioned as is Judged by the most thinking People chiefly by want of Silver and Gold for a Medium of Trade in lieu whereof the Government have made and Issued out near Two hundred Thousand Pounds in Bills of Credit ~

The Fishery of this Province (which indeed is the best and chief Article of their Trade) is much increased since the Cession of Nova Scotia. As to the remaining part of this

Question I must beg leave to refer your Lordships to Governour Phillips those places being in his Government –
To the 5th Q

To prevent illegal Trade I do my utmost Indeavours to put the Laws now in force relating to the Trade of the Plantations in Execution; and also take all Imaginable care that the Kings Officers may be protected in doing their Duty – And I am also of Opinion farther to prevent illegal Trade If two fishing Shallops were Imployed, under the Inspection of the Surveyor General or Principal Officer in each Port (the charge of building which would be about Three hundred pounds Sterling) to be Manned & Victualled by the Station Ship as there may be Occasion and a Custom House Officer on board, would be of great Service. But if this is not thought practicable the Appointing more Waiters in each Port as four at least in this Port (whereas there is but two) which I believe might answer the End and very much prevent the running of Counterband Goods –
To the 6th Q

According to the best Inquiry & Information I find belonging to the Massachusetts Province and mostly built in it nearest One hundred and Ninety Sail of Ships and other Vessels being in all nearest Eight Thousand Tunns and Navigated with about Eleven hundred Men. Besides about One hundred and fifty Boats with Six hundred Men employed in the Fishery
To the 7th Q

As to Manufactures, the Inhabitants in some parts of the Province work up their own Wool and Flax and make an Ordinary course Cloath for their own use without exporting any. But the greatest part both of Woolen and Linnen Cloathing that is wore in the Province is Imported from Great Britain, and some times Linnen from Ireland; and considering the Excessive price of labour the Mercht can afford what is Imported Cheaper than what is made in the Country~There are also a few Hatters set up their Trade in the Maritime Towns~And the greatest part of the Leather used in the Country is Manufactured among themselves ~

There has been for many years some Iron works in the Province that have afforded the People Iron for some of their necessary Occasions: But the Iron Imported from Great Britain is Esteemed much the best, and the Shipping wholly use that which is Imported. And besides the Iron works of the Province are not able to Supply as to the Common use the twentyth part of what is wanted ~

To the 8th Q

Upon the best Computation I find it to be nearest Two hundred and twenty Thousand pounds this Country Currency which is about One hundred Thousand Pounds Sterling according to the present course of Exchange between Great Britain and this Place ~

To the 9th Q

The Trade of this Province is principally to Europe by Codd Fish to Spain Portugall and the Mediterranean the produce whereof is remitted chiefly to Great Britain either p bills of Exch^a or Gold ~

Great part of the Trade of this place is directly to Great Britain by Whale Oyle, Finns, Furrs, Turpetine and other Naval Stores ~ Trade from hence to any Foreign Plantations is Inconsiderable, except that to a Dutch Plantation called Suraname which is carried on mostly by exporting small wild Horses not fit for Service here, nor Saleable in our English Plantations, for which is brought back in return chiefly, Molasses, In which Trade may be employed twelve or fifteen small Vessels ~ As to the Trade we have with Barbados Antego &c^a the Account of the Export and Import which I remitt yearly will make that Trade appear in it's proper light ~

To the 10th Q.

The French Plantations in our Neighbourhood are the Country of Canada and the late Settlement at Cape Breton ~

Canada is a vast Tract of Land lying on each side the great River of the same name, begining at the Mouth of S.t Lawrence extending up to Quebec from thence to Monreal, from thence up to the great Lakes and so to Messasippi River as the French pretend in all which vast Country they have not above 1500 Effective Men and about 5000 Souls~They have Thirty Comp.as as they affect to reckon, but I'm very credibly Informed they dont make 12 Men one Company with Another~The Government of the Country is like other French Governments Despotick & mostly Military M.r Vaudrovil the Governour has the Character of a very good Officer ~ They have also an Intendant General who manages the Civil Affairs and is a Sort of Check upon the Governour ~

Quebec is the principal Town in Canada a handsome well Fortifyed Town but small, but I have said something of that City already under a former Query~Their next best Settlement is Monreal of this also I have spoken before. There lives the Governour Maj.r Ramsey a Scotchman. The Trade of Canada consists chiefly of Beaver & some other Furrs which is managed by a Comp.a who are Supplyed by the Indians and French Hunters as far almost as Messasippi River and some even from Hudsons Bay: tho' by what I can learn there are but few Indians in those parts it being a Desart Cold Country. The value of the Furrs Exported from thence to France annually may be computed at Sixty Thousand Pounds Sterling; They also Export to the French West Indies some Flower Pease and Lumber to the value of about Twenty Thousand pounds Sterling annually. If the Furr Trade of Canada should fail the Country would be but of little worth for it does not afford English Grass, Cattle, Corn equal to other Countrys that lye more Southward and hardly any fruit at all   The Navigation up that river is very Inconsiderable Except once a year when the Ships comes to Quebec-As to Cape Briton of wch place I have also spoake before, to which I have nothing to add, but that the French have there a very considerable Fishery for these two or three last years having in the Season from Sixty to Eighty sail of Ships besides small Craft loading with Fish &c^a

Sir

I Received your letter of the 6th Ins^t inclosing among other Acts Passed in His Majesties Province of Massachusets Bay, in May 1718, An Act for Granting unto His Maj^{ty} several Rates & Duties of Impost and Tunnage of Shipping on which Act the Lords Comm^{rs} of Trade & Plantacõns desire the Opinion of the Commissioners of the Customs – And having laid the same before them, they have made the inclosed Observations thereon which they direct me to transmitt you and to returne you the Acts above mention'd, be laid before their Lordships

    I am Sir

      Your most humble Servt

Custom h: London

  14 March 1719   Cha Carkesse

Wm Popple Esq.

Observations on the Act for granting to His Maj^{ty} several Rates & Duties of Impost & Tunnage of Shipping made at Massachusets Bay in New England.

By the act of Trade 15 C. 2. no Goods can be Imported into any of the Plantations but from Great Britain, (salt for the Fisheries, Madera & Azores Wines Servants horses & provisions from Ireland excepted: And also except Irish Linnen from Ireland p act 3 & 4 Annae) and thô Madera's & Azores Wines &c. may be carried into the Plantations from other places in Europe than Great Britain yet it must be in British Shipping duly navigated. Wheras this Act seems to allow their being Imported into New England in any shipping there being no words to restrain such Importation to be in ships allow'd by law to Trade thither.

This Act which lays a Duty on Wines not Madera or Azores Imported from the place of their Growth is contrary to the Act of Trade 15. Car. 2, if they be not imported from Great Britain and likewise all other goods (except as aforesaid) not Imported from Great Britain is contrary to the said act.

This Act lays a double Duty on all Goods Imported from any other Ports than the places of their Growth or produce which will be a prejudice to the Trade of Britain & the other English Plantations.

This Act seems to give liberty to all persons who have Goods consigned to them to make Entrys &c which may give liberty to Aliens or persons not made free Denizens to Trade as Merch[ts] or Factors which is contrary to the Act of Navagation 12. Car. 2.

By this Act the Ship, with her Tackle apparel and Furniture, is liable to answer such Penalties & Forfeitures as the Master shall incur by not observing the Directions of that Act. Which seems to be very unreasonable and a great hardship on British Owners and other Plantation Owners of Shipping to forfeit their Ships, through the Default or Neglect of the Master, by a law made in the Plantations,

The Duty laid on all Shipping, except as in that Section is particularly mention'd, seems to be an unreasonable law and a great hardship on British Owners and other Plantation Owners of Shipping.

Signed by Order of the Comm^{rs}

Custom ho: London   Cha Carkesse S$\tilde{c}$y
14 March 1718

End: *Massachusetts*

L^r. from M^r. Carkesse of y^e 14th March 1718, with the observations of the Comm^{rs} of the Customs upon An Act *of y^e Massachusets Bay, pass'd in 1718, for granting to his Ma^{ty} several Rates & Duties of Impost & Tunnage &c*

      Reced 14th March 1718/19   Read 17th. Do.

End: *Massachusets=Bay*

Copy of an Order of Council, dated the 26th May, 1719, Signifying y^e Lords Justices Disallowance of an Act for Granting *several Rates & Duties of Impost & Tonnage of Shipping: & that M^r. Secretary Craggs give y^e Govr. of y^e Massachusets-Bay, a severe Reprimand for Consenting to y^e Passing an Act so contrary to his Instruct^{ns}*

               Rec^d. June 30th } 1719
               Read July ye 3^d.

At the Councill Chamb^r. Whitehall
The 26th of May 1719
Present

Their Excellencys the Lords Justices Councill Upon reading this day at the Board a Representation from the Lords Commiss^{rs} of trade & plantations dated the 24th. of Aprill last in the words following vizt.

"Memo^d Here was inserted the said Represen^{tn} at length,

"relating to the Massachusets Act, past in May 1718,
"Entituled An Act for granting unto His Ma^{ty} severall
"Rates & Dutys of Impost Tonnage of Shipping.
Which Report being taken into Consideration Their Excellencys the Lords Justices in Councill, were pleased to Declare their Disallowance and Disapprobation of the said Act, and were further pleased to order as it is hereby Ordered, That the Right Hono^{ble} James Craggs Esqr His Maj^{ts} Princip^l Secretary of State, do write to the Governor of the said Province of Massachusets Bay in conformity to the said Report, and give him a severe Reprimand for consenting to the passing an Act so contrary to his Instructions and to the Laws & Interest of England.

A true Copy
Edward Southwell.

Queries to Co^l. Shute Govr of the Massachusetts Bay in N=England.

No 1— We desire you to Inform us, what Number of Inhabitants there is at present in the Province of the Massachusetts Bay, under your Government? distinguishing the Number of Frenchmen, Women and Children, and of servants white and black; how they are Increased of late years; and what number of Servants, Men and Women have been Imported of late and from whence? what Forts or places of strength are there? and in what Condition are those Forts?

2 What is the Strength of the several Nations of Indians in your Neighbourhood? and are their Inclinations for us, or for the French?

3 What is the condition of the French Settlem^{ts} at Canada and Cape Breton? and how may they affect any of his

Majestys Plantations and what can be done to prevent any hazard or inconvenience from those Settlements?

4 How and in what particulars is the Trade of the Province increased or decreased of late years and what has been the reason of such Increase or decrease? and what Changes has been observed in the Fisher's since the Conquest or Cession of Nova Scotia to the Crown of Great Britain, and what Scattered Settlements are there either of French or English along that Coast without the Bay of Fundy?

5 What are the present Methods used to prevent illegal Trade? and what farther Methods do you think advisable for that purpose?

6 What Number of Ships or other Vessels are there belonging to the Massachusetts, where built? and what number of Sea faring men?

7 What Manufactures are settled in the said Province of any sort whatsoever? what Mines are there? and what Improvements made in the working of them?

8 What is reckoned to be the Annual produce one year with another of the Several Commodities in the Massachusetts?

9 What Trade has that Province with any Foreign Plantations or any part of Europe besides Great Britain? how is that Trade carried on? what commodities do they send to or receive from such Plantations, or any forreign Nation in Europe?

10 We further desire that you would send us the best Accounts you possibly can get concerning the French Plantations in your neighbourhood; what is the Number of the Inhabitants, and of the Militia, or what other Military Force is, in each of those Plantations? what are the several Commodities produced in them? and how much is the Annual produce one year with another of such Commodities? what Trade is carried on to and from these Plantations?

what form of Government is Established in them, and what Methods are used to encourage and Improve the products and the Trade thereof

By their Lordp? Command

Whitehall June 4th 1719   Wm Popple

End: Massachusets
Answer to Several Queries relating to the State of the Province of the Massachusetts Bay.
referred to in Col? Shute's letter to the Sec^{ry} Dated 17th Feb: 1719/20   Reced d?

Boston June 26th 1719

'S^r

I beg leave to Acqu^t their Lordships that 5 years since I Obtained Execution against one Elisha Davis of Haverhill in the County of Essex Planter for Destroying one pine tree marked wth the broad Arrow which would have made a mast of 32: inches diameter, the Execution was laid on his Estate, wch he had made over before hand to avoid the Law, then he was Imprisoned, but he broak Goal Just as I departed for England,

The Lawyers say I cannot proceute now being out, I lay that Judgment not being Satisfied I can, they are like wise of Oppinion that a Subject cannot be in one writt with the Queen, or King it being in the Late Queens reign, the Act of Parliament gives one moiety to the King his heirs and Successors the other to the Informer that shall Sue for the same. the Lawyers are at a loss how to draw the writt or lay the action, the Execution orders the forfeiture to be paid to me, nor could it be other ways here being no other Officer but my self, So that the property of ye Execution cannot be altred, and if I recover the forfeiture I must be Accountable and will give Notice thereof accordingly.

I have another Execution against John Sincler, and Jeremiah Bean, both of Exeter in the Province of New Hampshire Planters for cutting down and destroying one mast tree of 28 : inches diameter which would have made a Bowl spritt this Execution was laid on their Land as the other above. these in my absence have re entered on the land and are now in Possesion the same Objections are made to this Likewise I humbly pray their Lordships directions and oppinion in this great affair, for should these Criminals go unpunished Instead of dettering others it would Incourage them, who Inclined to such vile practises, of this Sort there are great numbers

I have vsed my vtmost Endeavours to bring these Offenders to ye obedience of the law thô they have proved Ineffectual. I have none to make my complaints or adresses to but their Lordships in behalfe of his Majesties Intrest: If those Offenders are made Publick Examples of, It will do his Majesties Intrest very Eminent Service in General.

My prayer to their Lordships is, that they would be pleased to give theire order and directions to the Attorney General here to proceute those Offenders with the Severity of the Law, as well those in New Hampshire (there being No Attorney Gen^{ll} as him in this Province, and a short time to the Gover^r to see it put In Execution, or other ways as their Lordships in their Great Wisdoms shall see most necessary for Obtaining the End hereby Intended.

The Assembly here after more than a months sitting with great perswasion and arguments and dificultys were prevailed upon to droop the duty upon English goods Imported here. I offered and gave the Gover^r the same Act that I got pass'd in New Hampshire relating to the preservation of the Tar Tree, but It was not minded but shall Endeavour for it the next Sessions

I am very well Informed here that the Agent offered my Post to M.ʳ Coram, but he asked so much money that Coram refused, what M.ʳ Burinston gave I cannot tell, but by his leter to me it appears very much like it for he says he was wholy a Stranger and Knows nothing of the Employ but is a perfect stranger to the Employ and Every thing belonging to it this he writes me, but what he gave for it I cannot tell, but the Agent made the most he could of it certainly, and now advisses him in the best manner he can, but the Agent missed his mark very much, for upon his knowing the Contents of the leter your Honour sent me from their Lordships or whether he Knew of the recomendation made to the Treasury in my favour I can't tell but he tells me what was done in his leter for me, upon this he kept the leter you gave for me, and goes forthwith to M.ʳ Burinston acquaints him what was done in my favour, he Imediatly sends a Deputation to M.ʳ Rob.ᵗ Armstrong knowing that the sallary was precarious till he had a Deputy on the Spot, the Agent Keeping my leter till about the 15ᵗʰ of Aprill and then put it on board one Cap.ᵗ Osburn who arrived the 8 June, by which managment M.ʳ Armstrong had the Deputation before I had your leter.

the Agent as he was the only person to Act this base and falce action, in the Infancie of it gave out that M.ʳ Burinston was a man of very great Intrest with the King and might have had this Goverment if he could have acted by Deputation at another time he was a Germain Count, &c. from which I must degress, for had M.ʳ Burinston been a person of common Intrest certainly he could have gott Instructions for his Deputy for the Agent must know better, I think, and to put in an Improper person at last lookes very far from a man of such Intrest, the Agent has screen'd him by his making him a great man and of such great Intrest, wᵗʰ the King that it has kept my friends from atempting to restore me so now he will droop him I suppose and since he could not procure any one for a deputy before he will be at a very great loss to find a person now Knowing in the raising, and manufacturing of naval stores, Knowing in the Production of all those woods here, and knows the Country, the people, & the woods, and I hope he must pass his Examination as I did after 20 years Experience and have the approbation of the navy, the admiralty, and their Lordships. I humbly hope it will be no Dificulty at this time for their Lordships to restore me, for Mr Burinston has no Intrest but the Agents; and now he has got his money and keept him in so long he now must stand on his own Intrest, the Assembly here has not given the Agent any money, and are very angry with him and say they will have no more to do with him.

· I cannot omit giving your Hon^r an account of the Growth & Progress of the Woolen Manufacture in this Province In a great many sorts, as Cloths, Serges, Shaloons, Kerseys, all sorts of Stuffs allmost and some Linnen and there is scarce a Country man comes to town or wooman but are clothed wth their own Spining Every one Incourages the Growth and Manufacture of this Country and not one person but discourages the Trade from home, and says tis pitty any goods should be brought from England, they can live wthout them

There is one thing which very much helps In this most pernitious trade to Great Britain, and that is Cotton wool Imported here from the west Indies, which is mixed with wool & flax and they make both woolen and linnin there with. If it should be agreeable to their Lordships oppinions to prohibit the Export of any Cotton Wool from the West Indies Into this & Road Island Goverm^{ts} It would prevent near the halfe of the Woolen, and Linnin, that is wrought up in these two Goverm^{ts}

There Is on an Island at this day called Nantucket about 12 or 14 leagues from Cape Cod more than twenty thousand Sheep, and all that wool for want of the Officers looking after the proceuting the Act wch makes or renders all wooll watter bourn seizable, by which the wooll is brought Into this Goverm.^t and supplys all those parts with wooll which raises little It is the same case at Road Island wch breeds many thousand sheep, and upon an Island called Block Island about 5 leagues from thence many thousand more and In the Naraganset Country more yet.

Here has been many years a Jealosie, of some March^{ts} Shipping some of those woolls above mentioned for france, and I querey whether the Carieing of such wooll to france, be a greater Prejduce to the Manufacture of Great Britain, than for the People here to Spin and Cloath themselves with such wooll.

If some care be not soon taken those people here will be able to live without Great Britain in a little time than there ability Joyned with their Inclinations will be of very Ill Consequence, I cannot say here are any that have a duty full regard to England or promotes Its welfare thô: It gave them breath.

I Beg your Hon.^r would be pleased to remind theire Lord^{ps} of my being of the Council and the first of those now to be appointed If it be only for the Insewing winter I am well assurd it will be a great advantage to his Majesties Intrest In Generall and by it the People will see his Majesties Supports his Officers for Defending his Just right and Intrest; There is one of the Council that Died in May last Theodore Atkinson of New Castel.

I have further Considered of the Settling of Annapolis Royal and humbly propose for to Incourage or Introduce the Sowing and curing of hemp there, That the Tenure and holding of the lands there should be, so many hundred weight of hemp according to the Quantity of Land Granted, and that all the french, that would Sware alegence to King George should be under the same Tenure this wold give life to the Sowing of Hemp, there being so much land proper for it, and none would refuse land on these conditions, others near the Woods should be Obliged to Deliver one or two Masts Anually of such a Diameter at such a place as should be apointed, and if it could or should be proved upon them that they Cut any Mast tree without leave such person or persons should forfeite his or their Land so held or had from his Majestie.

These Tenures one would Incourage Hemp, the other preserve the woods Infalible & to make it more firme the Informer should have ¼, ⅛ of the Offenders land or how or else as It shall be order'd, that Cuts a mast tree wthout any Diameter Sett or fixed, for all must be Saved Except Those Trees wch he or they should have leave to Cutt for under a pretence of cutting such a Diameter they Cutt what they please as Is done here to his Majesties Irreparable Loss;

There are many persons now settled at Annapolis who have built houses and have Improved lands all ready theire Titles thereto cannott be good till a proved by such an authority and under such a seal as your Lordships or his Majestie shall appointe No Saw Mills to be built without leave from his Majestie or the person by him appointed to give leave who should be a good Judge of the Peace, and Concequencies that may attend such Leave

Others if a Proper place for the product of Tarr should pay so many barrells of Tar anually or forfeite his Land, others Terpentine or according to what was most natural produced, as may be Easily seen upon a Survey of that place, the like may be Done at Menes and Sheconneto about ten or fivteen Leagues from Annapolis.

If I shall be thought worth by their Lordships to Lay out this place I will do it with all Faithfullness, and the man of war might Carrie me and Assistants thither and back, wch will save the Hire of a Sloop the Gover^r to assiste with a guard, at all times when required the boats and other things must be had which may be had there I suppose, the spring and fall

is the proper time to do this worke in, all which is most humbly submitted to their Lordships Great Wisdoms, by your Hon^{rs} most obedient and most humble Servant
J Bridger
Boston July 9th 1719./

In Council
Voted
 That the Thanks of the General Assembly be given to Jno Bridger Esqr for his good Service in projecting & promoting two Acts for the Encouraging of Naval Stores within this Province which so Immediately concerns His Majesties Intrest./
May 2^d 1719   Richd Waldron Cler Con

 Province N: Hamp^r May 8th 1719/
 The Above is a true Copy from the Council files
compared   p Richd Waldron Cler Con
 Examined p the Originall
May 23^d 1719   p J Bridger

End :   *New=England*
 Two letters from Mr Bridger late Surveyor of the Woods on the Continent of America to Mr Popple, dated at Boston, the 26th of June & 9th of July 1719.

Boston July 9th 1719/
S^r
 I have since my last Concidred the Setlment of Annapolis Royal, and have given their Lordshp^s my thoughts how Naval Stores may be raised there, with some certainty ; to be added to, or Amend, as shall be thought most proper for his Majesties Intrest./

I pray your Hon:rs favour and Intrest w:th their Lordships, that I may be Employed in that Service, which I hope will be no hinderance to the preservation of the woods the most proper seasons being after the people are out of the woods In the Spring, or before they go in, in the fall./

M:r Armstrong who M:r Burinston appointed his deputy has no Instructions to Act by therefore I shall not suffer him to act in that station, as to his being an Improper person I leave that to their Lord:ps determination, but had M:r Burinston been a person of such Intrest, as the agent first gave out, he could not have failed of having Instructions Granted him upon his application and tis my humble oppinion, that it is not dificult to restore me againe, his being in above a year and at last to appoint such a person under whose care the woods must have been Ruined. I made an Offer to him rather than to want I would serve for 150^1 a year; but his neglecting that, and puting in such a person, and his taking no care to comply with his Commission, I hope will open a way for my being restored./

S:r Your Inestimable friendship to me lays me under the Deepest sence of gratitude which I in the most humblest manner shall forever own, praying for your long health and life, and the Continuance of your good Offices I am

With the most Senciere and greatest regard

Yo:r Hon:rs Most Obedient serv:t

J. Bridger.

I most humbly aske pardon for my long leters w:ch I could not avoid and hope they will be read

Boston July 17:th 1719

S:r

I had not troubled you with any more accounts of this nature, but the continued malice of M:r Cooke & now he is a representative labours with all his Envie, subtilty, and Intrest, to Delude his fellow members, and by vile artifices, has brought a great number over to his Oppinion, having lay'd a very long leter before the House of Representatives and a memorial Directed to the Spaker wherein he wholly Insists against the Intrest of the crown that being Chiefly aimed at and his Majestys Just rights & Perogative Invaded in the Province of Main & Denies all claime, right, or Power, of the King or his Officer, in and over the woods belonging to and being in the said Province, Notwithstanding ye charter reservations, and the Act of the 9th of the Late Queen, wch act is according to the restrictions in said Charter, wherein the Province of Main is particularly Named/, The chief Strength of Mr Cookes Arguments, consists in this, That that Province was purchass'd and annexed to the Province of the Massachusetts in the year 1677. but I find this easy to answer, by Observing that his late Majesty King William of Glorious Memory in New Charter wch he granted thought fitt to Incert abundance of considerable Limitations, and alterations, amongst wch this is not the Least Material, And if the Province of Main be under ye Charter of the Massachusetts, it must be liable to the Reservations, and restrictions, of that Charter. What confirms me in this Oppinion is, that the Kings Right was never called in question till Mr Cooke (that Incendiary) with unparlleld Insolence, has Endeavoured, to poyson the Minds of his countreymen, with his republican notions, in order to assert the Independency of New England, and Claime greater Privileges than ever were designed for it:/ I find by Mr Cooks long leter and Memorial he has not taken any Notice of my 2^d Memorial and on further Examination, find that the Gover^r never delivered it to any of the Council nor layed it before them nor the Assembly, which has very much surprised me, had that Memorial been laid as I design Cooke had been long since

Silenced, or been In a nother place; but y`t` never, being laid Either before the Council nor Representatives, nor was I ever in place to make any other answer, Depending that I had Fully answered in s`d` Memorial; & pray leave to Inclose a Copy of my 2`d` Memorial for their Lordships reading and consideration, I am

   Your Hon`rs` Most obedient & most humble Serv`t`
            J Bridger

S`r`

I have some other affairs of Importance to Lay before their Lordships but the ships sayling now, I most ommit till the next Oppertunity

End : To the Hon`ble` William Popple Esq`r`.

End : Letter from M`r`. Bridger, late Surveyor of the Woods on the Continent of America, to M`r`. Popple, dated at Boston the 17`th` of July 1719, with Copy of his Mem`l` to Col`o` Shute, Gov`r` of New Engl`d` concerning the Right of the Crown of England to y`e` Woods in y`e` Province of Maine

 Rec`d` Aug`st` 28`th`   Read Sept`r` 10 1719.

E :   New England

Letter from M`r`. Bridger Surveyor of the Woods in America to the Secretary, Dated the 8`th` of April, 1720

R`d`. June 17`th` Read Sept`br` 5`th` 1721 1720

           Boston July 23 1719.

S`r`

Since my last to yo`u` of y`e` 17`th` Instant one James Smith, Judge Advocate here was suspended by the Gover`r` about 3 weeks since for what reason I know not,

Smith by way of revenge upon the Gov`r`. with the assistance of some people here who has loaded him with Complaints against the Gover`r` upon many Occasions, is gone home

Mr Cooke not to be behind his neighbours, has scraped together all his old Complaints and afidavits procured by him self when Clerk of the Superiour Court In the Province of Main last year, some 12 years since, some 8, some 6, some 4 years agoe, some when I was not in the Country, all these against me: In order to Lay them before their Lordships and thereby render me Obnoxious to their Lord^{ps} and unfitt ever to serve the King againe as Cooke setts forth to the Assembly.

I pray you to Observe to their Lord^{ps} that what ever papers Cooke has sent p Smith pretending to have been done by the Assembly is not true, but has prevailed on some of that people to signe something by way of Leter persuant to An Order from the Assembly, or by way of Memorial, or Remonstrance, & by the way of Committee against me which the Spaker nor none of the other Assembly men so much as knew of therefore never consented to much less signed. This James Smith is the person that would have been Surveyor of the woods.

I most humbly pray leave hereby to give you some knowledge of this mans Designe wch is General, against all or any boody whereby he might obtaine something, and by the same see the Lible, and continued Malice of Mr Cooke not many days since asserted to the Gover^{rs} face in Council, that the King has no Right Claime or title to any woods in the Province of Main, this I has from the Gover^r

I am Your Honr most Obliged and most humble Servt

J Bridger

Sr   I sent all the Affidavits last year to you, that I thought most material against myself

Smith sayled on friday last in one Capt Osburne by whom I wrott you

End: For his Majestys Service
   To the Honble William Popple Esqr Secretay to the Right

Honble The Lords Commissioners for Trade & Plantations In Whitehall

New England
Letter from Mr Bridger Dated 25th July 1719 relating to Mr Smith, the Judge Advocate, there, being suspended by the Govr & his coming to England, to complain against the Govr & Mr Bridger & being assisted therein by Mr Cooke.

A Memorial of the Governour Council and Assembly of Her Maj^ties Province of the Massachusetts Bay in New England for their Vindication against the Suggestions and Insinuation of Any who may accuse them of harshness and severity towards such as are of different perswasions from us in matters of Religion

It must alwaies be remembered That the Professed chief Design of the first Planters of this Country was Religion & the Gospellizing of the Wild Ignorant Indians Natives, to bring them to the knowledge and Obedience of the only True God & the Saviour of Mankind, as is declared and set forth in the Royal Charter or Letters Patent Granted them by His Majesty King Charles the first.

The Gentlemen the first undertakers in this Noble design were generally Persons of Education Piety figure Esteem & had plentifull Estates in the several Counties & places within the Kingdom of Great Brittain from whence they came; Yet chearfully parted from their Native Land & Enjoym^ts ventured themselves with their Families & servants over the Ocean into a Wild Desolate Wilderness at so great Distance, to pursue & lay the foundation of that Glorious work; In which they laid out themselves & Estates, not murmuring or repining at the unaccountable hardships, dangers & difficulties they were necessitated to Undergo, as well thrô the Intemperature of the climate as many other wayes for the subduing & cultivating of a rude Wilderness & to secure themselves from the Violence & Insults of the Barbarous Natives; To whose Spiritual & Eternal, as well as outward, good they had a special regard.

They early and very soon, by order & direction of the Government disposed themselves into Vicinitys, not only for their better Security & regular carrying on their secular Affairs but more especially for divine Worship. And it was the pious care of the Governm^t to make & Enact good and wholsome Statutes & Ordinances for the reforming of Manners, & the Propogating of Religion & to see to the due Execution of them. And in Grants of Lands for New-Settle^{ts} or Townships, A Proviso or condition is & has been inserted That the Grantees do procure & Support a Learned Orthodox Minister to dispence the Word of God to them.

Upon these their just & pious Endeavours the Plantation Increased, Towns & Churches were orderly settled & by the Blessing of God it is become a province, not of the least name among Her Maj^{ties} forreign Plantations: To the Enlargement of Her Ma^{tys} Empire, & Advantage to the Crown.

Under the present Constitution by Letters Patent Granted by their late Maj^{ties} King William & Queen Mary of Glorious Memory, The Governm^t have taken alike care to Enact good & wholsome Laws for the Support of Ministers & Schools, and that no Town or plantation should be unprovided & destitute thereof. As also for the suppressing of Vice prophaneness & Immoralities; Which Laws have the Royal Approbation. And the Governm^t have Enforced the Execution of them, by Issuing forth Proclamations from Time to time; Therein Comanding all Justices & other

Inf.⁺ Officers strictly to Observe & perform their respective Dutys in that regard; & to make diligent inquiry & detect all such who shall presume to trangress the same, In Imitation of the most deservedly commendable Examples of Her Maj.⁺ʸ & Her Late Royal Predecessors by their Royal Proclamations And in Countenancing Encouraging & promoting of Societys for the Reformation of Manners who by their Letters have recommended the same to be pursued here

Whatever complaints may have been made of over much rigidness & Severity practiced by the former Governm.⁺ toward persons of different perswasions in matters of Religion, perticularly those called Quakers.

We go not about to plead their Justification in things wherein possibly an over warm zeal may have carried them too far. There is none in yᵉ present Governm.⁺ that were concerned at that Time; And it cannot be expected we should make that answer for them as they could have made for themselves: nor are those that go under the denomination of Quakers now such as were then; who were some of them open bold disturbers of yᵉ publick peace, & their Principals Notoriously known to be Heretical but are much refined both in Principals & Conversation.

We strictly observe & yeild due Obedience to the Directions in the Royal Charter to allow Liberty of Conscience in yᵉ Worship of God to all Christians except Papists. Nor have we any Sanguinary or Pecuniary Laws against those who are of Diffirent perswasions from us in that matter.

The Laws of this Province provide only against Irreligon & Prophaneness That the People are not brought up in Estrangment from God, and perish for want of Instruction; But that the Publick Worship of God be upheld in the several Towns & Plantations That the Lords Day be duly observed & not openly prophaned by persons attending their Secular Imploym.⁺ Or, which is wose, by Revellings, Drinking & other Debaucheries, which is too sadly true in some places, not far distant from us.

And we justly fear that Infection has too much taken in some later settlem^{ts} begun in the remoter parts of this Province that have been destitute of the Ministry; being planted by a mixt company many of them vain profligate persons, of disolute conversation who combine together to Obstruct & oppose the Endeavours of the better disposed part of ye Inhabitants for ye Obtaining of a Learned Orthodox Godly Minister to come unto them. And out of a Sordid Spirit refuse to contribute to his Support, althô, Encouraged by Assistance from the Governm^t in their begining chosing rather to continue in Ignorance & Irreligion than to be at the lest Cost to have the meanes of knowledge & the preaching of the Gosple among them; But reject it thô freely offered, To the just Scandal of the Indian Native Tribes who have their Settlem^{ts} near them, & their several Assemblys & Ministers who preach constantly tò them; and Shame such disolute English to ye last Degree, by their Sobriety & better manners.

They are strengthened in this their Opposition in some places, by the Quakers thô but few in Number to the rest of the Inhabitants by their Aversion to Orthodox Ministers & labouring to Infuse their Wild delusions into them & the plea of Liberty of Conscience wch they make for themselves, but disclaim them as not of their Society; Their manners are so openly Vile; But if any time they come to their Meetings, thô only to Observe their Devotion (for which they afterwards ridicule them) & arrive to that Morosness as to deny the Courtesy of pulling off the Hat & shew an indecent unmanerlyness to their Superiours, then they Shelter themselves under the Umbrage of ye Quakers if they be demanded a penny for the Support of a good Minister; Thô at the same Time the Quakers are Ashamed to own them.

This Government have at no times imposed upon any in matters of Worship, but as is before said, allow Liberty of Conscience, as they are commanded yet account it their Duty to God to Her Majesty & the Souls of the People under their care, by proper and the most easy methods to see they be taught the knowledge of God & Jesus Christ; And to reclaim them from immoralities, Vice & Prophaneness. These are the Ends the Laws are pointed to, & to Constrain their Obedience and no further
A true Copy as of Record Examined

p I Willard Secr[y]

End :   *Massachusets=Bay*
Several Affidavits & other Papers [X in number,] relating to the Difference between M[r]. Bridger, late Surveyor-Gen[l]. of y[e] Woods in North=America & M[r]. Elisha Cooke, formerly one of y[e] Council for that Province.
Rec[d] with M[r]. Dumer's Memorial
Rec[d] Feb[ry] 25th   Read March 30th   1719-20

The Intrest of the Crown is grown so very low, and the Prerogative trampled on to that degree, That no good officer, or a lover of his King and country can be Silent: but Duty and a Strict adherence to his most Sacred Majesty, Armes me with Due resentm[t] to Lay it before their Lord[ps] in a true light and Nothing but fact shall be related, Therefore by their Lordsp[s] to heare it read.

The Clause in the Charter of New England for the Preservation of the Woods Saves no trees but 24 iñ in Diameter and upward, all the young trees may be cut at the pleasure of the people and tis at their choice whether ever they let a tree grow to be 24 iñ Diameter or not, wch Clause is the Distruction rather than the reservation of the woods, there is an Act of Parliament and an Act of this Province that has the Same Clause in them, which must be repealed, for the Small trees being in Demand at home in Great Britain, the people cutts all these trees under 24 Inches Diamt^r and plead the act for it, and I am Obliged to be Silent, the large trees they cut at pleasure wthout regard to Acts of Parliament the Royal Lycense or my Warrant, as I shall make appear hereafter.

I shall say nothing of Mr Cooke but what relates to his actions this winter, Mr Cooke having purchased two old grants for land that were granted by the Government of New England In the years 1641: & 1671 Never taken up till now the first for 800 acres the other for 500 acres of land, and to prove his assertion, that the King has no woods here, has laid out these two grants of 1300 acres of Land In the Province of Main, without all the Townships or town Bounds, in his Majestys woods as I allways thought & preserved as Such, but Mr Cooke bids Defiance to any Right or Title the King has to any woods.

The Province of Main was a Distinct Goverment 40 years after the first of these grants and many after the last, I was upon this Spot of land last winter was 12 months that he has laid out & lie in the Best parcell of Pine trees I ever saw in this Country, Now if Mr Cooke is allowed in this action he has fully proved that his Majesty has no woods for all within the townships are the peoples, and if all without are as Mr Cooke says they are by Consent of the Goverment the King is Shoved out, there being none else. These old grants being of no value to the owners or possessors Mr Cooke purchasses them for a very Small Sum and has got them Confirmed, he has Sold a part of this 1300 acres for 300^{ll} this is to my Knowledge true having Read the Deed, Cooke gave a Generall warrante to the purchasser: and why not any other old grant or any new grant be laid out in the woods as well as

M! Cooke. Certainly if one can, all may: one of these grants was Consented to by Co!! Dudley in 1710 but never laid out till now, the other was Consented to by the Present Goverment in No! 1718 Since the woods was Denied to be the Kings, and Thus he has proved what he asserted I have Inclosed Copy of the original and Confirmed grants for their Lordships perusall.

I have this winter Discovered a Sort of People that under pretence of Getting masts Destroyes more trees than any people, these men are Employed by the Agent of him that Contracts w.th the Navy one M! John Taylor; 8ber last his Agent M! David Jefferies comes from Boston, to Contract for a great number of masts, he takes no Notice of the Royal License, Nor me, Employs 5 Setts of Men to get what Masts he pleased, and what Number, these people goes Into his Majestys woods (as I think they are) and to cutting down of mast trees, which I forbid to Cut one tree without leave according to the Act of Parliament & Royal Lycense Imediately all these, Save 2 Setts, came to me for Leave which they had there 2 setts have been In the Kings woods, & have fell'd above a 150 trees notwithstanding I forbid them, before the Agents face & before the Leiv.t Gover! and to Several of their friends, and all the ways possible I could, but all in vaine for they at last Bid Defiance to me and laught at me.

Thes setts of men, they say to a Country fellow do you get me Such a Tree and I will give you 4.li according as they agree More or less, and so to another and another &c.a away goes all these fellows, ranges where they please, under the Notion of Mast men as they call themselves, and Cutts these trees Into loggs and often Supplys their Neighbors with loggs till they have Cutt enough, or what they Want yet the Tree agree'd for is not minded nor are they Seldom or never gott, this is the practise I am very Sure of it.

on the 6.th of the last month I applyd to the Leiv.t Gover!

here for a guard of horse wch he Imediatly granted, and on the 9th with the Sherife having the Gov^{rs} Warrant, psuant to a Warrant before obtained from the Lords of the Admiralty, I went into the Country and Seized Sixteen of the Trees Cut in his Majestys woods, for his Majestys Service, but the owners told me publickly they would Hew there the next week, I have given the Acc^t to the Lords of the Admiralty and hope they will not release the Seizure, for it will be to the great Damage of his Majesty, it being made so Publickly That all Expects the Issue, if released no bounds or laws will reclame the people for the future. The offenders Names are Timothy, and Paul Gerrish, and Thomas Hanson, all of this Province of New Hampshire and Men of Estates I could have Seized more, but would not fearing it might have hindred the Loading of the mast Ships Expected this Spring wch these will not, these very men have Cutt 12 large trees on that land Cooke has sold, but they Dare me to it, and Say I Durst not Seize one of them trees, nor shall I without order, for every one is upon me and against me, and that the King has no woods here which puts me upon my gard in this respect. I have Inclosed a bill for the prevention of all those Eviles if it meet wth their Lordships Approbation will Entierly Secure all the woods, and make it possible for the officer to do his Duty wch now tis not,

The first paragraph in the Bill is that all the woods without the Townships are to be reserved as his Majestys, and to Support this, I humbly answer, That it is of absolute necessity his majesty has Some woods, to Supply the Navy with Masts &c^a if this be granted I then say

That all the woods without the Townships are not a Particular, or any properity, if So the King takes no right from any man only Secures the woods to him self, So no body is damaged thereby, and In case there Should be a Necessity, for laying out a New Town for the Benefit or good of his

Majestys Subjects, there is a Clause in the Bill, That the Gover.̇ or Leiv.̇ Govern.̇ with the Surveyor of the woods, to lay out a proper place in these woods to be reserved; why the Gov.̇ or Leiv.̇ Gov.̇ with the Survey.̇ should lay out this place is, That as tis the Prorogative of the Crown his Majestys Officers are the properst for that Service, but let that be put in whose power it will, tis no great concern So the woods therein be preserved to the use of ye Crown There are no woods Else can be preserved, for all within the Town bounds are the peoples, and all wthout too M.̇ Cooke Says, but that I submit to their Lordships, I hope I have hereby given Sufficient reasons, that these outwoods may be his Majestys

This forbiding to Cut a Pine tree, is like the forbidden Tree, thô the Tast was Death, that did not deter it, but all thereby was lost.

There is in this case but one Tree reserved, yett these people will Cutt, thô they loose their all, their Idol the Charter; for no mens actions will ever Submit, while the apprehension rebel, and those Disturbers of Government, have always laid their first Train in Contempt, and endeavouring to blow it up in the judgements and Esteem of their fellow Subjects, Contempt of his Majestys Authority, like the Planet of Saturn, has first an Ill aspect, and then a Destroying Influence how Studiously has these people layd about them ever Since, In the Assembly and in all their publick meettings, to Cast a Slur upon the Kings rights and Title, and to bring under a Disrepute the Prorogative amongst the Country people, the pyson is spread thrô the whole, to his Majestys great and never to be recovered loss unless the bill recovers it.

There are many other ways by which His Majestys woods are Destroyed, and will be in spight of fate, as long as there is but one person to Secure so vast a District, against 40000 men scatered thrô the whole and tis in any of their Powers to goe and Cut Down what tree they please it is as Impossible for one Officer to Secure all these places, as tis for him to be at them all the same Moment of Time, besides the New Settlements making Every where no less than three In this Province. In the province of main tis all going to be Setled, if this be rightly Considered, they will be of my Oppinion. This affair being of the first consequence, as it is either Supported or Neglected, that can befall a Kingdom, Whose Safty, Whose Strength, Whose wealth, and Whose Glory, Depends on Naval Power, and have Dominions of its own, (which were they made more Dependant) could Supply, and Support, this Naval power forever, this is a happines no nation else can boast of.

These may make Great Britain, and his most Sacred, and most Sereen Majesty King George a noun Substantive, and not Depend upon any Nation under heaven for Naval Equipments, I am well assured the Bill will Entierly save all the woods if passed as tis drawn, that is to the same purport, and thô I am never restored I have done the Duty faithfully 2 years the 19th June

The paragraph in the Bill wh. Obliges the Person, that Employs the Labouror, to pay 6/8 ps every Sound Tree; is for the reasons following it will first, bring the people to acknowledge that they are his Majestys woods which now they do not. The Surveyor will then know how many trees are cut and by whom, it will give a great Cheque to the Employers of these Labourers being under oath and let the Contractors agent know that the woods are under the Direction and Protection of the Survey^r and not for him to Employ Men before hand and at his pleasure, which has been practiced without the knowledge of the Surveyor and greatly to his Majestys Damage, by Cutting what he pleased to order without taking any Notice of the Royal Lycence or Acts of Parliament, for these reasons I hope that paragraph may stand, which is all I need answer for the rest carrys their own reasons in them I hope.

Thus I have playd the Misser who never Discovers the hidden treasure till near Death.

I have herein, and Inclosed all my Experience all my Judgment and Contrivance resulting from thence, for the good and Support of his Majestys Intrest here, under the Strictest Duty, as a Servant, and a Subject, and in the most obedientest manner to their Lordships, and In these have made known all my Treasure which for 23 years I have been Colecting in this Country, the Difference is the hiden treasure could not Continue life, Thô the Lords of the Treasury Can Continue their faithful Servt and thô it can be true that I have out lived his Majestys Intrest here I humbly hope I have not out lived their Lordships favours nor forfeited their good oppinions.

Humbly begging their Lordships to represent my hard Case to the Lords of the Treasury for an alowance or my Salary, No person appearing to Superceed me.

There is yet another sort of People called Loggers which live every where and go where they please, these are the Common Enemies to all and Does great Damage to the Woods. they have now a Tacit Leave to go into the Woods upon, the notions that they may Cut any Tree that is not marked, wch this bill Intirely cutts them off, Nor is the marking any Tree of any regard, for an Ignorant man will fall that tree soonest, for says he tis good for the tree is marked and Down that tree goes a Crafty man when he sees a Tree marked, he Imediately Cutts out the marke and Tree Down & Into loggs and so tis of all, for tis only an Amusem^t and a Deceipt Instead of a gard, for no man Carrys a Witness with him when on Such vile actins, and tis as impossible to marke all the good trees, as tis to Count them all.

What is related being Truth their Lordships will see the

true State of his Majestys Intrest, and if no more officers or Deputys be allowed, nor more power given to the officer I can't pretend to Secure the woods as they ought to be, much more a Stranger, for he will Not be Able to Do any thing till by his own Knowledge, and Traviling he learns his Duty, for these people will keep him Ignorant most Certainly, and tis hard to learn, where all will obstruct, there are many other things I would have laid before their Lordships, but must heartiely begg their Pardon for this long Narration, and pray the Continuance of your honours good offices in my behalf for my Case is very Severe wch I beg may be Considered to my reliefe for I cannot Subject my self, and Expect to be Troubled for the Money that has Supported and feed me.

Some reasons why 50^{ll} is put In lieu of 100 in the Bill answer.

That a hundred pounds Sterling keept their Neighbours from Informing against them knowing it would ruine them if they should Informe, now the Sum is less, they will Informe and the people will be able to pay that when they could not pay a 100^{ll} Ster^{ll} but if it be not agreeable I humbly Submitt it.

And as to the Woods, there was never any other woods but those without the Townships, ever thought to be his Majestys, nor has there been any other preserved So that I humbly hope it will not meett with any Dificulty in the passing, by reason twill Secure them better than ever before; and without it, will every day be worse for the People are grown so Numerous and so bold that nothing but an Act of Parliament well Executed upon offenders will be able to restraine the Liberty they take.

I have only to add my most humble Duty to their Lord^{ps} Praying the Continuance of the favours by representing that I have Done the Duty two years the 19th of June next without any Salary, and Whereas there has not any Person yet appeared to superceed me here, I am as much Surv.[r] as ever, there being no other Commission but mine In America & if M.[r] Barington Continues In England his Commission Shall never be good or In force here, and that he Designes to act by Deputy is Impossible, it never being the Intent or meaning of the Crown. I am sure here is business Enough for many persons that understand the Duty, but how many Ignorant persons this Service will require I cannot say.

I am

   Your Hon.[rs] Most Obedient and Most humble servant
April 8.th 1720.   E. J. Bridger

M.[r] Blechynden to the Lords Commissioners for Trade and Plantations.

      Salem in New England 20.th August 1720
My Lords

I am directed by my Hon.[ble] Masters the Comm.[rs] of His Majesties Customes bearing date the 31.st Oct.[r] Last (w.[ch] did not come to hand till the 5.th ult.) to lay before your Lordships what progress is made in New England, in the Manufactures of Woollens and linnens and how the Same are Encouraged.

As for the Woollens, the Country in Gen.[ll] make it for their own use and weare it commonly themselves here are Several Fulling Mills they make very good Druggetts Cambletts & Serges which are Sold to the Shops and wore by the meanest Sort of People as for the Tradesmen they are very Ambitious of appearing above themselves and will not be seen in anything beneath the Merch.[t] or more Substantiall which, is in the Produce of Europe.

As for the linnen Manufacture the Comon people wear what they call Homespun which is made of Cotton and Linnen, tho wee have had lately Some hundreds of Irish Familys Setled at the Eastward which make as good Linnens and Diaper as in Ireland itself. This is what I have at present to offer to yor Lordships upon this Head and hope yor Lordships will believe that while I have the Honr to be Colletr of his Majesties Customes in these Parts I shall take all possible Care to prevent as farr as in mee Lyes the Exportation of any woollens and to informe yor Lordships from time to time what I think detrimental to the Trade and Manufactures of Great Britain as becomes

My Lords
Your Lordships most dutifull and most
Obedient Humble Servt
Chas: Blechynden

E: *New England*
Lre from Mr Chas. Blechynden relating to the Woolen Manufacture in New England Dated at Salem Augt. 20th. 1720.

To the Right Honble The Lords Commrs of Trade & Plantations, Att Whitehall   Recd 23rd Septembr 1720   Read July 5, 1722

Letter from J. Dummer to Wm. Popple Esqr. of Oct. 11, 1720 with his answers to the Circular Querys, relating to the Massachusetts=Bay

(Enclosure)
Queries for Mr. Dummer.
Massachusets–Bay & New Hampshire

14th. What Forts & Places of Defence are there within that Province? and in what condition?

Castle Willm is the Cheif which defends Boston Harbour & is kept in very good condition. There are other little Forts in the Province of Main. There's a little one in Brunswick at ye head of Casco Bay called George's Fort, which has in it 15 souldiers, and a Capt. Lieu.^t & Serjeant. It is built of stone & lime, with four bastions, having 14 pretty large cannon mounted on ye Walls: There's another at a town call'd Augusta about 22 miles from Brunswick: & a third at Winter harbour a place about 4 miles westward of Casco. There is also a Garrison in Arowsick Island, where the inhabitants keep guard by turns, there being no Soldiers in pay.

15. What Number of Indians have you, & how are they inclin'd?

We have but very few Indians well affected to us that are able to go to war, excepting the Iroquoise (who are call'd the 5 nations) & they onely guard New York & keep a constant newtrality with the French Indians.

16th What is the strength of their Neighbouring Indians?

We reckon the Eastern Indians (as they are call'd) not to exceed five hundred fighting men. These are Situated at Penobscot & towards Nova Scotia. But the Canada Indians who some times come down upon our Western Setlements consist of many Nations, as the Hurons Illinois & others.

17th What is the Strength of your neighbouring Europeans?

We have none but the French of Canada, who can't hurt us but by Surprizing our Frontier Setlements, & so preventing the growth of the Colonies. Their Number is inconsiderable, compar'd with the British Subjects.

The same queries for New Hamshire.

End:) Queries for Mr Dummer, relating to the Provinces of the Massachusetts Bay & New Hampshire.

(SEAL) Additional Instruction for our trusty and well beloved Samuel Shute Esq! our Governour and Commander in Chief in and over our Province of New Hampshire in New England in America or for the Commander in Chief of the said Province for the time being, Given at our Court at Hampton Court the 27th Day of September 1717. In the ffourth Year of Our Reign.

Whereas by our Instruction to you you are required not to pass any Law of any Extraordinary or Unusual Nature and Importance whereby our Prerogative or the Property of our Subjects may be prejudiced without having either first transmitted unto us a Draught of such a Bill or Bills and our having Signified our Royal Pleasure thereupon, or that You take care the passing of any Act of an Unusual and Extraordinary Nature, that there be a Clause Inserted therein Suspending and deferring the Execution thereof untill our Pleasure be known concerning the said Act.

It is our further Will and Pleasure that you don't for the future pass any Act which may any ways affect the Trade or Shipping of this our Kingdom without a Clause expressly declaring that the said act shall not be in force, untill it be approved and confirmed by us, our Heirs or Successors and you are to Signify our Pleasure herein to the Councill and assembly of our Province of New Hampshire in New England under your Government, and to take Care that the same be punctually observed for the future upon pain of our highest Displeasure. G. R. A true Copy from the Original

E: *New Hampshire*

Lre from M! Newman inclosing the Extract of some Lres from Col? Shute Gov! of New Hampshire relating to the Powder Money

Recd Febry 2d Read 8th Febry 1721/22

Letter

Col. Thos Westbrook to Lieut. Gov. Dummer. March 23. 1722/3

St Georges March ye 23^d 1722/3

May it please yor Hono^r

My last Inform'd yor honour of my Arivall in Penobscot river, and would Crave leave to acquaint you that on ye 4th Instant I sett out to find the fort, and after five dayes march thro' ye woods wee Arived abrest of Severall Islands where ye pilot Supposed ye Fort must be; here we were obliged to make four Canoo's to ferry from Island to Island and Sent a Scout of 50 men upon discovery, on the 9th Instant who Sent me word they had Discover'd ye Fort & waited my Arivall, I left a Guard of a hundred men wth the provisions & Tents, and with the rest went to ye Scout being forc'd to ferry over to them, they had, & wee cou'd see ye Fort but not come to it by reason of a Swift River, and ye Ice at ye heads of ye Islands not permitting the Canoo's to come round. we were obliged to make 2 more, wth which Wee ferry'd over, and by Six in the Evening Arrived at ye Fort, Leaving a Guard of 40 men on the West Side of the river, to facillate our return.

The Enemy had Deserted it in ye fall as we Judge and Carry'd every thing with them except ye Inclosed papers, nothing matteriall was found. The Fort was 70 yards in Length and 50 in breadth. Well Stockado'd 14 foot high furnisht with 23 houses Built reguler; On the South Side close by it was their Chappell, 60 foot Long and 30 wide Well and handsomely finish'd within & without and on ye South of that ye Fryers Dwelling house.

We Sett fire to them & by Sun rise next morning Consum'd them all. Wee then return'd to Our first Guards & thence to Our Tents, & so proceeded to ye Sloops being Judged to be 32 Miles Distant. Mr Gibson & Severall other

Sick with a Guard not being Arived; And when they Arived, Wee fell down the River. At ye Mouth whereof on ye 16th Current at 3. of ye Clock in ye morning the Reverend Mr Gibson Dyed. Wee Arived at this place the 20th Instant where we Decently Interr'd him, and three more of our men with ye usuall form, Wee have 50 men now Sick which has Exhausted our Stores for ye Sick, I have Wrote to Mr Treasurer Allen for a fresh supply or ye men Will, & do already Suffer Extreamly for want. I have made bold to give Liberty to Liev^t Buckminster to Wait on your honour for Leave to See his family while ye forces are Recruiting. Liev^t Hilton has been Ill all this March and is now grown so weak that I am Obliged to give him a furlow home, and at his request Given ye Charge of his men to Liev^t John March a Gentleman of great care & good Conduct and One I hope yor honour Will favour wth a Liev^{ts} Commission. I have not heard from Capt Harmon Since I left him, only as Capt Penhallow Informes mee he met him at York, & that he return'd from his March in 5 or 6 days, thô yor Hono^r Will See by the Inclosed his Instructions from mee & what Orders he had. Your honour Will Excuse my not Sending a Journall of our proceedings hitherto as I fully purposed to do, but am prevented by the badness of the Weather & Incumbrance of our Cabbin by Mr Gibsons Sickness & Death but shall not fail to do it p next op^{r}tunity. Wee are now preparing our whaleboats wth Clabboards &c to be in a readiness for pitching them as soon as any shall Arrive that we may be ready for a March as soon as wee are furnished with provisions, with all Dutifull Respect I am

  Yo^r Hono^{rs} Most Obedient Humble Servt
          Tho Westbrook

Letter from Gov. Shute.

Sir

Since my last Letter to you, I have rec^d Advice from Cpt Heath of a Party of eleven Indians that appeard the 25 of March at Richmond & Shot one of that Garrison thrô the Body, Cpt. Heath is of Opinion that there are only a Scout for Discovery & that there is a greater Number near at Hand; You must be very vigilant & careful, & employ your Men in the best Manner you can for the Annoyance of the Enemy & Defence of the Frontiers, & if any Place should be distress'd Let them have speedy Relief. It is necessary that there sh^d be a Vessel of some Force to carry Supplies to Richmond, and therefore you must Order the Sloop that was Strattons for that Service.

Ap. 10, 1722.

Votes of the House of Representatives (at the Session of the General Assembly held at Boston March 15th 1722)

Mr Cooke from the Committee Reported, That they having at sundry times made enquiry of the Situation and Circumstances of Fort Mary at Winter-Harbour, are humbly of opinion, That that Fort is of no Service as a Barrier or Security to the Inhabitants of that Town, nor any Bridle to the Indians. And there being now, as we are informed, but five centinels, and three of them old Men, the Guns belonging to the Garrison both Great and Small unfit for Service, and that in dry Seasons they are obliged to go two or three miles for Water for the use of the Garrison.

The Committee are therefore of opinion, That that Fort, being of no Publick benefit, It is for his Majesty's Service, That it be slighted and no longer continued. And that no pay or Subsistance be allowed and paid out of the Publick Treasury for any Officer and Soldiers there, after the 12th day of July next, and that Mr Treasurer Allen be directed to take speedy Care that the Provisions, Ordnance, Arms, Ammunition and all other Stores of War at that Fort, be Transported to Boston and lodged with him.

Read and accepted.

Marginal * Contrary to the Charter without consulting me
note & the fort so advantageous y^t the Country would have been undone if demolish They did not lyke the Commader.

27 June 1722

Elisha Cooke Esqr from the Committee on the Petition of John Smith &c Reported, The Committee having had Consideration of the petition of John Smith, &c. Proprietors of the Town of North Yarmouth, and the several Papers therewith Exhibited find that on the 26th of July 1684 Thomas Danforth Esq. President of the Province of Main, and by Order and Authority of the Colony of the Massachusetts who had purchased that Province of the Assigns of Sir Ferdinando Gorge did Give, Grant, Bargain, and Confirm unto Messieurs Jeremiah Dummer, Walter Gendall, John Royal and John York, Trustees on the behalf and for the Sole Use and Benefit of the Inhabitants of the Town of North Yarmouth mentioned in said petition. And that a Settlement was begun, but broke up by the Indian War. The Committee are therefore humbly of Opinion that Five Suitable Persons be appointed and constituted Trustees in the room and stead of Jeremiah Dummer and others first mentioned to carry on and perfect the Settlement of that Township according to such Rules and Methods as was then proposed, having special

Regard to the Original Proprietors and Settlers; and that the Number at present be sixty at least, and that the Town Book now in the hands of Capt. Samuel Phipps of Charlestown be put into the Hands of this Committee, a fair copy of all to be drawn out and sent to North-Yarmouth (the Original to remain in Boston) for the present), under the Custody of a Clerk to be appointed for that purpose, that Attested Copy's may be given to such as want them. The Charge of this Committee to be born by the Proprietors and Inhabitants of said Town.

Elisha Cooke, per Order of the Committee.

Letter from John Penhallow to Gov. Shute. July 4, 1722

George Town July 4th 1722

May it please yr Excy

I recd yr Excys Letter of Express of ye 20th ult: but Last night, this morning I Dispatched away my whale Boat up the river & Called the Inhabitants. I also order'd ye Boat to Richmond to direct the Officer there to keep good Guards, inasmuch as I had then but Just heard of Capt Westbrooks being Attacked at St Georges & the Dama that was done there, but as soon as the Boat had got as far as Merrymeeting Bay they Saw about 30 of the Indians, who as soon as they found 'emselves discover'd man'd out their Canoos in chase of the Boat wch was then obliged to return & soon got Clear of them, the Houses in the Bay were Just then Sat on fire, & after the Boat return'd to me wth the above Act, we Observ'd Smokes to rise in Long reach, & Mr Allen ye bearer being at his own House about three Miles of, I was willing to try to save him, & Immediatly man'd out ye boat wth fresh hands & releaved him, who had been in defence of his House about two Hours, it happen'd we did not Loose a man tho they fought the Indians about half an hour before they could get m^r Allen away, it's probable our men wounded if not killed some of them. There is five Garrisons in this Town but can keep but three wch will defend One Another & we are in a good posture of Defence. I am further Strengthening 'em according to y^r Ex^{cys} order, they are within Shot of one Another & some good Houses between that we are able to recieve & Entertain a good Number of men.

Mr Allen who now Comes up will give your Ex^{cy} a more particular Ac^t of his Loss & what happen'd to him this day, I have divided my half Comp^a that are here among the three Garrisons for their better defence, am fortifying for the security of the Stores, would pray y^r Ex^{cy} to order me two Swivil Guns to fix in the fflankers for the Security of the Same, there are here Several smart Lusty Young men that have been robb'd of all they had by the Indians, who would be glad to be in the Service if y^r Ex^{cy} would be pleas'd to admit of it, they Cannot possibly Subsist here without, I have detained 'em till y^r Ex^{cys} order inasmuch as their going off now will weaken the Country

I am y^r Ex^{cys} Most Dutifull & Most Ob^t Hum: Servt

[Superscribed]

On His Maj^{ts} Especial Service To His Excellency Sam^{ll} Shute Esqr Capt Genl, Govr & Command^r in Chief of the Province of the Mass^a &c^a

p Mr Allen. In Boston

Letter from John Wheelwright to Gov. Shute July 6, 1722.

May it Please your Excellency

That whereas the late disturbance given by the Indians hath put us here all in a great Consternation and sum places in great Confusion of which I can do no less but Informe your Excellency and of our present state: The people Eastward, Arundoll Bideford & Scarbrough seme to be under discouragments they being but in a mean way of Defence I mention nothing of those farther East they being more Imediatly under the Care of Maj^r Moody: This town are Generaley in Garison but vnder many difacaltys too many to bee Inumerated and are but short of Amonition York Kittery & Barwick remain yet Generalley at theire own perticuler Houses) I have latly given orders to every place for theire repairing of theire respective Garisons assigned them in each town the last year by your Excellencys order to the Militia here: and that all be vpon theire Guard of Defence and go armed to prevent a tame and Gentle submition unto any that may in a violent manner attemt to seize or disturb them in their lawfull Imployment or business/ I humbly pray your Excellencys direction^s and Comands for the managing these difacult affairs at this Juncture and shall be ready to attend and observe them to the utmost of my power / And am

  S^r your Excellencys most Dutifull & obediant Servt
        John Wheelwright

Journal of the House of Representatives

[At a great and General Court or Assembly of His Majesty's Province of the Massachusetts-Bay in New-England, Begun and Held at Boston on the 30th day of May 1722 &c]
      July 8, 1722
At a Council held at Fort George in New-York.
Part of a Letter from the Governour of Boston viz:
" I find Commissioners will not be appointed to come meerly
" to treat upon a Neutrality – if they may have the liberty

" to engage Five of the Mowhaws to go to the Eastern
" Indians, and acquaint them that they will take part with
the English in case a War should break out, Our Commissioners will wait on you at the time appointed."

Upon taking which Expressions into Consideration, This Board are of Opinion, That the Five Nations ought not to be engaged to leave this Province and concern themselves with the Eastern Indians since it may draw an Indian War on the Frontiers of this Province in its Consequences. That no more can safely be treated of by the Commissioners of Boston with the Five Nations then to renew the Covenant Chain with them, and to engage them to be no ways assisting or encouraging the Eastern Indians in the presence of the Governour of this Province or Persons appointed by him. And that they hold no private Conference with them directly or indirectly.

Letter from Th^{os} Westbrook to Gov. Shute Sept. 23, 1722.

Falmouth Sepr 23^d 1722

May it Please your Excellency.–

I take this Oppertunity to Inform You that I Arrived at Piscataqua at 10 a Clock in ye Morning The. 15th Instant & Immediatly Waited on ye Lt Governour Of Whom I rec̃ed a Confirmation That There was 5 or 6 hundered Indians at Arrowsick upon which I Immediately returned to ye Sloops In Order to Sail but the Wind proving Contrary I was Oblidg'd To Stay till ye Next Morning. 3. of ye Clock And then proceeded to Arrowsick, where I Came to an Anchor at One a Clock on Monday Morning. I Waited upon Coll Walton who Told me ye Indians were Withdrawn & that he Intended to March that Day with 180 Men To Waylay the Indians In Their Carrying Places and Desired our

Company. Butt In as Much as the Indians were withdrawn I was willing To make my best way To St Georges fearing ye Enemy might Attack it. Tuesday About five a Clock we Came To Sail & Came To the Mouth of St Georges River on Wednesday Morning And not having a fair Wind went up In five whaleboats To the fort which I found In good Order the Indians having Attacked it ye 24th of August and Kill'd 5. Men y^t were out of the Garrison They Continued Their Assault 12 Days. & Nights. furiously Only now and Then under a flagg of Truce They would have perswaded them to yeild of the Garrisson Promising Them to give Them good Quarter's and Send them To Boston. The Defend^{rs} Answ^{rs} Were That they Wanted no quarters at their Hands. Daring them Continually to Come on, and told them it was King Georges Lands And That they would not Yeild them up but with the Last Drops of Their Blood, The Indians Were Headed by ye fryar who Talked with Them und^r a flag of Truce. and Likewise by Two french Men. as they Judg'd them to be. they Brought with them five Captives y^t they took at St Georges 15th June last. and kept them During the Seige. But upon their Breaking up. Sent Mr John Dunsmore One of the Said Captives to ye fort to know Whether they would redeem them or no, Our people Made Answ^r they had no Order So to Do, neither Could they do it upon which Mr Dunsmore return'd to the Indians and they Carry'd the Captives Back to Penobscutt Bay and Then frankly released Three of Them Vizt Mr John Dunsmore Mr Thomas Foster and Mr William Ligett.

One Joshua Rose y^t was Taken at ye Aforesaid Time and place And whom the Indians had left Behind at Penobscutt Fort. Made his Escape. & After Six Days Travell Arived at ye Fort ye Second Day After the Seige Began he being Oblidged To make his Way Through the Body of ye Indians To Gett To The fort and was Taken In at One of the Ports,

I now Detain the four Captives to be as Pilotts to Penobscutt Fort Untill I Know your Excellency's Pleasure About them. They Inform me that the Indians have rebuilt Their fort at Penobscutt Since the 15th of June Oblidging Them To Work on it It Contains Ab^t 12 Rodd Square Enclos'd With Stockado's of 12 foot High it has 2 Flankers on the East The Other on ye West and 3 Gates not at That time Hung they Have Likewise 2 Swivell Gunns. It is Situated On an Island In a fresh water River Twelve Miles from ye Salt Water The Captives Judge their is no way of getting to the Island but by Canoes or flatt Bottom'd Boats & it is Impossible to Carry up Whale boats by reason ye falls are 8 or 9 Long & Very Swift. That They Saw 12 or 13 Barrells of Gun Powder Brought To The fort By the Indians as they Said from Canada Ab^t The Middle of July, They have a Meeting House within a Rod Thereabouts on ye Outside of ye South Wall of the Fort. it Being 60 foot Long. 30 wide and 12 foot Studd With a Bell In it which They Ring Morning & Evening~ The s^d Rose Informs me They had a Considerable Quantity Of Corn Standing when he made his Escape. After I had Viewed ye Garrison I return'd In ab^t an Hour & ½ to my Sloop Lying In ye Mouth of the River and Sent up one of them With a few Hands upon Deck as to Carry up stores To The fort and Sail'd with the Other Sloop for Arrowsick full of Men; To Induce the Indians Spy's To Beleive that We had Intirely Left the place, and That there was no Design, against Penobscutt, and Likewise To Inform Coll Walton of ye State of Affairs, not knowing but that he Might have Orders To Make an Attack upon Them.

This Being all y^t is Materiall I make Bold to Subscribe my self

  Your Excellencys Most Obedient Humble Servant
         Thos Westbrook

P. S. The Captives Inform'd me That ye most part of ye Indians food During ye Time of ye Seige was Seals which they Caught Dayly Keeping out a party of Men for that Purpose They Also Inform us & do Assert That there Is great Quantity's of Sturgeon Bass and Eels to be Caught Even Close by ye Island where Penobscut Fort is.

Coll Walton Desired me to Come Along with him To This Place To see what forces that he Could Draw, which I Did Accordinly and Brought Mr Dunsmore and Rose along with Me. The Garrisson at St George has Expended most of their Amunition During ye Late Seige and I Desire your Excellency To Send p^r ye first Oppertunity 4 or 5 Barrells of Gunpowder with Ball, Swan Shott and flints Answerable for ye Indians are resolved To Take ye fort if Possible. If there be no Oppertunity of sending it to St Georges please to Order it to Arrowsick and I will fetch it in my Whaleboats.

[Superscribed]

To His Excellency Samuell Shute Esqr
Capt Generall and Governour In and Over His Majesties
Province of the Massachusetts Bay. In New England
At Boston/   On his Majesties Service These

Letter from Zach Trescott to Judge Dudley Oct. 1, 1722.

Safransway Octo. 1 – 1722.

Honered

S^r As you have all ways ben my frind on all ocasions: I am the moor incuraged to write to you in my present curcumstances I am now after maney removs with the canada indiens at Safransway hamelton with the mohaks Edgar and loue with the indins at worenock Hansard at cabeck.

S^r I humbly intret of you to interseed with his exelency the govener to send the three naregwock indiens and thay will let us 5 go free I cannot think it aney atvantage to the govmant to keep 5 men here for three indiens.

S^r I beg of you to do what you can for me I beleve the best way will be to bring the indiens to albeney I am S^r your most humble servant

Zach Trescott

S^r if you would pleas to write me a line to let me know how things are you may direct it to Mr Jacob Wandol an Albaney gentman who is now at moreal to larn the french tongue who will send it to me

Z. T

[Superscribed] —To Judge dudley in Roxbury

Mr *Sharpe to the Lords Commissioners for Trade and Plantations.*

My Lords

In obedience to yor Lordships Reference I have Reconsidered the Charge Exhibited by me to yor Lordships Agst Mr Armstrong, Collector of his Maj^{tys} Customes in New Hampshire in New England and Deputy Surveyor of his Maj^{tys} Woods in America and upon the most Impartiall and minutest Inquisition, I Cannot find occation to Recede in the least from what has been allready said; but Rather to agravate his Crimes by Repeating his own Imprecations but he is without doubt unfaithfull in his trust as will appea$\tilde{}$ to yor Lordships thus— In the first place, He made Seizure of

Some Goods of Capt. Henry Slopers, who giving him some Moidores; as the S.ᵈ Sloper told me, and the S.ᵈ Armstrong Confessed he had Received; the goods were never more Enquired after. Secondly, The s.ᵈ Armstrong in Conversation Said; that Capt Henry Sherburn Was an ungrateful person: for that tho he had permitted Sherburn To Run great Quantitys of Spanish and Itallian silks; and Spanish & french Brandys & wines; and many other Things out of east India ships homeward Bound which Sherburn mett at Sea; Yett the S.ᵈ Sherburn never gave him anything Equivalent; but a Peice of Silk for his wife and some Brandys and Wines and Tea and muslin. Thirdly, The S.ᵈ Armstrong Seized Some Spanish wines part belonging to M.ʳ George Jaffrey and another part to M.ʳ Tobey; the first was Discharged and the latter Detained by Armstrong M.ʳ Jaffrey telling M.ʳ Armstrong to his fface in my hearing: S.ʳ if you keep my wines you shall not enjoy your Place; for I'll write to England you Know I have Enough against you; and you will be Removed as Soon as my Letters are Received; this is allso Confirmed by Studlys affidavit. Fourthly, He Suffered two Thousand or therabouts of his Majestys mast Trees to be Cutt Down Which were afterwards Cutt into Loggs Then Seized by order of Assembly & Sold. Tis Submitted whether he Could Be ignorant in this Affair if he had attended his Duty; the like never happening in any former Surveyors time This is allso Confirmed by Cap. Husk. Fifthly, he has permitted Command.ʳˢ of Vessells Bound to Spain, to carry Masts and other Timber fitt for Building Ships; which I believe Gives the King of Spain that Encouragem.ᵗ for Increasing his Navall Power w.ᶜʰ we are Dayly Alarmed with in our Dayly news papers. Sixthly, He uttered himself in the following manner In relating a Story Disagreeable to him as I informed yo.ʳ Lordships concerning Coll.ᵒ Philips Is it not a shame Says he that we must be Governed by Germans and have such a fine English Prince of our own; but I hope I shall yet Live to See the Right Heir upon the throne

Besides that he is a noted Irish Jacobite I subscribe my-Self with the profoundest Respect

   My Lords

  Your Lordships most Devoted most obedient & most
     humble Serv.\! Rich.ᵈ Sharpe
London Nov.ᵇʳ Yᵉ 16: 1722.

E: *New England*

Letter from M.ʳ Sharpe containing articles of Complaint against M.ʳ Armstrong Collector of the Customs & Dep.ʸ Surveyor of the Woods in New Hampshire Dated Nov.ʳ 16, 1722 Rec.ᵈ 16ᵗʰ Novem.ʳ 1722. Read do.

Letter Col. Tho.ˢ Westbrook to Lieut. Gov. Dummer

        Portsm.º Decem.ʳ 16ᵗʰ 1723

May it please y.ʳ Honour

M.ʳ Secretary Willard wrote me yᵉ 27ᵗʰ of the last Month that it was y.ʳ Hon.ʳˢ pleasure forthwith to know w.ᵗ men are Entitled to be released or exchanged are desirous of it and who (that are so Entitled) are Willing to Continue in the service I have made it my business since the recept of his Letter w.ᶜʰ came not to my hands till the 10ᵗʰ Ins.ᵗ to Acquaint my self with what your Hon.ʳ would be Informd of, but not knowing certainly what entitules a man to a release (tho' I suppose it to be a two yeares Continuance in the service) I have therefore herewith Inclos'd to your hon.ʳ lists of all the persons (save some few which I have sent to the Officers for but are not yet come to my hand) who have been in his Majesties service two years & upward the lists mentions yᵉ Captains names to whom they belong the Towns from whence they came & likewise shew wether the men were Imprest hired or Voluntiers and the time of their entrance into the Service, who are willing to Continue in it which are I think but three or four & all the rest are desirous of a dismission what remaines I shall send y^r Hon^r as soon as possible. Cp^t Harmon returnd from his Cruise a Wensday last, I have not received his Journal. I shall transmitt it to y^r honour as soon as I do wch will be next week, he Informs me that while he was at Mount Desart he was advis'd by Cp^t Elliot who was in a Sloop from Canso of a party of Indians on an Island call'd Titmanan (I think) wch is but a little to the Eastward of Mount Desert, but out of ye limits of his Instructions as he Conceiv'd wherefore he proceeded not after them. I came hither a Saturday night last from York in Ord^r to send y^r honour this Dispatch, and am now hasteing to Berwick with all possible Expedition. I am Honb^l Sir

    Your most Obd^t humb^l Servt
      Thos Westbrook

P. S. If I Receive no further Instructions I shall Improve Cp^t Harmon on Amus Coggin river & East side of Saco after his men are a little refresht but if wee Cou'd be left at large I am humbly of Opinion that Eastward is the only place to Catch Indians.

    T W

Letter Col. T. Westbrook to Lt. Gov. Dummer

      Yorke Jan^{ry} 28th 1723/4

May it please your Hon^r

  Haveing already acquainted Your Hon^r with the recp^t of some of the new raisd men, I have Sent this to Acq^t your Honour that one of them (Viz^t Elisha Dow who

I receivd from Coll{n} Noyce and posted under Lieut? Oliver at
Berwick) deserted the 26th Inst?, as soon as I heard of it I
dispacht the bearer with a Warrant to have him Secur'd, and
to wait on your Hon{r} with this after he has made diligent
Search —

I have receivd no more men since my last

I am yr Hon{rs} Dutiful humble Servt

Thos Westbrook.

Letter Col. Thos. Westbrook to Lieut. Gov. Dummer

George Town April 6, 1723.

May it please your Honour -

You have herew{th} an Account of my proceedings Since my
Last, I waited at St Georges. in hopes yt Mr Talbert whould
have Arrived there with provision So that I might have took
a Suitable Number of men to ye Eastward, but his Not Coming Oblidged me to come to Kenebeck. and at ye Mouth of
the River I met him & left him there & came hither where I
had Appointed Sundry of the Officers to meet me whome I
met. I immeadiatly Enquired into ye State of that part of
the Army wch I found in a Miserable Condition, on wch I
call'd a Council of Officers to know what might be best for
the presant Service of the Government, the result whereof I
send your Hon{r} a Coppy Inclosed. I detained 140 men at
St Georges in Order to go further East when I Should be
Inabled by receiving provision, but when I came away from
there I left 30 or 40 of ym Exceeding Sick. ye most p{t} of ym
I hope on my return I shall find So many well men as to
return, down East over ye same Ground. I went before in
part; & Spend about 3 Weeks and then return to George
town on Kenebeck river, to know Y{re} Honours further pleasure about the fforces left at Kenebeck river, & West of ye

Same. I formerly Wrote y^t I heard nothing of Capt Harmon but only by Word of mouth by Capt Penhallow I have Since Seen him & he has given me his Journal & tells me he has Sent you a Coppy of ye Same. & at the Same time he Shews me a few Lines wch you had Wrote to him on which I rejoyce that he has given so good Satisfaction. I now Send part of my Journal Imperfect being not Compleated to this day. wch I intended. wch you will please to Excuse. I trust your Hon^r will look over all faults — I having not had time to keep my Journal forward by reason of ye many y^t are Sick and Inconveinances Aboard. Mr Wittemore who has heitherto Assisted me in Writing. is Sick, & has been so for a Considerable time. as for my own part I bless God I Still retain my health in a great measure & had a Design if ye Army had remained so to have kept marching Constantly in the back of the country wth part of ye Army to Intercepted the Enemy in there hunting Ground, & on there Carrying places for this time of ye Yeare being one of their cheif times for y^r Hunting, & with the other part, I intended to have kept them on ye Sea Coast in Order to Intercept there fishing & fowling I have not received a Letter from y^r Hon^r Since the 30th of Jany I am Induced to beleive y^t you Wrote me a line because Sundry of the Officers tell me they have received Lett^{rs} from you. Liev^t Allen Informes me he Desires a Dismissôn for himself. Capt Heath Still Informes me of ye faithfullness of Mr Coleby one of his Serj^{ts} whom you Order'd a Commission to be Wrote for. I beleive the Mistake was In the Penman, for I found 2 Commissions for Capt Heath, But none for Mr Coleby. Capt Heath tells me he Should rejoyce if you would give him a Commission to be his Liev^t Liev^t Winslow, Notwithstanding being dropt. went East with me & Marcht to Pernobscout. I doubt not but he will make a good Officer, & I hope y^r Hon^r will bear him in Mind when there is an Oppertunity to Improve him

Liev^t Moulton Informes me he has Wrote to you for a Dismission from ye Service & likewise Urges me for leave to go home. I tell him I doubt not but you have Thoughts of Advanceing of him as soon as Oppertunity will permitt. by what Experiance I have had of him & ye Carracter I here of him I doubt not but he will make a good Officer. s^r my Extream hurry at present Will not Admit of any Enlargement Crave Referrence to Capt Temple & Capt Harmon who have yor Liberty for coming home. I am
    Yo^r Honours Most Obed^t Humble Servt

[*Indorsed*]
On His Majes^{ts} Service To the Honourable William Dummer Esqr Liev^t Governo^r & Commander in Chief of the prov. of the Massachusets Bay In Boston

To the Kings most Excellent Majesty in Council
  The humble Memorial & Petition of James Woodside late Minister of the Gospel, at Brunswick, in New England.
Sheweth
  That he with 40 Familys, consisting of above 160 Persons did in the Year 1718 embarque on a ship at Derry Lough in Ireland in Order to erect a Colony at Casco Bay, in Your Majestys Province of Main in New England.
 That being arriv'd they made a settlement at a Place called by the Indians Pegipscot, but by them Brunswick, withīn 4 Miles from Fort George, where (after he had laid out a considerable sum upon a Garrison House, fortify'd with Palisadoes, & two large Bastions, had also made great Improvements, & laid out considerably for the Benefit of that Infant Colony) the Inhabitants were surpriz'd by the Indians who

in the Month of July 1722 came down in great Numbers to murder Your Majesty's good Subjects there.

That upon this Surprize the Inhabitants, (naked & destitute of Provisions run for shelter into your Pet^{rs} House (which is still defended by his sons) where they were kindly receivd, provided for, & protected from the rebel Indians.

That the S^d Indians being happily prevented from murdering Your Majesty's good Subjects (in Revenge to your Pet^r) presently kill'd all his Cattel, destroying all the Moveables, & Provisions they could come at, & as Your Pet^r had a very considerable Stock of Cattel he & his Family were great sufferers thereby, as may appear by a Certificate of the Governour of that Province, a Copy whereof is hereunto annexed.

Your Pet^r therefore most humbly begs that in Regard to his great undertaking, his great Losses & sufferings, the Service done to the Publicke in saving the Lives of many of Your Majesty's Subjects, the unshak[en] Loyalty & undaunted Courage of his Sons, who still defend the S^d Garrison. Your Majesty in Councel will be pleas'd to provide for him, his Wife & Daughter here or grant him the Post of Mr Cummins, a Searcher of Ships in the Harbour of Boston N England, lately deceas'd that so his Family, reduced to very low Circumstances may be resettled, & his losses repair'd where they were sustain'd.

& Your Pet^r shall ever pray &c.

I do hereby certifie that the Revd Mr Woodside went over from Ireland to New England with a considerable Number of People, that he & they sate down to plant in a Place they called Brunswick in the Eastern Parts of New England there he built a Garrison House, which was the Means of saving the Lives of many of his People in the late Insurrection of the Indians in July last. That his Generosity is taken Notice of by both Doctors Mathers & that the Indians cutt off all his Cattle, whereby he and his Family are great Sufferers

Samuel Shute

Copia vera

London June 25. 1723

E: Memorial & Petition of James Woodside to His Most Excellent Majesty in Councel.
June 1723

Lieu.^t Govr Dummer to the Lords Commiss.^{rs} for Trade and Plantations.

My Lords

Haveing directed the Secretary of the Province to transmitt to your Lordships by this Ship Coppyes of the Acts Orders resolves & votes of the General Assembly & of his Mag^{ts} Councill which have passed from the last of Sep.^t to the last of ffebruary I thought it a proper occation to psent my humble Duty to your Lordships & to Express the Satisfaction & Alacritye with which I shall receive & Obey your Lordships Comands Soe long as I have the Honour to Serve his Mag^{ty} in my psent Station

Since the Departure of his Excellency Govern.^r Shute I have received advice that ffive English Prison^{rs} taken the last Summer uppon Kennebeck River were Carrid to Canada amoung the ffrench & some of them to the Towne of Quebeck the Metropolis of that Governm.^t where they are now detain'd Prisoners which I looke uppon to bee Such a Countenance & Encouragement given the Salvages in their rebellion as I thought it necessary to acquaint your Lordships with & that wee should have a much nearer prospect of reduceing those rebels did not the ffrench (at least undehand)

Sustaine them. there is nothing further in the Affaires of this Province propper to trouble your Lordships with at psent.

 I am My Lords
   Your most Obed.^t & Most humble Servt
Boston 22 May 1723   W^m. Dummer

E: *Massachusets Bay*
  Letter from Mr Dummer Lieu.^t Govr of the Massachusets Bay Dated the 23.^d of May 1723.
Reced Aug. 14.th 1723 Read July 23.^d 1724

    Defence of Robert Armstrong.

   To the Right Honorable the Lords Com.^{rs} for Trade & Plantations.

The Defence of Robert Armstrong Deputy Surveyor of His Majesties Woods in North America and late Collect.^r of the Province of New Hampshire.
     Is most humbly offer'd
May it please Your Lordships

The complaints against me are of three Sorts: That I have been unfaithful in my Office of Collect.^r That I have suffer'd His Majesties Woods to be destroy'd contrary to my Duty as Deputy Surveyor, and, That I am a Man of Disloyal Principles, and a Noted Irish Jacobite. As this last Charge affects me most nearly, I shall beg leave to begin with That.

Richard Sharp is the person that brings this Charge and says, that I deliver'd myself in the following manner (relating to a Story disagreeable to me concerning Col.^o Phillips) Viz.^t "Is it not a shame we should be govern'd by Germans and Dutch, and have such a fine English Prince of our own, But I hope I shall yet live to see the right Heir upon the Throne", and then adds, That I am a Noted Irish Jacobite.

To this I reply, first, That the Accusation is very general and uncertain; neither mentioning the time nor place nor Company before whom these words were utter'd, which are Circumstances that carry at least a presumption of the ffalsehood of it.

2dly That my accuser is a Person of very profligate Character & had a particular Malice against me, and had often declared that he would, upon his arrival in England endeavour my Ruin.

His Character, I prove, by Col? Armstrong, who has already acquainted Your Lordps, That he was so profligate that no person of Reputation would admit him into their Company: By a letter from M? Bacon my Successor to his Brother S? Edmund, wherein having assured him of my good Behaviour, He declares That Sharp was a Man of a wicked & scandalous Character, & that no Credit was to be given to him; By two letters from the Lieu! Gov. Wentworth, one to M? Secretary Carbass, & the other to M? Jeremiah Dummer in London; and by another Letter from M? Samuel Dummer Naval officer at Boston to his Brother the S? Jer. Dummer.

His Profession was that of a Quack Doctor as appears by one of his printed Bills ready to be produced.

The Ground of his prejudice to me was occasioned by an Action I brought against him for Male practice in his profession, he having my Wife, (then ill) under his Care; and it was upon the clearest proof of his vile Character attested by the greatest Physicians & Surgeons in Boston that I recover'd of him thirty pounds for damages; I have this attestation to produce.

His particular Menances to ruin me in England are sworn to by the Rev? M? Emerson Minister at Portsmouth in New Hampshire; and M? Story where he lodged.

To prove my General Character of Loyalty & Attachment to His present Majesty, I have a Cloud of Witnesses Particularly, A Certificate from the Govern.ʳ & Council of his Maj.ᵗⁱᵉˢ Province of New Hampshire, & another from the Bench of Justices there. As also, a Letter from the Lieu.ᵗ Gov.ʳ of New England ffrom the Secretary of that Province, ffrom the Judge of the Court of Admiralty, ffrom the Survey.ʳ General & all the officers of the Customs; And, ffrom the principal Merchants of the Country, who have known me more than Twenty years. And if all these be not sufficient to establish my Character ag.ᵗ the Malice of one Infamous Man, I must then have recourse to Col.º Hunter Govern.ʳ Shute Gov.ʳ Phillips Col.º Armstrong M.ʳ Dummer M.ʳ Newman and the Principal Merchants on the Exchange trading to New England, who will be ready to do me Justice.

So that, May it please yo.ʳ Lordsps, if it were possible (after these Proofes to the contrary) for me to have been a Jacobite yet I must have been a very secret conceal'd one and not a Noted Jacobite, as this false witness affirms, And I must beg leave to take notice of the Infatuation of the Man in not being contented to call me a Noted Jacobite; when in truth I was neither born in that Kingdom, nor ever lived there, nor any of my ancestors. that I know of.

Having thus, my Lords, as I hope abundantly justified my General Character of Loyalty and ffidelity in the Posts I sustained; I shall proceed to vindicate myself from the Particular accusations bro.ᵗ ag.ᵗ me.

Cap.ᵗ Bolam's letter, upon Yo.ʳ Lordships ffile, That I stopt his Ship, laden only with Lumber, and demanded fforty pounds above my stated fees, and that he at last gave me Twenty pounds to let her go. It is said, laden only with Lumber, to insinuate that I stopt his Ships arbitrarily, & without Cause, only to extort money out of him; whereas I have his Clearance to produce, whereby it will appear That he had on board fforty eight Masts, and some above 24 inches; which made it my duty to stop the Ship, and I made him give Bond according to Act of Parliament That he should on his Arrival in England tender them to the Crown: And in consideration of my extraordinary trouble which he thereby occasioned me, He left me upon his sailing Twenty pounds, N: Engl^d mony, which is ab^t seven pounds Sterling which He has declared upon Oath was Civility mony, and what I well deserv'd. It further appears very plainly, that he was influenced by Capt Huske to make that Complaint ag^t me; (either wilfully ag^t his own knowledge, or as I am rather apt to believe inadvertently) by one particular, which is This: In the Complaint which he sign'd with the said Husk and Sharp, He charges me as being notoriously disaffected to the Governm^t whereas in his Affidavit he affirms he never heard either in New England or elsewhere, that I was in the least suspected to be Disaffected to His present Majesty, but really believes the contrary, And that what the said Sharp had sworn to that purpose was groundless false & malicious. What credit therefore is to be given to his Information is humbly submitted to yor Lordps. And for Yo^r Lordpps further satisfaction, I hope to bring him personally before your Lordships. In the mean time it is not pretended but I did my duty faithfully to the Crown, in not suffering the Masts to be exported till I had taken the proper Bonds in that Case.

The next accusation is a Paper in the name of James Stoodly Master of the Sloop Endeavour from Cales & ffyal, which charges me with Seizing a Quantity of Wines on board the said Vessel & then releasing them, having a particular part to myself.

I must beg your Lordpps to view this Paper, it carrying apparent marks of Imposture; His name tho' but a dissylable is spelt false in four letters; The Justices name is set to it instead of the Deponent's; And the Captain of this pretended affidavit is Coram Ellis Huske & John Ray, instead of the Justice; They are both private men, and one of them Viz.[t] Ellis Huske the very man who has stir'd up all this Mischief ag.[t] me.

I heard of this attempt before I left New Hampshire, and therefore cited Cap.[t] Stoodly before the same Justice, whose name is to the Paper; where he made Oath That Ellis Husk often prompted him to make such an Affidavit, but he refused it, the matter of it being entirely false; I have also the Justice's own Affid.[t] taken before another Justice of the Peace & one of His Majesties Council for that Province, That the said Husk did bring before Him the said Cap.[t] Stoodly with an affid.[t] ready drawn & prest him to swear to it but he refused it. Both these affid.[ts] were authenticly taken, and for a further Confirmacon of them are attested by the Publick Notary; To this I am ready to add my own Oath That I never Seized the Ship: and the wines being a small Quantity mencon'd in the affid.[t] for the Ship's Stores & a few presents, and I never had the value of a single Bottle from either the Master or Owners for myself.

I come now in the last place to the Articles drawn up by this Ellis Husk himself ag.[t] me, which are General Charges, & those not sworn to.

To invalidate this man's Evidence, I pray Your Lordps to consider

First, That I have just prov'd him guilty of attempting a Subornation of Perjury ag.[t] me, both by the Oath of the Justice of Peace & also of the Person, whom he would have suborn'd

2.[dly] This is the same Person, who has accused me of being a Notorious Jacobite, which I have already prov'd to be false by all the principal Persons in both Provinces & by the worthy Gentlemen who appear'd before yo.r Lordships in my Vindication.

3dly It is the same Person who has charged me as one noted for being guilty of Perjury upon Record, and yet no other Person in the Province knows any thing of it, I having produced to your Lordships, attestation of my honesty & Good Character from the Governour & from all the Judges & Justices who must have known this had it been fact, nor does my answer produce a Copy of this pretended Record, or mention any Punishm.t inflicted on me upon my conviction, which surely he ought to have mention'd; I must therefore flatter myself, that yo.r Lordship will not give the least Credit to the Testimony of a Man who has been guilty of such flagrant Malice, and improbable falsehoods.

4thly It is the same Man, whom I prosecuted & brought to Two Trials for having cut down trees contrary to Act of Parliam.t The last Trial Gov.r Shute & Lieu.t Wentworth were both present at, a Copy of the Proceedings I sent to your Lordships And this is the true & only Cause of his inveterate Malice.

It would, My Lords be an insupportable Hardship if such a Man's evidence should be taken ag.t an officer, who has faithfully done his duty, and for that very reason only because he has done it, and it would discourage any officer for the future from discharging his Trust. Had I conniv'd at Capt. Husk's illegal Practices it is very plain he would never have complain'd agt me.

His charge of my suffering many Mast Trees to be cut into Logs being a bare assertion I can only confute by as plain a denial of it; And the attestations of Col.o Wentworth Lieu.t Gov.r M.r Minzies, Judge of the Admiralty, & several other Persons of Distinction; who declare not only my fidelity & diligence in preserving the Masts, but particularly that I had brought on me the Malice of several Traders & especially of

Ellis Husk for selecting & prosecuting them according to my Duty.

There were no Trees converted into Logs in my Time, save 300 which were cut in Mr Bridger's time; The great Waste made then, and the care I have taken since to preserve His Majesties Woods will appear by the Affidavits of Edwd Hall, Capt. Elisha Plaisted & Capt Benj.^a Wentworth (who were imploy'd) as Deputies under Mr Bridger and since by me) and likewise the Certificate of Mr David Jeffries who has been many years Agent & ffactor for supplying His Maj^{ties} Navy with Masts. The care I took of those Trees will appear from Col.^o Wentworth's Certificate & the Copies of my Proceedings in getting the said Masts appraised & exposed to Publick Sale.

There is one particular article w.^h Capt. Husk charges upon me, That he being ready to sail with the Ship Lancaster for Great Britain laden entirely with Lumber, I stopt him a Month because he would not comply with my unreasonable Demands. This is false in every part of it, for ffirst, she was not laden nor had any sails bent to the Masts, nor the Ship's provisions on Board when he demanded his Clearance; as I am able to prove by my officers affidavits whom I sent on board to view the Ship. And Yo.^r Lordships will please to observe that it would have been no way proper or safe for me to have clear'd the Ship till she had her full lading, and was on the point of Sailing. In the next place, it is false that she had nothing on board but Lumber; for it appears by her Clearance which I have, ready to produce, that she had on board 27 Masts from 18 to 23 inches and 21 Bowsprits, & therefore I could not give him a Clearance without Bond, these being enumerated Comodities. I must likewise take notice to Your Lordships That he had an ill design in demanding his Clearance at the time he did, because it was near a month after he sail'd or was ready to sail.

What this man says, that I suffer'd Capt Macphedris and Capt Sherburn to export Masts directly for Spain, is equally false; It is true May it please Your Lordships, That there have been Ship loads of Plank & Timber carried from New Hampshire to Lisbon, & that I have clear'd those Ships, because there was no Act of Parliam.^t to forbid it, tho' at the same time I did it with extreme Regret; ffor a proof of this, I humbly refer myself to my letters to your Lordships for several years running, and in particular my letters of the 20th Novr 1720 & the 20th Octr 1721 in which I complain'd of this practice as an Injury to Great Britain, & therefore inclosed in those letters the Specimens & Quantities of Plank & Timber so exported, which I presume no officer ever did before me, And for this Information I received the Great Honour of Your Lordships thanks. If there were any Masts exported to fforeign parts while I was upon the Spot as Deputy Servey.^r it was by ffraud & Stealth; And this very Complainant was the likliest man to be guilty of it; he having practiced that Trade & also insinuated to others, That the King had no right to the Woods there, and built a Ship for the Carrying on that very Trade & made two Voiages since I came away, as Capt. Bolam can inform yor Lordships.

My Lords, having thus gone through my Defence, I must humbly beg leave to observe to yor Lordships.

That it is Two and Twenty years since I first went to New-England as Secretary to the Earl of Bellomont, being recomended by the late Sir Matthew Dudley, & was soon appointed Naval Officer for N. Hampshire. But His Lordship dying in a little time, I came home & making a Representacon of the State of the American Woods & of the nature & produce of the Northern Colonies, and how they might be made more beneficial to the Mother Kingdom; a new Establishm.^t of the Customs was thereupon made, and I was presented to the then Lord High Treasurer to be Survey.^r General of the Customes in N. America.

His Lordship having promised (to another) This place, appointed me Collect.^r for New Hampshire assuring me that I should be better provided for, and in that office I have continued till now being fifteen Years. I might also mention that it was upon my Memorial, that an Encouragement was given to raise Naval Stores in America, which presently sunk those imported from the East Country to half the value.

For your Lordships further satisfaction as to my former Services, I humbly refer to the two Presentm^{ts} from those Com^{rs} of the Customs to the Lord High Treasurer dated the 25th June 1709, setting forth at large all my former Services; and likewise to their Original Certificate annexed to the same.

Upon the whole, My Lords, I most humbly hope and pray That after having for so many years faithfully serv'd the Crown, & laid up nothing for my Support, (and having the Misfortune of being cast away in coming over) I may not be blasted in my Name and Character & ignominiously turn'd out of His Majesty's Service upon the accusation of Two men, One of them being infamous & Both, of declared Malice ag^t me.

All which is humbly Submitted to your Lordships

By your most obedient humble Servt

6th January 1724.   Robert Armstrong.

E: *New Hampshire*
     Mr Robert Armstrong's Defence With Sev.^l Papers referr'd to Preferr'd 5. Jan: 1724.

Recd Janry 12 Read Febry 25 1724/5

Letter Lt Gov. Dummer to Mons. Vaudreuil

Boston N E Jan^{ry} 19, 1724

S^r

Your Letter Dated Quebec Octob^r 29th p Henry Edgar one of the English Captives came safe to me on perusall whereof I am greatly surprized at the matters contained therein, which are so unjustly represented that I cannot satisfy my self to pass them by unanswered.

In the first place As to what you say relating to the Death of Mr Ralle the Jesuit which you set forth as so inhumane & barbarous, I readily acknowledge that he was slain amongst others of our Enemies at Norrigwalk, And if he had confin'd himself to the professed Duty of his Function vizt to instruct the Indians in the Christian Religion, had kept himself within the Bounds of the French Dominions & had not instigated the Indians to War & Rapine, there might then have been some ground for complaint. But when instead of preaching peace Love & Friendship agreeable to the Doctrines of the Christian Religion he has been a constant & notorious Fomenter & Incendiary as flagrantly appears by many original Letters & Manuscripts I have of his by me to the Indians to kill burn & destroy, and when in open violation of an Act of Parliament of Great Brittian & ye Lawes of this Province strictly forbidding Jesuits to reside or teach within the Brittish Dominions he has not only resided but also once & again appeared at the head of great Numbers of Indians in an hostile manner threatning & insulting as also publicking assaulting the Subjects of His Brittish Majesty, I say, if after all, such an Incendiary has happen'd to be slain in the heat of Action among our open & declared Enemies, Surely none can be blamed therefor but himself, nor can any safeguard from you or any other Justify him in such proceedings; And I think I have much greater cause to complain that Mr Willard the Minister of Rutland (who never had been guilty of the Facts chargeable upon Mr Ralle) who applied him self solely to the Preaching of the Gospel was by the Indians you sent to attack that Town, assaulted, Slain & Scalp^t & his Scalp carried in Triumph to Quebec.

As to the next Article you mention "That St Georges "River was in the year 1700 by order of the Two Crowns "mark'd as the bounds of the English & French Lands "whereby it appeared that Penobscot was given to you, & "that one La fevre had a right to the Land thereabouts & that "all Vessells paid a Duty to him & that Mr Capon Envoy of "Engl^d when K: George came upon the Throne went to ask "the Penobscot Indians to Submit themselves to England "which they refused," I have no difficulty to answer to each of the aforesaid points, & as to the Last relating to Mr Capon you labour under a very great mistake to mention him as an Envoy of England he being far below any such Character, & only an Inferiour Officer, Comissary or Victualler to the Garrison of Annapolis, & some time after that was taken & yielded up to the English sent by the Lieut Govr of that place to visit the French Settlements within that district & to require the Oath of Allegiance & Fidelity from them to Queen Anne, but he had no occasion to come and entice the Penobscot Indians to submit themselves to England, for they as well as the Narigwalk Indians & many other Tribes had done that long before even in the year 1693 at a Treaty with Sr Wm Phips Govr of this Province, by which Treaty I can make it appear that they not only submitted themselves as Subjects to the Crown of England but also renounced French Interest & quitted claimes to the Lands bought & possessed by the English, But since King George came to the Throne Mr Capon has not been in those parts at all as I am inform'd by the People of that Countrey. As to St Georges River being the Bounds & La ffevres pretended Right, it seems very wonderfull you should make any tion of these things or lay any weight upon them at this time, when if the Case were formerly as you now represent it which I do not allow, all such Claim & pretention is wholly superceded & at an end whereof you may soon & easily satisfy your self by consulting the Treaty of Peace at Utrecht concluded between the Two Crown in the Year 1713. by the twefth Article whereof it is provided " That all " Nova Scotia or L Acadie with its antient Boundaries &c " together with the Dominion property & posession of the s^d " Isl^{ds} lands & places & all Right which the most Christian " King, the Crown of France or any the Subjects thereof " have hitherto had to the Isl^{ds} Lands & places & the Inhab- " itants of the same are yielded & made over to the Queen " of Great Brittain & to her Crown for ever " Now by the afores^d Resignation the French King quitted all Right not only to the Lands but also the Inhabitants whether French or Indians or whatsoever they were & transferr'd the same to the Crown of Great Brittain for ever, whereby you are entirely cut off from any claim to the Subjection of the s^d Indians from thence forward.

And We are not ignorant how far the French King understood the Countrey of L'Accadie to extend Westward by Patent granted to Monsr D'Aulney though you seem to be a Stranger to it.

" As to the whole Nation of the Indians exclaiming against some of their Tribe as pretending they were Suborned to give Deeds for their Lands, if it be matter of Fact that they do so which is hard to be conceived, it is a most unjust Imputation & must argue a wonderfull deceitfullness & self contradiction in them, since they have upon all Treaties when the whole Tribes were together constantly acknowledged & submitted to the English Titles & posessions which they had by honest & lawfull purchase acquired.

As to the building of Forts any where within the Brittish

Dominions, I suppose you will not Scruple to acknowledge that the King of Great Brittain has as good a Right to erect Fortresses or places of Defence within his Dominions as the French King has in his, & therefore when you shall please to give me Instances of the French Kings applying himself to the Indians for leave to build a Fort or Forts for the Defence of his Subjects, I shall then give you a further Answer to that Argument. And in the mean Time I must tell you We have alwaies treated the Indians with Sincerity, & never thought it proper to make Apologies for Building Forts within our own Jurisdiction (as you insinuate) but on the Contrary in all our Treaties with them have asserted our undoubted Right so to do.

You likewise signify that we must blame no Body but our selves for the Violence & Hostilities committed against our Nations by the Indians, but Sir, if the Blame must ly where it ought, we must impute their Outrages & falseness & Ill Conduct towards us not so much to their own Inclinations, as to the Instigations of the Jesuit Ralle & others under your Government whereof we have had sufficient information from time to time, as also of your own forcing the Indians against their Wills upon our Fronteirs to destroy & cut off our people, which cannot be otherwise lookt upon than as a Direct & notorious Violation of the Treaty of Peace at Utrecht

Nevertheless Sir after all, I have much greater Inclination to live in Amity & good Correspondence with you than otherwise, & therefore I have sent Col^o Sam^{ll} Thaxter one of his Maj^{ties} Councill & Col^o William Dudley Speaker of the House of Represent$^{v.es}$ who are commissionated to confer with you pursuant to such Instructions as they have rec^d from me And I desire you will give Credence to them accordingly.

I am S^r Y^r most humble &
most Obed^t Servt
Wm Dummer,

Letter Capt. Saml Hinckes to Lt Gov. Dummer.

Fort Mary Jan^r 25th 1724/5

May it please your Hon^r

This comes with my Dutie & humble Service and may Acquaint your Hon^r That Corr^l Westbrook with all ye Rest of the officers Called in here are passed forward & according to y^r Hon^{rs} Direction, ye Corr^{ll} Sayes I shall have men as soon as possible, but am not backward in my Endevours having sent a man on purpose to New Hampsh^r for thre men. my misfortune in this affair Lyes in Conception that if they inlist in the Kings fort they can^t be Cleared in a years or I could have Enough if your Hon^r Sees Cause I may Discharge them in 12 months; I would not trouble y^r Honour for men, which Hetherto I have found the fort mostly with, at my charge.

Capt Heath has taken a Rough Sceam of My fort & well, which cost so much money & Labour) & all thats Necessary, Except Cape porpus & Cape Elizabeth between two which bayes I Lie in sight, & will send forward to Mr Pell, (Dedicated to y^r Hon^r/ & in order to be lanskipped, & as he informes me I must pay 30/ shillins So I have ordered the money to m^r Pell. What news offers Coro^l wrote y^r Hon^r from hence he is now at Casco & Corn Harmon.

if any thing new offers I shall Dutiefully acquaint Y^r Hon^r

One Benjamin Downer a soldier of mine came from Norwich west of Boston & while I was at Boston he run from the fort, he carryed of Six pounds, & gave order to Capt Jordon & to me to take his pay, but Mr Jordon gott it out of my Role, I must petty my selfe that other men take away my poor previledge.

Downer has forged a Discharge & shown it also my name in Severall papers Some have by me as furloes & I hope your

Hon^r will give orders to Comanding Officers to Secure him, for the service I heard of him being at Newberry & Capt Kent can Secure him, he was born their & his friends are at Nowich.

I hope y^r Hon^r will forgive my Teadiousness & give me leave to se my family for 15 Dayes, for I have been sick a season & was all the time at Boston So I am Y^r Hon^{r}s Humble Servt

    Sam^{ll} Hinckes.

Letter L^t. Gov. Dummer to Lt Kennedy

Sir,

I have given Saccamakten one of the Hostages Leave to go Home & visit his Friends vpon his Parol To return in about Six Weeks. You must send out a Scout with him under a discreet officer as far as may be convenient, & so that he may be conducted in Safety out of ye Reach of any of our Parties that may be in the Woods, And when your People Leave him let him be furnish'd with twenty Days Provision to carry him to some Indian Settlem^t.

Agree with him for some Signal to be made upon his Return, And thereupon receive him kindly be with him & if they think proper to accompany him And if two or three other Indians offer to come in peaceably with him, receive them likewise kindly Advising me immediately of it And send them to Boston by ye first good Conveyance

 Feb. 4. 1724

 To L^t. Kennedy

Passport

Whereas Saccamakten (one of the Indian Hostages) has obtained my Leave to visit the Indian Settlem^{ts} & see his

Family & Friends in those Parts upon his Parol to return back in the Space of forty Days; These are to Require all officers Civil & Military & to desire Persons within this Governm^t & all his Majesties good Subjects to suffer the said Saccamaksen to pass forward to Penobscot or other Indian Settlem^{ts} without Lett or Molestation & to return back to the English Fort at St Georges River Provided he pass & repass peacebly without offering any Injury to his Majesties Subjects:

Letter Col. T. Westbrook to Lt Gov. Dummer Feb. 8, 1724/5

May it please Your Honour

    Yesterday Capt Bane returned from his March he has made no Discovery of the Enemy Since last Fall in any part of his March, He informs me that Persumscot River and Sebagook Pond was so open that it very Much hindred him from getting to Madumbessuck and the hunting Ground thereabout. I have Sent for about twenty five Men who are to meet Me at Saco Falls on the eleventh Instant in Order to make ye Second attempt, whom I design shall march away light So that they may get there if possible, I design likewise another Party to follow them up Saco River to carry Provisions with Sleds in order for thier return. I Judge it is Your Honours desire to Search that Ground well in order to Intercept & Destroy those Fellows. Notwithstanding Persumscot River and Sebagook Pond was so open the other Ponds and Rivers are generally fast —

    I am Your Honours most Obedient Servant
                              Thos Westbrook

Falmth Feby 8th 1724/5

Letter Col. Westbrook to Lt *Gov. Dummer*

Fort Mary Febr. 16. 1724/5

May it please/
Y^r Honour /

I Believe Cap^{tt} Heath Marched Exact to ye Time y^r Honour Ordered on his Return I shall Emply the men on This side off Cannebick River persuant to y^r Hon^{rs} Orders,

Leiut Brown Marched for pigwoket the 13th off this instant with twenty nine men –

Rec^d the inclosed the 15th of this month About nine a Clock at night.

I am Y^r Hon^{rs} most Dutifull Serv^{tt}

Thos Westbrook
post

I have advised the front, teer's to be on their gaurds, untill y^r Return off Those Indians.

The place where the indian stop'ed That Did not Come into the Fort is about seven miles Distant

I am Dispatching Cap^{tt} Slocum immediately with Cap^{tt} Bean for georges Their Being an interpreter wanting.

Letter Allison Brown to Col. T. Westbrook March 23, 1724.

Arundal Mch 23^d 1724

Sir

This day being up at Mr Perkins Sawmill and returning back five men together a Scout of Indians fired on them and wounded Sarj^t Sam^{ll} Smith very badly. I being Informd went directly out and could not meet with them but brought the wounded man home. from S^r

Your Hum^{bl} Servt
Allison Brown

To Coll^o Thomas Westbrook
    A True Coppy   Town Clerk

Falmouth M^ch 24. 1724

Sir

You are to see y^t the Soldiers under your Command keep a very strict watch & ward lest the Enemy should Surprise any of our people wch is to be feard

Given under my hand

A true Coppy   Thos Westbrook

Letter Col. T. Westbrook to Lieut. Gov. Dummer

Falmouth March 29, 1724

May it please your Hon^r

My last Inform'd of my Arrival here and my makeing the best of my way to visit all the Frontiers but I have been stopt by a long and Tedious storme, notwithstanding I wrote Orders to all the Officers on the 24th Ins^t about eleven a Clock, and about three a Clock in the Afternoon, wee heard an Alarm from the Westward, but could not hear the Occasion of it till the 27th Currant, whereof I Enclose a Coppy. they have taken a great deal of pains to get a Doctor for the wounded man, they went to Portsmouth and brought one as far as York, and there he was taken sick, so they returnd and went as far as Greenland but could get none from thence, they came to ffalmouth for Docter Negus, who was taken sick the 27th Ins^t. and died the 29th between Eight & nine a Clock in the Morning. wee have had an Instance of the like Sudden death in the past week, a Stout man about twenty five years of Age was taken sick and died in about forty hours – we stand in Absolute necessity of two Docters to visit the sundry sick among us and likewise to Dress the wounded man Docter Bullman haveing his hands full at Richmond & Arrowsick. I doubt not but your Hon^r will take speedy care to send them. I wait with patience as it is my duty to hear what your Hon^{rs} pleasure is relating to the Affairs in the frontiers. If Docter Moody be not Engag'd he would be very Acceptable in general wee haveing had Experience of him last Summer and his Practice generally Attended with Success

  I am your Hon^{rs} most dutifull and Humble Servant
           Thos Westbrook

Letter Richard Davenport to Col. T. Westbrook

Mr Cor: nal: tomous: wes: brok: Sor: idono: Pray: that: yov: will:: let me: have: a: Pass: to boston: Se: in: that: i dont know: what: capten: iam: under: and: i Pray: yov: to: Send: me: a few lines: how things: be: your: most: humbel: Sarvent
      Richard: davenport
      [Superscribed]
      To the Honble Thomas Westbruk
      Corinall and Command^r of his Mag is ties forces

Col. T. Westbrook to Lt Gov. Dummer

            Falm° April 1st <u>1724</u>

May it please your Hon^r
     My last of the 29th of March Inform'd of the death of Docter Negus, and sundry sick people that wanted a Docter and not haveing heard from Richmond in Eight or Ten days I had some small hopes that Docter Bullman might be spard to make a visit to Falm° to give directions what might be best to do for the sick but when the

Express arrived there they found two men had lately died and that Cap^{tn} Heaths brother and two or three men were still sick Captain Penhallow writes me that there were several sick at Arrowsick so y^t Docter Bullman could not be spared. Here is no less than Ten or twelve sick, several of them are recovering Cap^{tn} Penhallow Judges y^t the Indians was about there garrisons on the 29th of March. I directed Cap^{tn} Gray to write to Cap^{tn} Heath to let me know what forwardness he had got the garrison in, In answ^r to it he Informs him that the house design'd for the Maquois, he hop't would be finisht in ten days, and all the rest of the work by the last of May, I suppose the bad weather and sickness has put him back.

The Inclos'd is a request of Mr Davenport for a pass to Boston, he being but just come down and it being a sickly time amongst us I thought it best to Inform your Hon^r of his request. According to your Hon^{rs} Ord^{rs} to make him a Sarjeant I have done it and shall rejoyce if he shou'd carry himselfe so that he might be worthy of a better post.

I am your Hon^{rs} dutifull Hum^{bl} servant
Tho Westbrook

P. S

I wait for a wind to go westward as far as York so that I might get to Berwick to visit all ye frontiers.

Letter Col. T. Westbrook to Lt Gov. Dummer

Falm^o April ye 2^d 1724

May it please your Hon^r

I rec'd your Letters & orders dated the 20th of March last on the first of this Ins^t and am heartily sorry we have not a sufficient numb^r of men to pursue every part of them for wee have not more than will be sufficient to way lay Saco & Amuscoggin rivers & keep our garrisons, for in my Letter of the 05th of March I gave an Account of as small a number as I thought necessary to be on those rivers and which are as many as I can possibly draw and leave the garrisons and Towns their Quota as your honr has ordered, there being but three Compys to march which if full is 150 and your Honours orders is that the garrisons of York Wells and Berwick be not lessned which I believe are as few as can be for their security, all the other Towns and garrisons are not better provided for altho more Exposd, and had I rec'd the 114 men according to your Honrs Letter to me some time since I should not have had more then the 3 Compys full but I want Twelve of them and I believe your Honr has dismist ten or Twelve more and it has pleas'd God to take of Eleven or Twelve by death so that the raising of 30 men more will but make up the old Number theres 15 men out of the Marching Compys to Cover Dunston, Scales and Mitchels and they are daily beging for more and my orders is to Call them off to march which if done they must draw off also wee have not then 30 men sick so that they are not fitt for any service but must be tended, I have lookt over my Journal and Enclosd an Acct of those deceast, taken Captive, & deserted, since I gave in my Account, by This and what I have already writt your Honr may see how wee are decreast. The thirteen men that I enlisted to stay at Georges on Acct of the proprietors in the fall I promist to release in the Springe and they now Claim it of me wch I must Entreat yo please to Enable me to pform

    I am your Honrs dutifull and Humbl Servt
        Thos Westbrook

P. S.

April 5th   Since the above was written I am got to Cape Porpoise I believe I Can Enlist the number of Thirty men &

more generally young men and such as must leave the County if not Enlisted. Some of them may be desirous of a dismission in a Short time others may be willing to stay longer so that what I Enlist shall be Conditionally either to be dismist in a Short time or to stay longer as your Hon^r shall See cause and their Inclinations shall lead them as to the time. The wounded man died the 1st Ins^t I am afraid for want of a Docter Sarj^t Brown was obliged to press a Sloop to carry him to Portsm^o

Col. T. Westbrook to L^t. Gov. Dummer

Yorke April 6th 1724

May it please your Hon^r

My last of the 12th Currant gave an Acc^t of my being at this place & the measures wee were takeing, the people are not steddy in what they pretend, one day they say they will Enlist, another they don't know, and want promises how far they must march out of Town, finding them of so many minds, I have sent Coll^o Wheelwright your orders to Impress fifty men, wch are wanting to Compleat the Comp^{ys} & to make up Thirty more, notwithstanding wee have Enlisted sundry.

Your Hon^r will see what is wanting by the Inclos'd List$_*$ Cap^{tn} Harmon as he Informs me he has not had time to make up his Accounts with the Treasurer this long time, he desires to wait on your Honour to ask leave, which I have Consented to, it being such a time that there is no marching far into the Country the Swamps & Rivers being so full of water, of which he will be able to give a more pticular account, and also of the State of the Army and the present Affaires.

I am y^r Hon^{rs} dutifull Humb^l Servant
Thos Westbrook

P. S

* I mean your Honour will see by the Inclosed list and the Acc^{ts} I sent in my Letters Dated the 1st & 11th Currant, I cannot send Capt Moulton to Richmond till Cap^{tn} Bourn comes to receive the men and arms.

Letter Capt. Johnson Harmon " to Col. Westbrook."

York ye 8th of April 1724/

The reason I sent not the men you orderd, To Serj^t Brown, All were in the Woods, till yesterday, Since I saw your Order, I had none but Sick and Creeped, I now Send Corp^{ll} Aver'll with Six men, as p^r your Order, My men are allmost off their Leggs many Sick att this Time. I hope to See your Honour this Way in a Short time, I shall do all I can with what Men I have able to Send. I heartyly Wish your Hon^{rs} Wellfair, With the Enclosed you'ave this, which is All,

From your Humble Servant att Command

Johnson Harman

A True Coppie
P. S   I have discovered nothing Worth Mentioning

J H.

Col. T. Westbrook to L^t. Gov. Dummer

Kennebunck April 11 1724

May It Please your Hon^r

I rec^d your Lett^{rs} and Orders ye 9th Currant, By Ensign Pyke which were dated on the First & Second of This Instant. I have Enlisted some men, and wait

A Few Days for the answer of Sundry more, I have sent Orders To Cpt Harman, To Enlist Some, he being where the Boddy Of The Inhabitance live, If these measures do not do in A Few days I shall send Coll Wheelwright his Orders, I Shall make the best of my way To York & Berwick, to morrow If The Weather will permitt, I have Gaurded ye People of This place, This Week with a Small number of men to Gett Down their Lumber: The Indians were Like to Catch A Man, att Wells ye 9th Currant. The Inclosed is a Joppy of Cpt Harmans Lett^r, Which gives the State of his Company which I Fear will in Some Measure defeat your Hon^{rs} Projections att pressent

  I am Your Hon^{rs} Dutiful and Hum^{bl} Ser^t

          Thos Westbrook

P S May It Please your Hon^r Paper is Very Scarce, with Me ——— ——

[Superscribed]
On his Maj^{ties} Service To The Honble William Dummer Esqr Lieu^t Govr and Comånder in Cheif &c in Boston

Col. T. Westbrook to Lt. Gov. Dummer

          York April 13th 1724

May it please y^r Hon^r

    Since mine of ye 11th Ins^t I am come to this place Capt Harmon is Endeavouring to Enlist men, so wee shall see w^t men will Enlist in a few days — Capt Harmon has 12 men sick and sundry of Capt Moultons there is two more dead then I gave an Acc^t of being in great hast I must beg y^r Hon^{rs} pardon I cannot be more pticular the Sloop being under Sail

  I am your Hon^{rs} dutifull humb^l Servt

          Thos Westbrook

Col. T. Westbrook to Lt Gov. Dummer

Yorke April 16th 1724

May it please your Hon^r
 The bearer hereof Samuel Choate is troubled with Convulsion fitts, & therefore uncapable of Service. I have pmitted him to wait on y^r Honour, he was dismist the Service on this Account in Coll? Waltons time & now has taken Six pounds of one Kembal of Bradford & came in his room

I am y^r Hon^{rs} dutiful Hum^{bl} Servt

Thos Westbrook

[Superscribed]
On his Maj^{ties} Service To the Honb!. William Dummer Esqr Lieu^t & Comander in Cheif &c at Boston

Letter Wm Peperell & others to Col. T. Westbrook.

Hon^d Sir
 There is a house Lately made defenceable near ye head of York river built by Mr Robert Cutt and some few Inhabitants reside there the keeping of which house will be a very great Annoyance to ye Enemy and will be a great Security to the greatest part of Kittery and all the Inhabitants on the south side of York river it being the place where the Indians frequently come in with their Scouts. You being at ye head of the forces doubt not but it is in Your power —

therefore our humble request is that Six or Eight Soldiers be posted there for the reasons above said.

      Wee are Sir y^r Humb^l Serv^{ts}

April 20th 1724   Wm Peperell
To the Honb^l Thos Westbrook Esqr Jos: Hammond
Comander in Cheif of ye forces   John Leighton
in ye County of Yorke   Nicho^s Shapley

Richd Gowel	Jno Tompson	Stephen Tobby
Elihu Jimmison	Richd Cutt	Wm Peperil Junr
Nich^o Morril	Geo: Jackson	Wm Fernald
Roger Dearing	Nicholas Weeks	Thos Jenkins
Clement Dearing	Eben^r Moore	Sam^{ll} Came
Joseph Moulton	Joseph Sayward	Joseph Young

A true Coppy   Jon^a Bean

Col. T. Westbrook to Lt Gov. Dummer April 21, 1724.

May it please your Hon^r

   Leiu^t John Lane has been so Imprudent to suffer his men to kill sundry Creatures belonging to the people of the County of York as soon as I heard of it I sent for and examind him before Capt Moulton & Captn Harmon he did not deny the fact, but own'd it and made satisfaction to the people rece'd the damage and promises to amend for the future, I informd him I must acq^t your Hon^r of him and if he desird it I would give him liberty to wait on y^r Hon^r and so more p'ticularly informe. I am heartily sorry for his Imprudence

York April 21st 1724   I am your Hon^{rs} dutifull Servt
              Thos Westbrook

P—— S——

I gave Franklyn a written order not to let Anderson go ashore till he had known y^r Hon^{rs} pleasure concerning him, notwithstanding he took him ashore at Casco where he made his Escape from him. Ens^e Wright found him at Piscataqua had him before Justice Penhallow who committed him to Portsm^o Goal the keeper gave him the liberty of the Yard to walke in, wch gave him an Oppertunity to make his Escape and wch he never gave ye authority notice of till Six days after.

[Superscribed]
To the Honb^l William Dummer Esqr
Leiu^t Govr & Comander in Cheif &c at Boston

Col. T. Westbrook to L^t. Gov. Dummer.

York April 21st 1724

May it please your Hon^r

I receiv^d the Inclos'd at one a Clock afternoon, I have receiv'd but Twenty Two of the Fifty men Coll^o Wheelwright was to Impress, I design to get out a Scout on Saco and Amuscoggin rivers as soon as possible, I wrote by Capt Harmon wch will Inform your Hon^r there is sundry scattering garrisons which I expect will be Surprised if not calld in by the Coll^o of the Regiment, The people generally preach up peace to themselves if the Indians do not knock some in the head in Six or Seven days.

I am your Hon^{rs} dutiful humble Servt

Thos Westbrook

P——— S——
I mean what is wrote by Cap^{tn} Harmon will give a more pticular Acc^t relateing to Coll^o Wheelwrights impressing men the 19th Ins^t ab^t sunsett I went to Piscataqua & arrived here again on Monday following.

A Sloop man that lately arriv'd here brings news that a gentleman in Boston that the Maquois had offered to bind themselves and Estates over as a Security that they keep ye Indians off us, which very much Lulls our people in Security :

[Superscribed]

On his Maj^{ties} Esspcial Service To The Honble William Dummer Esqr Leiu^t Govr & Commander in Cheif &c at Boston

with Speed

Letter from Nathan Knight

Black poynte Apr^{ll} ye 19th/1724

S^r

This is to Inform you that the Indans yesterday Kild Mr Michell of Spurwink and tooke Captive two of his eldest Sons and this morning we hard fourteen or fiftean guns up at Winicks neck up black poynte Reaver

Nathan Knight

Col. Thos. Westbrook to L^t. Govr. Dummer April 26, 1724

May it please your Hon^r.

This morning about Eight a Clock I rec'd the Inclos'd wch gives the Acc^t of three mens being killd at Kennebunk they were trackt on the back of this Town the 23^d Ins^t & two seen at Cape Nettick the Same day; Lieu^t Jno Harmon marcht with thirty one men the 23^d Ins^t to Berwick & from thence to march through the wood to Osibye River and then to fall down Saco River to the most likely places of the Indians passing and repassing there to Spend a Months time before he returns, his men not being able to carry Provision enough to last them y*e* Scout, I have ordered him about sixteen dayes hence to meet a Scout of men at Saco Sammon falls by w*ch* I intend to send him Provision Enough to Enable him to tarry out the time.—Cap*tn* Moulton with part of his Comp*y* marcht to Joyn the Remainder at Richmond and immediately to proceed up Kennebeck river there lie in Ambuscade for the same term of time ~

Cap*tn* Harmons Comp*y* is likewise on their march to Royals river and from thence to proceed to Amuscoggin river where they are to tarry dureing the same term of time.

I proposed to some of the Commission Officers of the Militia that when our Scouts are lodg'd that they rally together the Inhabitants & that with the remainder of the Soldiers & part of them they range the woods on the backs of the Towns In hopes to find them out or else drive them to our Scouts but I have recd no Answ*r* from them.

York April 26*th*, 1724   I am your Hon*rs* dutifull
         Humble Servant
          Tho*s* Westbrook

P—S—

Those Scouts & that I propose to send to Saco Falls with provision are all the men I can find Capable to march into the Country, there being many Sick & weak among us.

To the Honb*l* W*m* Dummer Esq*r* Leiu*t* Gov*r* &c

*Capt. Joseph Heath to L*t*. Gov*r* W*m* Dummer*

         Richmond April 27*th* 1724

Honourable S*r*

   Yours p*r* Ensigne Clark I had the Honour of Receiving– The large house for the accommodation of the Mohawks is up & finished Except the Chimneys for which the brick are making & will be Ready in few Dayes. In case the Mohawks come Down I Believe they will expect Such things as they Shall want will be Lodg'd here, I Desire therefore that Such Necessaryes as your Honour shall think it proper to Supply them with may be Sent, with instructions for my Goverment in Disposing there of, as well as the provision & ammunition I am to Deliver them from time to Time. I have lately buryed three of my men who Dyed Suddenly with a pluretick Fever.

Collo[l] Westbrook Order[d] me to Dismiss 16 men of my Company & Sent me but 14 of the Recruits, he also Detein[d] an other of my men (Viz Ebenezer Nutting) as an Armorur at Falmouth, & I understand the Recruits are all Dispos[d] of; Nevertheless I Don't mention this by way of Complaint against the Colo[l]. in the least. But only to Discharge my Duty in acquainting your Honour with y[e] State of this Garrison

The Season to Expect the Enemy is now come & they are gathering to gether, And in order to be Enabled to Entercept some of them And also Fit out a party of y[e] Ablest, to march with y[e] Mohawks (if they come & your Honour thinks it proper) I should be very Glad to be made up a full Company
 But Humbley Submit And with Dutifull Respect
  I am Your Honour most Humble Obedient Servant
          Joseph Heath

[Superscribed] On His Majesties Service
 To The Hon[ble] William Dummer
 Lieu[t] Governour & Commander in Chief of his Majesties Province of the Massachusetts Bay in New England
   present In Boston. pr Cap[t] Gyles.

Letter Col. Tho[s] Westbrook to L[t]. Gov. Dummer

May it please your Honour

The house that the Gentlemen Sett forth lies about **a mile** and quarter from Major Frosts garrison **so** that the **posting** some Soldiers there that they might have a Communication one with another would be very much for the security of all the lower part of Kittery and the people on the south side of York river and to the people in getting their hay out of the marshes.

It being so great a Service to so many people I have presumd to lodge five or six Ineffective men that were not fitt to march till your Hon[rs] pleasure be known in that Affair.

    I am y[r] Hon[rs] dutifull Humble Servant
            Tho[s] Westbrook

York April 28th 1724

Capt. J[no] Penhallow to L[t] Gov. Dummer

        George Town Ap[l] 29th 1724

May it please y[r] Hon[r]

I rec[d] y[r] Hon[rs] Letters of March 20th, One respecting Sam[ll] Hopkins, whom I Percieved had made a Compl[t] he was not discharged with y[e] Other men, altho he was intitled to a Dismission~it can be no Little perplexity to your Hon[r] to be troubled wth Such Matters.

Your Hon[r] will find p my List I return'd him a man that was in y[e] Service above 2 years, & was therefore directed to be dismissed p your Hon[rs] order, but inasmuch as y[e] men did not Arrive here (to exchange others) 'till sometime in Feb[r] he took Occasion to write to your Honour by way of Compt[t]; he was one of the men I dd into y[e] Marching Comp[a] under y[e] Comm[d] of L[t] Bourn & was dismissed as soon as y[e] New recruits Arrived here, so y[t] I am no ways Culpable, but in Case he had not been dismissed it had not been my fault, that Matter being Committed to y[e] Col. Yet althô he was discharged he hired himself into y[e] Service in y[e] room of Another that was released.

p your Hon^{rs} Other Letter am inform'd your Hon^r has taken into Consideration the State of this place & pursuant to your directions I have order'd the Inhabitants into Garrison.

I Rejoyce your Hon^r has a Reguard to Small point, of wch should speak were I not a person Interested there, yet would Crave leave to Say, its a place of Importance it being a Cover & Security to the fishery &c^a it will be a Damage to ye Government Such a place should be Slighted, Especially Considering there is so good a Garrison wch every body will Say is ye Best in ye province, save Castle W^m & more Easily defended with a few men

The Latter end of May will be above 6 months Since I made up my Roll, if your Hon^r thinks fit I should come to Boston in May Sessions for that end, I would pray your Honours Liberty by the Next Sloop.

I am, Y^r Hon^{rs} Most Dutifull & Most Ob^t Servt
John Penhallow

we have Nothing New respecting the Indians Except a Small Scout we fired at about our Garrisons about 8 Nights past —

To The Hon^{rble} Lt Govr Dummer.

Col. T. Westbrook to Lt Gov. Dummer May 1, 1724.

May it please your Hon^r

The Enclos'd is a Coppy of an Impertinent letter from Mr Peter Nowell Representative of York, which I am almost ashamed to trouble your Honour with neither should I have presum'd to have done it had it not seem'd to have reflected on your Honour he asserting that your Honour promis'd the men should be dismist in Convenient time to help to put their seed into the ground his daily declareing he has brought a present dismission for the men has Created a great deal of uneasiness among the people— I have nothing material to Acquaint your Hon.ʳ with since mine of the 26ᵗʰ

I am your Honʳˢ dutiful humble Servant
Thoˢ Westbrook

York May 1.ˢᵗ 1724
To his Honour the Lieuᵗ Govʳ

I rec.ᵈ yʳ Honʳˢ p mʳ Nowell and shall observe your ordʳˢ therein on their return wᶜʰ will be in a Month or Six weeks

T W

[Superscribed]
On His Majᵗⁱᵉˢ Service
To The Honᵇˡ William Dummer Esqʳ Leiuᵗ Govʳ
& Commander in Cheif &c in Boston

Jeremiah Moulton to L.ᵗ Gov. Dummer

Richmond May 6ᵗʰ 1724

Honourable

Sʳ I Take this Oppertunity to Tender Humble thanks for the Late Expression of your Honours Favour & Goodness towards me And shall Endeavour to the uttermost to act worthy of yʳ Good Opinion

I have been in the woods Continually Since I came from York an accᵗ of which Collo.ˡ Westbrook Saith he will Send you to which please to be refer'd

I have two Rolls to bring before your Honour And the Souldiers Contained there in being in Suffering circumstances for want of their pay, I intreat a permission to come and present them At this Session If it be thought proper.

I Am Your Honours Humble Obedient Servᵗᵗ
Jeremiah Moulton

Col. T. Westbrook to L! Gov. Dummer **May 16, 1724.**

May it please your Honour

According to my letter of the 26th of April w[ch] Informs that Leiu[t] Harmon marcht the 23[d] and was not able to carry provision enough to stay out the time your Honour had ordered, I ordered Sarj[t] Brown with Twenty men to meet him at Saco Sammon Falls who mett Leiu[t] Harmon on his return, who was not able to stay by reason of so much bad weather and all the back of the Country so full of Water Especially the Intervale land on the Rivers where he was to way lay, they were oblig'd to march nine miles together up to their Middles in water, and some of the men fell into holes and had like to have been drown'd they Inform me, Brown notwithstanding is gone about Twenty Miles up Saco River there to stay a few days and way lay two Rafts where Leiu[t] Harmon had perceiv'd the Indians had come over the River, I doubt the Scouts on Amuscoggin and Kennebeck Rivers will meet with the same disappointments, I am sending Cap[tn] Harmon as soon as the Country Sloop comes down which I supposed would have been here ere this had there not been so many Easterly winds with what men I can make down to the Islands to range there these moon light nights it being the time of the Indians gathering Eggs and Catching Sea Ducks as they sitt, the Officers are very desirous to go and make up their Rolls in a little time therefore desire y[r] Hon[r] to send directions thereabout

York   I am your Hon[rs] dutifull Humb[l] Serv[t]
May 16th 1724   Tho[s] Westbrook

Capt. John Penhallow to L! Gov. Dummer

George Town May 18th 1724

May it Please your Honour

Yesterday morning about 9 of y[e] Clock three of my men going, within a Gunshot of y[e] Garrison (to drive up some

Cows) were ambushed by about 50 or 60 Indians whom we Judge fired upon the Enemy, who Immediatly discharged upon 'em about 20 guns, & then ran directly upon our men, after that they fired upon this Garrison sometime, while a party of 'em were destroying the Cattle, they tarryed here three or 4 hours before we discovered 10 Canoos going off, who landed about a Mile distant from us upon this Island, I then Mustered of our Little party what I Could Venture to draw out of ye Garrisons, wth the Assistance of Capt Tilton & five or 6 fishermen, I went out to bring off the dead men, Supposing they had been kill'd, & after we had Scouted an hour or two about a Mile round upon this point, we return'd with-out finding them, so that we Judge they Carried 'em off alive.

The Indians are Still about us, this morning before Sun rise Severall appeared runing into the woods, who Skulked near ye Garrison Last night ~ I expect we shall have 'em about us till we have Some reliefe, our weakness being now discovered. the Men being posted in the three Garrisons I Could not at this Juncture Send off a Boat wth Intelligence without danger of having her Surprized as well as runing ye hazard of Loosing the three Garrisons, So that I have desired Capt Tilton to be the beare thereof as far as Falmouth otherways must have run ye risque of Sending off a Boat.

I hope we shall soon have a recruit from the Col: as your Honour has inform'd me, in the meantime, shall be as diligent & Carefull as possible

I am Y^r Hon^{rs} Most dutifull, & Most Ob^t Hum: Servt

John Penhallow

the Names of ye men taken are
Viz^t Morgan Miles ⎫
    Thomas Gillis ⎬
    Corn^s Pass ⎭

Col. Tho.ˢ Westbrook to Lᵗ. Gov. Dummer May 20, 1724.

May it please your Honʳ

I came to this place about Ten a Clock forenoon where I heard that there was a Packett gone along the day before to acquaint your honour that the Indians had been at Arrowsick and killed or carried away three men Its said there was Fifty of them seen I cannot say much about it not haveing my Letters they being carried along also.

I have dismist forty Two of the new rais'd men and shall dismiss the rest as soon as they return.

The Indians are seen frequently all along our frontier from Arrowsick to Kingstown where they killd or took four people on the 16th Insᵗ the Inclos'd is a Coppy of Sarjᵗ Browns Journal

                I am your Honours dutifull humble Servᵗ
                            Thoˢ Westbrook

Arundal May 20ᵗʰ 1724.

Letter from Lᵗ. Gov. Dummer to Col. Thoˢ Westbrook May 21, 1724.

Sir

I recᵈ your Letter by Cpt. Cox with your Projection respecting a Decoy for the Indians by Sending a Number of Soldiers in the Fishing Vessels; Wᶜʰ I approve of & Direct you to man the said Fishing Vessels accordingly & send some Commission Officer with them: I hope Cpt Bourne & his Indians will be with you in a few Days & yᵗ you l Imploye them dilligently according to my last instructions Concerning them & that some notable Impressions be made on the Enemy in the Eastern Parts, as have of late ben made Westward Where our Forces have behaved themselves with a Gallantry worthy all our Soldiers Imitation. And wch by good providence has ben attended wth answerable Success in the Destruction of a great Number of the Enemy

Y^re humble Servt

Boston May 21, 1724 Wm Dummer

Col. T. Westbrook to Lt Govr. Dummer June 2^d, 1724.

May it please your honour

This morning about Five a Clock at Mr Yorks garrison at Pernooduck the Indians killd one man and wounded another there appeared Nineteen I was at Falmouth Side with Eight men with whom I immediately put of a whale-boat and went to their assistance, but the Enemy were drawn off, wee Immediately pursued them with about fifteen men about a mile & halfe but could not come up with them, our number being so small, wee concluded it best to return, It is Judged that there was Canoes seen comeing from the Eastward on last Sabbath day night by Captain Franklin

Falm° June 2^d. 1724

I am your Hon^rs dutifull humble Servt

P. S. Thos Westbrook

Since I wrote my letter I find wee want five or Six more men then what I then Inform'd y^r Hon^r. off T W

Col. T. Westbrook to Lt Gov. Dummer

May it please your Hon^r

My letter of the 21st of last month wch gave an Acc^t that Leiu^t Bean was not returned — This accompanys him with a Coppy of his Journal by wch your Hon^r will be Inform'd of his march —

Cap^tn Harmon went East among the Islands the 26th of last month in quest of the Enemy with fifty five men. I am this day sending the Sloop down to Monheigen Island where he is to repair to in case he want anything.

I sent Leiu[t] Lane from this place the 30th of last month with twenty four men a Scout on the backs of the Towns from this place to Berwick only to stop at Saco Falls to guard the people to get down their Logs.

Wee have not heard anything of the Indians for some time past so that its generally thought they are getting into a body — Mine of the 20th of last month gave an Acc[t] that I had dismist Forty Two of the new Imprest men there is dismist thirteen Since. I have p'mitted Leiu[t] Bean to wait on your Hon[r] by which he is in hopes he may get his back wages for his being Pilott, whome I have Improv'd according to your Hon[rs] orders from the date of his Warrant to this day –

I am y[r] Hon[rs] Dutiful and humb[l] Serv[t]

Tho[s] Westbrook

The number of men as near as I can get the Acc[t]
that are now in the Service is about Four hundred.

Falmouth June 2[d] 1724

Col. T. Westbrook to L[t] Gov. Dummer

May it please your Honour

Captain Harmon is return'd from his Cruise, whom I mett at Monheigon, he informs me, your Honour has given him leave to go to Boston to make up his Roll. the Enclosed is a Coppy of his Journal by which your Honour will be Inform'd of his Cruise

I am your Honours Dutiful Hum[ble] Serv[t]

Tho Westbrook

Sagadahock June 5th 1724

P- S-

I have ordered Cap[tn] Harmon to send the remainder
of his Comp[y] to Saco to Joyn Lieu[t] Lane, whom I gave

your Honour Acc^t of in mine of the 2^d of this Ins^t he is to take with him Mr Stephen Harden as a Pilot who is an Expert one on Saco Kennebunk and all the rivers as far as Winipeesiaucut Ponds he haveing hunted on that ground for many years past, He was Pilot to Lieu^t Jno Harmon on his last march who says he never Saw a man have more Judgm^t in the Woods than he

T W

[Superscribed]
On his Maj^{ties} Service
To The Honble William Dummer Esqr Lieu^t Govr
& Commander in Cheif &c at Boston.

Col. T. Westbrook to Lt Govr Dummer June 6. 1724.

May it please your Honour

Cap^{tn} Harmons Company is ordered on the backs of the Towns between Saco and Berwick as I gave an Acc^t of in mine of the 5th Curr^t the rest of our men are ordered to Cruise in Casco Bay amongst the Islands Pemequid and East as far as Musconkus and from thence back into Damariscoatty and Sheepsgutt rivers and to Mountsweeg bay so on the back of Arrowsick to Kennebeck river up to Richmond and so to keep on this Cruise till your Hon^{rs} pleasure be known Indeavouring to hinder the Indians from passing and repassing with their Canoes for its Judgd since wee have not had men to pass in our boates that they frequently pass by water, when they came to Arrowsick they went off in their Canoes to Casco bay as it is Judg'd — Capt Franklin waites here for a wind to carry provision to Georges. I hope your Hon^r will ord^r what must be done relateing that garrison — the above Cruise is ordered by the advice of the officers present Viz^t Capt Harmon, Capt Penhallow, Capt Heath, Capt Moulton, Leiu^t Kenady

     I am your Hon^rs dutifull Humb^l Servt
           Thos Westbrook

Sagadahock June 6th 1724

 P. S. Capt Heath haveing acquainted me with your Hon^rs Furlo comes up to Boston accordingly by whom I write **T. W**

     [Superscribed]

On his Maj^ties Service To The Honble William Dummer Esqr Leiu^t Govr & Commander in Cheif &c at Boston

 p Cap^tn Heath.

Col. T. Westbrook to Lt Gov. Dummer June 13. 1724.

May it please your Honour

 This morning about Ten a Clock Cap^tn Franklin brought us this Maloncholly Account Viz^t That the Indians on the first of May last way layd Cap^tn Winslow on both sides Saint Georges River as he was going to the garrison with Seventeen men in two Whalboates, whome Indians have killed or taken all but three that made their escape and got to the garrison they say there was a great number of the Indians, who fir'd on our people first from the Western side the river, as soon as they had fired they put off in their Canoes and fell on our people very furiously, so that our boates were oblig'd to part they over powering them with a superior number. Cap^tn Winslow endeavoured to land on the West side and so long as he was seen by our people fought boldly and bravely, And it is Judgd killd several of the Indians, Sarj^t Harvey landed on the East side hopeing to get clear of them but as soon as they landed there was another Considerable party mett him and shot him down after they had changd some shots on both sides our people were then obligd to draw off as well as they could, one of them did not get into the garrison till three days afterward he saw an Indian that day, our people trackt some about a week after not more than one hundred yards from the garrison. It is Judg'd there is a party lurking about the river and garrison still ~

Where they fird on our people first, they Judge there would not be less then Thirty Canoos besides three Ambuscades more One on the West and two on the East sides the River, Wee have not men to look for the Dead bodies of our friends so that our Enemies have a double triumph over us — Cap^{tn} Harmons Comp^y being at the Westward and the army is so decreast as I have already given your Hon^r an Acc^t of in part and shall be able to give it in full when I come to Boston.

I am your Hon^{rs} dutifull humble Servt
Thos Westbrook.

George Town June 13th 1724

P. S. Cap^{tn} Winslow went out of the garrison on the 30th of April to the Green Islands hopeing to meet with a Canoo or two of ye Indians ~

Capt. Joseph Heath & Col. T. Westbrook to Lt Gov. Dummer.

Boston June 24th 1724

Honourable S^r

Having your Orders to returne to the Fort at Richmond, thought it my Duty to Lay the State of that Garrison before Your Honour by Several Deaths & Dismissions my Company is reduced to Twenty men, And the fort being large & far from Relief, I would Humbley Suggest to your Honour Is in danger of being lost with out a reinforcement

& your Honours Designe of Sending Some able Souldiers to Scout with the Mohawks altogether imprackticable. The number of men posted at Casco Fort in y⁰ last warr, and the present Company at north field are presidents, & Seem to plead for a recruit to be Sent to richmond, which is farther in the Enemyes Countrey than Either of those.

All which I Humbley Offer to your wise Consideration & with Dutifull Respect remaine

Your Honours most Humble Obedient Serv^{tt}
Joseph Heath

May it please your Honour

Capt Heath has acquainted me with the above report design'd to lay before your Honour, which appears to me very reasonable

I am your Honours dutifull and most obedient Servt
Thos Westbrook

[Superscribed]
On his Maj^{ties} Service
To The Honble William Dummer Esqr Leiu^t Govr
& Commander in cheif &c in Boston

Zach Trescott to " Edward Hutchinson Esq."

Mont royal iune 29⁻ 1724.

S^r

I rec^d yours dated November 29 and return you harty thanks for intersesion with the French gent men for my redemption I have ben 13 months with His Excelency gouerner Voudreill I hope by the devine permision to set out for boston with in three weeks

M^r lorie hath writen hear that the hostages aear dead in boston preson which has put the indiens in a grate rage agains the English thay say thay aear poysoned and thear aear about 700 gon and going in small compeneys 10 12 15 20 25 in a company to al parts of New england the frontears and if thear be not grate care taken I fear thay will do a grate deal of mischef no noise from frans as yet but dayly look for it I am S^r your most obiged and uery humble seruant

            Zach Trescott

John Minot to Lt Gov. Dummer

           Boston July 16th 1724

May it Please your hon^r

 This Waits on your hon^r to advise you that the Two Coxes that were bound to the East are put into Marblehead where they are indeavouring to get more men having on board boath scooners but fourteen men, and our people here being so very uneasy about so many of their freinds and relations being now in the hands of the Indians are very backward to goe against them in a Hostile manner, they begg the favour of your honour, that there be some emediate measures taiken to redeme our people and Vessells out of their hand Mr. Cox tells me he will willingly taike on board anything that we shall send to redeme our men and Vessells out of their hands and if your honour will please to give direcktions to the two skippers to ackt according to the measures the Indians have proposed it will be a great Obligation uppon the Widdows and fatherless that are now in some hopes of some of their freinds remaining still in their hands this favour the distressed people in Marbleh^d desired me to aske of your hon^r

   I am Yo^r Hon^{rs} most Obed^t Humb– Servt

             John Minot

I would further say to your hon^r that our people would chearfully goe here what number your hon^r pleases to make reprisals on the ennimie provided they can meet wth y^m to advantage at sea but if they have hal'd up our Vesels into the Countrey as we understand they have it will be impossible to come at them without a flagg of truce and If your hon^r pleases I will go Down with them if your hon^r sees meet to act in this affaire its my humble Oppinion that its emediatly requisite a post be Dispatcht to Marblehead to Stop these two Coxes to reseive your Hon^{rs} orders I am Yo^r Hon^{rs} Most Obed^t Humble

Jn° Minot

they may call at Casco for Jos Beane & the Vessel that is there which the Indians desire to come.

[Superscribed]

To The Honor^d Willm Dummer Esqr Command^r in cheife of his Maj^{ties} Province of the Massachusets Bay

Letter Lt Gov. Dummer to Gov. Saltonstall, of Conn.

S^r

I wrote your Hon^r 30th Decemb^r last in order to obtain from His Maj^{ties} Government of Connecticut a supply of Forces to join with the Towns of this Province in covering some of the most exposed Towns in the County of Hampshire & thereby your own Out Towns from the Attempts of the Indian Enemy, At the same time in compliance with the desires of your Gen^{ll} Assembly of Octob^r last, An account of the just Grounds this Government had to declare War against the Eastern Indians was by the Secretary transmitted to you, as also our Treaty with the Mohawks & altho̅ nothing has yet been done on your parts in answer to our proposalls at that time, yet the Occasion still remaining & the

Generall Court of this Province being now again convened & having under their consideration the Defence of the Western Frontiers, they have unanimously desired me to renew my Motion to you on that Head. The Season of the Year being now come on when the Indians suppose they can make their attacks with the greatest advantage to them & the most disadvantage to us, & there being advices from abroad that there is not now an Indian Man to be seen in such places as they use to frequent gives us strong grounds to conclude they are preparing to make a violent Effort on some place or other as soon as they can meet with a fit opportunity for it, so that it appears absolutely necessary to have a considerable Force on the Fronteirs either to keep or beat them off: & this Province having Fronteirs of so large an extent we are exposed to a most heavy charge for the Defence of them. Now althô War has not been proclaimed against the Indians in Form by the Government of Connecticut as by this Government yet inasmuch as we are both embarqued in the same Bottom, are under the same Crown, our Interests are the same, inasmuch as His Maj.^{ty} has given his commands & directions to the severall Governm^{ts} on this Continent for assisting one another in case of a War & most especially inasmuch as our Western Towns are the immediate Barrier & Cover to yours & that if ours should be broken up or drawn off, yours would be exposed to the Fury & Ravages of the Enemy in the same manner as ours now are. We cannot but judge it highly reasonable & we doubt not but upon mature Deliberation you will do so too, that you should join your Forces to ours for the Mutuall Defence of both.

Besides the Forces which have been formerly posted in those Towns, I have upon the advices rec^d lately made a further addition to them, but these also are not sufficient to give the Enemy a warm Repulse & althō it appears by the

Votes of your Gen'l Court that you have 200 men in readiness to march yet that provision does not seem likely to attain the desired End, for you are sensible that the Indians alwaies make a Sudden onset & then retire forthwith so that if your forces remain as they now are before they can be got together & march to the places attackt the enemy will probably be got out of reach & so it will be too late to follow them. Upon all which considerations we desire Your Governm.^t will send 100 Men to be posted at Northfield Deerfield & Westfield in such proportion as shall appear most necessary, to continue there for a few months till the time of the greatest danger is over, if some part of them were trusty Indians who are used to the woods it might be an advantage.

This comes p̱ who it is hoped will wait upon you before your Generall Court rises & request you will make use of your Influence & Authority that what is proposed may be obtained whereby you not only do Service to the Crown will gratify a Province that is always ready to testify their Respect to you & will likewise oblige

Y.^r In the name of the Committee

~ Wm Tailer

In Council June 9, 1724.

Read & Ordered that this Report of the Draught of a Letter to the Govern.^r of Connecticut be Accepted

Sent down for Concurrence   J Willard Sec̃ry

In the House of Representatives June 9th 1724_
Read and Concur'd & that His Honour the Liev.^t Govr be desired to Express the Letter to the Govr of Connecticut as soon as Possible

W Dudley Speak.^r

In Council, June 9. 1724   Read & Concur'd

J Willard Secry

Samuel Hinckes to L^t. Gov. Dummer.

Fort Mary July 19, 1724

May it Please Y^r Hon^r

This comes in Company with a Letter from Leiut Beans to Coro^l Westbrook who was Sent here and arrived the 17 instant,) & in order to give y^r Hon^r an account That ye 18: I supplyed him with ammunition &c to hasten to Spurwink where the Enimy were & Burnt one Perryes house. Killed one Solloman Jordan near ye garrison of Leiut Jordan Lt Bean Hastned from hence 19 instant fought about 30: indians Killed one & Recovered his Scalp gun &c. took from them Beafe Blankets & Sundryes Drove the Enemy: & took about 25 packs & they Ran away naked, this day —

We Lost one Robert Brown of plymouth and one Simon armstrong was scarred on his head flesh wound, the Enimy fought smartly while they stood, Mr Bean & men are here & as to any particulars farther I beleive Corr^l Westbrook will forward, Mr Beans Letter to y^r Hon^r for whō I wrote the particulars & pray I may be Excused for my not inlargeing. I hear Mr Buckman's garrisen at N° Yarmouth is Burned & of Alarums their, this morning Large fires appeared up Saco River, at Cape porpus, we dont hear the Reason but guess the Enimy to be Every where, & having no incorragement that I may have men to fill my Complement up as yet I hope y^r Hon^rs not forgot y^r Direction you gave me to Leave a mem° in the Secre: Office that I may have them, by y^r Direction to Corn^l Westbrook & Especially one fit for a corporell.

the 14 instant went hence volenteers from piscatt^a after indian pirets as also sundryes & one Capt Salter from the Sholes & 4 men at green Islands, said Salter) since parting form his Conserts who arrived here to day) informes me he meet with the indian privateer a sconer once of Marblehead full of indians Extraordinary well fitted who Chased them 3 hours & she Takes all She Can come up with, so that the fishermen dont go East of this place or scarce to sea, with my Dutie is what offers from y^r humble Servant

        Samuel Hinckes
    [Superscribed]
To His Honour William Dummer Esqr Cap^tt Generall & Comander in Cheife In Boston
On His Majestyes Service

John Wainwright to L^t. Gov. Dummer

        Ipswich July 13th 1724

May It please Yo^r Honour

  Just now arrived a fishing shallop from the Eastward, the Skipper whereof appearing before me made Oath to the inclosed Declaration, which I thought necessary to Express to your Honour.

  The Skipper of the shallop informs me & I am apt to be of his opinion that there is a great probability of making reprizall of the shallop the Indians have taken if not of recovering the men & Surprizing Some of them, who are at present very bold in Enterprizing & boarding the fishing vessells on the Eastern Shore, There is a Sufficient Number of the ffishermen & other men & vessells now ready, who are very willing to go with all the Dispatch & Expedition your Honour may please to order down to the Eastern shoar & who I am fully persuaded will do their Utmost to decoy & surprize the Enemy, if they may have yor Honours Commands & Directions therein.

  They may have provisions Ammunition &c. as Soon as orders are given therefor. Mr Eveleth the Bearer is able to give a more particular Acco^t of the matter theres Time will allow to inform yor Hon^r in writing

    Y^r Hon^rs most Obed^t humble Servt
        John Wainwright

"*Letter to Capt. Durrell*"

Sir

Having rec^d Advice of sev^{ll} Vessels man'd with Indians infesting the Eastern Coast to the great Disturbance & Loss of those concern'd in the Fishery, I desire you to draw out of your Ships Company fifty or sixty of your ablest men which with such Men as I have Order'd to be impress'd here & in the Out-Posts to be all under the Command of your Lieu^t & Lett them forthwith proceed East in three small Vessels provided for that Purpose, Lett them keep near the Shoar & look into the Harbours as they go along & endeavour to get Intelligence of the Enemy, & decoy them by Sounding for Fish & Concealing their Men & such other Methods as are proper for that End & by all possible Means to find out the Enemy & suppress & destroy them as well as any Pirates that may possibly be on the Coast. I do not limit you as to the extent of Coast for this Cruize, But leave it to you & the Discretion of your Officer how far East he may proceed in wch he must govern himself according to the Intelligence he may meet. If he can hear of the Enemy on shoar & his Men be capable of Service that Way Lett Him land such a Number of his Comp^a as he shall think fit & prosecute the Indians vigorously on the Shoar. If after all proper Methods for the Discovery of the Enemy, There be no likelyhood of Meeting with them & intercepting them by Sea, He must endeavour to find out the Vessels the Indians have taken & if practicable secure & bring them off: Put one good Officer in each Vessel to be under the Direction of your Lieut. & to proceed by his Orders: They must return back in thirty Days; Unless Circumstances shall be such as to give great hope of Doing Service by Staying out longer.

Sir

I have rec^d your sev^{ll} Letters respecting Mr Banes Engagement & the March of the Forces to Kennebeck River, And am well satisfied with the Dispatch you have given to that Affair; There being such a Number of Troops in your Frontier, I have determined they sh. be employ'd (after the Marches to Norridgewock are over) on an Expedition to Penobscot & on the Sea Coast in those Parts. Therefore after a proper Time allow'd for the Soldiers Refreshm^t you are to proceed at the Head of them yourself to Penobscot & other Places to the Eastw^d where it is likely in order to w^{en} the Enemy to gett ye best Intelligence possible, & to project the particular Circumstances of this Affair & Send to the Treas^r to furnish you with every Thing necessary & Let me know your Thoughts immediately upon it, that so there may be no delay.

Col. T. Westbrook to L^t. Gov. Dummer

May it please your Honour

Cap^{tn} Harmon arrived this day with the Fryars and Twenty Six Scalps more from Norridgewock and brought Bombazees Squaw and three more Indian Captives retook three English boys, he Informes a great number of Indians are comeing on our fronteir Sundry from Canada and Two Hundred from Penobscutt for a more account I refer to him; They have taken Leiu^t Kenadys Coat at Norridgewock who resided at Saint Georges, which makes us doubt they have taken the garrison, I am Sending Cap^{tn} Sanders in his Sloop strongly guarded to that place and am likewise dispatching orders to all the fronteirs to be strict on their guard. Capt Harmon and the officers Judge, that by the modestes Computation besides the Scalps and Captives they brought in, what they killed and drowned there could not be less then thirty or forty, God has now been pleased to Crown your Honours unwearied Endeavours with success, which I desire to rejoyce at. I hope y^r Honour will smile on Cap^{tn} Harmon and favour him with a Commission for a feild Officer.

I am your Honours most Dutiful Humble Servant

Thos Westbrook

Falm° Augt 18th 1724
I have Imprest Mr Dokes Scooner
to convey Capt Harmon to Boston

Col. T. Westbrook to L^t. Gov. Dummer

May it please your Honour

I received your Instructions dated the 25th Curr^t on the 28th Ins^t and shall put them in Execution Immediately – I hope the Hostages will Pilott us through from Kennebeck to Penobscut which will be the best way to get to their Town undiscovered – As to Bombazeens widow I have examined her and she knows little or nothing about the Penobscut tribe and is so sick she is not able to travel. My advice to the Inhabitants and orders to the officers has always been not to go out with less then Fifteen or Eighteen men or more as the occasion may require but the Inhabitants are so obstinate they will go out not above Two or three at a time Two or Three miles from their garrisons if they cannot all have a guard in one day and the Officers of the Militia in each town do not take any care to regulate them, they refuse to help in watching in their garrisons at night where the soldiers are but Two or Three especially the Inhabitants at Perpooduck point I acquainted them it was your Hon[rs] orders but they refused to comply. There lies this difficulty with me which I can't tell how to get over –

Viz[t]. Wee must have a strong guard with our Whaleboates up Kennebeck River lest wee should not get through and be obligd to return, neither are wee able (in Case wee should get through) to leave a sufficient number of men to bring back the boates to Richmond without weakening the Army too much to pursue the march, besides it will be of absolute necessity to have some boates on our return with the Sloops at the mouth of Penobscutt river to search after the vessels taken from the Subjects of this Province w[ch] wee cannot have unless y[e] Sloops bring some with them from Boston or unless your Honour will please to send Fifty men more for the above mentioned designes Wee must have Two Doz[n] of falling axes to make either Rafts or Canoes to get from the Main to the Island where the Indians live and those men that have the charge of the Axes must have pistols sent them they not being able to carry their guns Packs and Axes there is wanting Thirty or Forty Firelocks for the men already in the Service which must be sent Immediately, I shall not be able to get the men so soon as my orders direct, to Richmond, by reason I sent a Company to releive Georges and Intercept the Enemy there and they are in quest of them now by the verbal Acc[t]. I had brought me this day from Cap[t] Sanders who is Just come to Richmond from thence and brought a Captive Leiu[t]. Kenady redeemed, as y[r] Hon[r] will see by the Enclosed which is a verbal acc[t] I received from one of my Sarj[ts] whom I sent Express to Cap[t]. Heath and who met Sanders going to Richmond from whom he had the Information —

When I had ordered the men to Scout at Saint Georges I had thoughts y[e] army would have mov'd that way – Here being only Docter Bullman that is Capable of marching with us and he being very much fatigued I must entreat your

Honour to send another Docter down to march that he may have some respite

    I am your Hon^rs most dutifull Hum^bl Servt
        Thos Westbrook

P— S—
I pray your Honours to excuse every thing amiss for I have been writing and dispatching orders from Sun rise till Nine a Clock this night so y^t my brains is quite Addled

Letter Lieut. Gov. Dummer to Secretary Willard
"*Sept. 1, 1724*"

S^r /

 Coll? Westbrooks Packett is enough to make one Sick what Hee has done allready as well as what Hee further insists on seems to tend directly to Confound our hopefull designes. What Hee sayes of a Strong Guard for the Whaleboat is a mere jest. 10. men is Sufficient for that, What Number of Men Can Hee expect to bee there at this time when Hee expects so many at Penobscutt.. Those 10 Men with the Whaleboats may have a Communication with Richmond fforts & Can't be better Imploy'd then by lying at such a pass to intercept a Smal Scout of the Enemye.. It was Impossible to express in more Strong termes My orders above all things that Hee should make no delay & yett Hee seems to have no Idea of it. for My part I will write no More to Him it's an unaccountable thing that without orders Hee should Send away a Number of Men to St Georges. I allwayes intended a March to Penobscott as soon as the fforces should be return'd from Norridgawalk & therefore would not hearken to anything that Could prevent it.

 Pray Communicate this Letter to the Bord this Day & write a Line to Westbrook that Hee make no further delay &

thereby ruine this Project if phaps it bee not allready ffrustrated by Intelligence gott to the Enimye, & Lett Him give such orders to His People about Georges as is necessary if it bee not done allready, & if Hee don't incline to go Lett Harman take his Command. The Pistolls axes and Guns you say are ready. Pray Coll? Fitch to get the men on Bord & Let the Vessell Sail to night or in ye morning.

Col? Westbrook Sends a long Story of New Projections to Amuse us they may bee putt to the Tryal in the Winter phaps when we have nothing else to do but now the is the time to finde them in their planting. for tho.- they may have gatherd their Corne by this they have not had time to dry it & Carry it away & an old settlement is not Suddenly broak up & quite deserted.

If the Councill are of opinion to stop Winnett & all the Annapolis Vessells for two or three days it shall be done

Y^r
W Dummer

Letter John Gray to L^t. Gov. Dummer

Falm^o Septr ye 8th 1724 –

May It Please your Hon^r.

By a Vessell Bound to Boston I take Leave of Obeying your Hon^{rs} Commands, in Sending My Com̄ission your Hon^r was pleased to tell me that you'd alter and Send another To me. I Heartyly Congratulate with y? Sr. In The Success your Troops has obtained over the Enemy. So may you prosper in all y^r Und'rtakins For the general good of your Goverment Is, and shall always be the Prayer of Y^r Hon^{rs} Most Dutifull & Obedient Ser^t Att Com̄and

John Gray

P S
My hum^{ble} Service To Your Lady
We have no Indian News here

Letter Col. T. Westbrook to Lt Gov. Dummer

May it please your Hon^r

I received your Hon^{rs} two letters not before the Seventh of this Inst One was dated the 28th of August & the other the 1st of Sep^t wherein your Honour blames me for haveing a project of my own. I do assure your Hon^r my letter of the 28th was in obedience to your Hon^{rs} order to me, in your letter of the 6th of Augst and was wrote the day before my Instructions came and if it should please God that I should return from this march, I doubt not but I shall be able to satisfie your Hon^r that I have not delayed my time Capt Slocom arrivd the 7th Curr^t with 24 fierlocks wch was not as many as wee wanted and sundry necessarys as Blanketts shoes stockins &c which the men could not march before they had y^m as to the boates I did not expect any for this Expedition, but have Swept all garrisons clear of their old boates they had to fetch their provision and have been mending them night & day ever since I received your Hon^{rs} orders— I must be obligd to send up part of the body first and a party of them to bring back the boates, I hope wee shall be on the march near ye time I wrote in my last Falm^o Sep^t 8th 1724

I am your Hon^{rs} most Obed^t Humb^l Servt

Thos Westbrook

P S

I did not receive your Hon^{rs} letter of the 6th of August till ye 27th of the Same Month by the hands of Capt Gray

Col. T. Westbrook to L! Gov. Dummer

Dated 60 miles up Kennebeck river on Dummer Island on grape Street Just by the great fish Market   Sep^t 12th 1724

May it please y^r Honour

We sent up part of the army on the 9th Currant not haveing Boates enough to carry us up all at once and arrived with the army here the 11th of this Instant where wee are detaind by rainy weather ~ As soon as the weather will pmit we shall be diligent on our march which I desire and hope will answer your Hon^{rs} Expectation ~ I ordered the Sloops to be at Penobscut in fourteen days from the 11th day of this Instant.

I am your Hon^{rs} most dutifull & Humble Servt
Thos Westbrook

P S
Written by the pure blood of the grape gathered on Dummers Island

L! Govr Wentworth to the Lords Commiss^{rs} for Trade and Plantations.

Right Honorable

I shall not trouble your Lordships with Copy of what wrote the 5th of Aprill, hope the Collector^s Acco^{ts} came safe which is the remaining Six months that makes up ye year to the 25th June as also Fort William and Mary Acc^t of Expence of Gun powder to the 5th day of July 1724,

I am not yet out of hopes of his Majesties Royall Bounty to ffort William and Mary, Our Stock being next dore to nothing, it would be a great pleasure to me to see something come that way our Trade being small, dos but a little more or less, bring the year about sometimes a little Over and other Years Under and in case we Should be attack^t by Our Enemies we have not above one Round of Gunpowder in the ffort.

I have been greately perplexd in my minde about it.

The Assembly of this Province Say the people are so oppresd with the Indian war that they cant pay the charge that ariseth thereby I hope your Lordships will not take it amiss in giveing much troble, this affair has been laid before your Lordships by Our Agent the last Year and your Lordships was pleasd to report in our favour, but it Stop't at the Board of Ordinance, as I would not be tho't Troblesome, so neither would I be Negligent of my Duty in reporting the truth, least any Acsident should happen (which God Allmighty divert) for want of recruites about the Midle of the last Month Capt Harmon with a party of Troops came upon one of the Chiefe of the Indian Towns and about one hundred & Twenty Miles from the Sea called Noridgeawag, and distroyed about one hundred Men, Women & Children, which is the greatist slaughter we have made upon them for many years, or indeed Even on the Eastern Tribes, I have Joyn^d the Massechuset Governo^r with fifty Men On a Second March to Penobscot, we have found out a new way to Penobscot, and So intend to attack em by Sea and land at the same time, This Indian war is greately Impoverishing to New Hampshire in particular & all the Towns in this Province Excepting Portsm^o & New Castle are in Close garrison Men Women & Children Crowded all to geather, and a full Tenth of the whole Province Constantly upon Duty, and Notwithstanding all possible cear is Taken Yet Every week some or other is Taken Captive or killed So that your Lordships may Judge how we are wasteing boath in Numbers, and allso the Impoverishing the pore Inhabitance. I am

With Greatist respect May it Please Your Lordships, Your Lordships Most Obed^t humb^{le} Servt

J : Wentworth

Province of New Hampshir
Septr 12th 1724.

Letter L! Gov. Dummer to Mons. Vaudreuil " Sept. 15, 1724.

S^r

Haveing Lately Seen your protection Commiss to Sebastian Ralle I thought it a proper ocation once more to write to you & to acquaint you that the Norrigawalke & Penobscott Indians are by long & often repeated Submissions the undoubted Subjects of the King of great Brittain who also living in his Territorys they Cannot bee any otherwise Accounted your Alleyes then by Virtue of the Allyance between the Crownes of great Brittain & ffrance & that therefore you Ought not to Concerne your Selfe in their affaires without my pmission & I Cannot but esteem it an open Violation of the Treaty of Peace & allyance our Masters have entred into for you to Commissionate Him to reside amounghst them. And you might as well pretend that ye Protection is sufficient to justify those of y^{re} religion in Committing the most flagrant Acts of Violence & Hostility in any other Parts of this Governm^t & whatever disputes there may be between us & those Indians Concerning the bounds of that Country it does not belong to you to engage your Selfe in their quarrell but rather to assist us to reduce them to obedience, when it shall bee desired but instead of that I am sorry wee must Charge you with having animated them together & others belonging under your owne Government to ffall in the most outrageous Manner upon the Subjects of the King of great Brittain in all Parts of the ffrontiers of these His plantations. I must also add that I have many assurances that the Indians would have long since made their Submission had they not been Stimulated by your pswations & encoraged by the protection & rewards you have given them. However I doubt not but Ere this they are Sensible of the ruine that is like to fall upon them if they psist any longer in their Hostilitys wherefore I resolved againe to recomend to you the good dispositions that ought to be Cultivated between the respective Governours of the Two Crownes that are so Strictly united in ffriendship & intrerest that no inconveniency or Jealousys may Arrise by our unequal Conduct here & that you'l give no further ocation for these disagreeable remonstrances but rather use your influence to the Salvages to a Peace & I thinke it proper further to acquaint you that we have hitherto restrained our Indian Allyes who have expressed great inclinations to revenge the Injurys done us upon those whoe abetted our Enemyes but are not sure wee shall bee any longer able to do it unless a Spedy Stop be made to Such practises.

Sir Your humble Servant
William Dummer.

Letter John Penhallow to L^t. Gov. Dummer.

George Town 8^{br} 16th <u>1724</u>

May it please y^r Hon^r
 S^r

 Col: Westbrook being indisposed at my Home, Orders me to give you an Acc^{tt} that he has Diligently Searched after the Vessells belonging to this Province (that were taken by the Indians) but Could find none, we were detained several days at the Fox Islands by bad weather, as also in this place.

 The Col: has not as yet rec^d any Orders from your Honour, concerning the Officers going to Boston to make up their Rolls, nor how to dispose of the Army.

 I am y^r Hon^{rs} most Dutifull & most Ob^t Humble Servt

John Penhallow

To The Hon^{eble} Wm Dummer Esqr Lt Govr Comm^r in chiefe

Letter L^t. Gov. Dummer to Col^o Wheelwright

Boston 18th Septem^{br} 1724

S^r

There is lately come over the lake a very Considerable Body of Indians, more then what are Suppos'd to be come upon the Western Frontier, tho there be a great Number of them there You'l do well to Charge the people within the District of Your Regiment, to be very careful when they go into their fields, not to expose themselves by going out Weak and without Arms, but that they associate in their worke in partys of 10 or a Doz. Men well Arm^d keeping a Centin! with their Guns, & I desire You$^{'l}$ forthwith Acquaint all the Garrisons as far as Capt Heaths at Richmond, to keep a Watchful Guard at this Juncture — I am Sr Y^{ur} Servt

Wm Dummer

Col^o Wheelwright

Letter "L^t. Gov. Dummer to Col. Westbrook.

Sir,

I hope this will meet you safe arrived at Falmouth after a successful Campaign

Upon Sight hereof you must forthwith dismiss Cpt. Bournes Comp^a of Indians & send them hither in one of the Sloops, That so they may lose no Time for Following the Whale Fishery, wch is agreable to my Promise made to them at Enlisting. Let Cp^t Bourne come with them to see them safe returned.

You must send a Party of fresh men that have staid at Home, in the Garrisons consisting of fifty or sixty effective Soldiers to make one more visit to Norridgewock Ameseconti & Parts adjacent near Kennebeck & Amerescoggin Rivers in

Order to surprize ye Enemy. It being probable the Corn left in those Parts or the Hunting may have drawn thither some of the Indians that escaped at Norridgewock.

The other Captains being probably fatigued wth ye past Marches Let Cpt. Heath have the Command of them & send with him other proper Officers & Pilots. Let this Affair be proceeded in as soon as possible.

Sept. 28. 1724.

May it please your Hon{r}

Wee have got through the body of the County from Richmond to Penobscut River but either by the willfullness or Ignorance of the pilot he brought us near Fifty miles below the Indian villages when wee came into our knowledge — Wee traveld up the river as high as the falls where there was a large River to Cross here wee found the freshetts very high by reason of the late rain. The army not haveing more than three or four days Provision sundry men haveing lost their bread in wadeing the rivers as I acquainted in my last of the 20th Currant and sundry men much Indispos'd it was likewise Judged that wee could not march to their Village and back to the falls where the Sloops were to meet us in less than Eight or Nine days whereon wee desisted and waited for the Sloops they not being come was oblig'd to go down the River in quest of them and verily beleive had not wee found two Indian Canoos and sent four brisk men to look for them some of the men would have perisht before wee could have got to them but the men found them and brought up some boates in which we got to them, and the freshet run so strong they could not possibly get up the river – Collo Harmon Capt Moulton, Capt Wentworth and sundry other officers are so much indispos'd that I am oblig{d} to let them go home I shall stay with the well part of the Army and search the rivers and

sea coves Well before I come off. The officers all desier to go to Boston to make up their Rolls and there is great necessity that Capt Moulton and Capt Bourn go their accounts lying very Intricate I desire your Hon^{rs} to make up my Roll.
Sep^t 28th 1724

I am your Hon.^{rs} most dutifull Humb^l. Servt
Thos Westbrook

"*Letter to Mass. Agents in London.*"

Gent.

We desire & direct you to solicit with all proper Earnestness & Speed the Matters contain'd in the Mem? of the Gen^{ll} Assembly to his Maj.^y sent last Winter to his Exc̃y: the Govr & by him (as we are inform'd) either presented to his Maj.^y or laid before one of his Maj^{ies} Principal Sec̃rys of State in Order thereto, A Copy of wch Mem° as also of the Journal of our Commiss^{rs} late Conferences with the Five Nations at Albany are herewith sent you :

By wch last, together with y^{or} other Advices from hence, You will find how much the Distress of this Province is increased, & what little Prospects We have of being brought safely & hon^{bly} out of the War or having any Assistance to prosecute it with Vigour & Success ; The Govr of Canada having (as he has threaten'd in his Letters) drawn many remote Nations ; viz, The Hurons & others with whom We have never had ye least Concern, into a Confederacy with the Eastern Indians ; So that our Western Frontiers have been more annoy'd this last Summer than the Eastern, Almost every Town in the County of Hamps. One Half in Middx. & sev^{ll} in Essex being driven into Garrison & much distress'd by this new Enemy : And althô We have had great Advantages over ye Indians by such a Slaughter of them at Norridgewock as has not been known in any of the late Wars, Yet by Inaction of the Western Tribes, the Enemy is become more formidable than before And the Service in the War & the Charges for the Support of it are so heavy as greatly to impoverish the whole Province; & drive away many of our Inhab^{ts} to the Neighbouring Colonies: all w^{ch} (Connecticut & New Hamps. excepted) being in perfect Peace & Prosperity them selves, sit still & see us languishing under all the Calamities of War without Affording us any Succour either of Men or Money In Consideration of wch You must earnestly Supplicate his Majesty That his positive Orders may be given to the sev^{ll} Governm^{ts} To furnish & maintain a necessary Force for our Assistance in such Proportion as his Majesty shall think fit to Order.

And whereas you will observe by the enclosed Conferences That the five Nations have denied to enter with us into the War partly under a Pretence of Waiting an Answer to their Message to his Majesty dd with their Belt, & for his Majesties Approbation of the Conduct of this Governm^t in Declaring War, & his allowance of their Engaging in it, You must humbly apply to his Maj^y for his gracious Answer to that Message, That so the Five Nations may have no such Pretext for Declining this Service, for wch they have given their frequent & solemn Engagem^{ts} & in Prospect of wch this Governm^t has made great Presents to them wch with the sums expended in the Treaties with them amount to many Thousand Pounds.

As was before observed to you, You must use your utmost endeavours to obtain his Majesties Consideration of this Mem^o And that he would be graciously pleased to direct his Minister at the Court of France so to represent the unjust & barbarous Proceedings of the French Gov^t in Encouraging & Exciting the Savages to this War, as that effectual Orders may be sent to the said Govr & others concern'd not only to withdraw their Assistance & Countenance from the S^d Indians in the Prosecution of their Hostilities, but to use their Influences y^t for ye future they live in Peace with his Majesties good Subjects in these Prov. And unless such Orders be given & effectually complied with There seems to be no other Method left us for putting an End to this ruinous War than We shall be obliged in our own necessary Defence to pursue the Enemy into the French Territories where they are not only shelter'd but rewarded for their Barbarities.

"And if matters sh^d come to this Extremity with us, We cannot promise the French (who have been the Fomenters of this War) better Quarter than the Indians, This last Hint you will observe & make what Use of it the State of our Affairs will require & admit of.

And if there be no Prospect of any speedy Relief by such Order to the French Govr; You must endeavour to know his Maj^{is} Mind as to what is hinted to you respecting the Pursuit of ye Enemy into the French Territories: You will give us the speediest Advices you can as to these Particulars, And unless such Orders be given & effectually complied with or Liberty given us to carry the War into the French Countrey & distress them as they have done us, We can see no Method that will save us from Ruine

Letter Joseph Heath to Lt Gov. Dummer.

Richmond Octob^r 7th 1724.

Honourable

Sr Having Your Honours Permission I was on the way to Boston But meeting an order from Lt Colon^l Harmon to march to neridgwalk Ammisquenty &c am attending that Service, Ready to march assoon as the Quoto of men appointed are Delivered me And Rejoyce in this Oppertunity you are pleased to give me.

This Accompanies the three Mohawks who returning from Penobscut were got as far as Falmouth in the way to Boston before my marching Orders came & so could not returne back.

I have Lay^d before the Treasurer an acct of what provision & other necessaryes I supply^d them with

It's Obvious to all the Army that these Mohawks proved them selves good men in the Late action at Neridgawalk Since which they have met with some Rough Treatment And in case they should not be made Easey with the method of Dividing the Captives & scalp money (which now they are not) I Doubt the Consequence will not be good. Thus much I thought it my Duty to premize to your Honour and Begging pardon if I have Ignorantly Exceded

  Remaine Your Honours Most Hum^ble Obedient Servant
            Joseph Heath

  [Superscribed]
   On His Majesties Service
To The Honble William Dummer Lieu^t Governour & Commander in Chief &c In Boston
p Capt Giles

Letter James Parker to L^t. Gov. Dummer Oct. 15, 1724.

May It please y^r Hon^r

I rec^d y^r Letter & with all Thankfulness acknowledge y^r Hon^rs favour In granting me Liberty to make my Deffence before you'd proceed against me. I am Sensible Major Moodey hath no great affection for me. but w^d Endeavour to Ruin me were it in his power. occasioned by an Old Grudge he has to me. The Select men of ye town of Falm^th gave me a permitt to sell Drink In October 1723 and I did presume to sell by vertue of y^r Authority Designing to take licence as soon as ye Court usually granting Licences sh^d come about, never ye less I was present^d & ye Court notwithstanding my permission from ye Select men proceeded against and fined me wh. I p^d This is w^t refers to ye first Conviction. Concerning my Recognizeing & ye forfieture by my Default, I never did Recognize nor know any thing of It. But upon y^s new Complaint I have waited upon Maj^r Moodey time after time for ye papers & Coppys of ye Evidence If any Such y^re be against me that so I may be able to make my deffence to the Court, but he tells me I am a Rogue & a Dogg & he'l give me none nor take any notice of me. I have waited upon him since I rec'd y^r Letter & ye matter is still ye same And for my Endeavour to Elude ye Law as he hath misrepresented to y^r Hon^r by my Enlisting into ye Service there was time Enough before such Enlistment for prosecution. If not I have Estate Enough for to answer all such forfietures or bonds of Recognizance as shall apear agst Me. So ye Sum of ye Whole Seams to be y^t he was In hopes y^t y^r Hon^r w^d have grant'd my Dismission without giveing me notice of It. Not y^t he was so strenuous to bring me to ye Court. Otherwise he w^d not have denied me ye Copys, but to do me a displeasure by misrepresenting to y^r Hon^r y^r Hon^rs most Hum^le & Obedient Servt

James Parker

Falm^th 8^br ye 15th 1724

Letter Saml Hincks to Lt Gov. Dummer

Hon^d S^r

The 8th instant in the Evening, Ten indians way layed The path near 3 garrisen houses in This town and Killed one Allen a Soldier (posted at Casco) sculped him & carryed his habbit & gun away & shot at a Boy who Escaped, and directly I alarumed The Town & adjacent places who all Took itt. at Saco falls we heard one great gun fired who cannot hear us. but Can't Learn The meaning, as yet Their is m^r parker up Their Loading, & I fear This Scout surprized Them.

Corr^l Harman some Dayes since, passed This Harbour, westward, with other officers. Corr^l Westbrook is Expected Every Day & in The Sloop this Comes is Capt Born with his indians, we have Lost no man in This march but are Disappointed

Your Honours humble Servant
Samuel Hincks

Fort Mary: Winter Harbour Octr 9th 1724

[Superscribed]
To His Honour William Dummer Esqr
Leiutt Govr Comand^r & Cheife// In Boston

Letter Lt Gov. Dummer to Capt Wheelwright

Bost 17th Nov^{br} 1724

I received your Letter by Express this Morning & you are hereby directed Immediately to draw out of the Souldiers Posted at York & Wells 50 good Men Well armed & Supplyed with Sutable proviss. for 5 Dayes or more if need bee & with them to March forthwith to Piggwacot in Search of the Indians Liveing there According to the relation you have from the Captive Peter Tallcott who made his Escape from them & is arived with you whome likewise Stephen Harden or such other person or psons as shall be knowing of the place & the Way to it & the Officer Commanding at Yorke is hereby Order'd without delay to furnish his part for this Service which 25. Men. & inasmuch as the Success in this

Expedition will in a great Measure depend under God on your dilligent dispatch & I expect from you that the uttmost Care bee taken therein.

So wishing you good Success I am Y^r

P. S. You are to take with you Mr Allison Brown of Cape porpus who is hereby Authorized to Act as Your Lieu^t, & inasmuch as You may probably not be Able to Muster the whole Complement of fifty good & able Men fit for the Service out of the Two towns aforemention'd Lt Brown is hereby Directed to bring with him 10 or 12 good Men from his Detachment to make up your Number.

Capt Wheelwright

Letter John Schuyler to Lt Gov. Dummer.

honoured S^r//

Some Time agoe one Monsr Daguiell, of mont Reall was here in Albany by whom I forwarded Your honours Letter to marq^s Vaudreuiell –

I had at ye Same time Some descours with said Daguiell Concerning ye warrs between New England and ye Indians I Told him of y^t unjustice and barbarity of y^{tt} warr, and Some further discourse Thereabouts, which it Seems s^d daguiell has partly Imparted unto Monsieur Lachassaigne Govern^r of mont Reall as I Can perceive by a Letter I Recei^d of Monsr Lachassaigne p the bearer hereof that Monsr Vaudreuill is very sory and weary of that warr and as far as I can perceive would willingly See one or two gentlemen Inpoured by New England Gov^{tt} to Endeav^r to make an End of that warr which would bee Very Acceptable in Canada. by this Conveyance Goes a Letter For Your honour from Govr Vaudreuill.

here are now some French Indians in Towne I designe to keep two of y^m about a 14 days or Longer which I Can Easy doe for Little or no Charge if his honour may write an answer to Govr Vaudreuill upon his Letter that I Can Soon dispatch itt.

This is att psent ye most needfull from
Your honours most humb^l Serv^{tt}
John Schūÿler

Albany 21th Novr 1724 –

Letter, Gov. Wm Burnet of N. Y. to L^t. Gov. Dummer.

New York 16th Decr 1724.

S^r

I received the favour of yours of the 30th Novr by the Express, on the 14th at Night, and have made all convenient Dispatch to return you an Answer, after that I had taken the Opinion of the Council which you will find enclosed, and in which Opinion I cannot but agree with them, Since I look on the Threatning the French Governour with the Insults of our friend Indians, in Case of his not complying, tho expressed ever so cautiously, naturally makes us responsible for what they may do.

And by our threatning to pursue the Eastern Indians to the uttermost, must be understood into Canada, which will be entring that Country in a hostile manner; and this my Instructions expressly forbid in these words.

"Provided always that you do not by Colour of any power
" or Authority hereby given you, commence or declare War
" without our knowledge and particular Commands therein,
" except it be against Indians upon Emergencys, wherein the
" Consent of the Council shall be had, and speedy Notice
" thereof given unto us.

And as to entering into a War with the Eastern Indians it is what Assembly of this Province did in 1722. refuse to contribute to, which Resolution of theirs I then communicated to your Government, and therefore need not now send you a Copy of it.

Under these Circumstances, a Message to the Governour of Canada, which this Government is not able to support by any one Action, in Case of Refusal, would be not only of no use, but of very ill Consequence by acquainting him with our feebleness.

I see no reason to expect that our Assembly will be prevailed upon to alter their Resolutions, But I cannot have an opportunity of trying that, till after Harvest next, it being impracticable to meet them while the River continues shut up, and the Affairs of New Jersey obliging me to meet that Assembly in the Spring: So that upon the whole, tho' my wishes and Intentions are to serve your Province to the utmost of my Power, I find myself intirely incapable of joining with you in the present Proposal, or any part of it: Being with great Esteem,

S^r your most obedient humble Servant
W Burnet

Letter Hez. Wyllys Sec^y of Conn. to Lt Gov. Dummer

Hartford Decemb^r 22^d 1724

S^r

I have Received yours of November 30th with the Enclosed Referred to therein and Wish that a Copy of the Act of Your Assembly respecting the Message to Canada had also been Inclosed which Your Hon^r Can Yet Supply.

I have Advised with the Gentlemen of the Councill that I could (at this Season with Convenience Speak with and am not Unsenceible of the great difficulty and Charge the Warr with the Eastern Indians hath bro^t upon the whole Province under Your Comand I Wish this Government were able to

Render the Circumstances of Your Province (in that affair) more Easie but as to what Your Honr Intimates respecting Sending Messengers to Canada Altho' that project Seemeth Likely to make Monsr Vaudrevill Senceible that his Conduct Cant be Justifyed neither will it well Support the french Cause when the Same Methods shall be Taken by New England against Canada the Letting Loose the Indians (as Intimated in Yours) will doubtless give Conviction when those things proper to Convince Reason fail And therefore tis to be hoped at Sight of it at a distance as Represented by Messingers may do something with that Governour.

But Yet would further propose to Your Honrs Advisement whether it may not be proper to Close the Message to M. Vaudrevill with a representation that it it is very Apparrent that our Indian Enémy have Such a dependance on him to Support them in the Warr that he Can Easily reduce them to Quietness and that his Exerting himself in So good a Work (as reduceing those Indians to Order would be) may hapily prevent many Mischieffs that Seem to Threaten us as well as the people under his Comand.

And also give us a Speciall Instance of his good Neighbourhood and if this or any thing Else proper to Insert in the Message to the Governor of Canada might gaine him to Influence the Indians to peace it would be well but if he Should Slight the Motion of being an Instrument to gain a peace for us I think he would Still be the Less Excusable and must Thank himself when he is Saught by other Means.

But Yet after all must Let Your Honr know that it is not in my power with the Councill to Comply with Your desire And if I Should Call our Assembly together (who Can only Authorize a person to go upon the Errand You mention I fear the Same Scruples (as when Colo Stoddard was with us) will Still be Started which were principally two. first that the Indians had been wronged in their Lands~ Secondly

that the Hostages received by Your Government of the
Indians were only to Secure the payment of Some Beavour
which the Indians Say they have Since paid and therefore
the Warr not Just on the English Side. These things our
people have had Confirmed to them by Many persons (and
Some of distinction) of Your Government I would Charitably
hope these reports are wholly groundless I should be very
Unwilling to Entertain Such things without the Clearest
proof. Notwithstanding which in Order to Sattisfy our
Assembly possibly it may be best to Send to me the fullest
Accounts that may be Come at Our late Very Hon[ble] and
Excellent Governo[r] Col[o] Saltonstall Sometime before his
death received One of Your Treaties with the Eastern Indians
which now Can[t] be found doubtless Your Treaties and other
Writings respecting the Eastern Lands if Comunicated to our
Assembly might be of Service and a Copy of the Entry made
when the Said Hostages were delivered up (which Entry
Certainly doth Include what they were received for) will
Certainly Sattisfy our Assembly how the Matter is as to the
Hostages Y[r] Hon[r] won[t] think it Strange that there is Need
to Sattisfy our Assembly in these things when You Consider
our people had the Said reports from Among Your Selves as
is above hinted and that what persons Confess against themselves is Easily beleived and in many things there wants no
other proof I have Insisted the more Largely that if possible
I might prevent all difficulties for I would Always Cultivate
that good Understanding that hath been between the Two
Governments.

  By Order of the Governo[r] of the Colony of Connecticut
      Signed p[r] Hez: Wyllys Secret[ry]
    [Superscribed]
  To The Honourable William Dumer Esq[r] L[t] Gov[r]
  of the Province of the Massachusetts Bay
  att Boston These

*Letter Col. T. Westbrook to L^t. Col. Johnson Harmon
Dec. 29, 1724.*

Sir

It is his Hon^r. the Leiu^t. Gov^{rs} order, on sight hereof you give orders that all the frontier garrisons under y^r Care be strict on their guard, and that you order a Scout of men from Pesomscutt River to Saco River, some distance above those Towns, And let a Scout of Fifty men be constantly kept from Saco River a Cross to Berwick, some considerable distance, (not exceeding Twenty Miles) above the Scout that are already allow'd to those people, a Loggin at Berwick and Saco River, and in Case you hear of the Enemy, you are to draw out a sufficient number of men according to the Intelligence you receive and pursue them. Capt Sanders will Sail this week for York with a Sufficient number of Snow Shoes and Moggisons. & in the Mean time you Must Make a Shift with those that are in the Hands of the Commissary at Casco which the Treasurer Acquaints the Leu. Governour are about One hundred as well as those in the several Towns where they are lodg'd
Boston Decem^r 29. 1724

      I am Sir yours to Serve
        Thos Westbrook
To Lt Col^o Johnson Harmon at York
  A True Coppy

Letter – Thomas Sanders to L^t. Gov. Dummer

     Agemogen Reach Febr^y 18th. 1725
May it Please your Honour
    Pursuant to your Honours Orders I made the best Dispatch I cou'd to land the Indians at this place, but

not finding any Indians here We fir'd two Gunns and the next day six Indians came to us who inform'd that the Tribe was at Mount Desert. We thereupon made sail and went up into a large Bay on the Back of Mount Desert where we found them. When they had done trading they Consented to our Departure and the twentieth of Jan.y we sail'd for St George's. Night coming on We harbour'd in Agemagen expecting next day to have gain'd St Georges but contrary to what the Indians told us & our own Expectations we were wholly debarred moving by reason of Ice. The Weather continuing extream cold at times we are still detaind but the first oppertunity I shall make all possible Dispatch home. Sundry of the Indians came seven or eight miles on the Ice to trade with us and as far as we can discover there is only Ice to be seen. I have no news to Communicate to your Hon^r so Conclude and am

    Your Hon^{rs} most Dutifull & Obedient Servt
        Thomas Sanders

Letter Edmund Mountfort to L^t. Gov. Dummer

      Agemogen Reach Feb^{r}y 18th 1725/6
May it please your Hon^r

These Serve to Enclose a Letter deliv'd me by the Cheifs of the Ind^{ns} for your Hon^r And as we are frozen up here I tho't it proper to send it by the first Opportunity not knowing but it was of importance; the Indians seem to be very well Satisfied in y^r Trade (but by preswasion of the Jesuit) disapprove of some Artickles in their Submission; but Capt Beane being present found y^t he misinterpreted them; & he inform'd you of the true meaning yr of wch was to their Satisfaction; the weather hitherto has been very Cold and all the bays are so frozen y^t y^{r}s no moving by water unless out to the Sea; having nothing farther at present to Add I Conclude & Am

    Y^r Hon^{rs} Obedient Humble Servt
     Edmund Mountfort

      Falmoth March ye 3 1725/6

May it please your Honour ye 26 of febuary theire came in fourteen Indens to St Georges and brought the express which accompanyes this and I as soon as posibel brought it to falmoth but through some Diffecelty for wee drew our boate ten miles on ye Ice for I was obliged to make our number of men smaller by reason of our Stores being spent wee have not had anything but bread above this month and but little of that for wee depended on Capt Sanders and he being disappointed Capt Gyles sent his Leu^t to take charge of the garison but I thought it not proper to deliver it by reason of so much Ice in ye river that I could not bring of ye men and my things: I hope it will not bee long before Capt Gyles will bee down with ye sloope and I shall deliver ye Garison to his sattisfaxshon and shall hasen to Boston to waite upon your Honour.

I am your Honours most humbel and obedient Servant att Command
    William Canedy

     Albany March 22th 1725

Honble S^r

 Yours of ye 16 Instant I have Received Last Night with ye Franch Packet.

I have been Very Much Wondert I had not a Line from y^r Honour Since I must be Some times at a Littel charges.

Ever Since I have heard of y^r Pease Made with ye Indians

I have always Inquier'd to heare of yᵉ Sᵗ France Indians but Cant Gitt no Other Intelligence from them but that there Designe is to Come to Albany in Order to Make Pease with your Honour Some time in June Next, but its Not to be Trusted it is Only flying Neuws

I have Consiedert yᵉ Case & take it to be yᵉ Proper Meanes & to send Two Discreet faithfull Pearsons to Gitt it Out of them who will be the Bearer of the Packet and Dont Doubt but they Will Come to a Certain Knowledge thereof, I Remain

   Your Honours Most Humͥ and Most Obedient Sarvᵗ
          John Schŭÿler

To the Honᵈ Will: [Dummer]

Letter S. Thaxter & W. Dudley to Lᵗ Gov. Dummer
March 26, 1725.

May it Please your Honour

This is the first oppertunity we have and this obtained by Secrecy & great Dificullty by one Cagnawaga indian only which is to informe Your Honour & yᵉ Goverment that all the easterne indians were gone before we arrived here which was on the third Day of this month after much hardship & Dificulty and that the Designe of those indians were to hunt some time & then to fall on the frontiers we pray God to Defeat & blast all their Designes if the frontiers particularly on Merrynack & Connecticutt were at this juncture strengthned itt might be for their Security and of great Service to the facilitatig the Peace with them we cannot partiularly Relate the treatment we have had here where we mett the Governour we have made our Demands and in as Strong terms as we can the Governour most of all insists on their land and is intirely Governed by Pere La Chace the chief of the Jesuitts we have Sent Down Captain Jordan to the indians places St Francois, Recancourt, Wewenock &c where he Saw a few indians and many Squaws they all aquainted him the indians were for Peace & Desire us earnestly to Stay for the indians Returne We have aquainted the Governour on his talk leading that way that the Goverments Desired no Grace or favour of him butt Demanded only justice and if he was not for that & would cause the indians to go to Boston or piscataqua to talk of & conclude a just honest & honorable Peace he must be looked on by God & man as the instigator of the warr which we could & Did prove by his & other letters and the hinde[r] of Peace Sometimes he tells us he has nothing to Do then again he is angry if any thing is Done or Said without him and Refuces to give his answer in writeing to our Demands in writeing how this matter will come out we cannot yett tell but hope for the Best if the Governour had that Stedyness & Sway he Ought only to have we should have nothing to Doubt.

We shall Dispatch as Soon as possible and gett home again And in the mean while we are your

Honours most Obedient hmble Serv[ts]
Sam[ll] Thaxter
W Dudley

Mont Reall 26 march 1725
verte

Honble S[r]

Col Thaxter and all the Gentlemen are in good health & pray the favour that our family & frinds may know the Same and that we hope to be back by the middle of May at furthest.

Letter John & Hannah Hunt to L! Gov. Dummer
March 30, 1725

To the Hounorable L^et Goviner William Dumer Esqyr

Ouer Humble Request to your Honer is that your honer wold Relase Ouer Son Jacob Hunt Hov is now att Richman fort for I am In grate wont of him I being uary Lame and haue no help and all so Liue uary Remote thearefore wold Pray your Honour to Consider me And Haue him Relased as Soon as Posoble and we wold Pray Your Honor to Send uss A Return whether ouer Request may be granted and in So doing you Will much oblige your Honours most Humble Saruants Dated att Almsbury March : ye 30 : 1725 –

John Hunt
Hannah Hunt

Letter, Col. T. Westbrook to L! Gov. Dummer April 4, 1725.

May it Please your Hon^r/

Capt Bourn will be able to acquaint your Hon^r. relating what I wrote from Spurwink the twenty eighth of last April, I sending him and Lt Dominicus Jordan to make Discovery. I have Enquired into the Affair of Mr Benj^a York mentioned in your Hon^rs Letter Dated April ye 5th and by Examining your Hon^rs Orders to me from time to time there is no men Allow'd him neither did the General Court vote him any in the Year 1723. Six men has been Allow'd at the Ferry Place and upon Enquiry I find by the Coll^o of the Regiment and the Select men of the Town that Mr Sawyers is the Establisht Garrison. Their houses standing not above three hundred Yards distant I thought it best to put part of the men in one house and part in the other and Mr Sawyer having five and York but three York is thereupon uneasy. I posted five men at Mr Sawyers because the Capt and Doct^r are there and the Doct^r has Occasion very Often to cross the River to Visit the Sick.

        I am Your Hon^{rs} most Dutifull Servt
Falm^o April ye 4th 1725

                       Th^{os} Westbrook

P. S. The Enclosd is the List of the ineffective men which I omitted to send with the other Account.

Letter L^t. Gov. Dummer to Col. Westbrook

                      Aprill 5th 1725.

Colo¹ Westbrook

I have two of yours of the 17th past & one of the 27th recv^d yesterday. the Councill have voted £12 – & no more towards the repairing of Georges ffort wch you are to husband to the best advantage In making the Lodgings Comfortable for the people & having visited your ffamily lett the next of the Sloop in the Countrys Service that goes east ward take in the Boxes & Nailes At Saco Mills & You may go down with them to see the repairs pformed as you proposed & as far as £12 – You may draw on the Treasurer for the s^d service rendering an Acc^o. thereof Capt Canada acquaints me that he has made the Wharfe allready which you spake of, to whome for his good Service in gallantly defending that Fort I have given a Commission for the same.

    Gett all your Whaleboats mended that are Capable of it (for it Will take time to gett New ones) & order a party of about 50 men under a dilligent prudent Officer downe to Penobscott Bay & as much further as you shall think for the Service especially at Passamaquoddy where y^r Lett^r. informs the Indians have bin ye last Winter under such orders as if well Executed they May by Gods blessing Surprise some of the Enemys if there be any of them there I have wrote a Letter to all the Collonells in y⁰ E. & W. to warn the People to be on their gaurd & to go out in Companys to their Work well Armed. I finde you have sent out divers parties of about 14 Men to Ambuscade the Indians in their lurking places it will be well if they pform it patiently & faithfully which I recomend to you to inspect well into & that they be releived from time to time by Fresh parties so as their Ambuscade be Continued without intermission untill you have further orders & that you require of the Several officers an Account of what passes in their turne, & minute down every thing any wayes worth notice.

You shall hear further from me very Soon. I shall be glad when Capⁿ Vo: with the Indians he promised to bring with are come to Penobscott. You shall hear from me in a Short time pray do every thing thats possible to keep us the Territòry of the Enemy

I am sʳ Yʳ friend & Sᵗ

Wm Dummer.

Letter John Gyles to Col. Westbrook

fort George April 14 : 1725

Colˡᵒ Westbrook

April 13ᵗʰ an Indian Dogg appeared on y⁰ North side of y⁰ River, a Gainst fort George, which my People shott, & by y⁰ Carkes of it is not Long since, it straid from y⁰ Indians, whear vpon I ordred a Larom to Notify y⁰ a iecant Garricons to be on thier Guard, for in my Opinion yᵗ huntars or a small scout of Indians ar sculking a boute & Came Down this River, if it might Pleas, a small Party of men to Reng Might —

This is from your humble Sarᵗ to Command   John Gyles
Sʳ since I wrote y⁰ a boue,— I Recd an accompt
from Maquaitt yᵗ a soldiar is missing, & Supposd
to be taken

Letter L̇ṭ Gov. Dummer to Col. T. Westbrook

This Comes by Mʳ Moses Markham your Clerk Who informes me that Hee has On divers Occations been Imployd by you in Affairs relateing to the Service wherein there has been no allowance - for his Expences which seems not reasonable & I think Hee should Make out a Just Account thereof Which being Avouched by you will doubtless bee Allowed him by the Government. & if you have Supplied the Birth Hee had with you by any other p son & there be any other vacancy Sutable for Him Lett him have it.

        I am Yʳ friend & Sᵗ
        Wm Dummer

Letter, John Gyles to L̇ṭ Gov. Dummer

May it Pleas your Honour
April 15 : 1725
    this Day a Soldier taken from Maquaitt Made his Escape to this Garrisson, who in forms me yᵗ he was taken by two Indians yᵉ 13 Currant, one of spake good English & askd him many questions Particuler Concarning myself & this fort, he being well acquainted with. & tould him he kild Moses Eaton, & a negro & an English Man at black Point, & he tould him yᵗ six Indians wear now gon towards falmouth to kill & take, and yᵗ our Gen¹men Commitionars wear Returnd from Canaday, and yᵗ yᵉ Indians wear Resolved for war. & yᵗ Many Indians & Mohewks would be Down this summar to Destroy yᵉ English & thier Cattle, and now thier wear 50 or 60 Indians with a friar at Naraugawock, & seueral Indians at a Vilig Vp this Riuer, (Part of his Discours I take to be. french Aier, tho My humble opinion is as I mentionᵈ in my mean Lins, to your Honour Decᵇʳ 12: 1724 Date) the Sund night after yᵉ Presonar was taken, yᵉ aboue sᵈ 2 Indians

after hunting & killing Seueral beauer & authers in y͏ͤ Euning they being tird, then Campᵗ about 15 or 20 Mils Vp this Riuer a boue our fort, and when sound on sleep, y͏ͤ youth James Cochron y͏ͤ Presonar, Ris & nockt them bouth in y͏ͤ head, & took of thier sculps one of he brought to this Garrison y͏ͤ auther lost by y͏ͤ way, and a fin gun in a small Riuer Passing ouer, I aduised y͏ͤ Presenar to giue a full accompt of to y͏ͤ Col¹¹ by y͏ͤ first he being now much tired, I have also Rote a gain to y͏ͤ Col¹¹ of affears since y͏ͤ Presonar Came in.

I though also to send to Capᵗⁿ heath for Men, to go up & secure y͏ͤ Canew & authers, that y͏ͤ Presenar Left wᵗʰ y͏ͤ Corps of, but it being difucult Sending to Ritchmond, I thought it Proper to mustar a few hands of my Little number & from Maquaitt, to Prevent y͏ͤ auther Indians getting y͏ͤ Plunder. April 18ᵗʰ this Day our People went Vp y͏ͤ Riuer to Vew y͏ͤ Indians corps & bring of y͏ͤ Plondar and if any further Discouery.

April 17ᵗʰ then Returned, but no fur ther Discoury, they brought of y͏ͤ auther gun hatchets kniues & Stove y͏ͤ Canew brought y͏ͤ auther sculp, skins & in all to y͏ͤ Value of 6 or 8 Pounds.

I have often Prayed for a Reinforcement of men to this Garrison, to scout & ambush this Riuer & auther Places which Depending on authers for it. I now renew my humble Request for your Honours feauer to this Garrison.

fort George April 16ᵗʰ : 1725 :

    I am your honours Most Dutyfull seruant
           John Gyles

I inclose a Copy of a few Lins to Colˡᵒ Westbrook of our furst Discouery of y͏ͤ Enimy

//y͏ͤ Indians also tould y͏ͤ Presenar, yᵗ Jnᵒ Legon & more Indians wear to y͏ͤ westward, & by & by go kill English, but Samson Leagon his brother was at Canaday, which y͏ͤ Presonar furst Enquired after Samson Leⁿ.—

//the Indians tould ye Presonar they took a Vew of this fort furst, but seeing no (Raspict) of, went to Maquaitt thier Lay all night by ye garrison, & in ye morning Dog^d ye soldiar a bout ¾ or a mile distant, then took him as they said, ye Presonar advised them to go back to ye garrison, & take an auther they s^d no, a nough Now & struck a (Coross) to this Riuer, towards thier Canew, as ye Presonar says —

Pray Pardon my Long Scralls.

York 16th April 1725

May it Please Your Hon^r /

We have no Account of the Enemy at present, but fear they are endeavouring to be reveng'd on us for their Brethren, I hope our constant putting Your Hon^rs Orders in practice will prevent them. I have no Sloop yet arrived here with Stores to send down to the Eastward according to Your Hon^rs Orders to distress them which I was in hopes I should have had some time ago. Lieu^t Jaques has been for some considerable time past very desirous with me to write to your Hon^r for his Dismission which at last has prevail'd he assuring me of his great necessity to be with his business and what damage he shall sustain if not granted Lt Coll^o Harmon tells me he had Your Hon^rs word to dismiss him when his business earnestly call'd for him which it doth at this time, Both of them thankfully Acknowledge Your Hon^rs favours to them from time to time. If Your Hon^r shou'd be pleas'd to Dismiss Lieu^t Jaquesh and Commissionate En^s Carlile in his room Lieu^t Coll^o Harmon informs me he will be very agreeable to him, and I do assure your Hon^r I have known him ever since I have been in the Service and have always found him a modest and sober Young man and very ready & faithfull on all Commands The last Orders I rec^d from Your Hon{r} were dated the 16th of last Month. Having nothing more that offers worth Your Hon{rs} notice

I remain Your Hon{rs} most Dutifull Servt

Thos Westbrook.

P. S. Lieut Coll? Harmon is very desirous if Your Hon{r} shou'd order any Sloop to guard the Fishery that he may Command her.

I have askd leave some time ago to go home for a few days my business there being very urgent but have not yet recd Your Hon{rs} Smiles.

Letter Lt Gov. Dummer to Capt. Bane " April 17, 1725."

Cp{t} Bane.

You must acquaint Sackaristis & the other Indian That at the Desire of Sackamaten (as well as their own) & allso Mr Minotts motion I permit them to visit their Friends & Families Upon their Promise to return again punctually in Fifty Days: That Sackamacten has much recommended him self to me by his Honesty & Faithfulness and therefore I shall alwaies treat him well, as I shall them If they prove them selves as faithful as he has done.

That Sackamacten has inform'd me That the Indians are desirous of Peace, If they find so, when they come among them And any of the Chiefs are disposed to come in to treat they may bring them in upon their Return & the Chiefs shall be well received & dismiss'd with Safety; That We shall be very ready to receive their Submission & let them live in Peace if they are desireous of it, Althô God has given us great Success against them of late, And our Soldiers are now so well trained & used to the War & have so good a Knowledge of the Indian Countrey, That We doubt not but that by the Help of God we shall force them to submit, If they continue obstinate: But we don't delight in War any otherwise than as the Injuries they have done us make it necessary.

That if the Indians have any Distrust of being safe in Coming in Because of our March to Penobscot & Cpt. Heaths burning the Houses, They make a wrong Judgment of yᵉ matter. they must not expect that I shall at all slaken the Prosecution of the War till their Chiefs come in: And that is the Method of all wise Governments, but when they come in yᵉ Name of their Tribes & express their sincere desires for peace then they may depend on it I will desist from all further Acts of Hostilitye & give orders Accordingly to all the fforces everywhere.

Be very careful to make them fully & clearly understand you.

Would have You to let nothing hinder You from Returning to Sᵗ Georges Fort So as to Receive the Indians at their Return thither To which purpose I have also Wrote the Colonel.

Letter John Minot to Lᵗ. Gov. Dummer

Portsmᵒ Aprˡ 20ᵗʰ 1725

May it Please your honʳ/

/ Having formerly tacken some minets of a Conference that I had with twenty of the Eastern Indians that were heads of those Tribes, my buissness allowing me a Leasure hour and hearing of yᵉ many miseryes and callamityes that acrew by reason of this unhappy Warr I think it a Duty incumbent on me to give your honʳ a relation of it; It was a few months before I left that part of yᵉ Countrey that if your Honoʳ should be so happy as to have a Treaty with them some things might be Effeckted that I have a great

Assurance would be for ye promoting & Establishing a Lasting peace and being Assured of your having the Publick good so much at heart & my rearl freindship and Intimacy with those people imboldens me to write, One morning as I was walking in ye town I met one of ye Saggamores he tould me there was a Com^a of Indians that desired to speake with me, when I came to them I found the number before inserted, & they were all elderly men — After a little silence one of them spake to me asking if I knew them, I tould them I knew they were the Leading men of Panopscoat and Nerigwalk they tould me the time of year allowd them to meet there, and they took this Oppertunity to talke with me uppon some heads which they sayd they would fully Communicate to me, taking me for their friend, & uppon it, tould me they were very much wrongd & Abus'd in many things and sayd if there were not some speedy methods taiken to prevent these abuses, and to perform our Promises made by Coll˜ Shute and the Saggamores that were at that Congress, there would be A Warr Acrue in a little time, and as I was there and heard what was said, desired me to remonstrate it to some of the Governm^t how they were agreived, and farther added that if they did not prove their cause to be just in troubling us this time they would desist, and that it only wanted their assent and ye warr began, but farther added that they were old men and warr was troublesome & they urgd peace provided the English would come into just methods with them and performe what was promis'd at that Congress — and that notwithstanding what the Jesuit should Excite them to, it would have no influence on y^m for it was Interest & not religion that Obliged them to live in peace & freindship with any People, Uppon which I tould them I was very much surpriz'd at what they said, and that their now speaking of Warr was Contrary to what they have often tould me of Living in peace and as Brothers with us, and that it was agreable to their former treatment of ye English in breaking their many truces that were made with them in Coll. Dudleys time & wth other Gentm. that had the Governm^t of the provinces: they tould me we were their Enemies & that we lookt on them as ours & when ever we were an Anoyance to them as we were now they made warr, giving me many Instances of our Breach of ffaith perticularly Capt Chubs treating with them on the Sabath day calling some of y^m togather (as he said) in a freindly manner & at the same time drew Pistolls and shot them while they had his bread between their teeth and another time of hard treatment by Coll Walton of Cochecho which your hon^r may not be unaquainted with, but said as those things were past they should be overlookt on bouth sides, And added that we could not have a greater Manifestation of their Intentions for a <u>Lasting freindship</u> then by their paying down the hundred & od skins for to Compensate in some measure for ye damages their people had done, when they might at the same time have come down on our frontears and made the same depredations that they had formerly done, And farther said that they had concluded on those methods which the Govr chearfully came into & unless they were Effected the peace would not last I askt them what they were they tould me I could not so soon forget what was said there, Asking me if I did not heare the Govr promise that he would be a Constant succor and help to them and that he would taike caire to prevent those Abuses that were Constantly impos'd on y^m by the Inhabitants in this part of ye Countrey and that to prevent these abuses he would build them a Traiding house or houses and Appoint some just men to Transact with them that should doe them justice, and said their people were Constantly made Drunk by our People selling y^m rum, and all the Laws and Severe penailtyes the province could inflict would never prevent it without this Trading house and thatt the Killing of ye Cattle and all ye Diffirences arose from our letting their rude people have rum, I then askt y^m how it would prevent it though I was very Sensible how it would / they tould me I was not unsensible of the nature of their trade and that when an Indian came downe with a quantity of beavour many of them that were drinking men would first ask for a skin in rum which was worth 7 or 8/ and that they often gave for one quart which is 30/ ꝑ g^l notwithstanding (sayes they) they are often deny'd and your people tell them: there is a Law of our Province against it, and you give us a great deale of uneasiness by breaking open our Doares &^{ca} this great profit on the rum sometimes will not prevaile but here is a Temptation sayes they that few or none of you will withstand – this Indian tell you he has a large quantity of beavour, and he nor any of his friends shall deale with you unless you grant this request & the Temptation of loosing sometimes ten pounds aday which I have known som Experience is dificult to resist & if the Trading house undersold every bodey else no body would be tempted to sell rum only for the profit they get on y^t Commodity by reason they give the people so great uneasiness after they are drunk with it. Another of ye same Community tould me he had lately gave 28/: bush^l for Corn and askt me if I were not A witness to it I tould them I was, that I was sorry it was so, they tould me the promises that were made by the Govr would prevent these impositions – Another of ye Same number tould me that afew Dayes past, he had stole from at a House up the River 30 saple skins which I had great reason to beleive was true, he tould me Two witnesses were enough in our Law to prove any thing, but he had brought three and could get no justice done him, saying he was Unhappy last night to drinke too much at the said mans house & that it was a villanous thing in him after he had got away agreat deale of his substance for rum to rob him of great part of what was left I tould him he must goe to the Govr to Boston for Justice he tould me it would cost him 50 skins to goe there, and that it was a great hardship there was no bodey appointed here to doe them justice & then askt me 'what Two oxen were worth. I tould him it was a wrong way to doe himselfe justice he tould me he had no other way & in a few days I heard the man had lost Two oxen. They farther added that there was a Trading house Appointed by the Governm^t formerly but that the man that kept it was a Rogue & made the yard ¼ to short and impos'd on y^m which gave many of them a Disgust against the Governm^t, & uppon ye Conclusion tould me they had never Broke their faith with the french but had allwayes liv'd in peace with them and that it was their kind treatment of y^m induc'd them to be their freinds & tould me that when once their people Experienced that we were a Constant Succor to y^m it would induce them to keep alasting freindship with us for sayes they your giving us a Present at once is soone forgot by our young men, but this would be a Constant Obligation on them that they would daily see their dependance on us. Its my humble Oppinion that some methods might be taiken with the Expense of about £500 p Annum that would keep them in perpetuall peace which I hope your Hon^r in your great wisdome will be so happy as to Effeckt I am

    Yo^r Hon^{rs} most Obedient Humb Servt
            John Minot

    [Superscribed]

To The Hono^r William Dummer Esqr Leu^t Govr of ye Province of ye Massachusets Bay &c^a Humbly present

Letter John Gray to Col. T. Westbrook.

Falm⁰ aprill 20. 1725/

Hond S͏ͬ

Ensign Woodside waits on you With the Acc͏ͭ of the Action Latly Performed By the Lad against the Indians, Who with a Party of Men, on the return of s͏ͩ Coughran Went to View the Corps of the destroyed Enemy, I did Imagine it might be proper To send him in Case of any dispute that might arrise referring to their Scalpes – of Which your Hon͏ͬ will be a sufficient Judge.

I am your most Obedient Ser͏ͭ
John Gray

M͏ͬ Woodsides has taken a great Deale of pains and been very Expeditious

Letter from Col. J. Wentworth

Portsm⁰ Aprill 21ᵗʰ 1725

Sr

Yesterday was with me a Young Man who is a Souldier in Your Servis by Cocharain An Ireish lad, Two Indians Took him at Maquoite and carried him up Amoscogen river a Day & halfs Journy The Second Night, this Cocharain found The Indians fast asleep went round em. feeling for a hatchet at length found one with which he Dispach͏ͭ em boath & has bro͏ͭ away there Scalps, but makes the Story more Manly, this Cocharain lost one of his Scalps on his March home So that wen he came to Our Garrison he got three men more of his minde and went up to the place w͏ᶜʰ they Judge Neer forty Miles from Maquoite, and there found the Indians as he had Saide, So the Took An other P͏ˢ of his Scalp and brings with, I Sent them Down Yesterday in Order to get apassage to Boston, where I hope you will See him this Evening.

it was a Manly Action and doubt not but you will reward Accordingly, but in these cases our hands are Tied up, which is Verry Greaveious to me, I think Such actions should be bountifully rewarded, it would animate attempts, which would Discourage our Enemies) The Young Man Tells me that our Gentlemen were returning from Cannada and that no peace.

I have a letter from Govern[r] Shuler who Tells me his three Reports Now lyes before a Committe of Councll, and all reported in his favour, and that he has the promiss of comeing over in better Cercumstances then before if you have any thing New shall be glad to Know it

I am D[r] Sir Your Most Obed[t] Humbl Ser[t]
J: Wentworth

Letter L[t]. Gov. Dummer to Capt. J. Gyles

"Letter to Col° Westbrook D° to Cap[t] Gyles
April 27th 1725"

Sir

I have enclosed a Warr[t] to the Commanding Officers of the Marching Companies to deliver to you thirty Men, You will see that they be good Men & well arm'd & fitted & after a short Refreshm[t] at Fort George You must march with them up Amerescoggin River in Quest of the Enemy taking with you Cpt Joseph Bane to command under you & as a skilful Pilot for this Service, And the said Cpt Bane is order'd to attend you accordingly. You must take with you as much Provision as you can conveniently carry, & march as high up the River as possible, & if you can find no Tracks or Signs of Indians on that River or the Branches of it, You must cross over to Kennebeck River if it be practicable (of which you will be the best able to judge) & March down that River to Richmond, Let your Motions be perform'd with great Silence & Secrecy, & be patient in Lying wait for the Enemy in such Places where it is probable they will pass: If any Opportunity of Service may present that may require a different Rout from I have here directed: You have my Leave to proceed accordingly.

I lay very great Stress upon y^{ur} Seeking out ye Enemy y^t may be in that River at this Juncture & expect that you perform some notable Service as may be expected from two such good & experienced Officers.

If you are of opinion that you may not be Safely Spared from your Garrison at this Season I Order that Cp^t Bean have the Command & psue these instructions & Hee may take Some Sutable good Officer to Command under Him

Mr Trescot is the bearer hereof whom I Appoint for the third Officer in this March And in Case You don't go Your Self he is to be the Second.

Warrant.

By the Honble the Lieut. Govr

These are to direct the several Commanding Officers of the three Marching Companies or of such of the said Companys as are at or near Casco Bay forthwith to detach out of them such a Number of Men from each as shall make up in the whole thirty effective Men to be deliver'd to Cpt. John Gyles who is to Command the said Party vpon a particular Service for which he will receive my Instructions.

Letter L^t. Gov. Dummer to Col. T. Westbrook

Sir

I have Order'd Cpt. Giles & Cpt. Bane with a Detachm^t of 30 Men from the Marching Companies to go in Quest of the Indians upon Amerescoggin River & Parts adjacent: If this should meet you at Casco or thereabouts, You will see that this Matter be expedited.

 I Can't be of any other opinion but there has been a great Neglect in the Officers at Falm? That a Scout was not immediately sent to ly for some Days about the dead Bodies of the Indians W^{ch} being upon a Carrying Place It was highly probable the other six Indians would pass that Way I desire you would strictly examine into this Matter & find where the Fault lies: for I am much ashamed that there should be so little of a Spirit among the Officers to make any brisk Attempts upon the Enemy w^n such proper occasions offer. I will finde out officers if it be possible of more spirit. You must Order that the Muster Rolls of the sev. Companies be made up as soon as may be that they be ready to pass upon the first Sitting of the Court: You must not let too many of the Captains or Subalterns be off from their Posts at a Time; but the Clerks or one of the Sergeants of the sev^{ll} Companies may bring up the Rolls, & make Oath to them. The Enemy being now about, The Frontiers must be carefully protected, & the Marching Forces be upon constant Duty in the Woods, & if any demurr should hapen that requires the officer to Clear up I shall pmitt them to Come downe w^n they will have time enough to doe if they make up their muster rolls forthwith, wch may be done directly. as farr as the Elect: Day.

 • I have no direct application from Coll^o Harman or L$\hat{e}$. Jaques for a dismiss^n which is proper in such Cases, & thô they are good Officers I Will not keep them from better opportunityes for their advantage if there should be any other Vessell & Company then what are allready in the service to protect the ffishery I shall be glad if Coll^l Harman serve

Letter Nathan Knight to John Gray

Worshipfull sir
These are informing you that by the noise of such a great number of guns which we hear in the woods hard by us killing the cattle as we supose, we understand there are a great number of the Indians in the place, and we are mightily afrayed haveing so few souldiers and the inhabitants utterly refuses unanimusly to watch[in] and to asist us, in such a strait, we therefor earnestly desire you would be pleased as you are a Civil magistrate we intraiet you to Sympathize with us in useing some present method to oblige the Inhabitants if possible to watch and asist us in this so perilous time under such eminent and iminent danger Dear Kind sir we repose much confidence in your favour and speedy care of us and oblige and help
     Sir Your humble servants
     Hugh Henry minister Nathan Knight
Black point April 28. 1725.
Sir I request fauour to deliver the inclosed at your convenience.
 [Superscribed] To Captain Gray at Casco these

Letter Col. T. Westbrook to Lt Gov. Wm Dummer

May it please y^r Hon^r
    You will see by the two Acc^{ts} Accompanys this that the Indians are down upon us in great numbers I am sending to Lt Coll^o Harmon and the Officers on the Frontiers to Muster what men they can to meet them but they being at such a Distance fear it will be to little purpose being in hast cannot Enlarge
    I am your Hon^{rs} most Dutifull Humb^l Servt
       Thos Westbrook

To the Right Honorable The Lords Commissioners for Trade & Plantations.

The Memoriall of Thomas Lechmere Esqr Surveyor Generall, & the Severall Collectors, and other officers of His Majesty's Customes In New England

Most humbly sheweth

That wee being obliged by your Lordshipps letter dated the 26 June 1719 to lay before your hon^{ble} board the proceedings of the severall Governments in our districts, cannot omitt the repeating of our observations upon the great Priveledges & advantages ariseing to the Dutch & French plantations in America being supplied with horses for the Mills, Provisions, Lumber &c. without which they cannot subsist, & in a more perticular manner the horses for their Mills to grinde their Canes, they having few or none of Watermills or Windmills, so consequently must have Cattle Mills, and the cheif returns wee have from thence are in Melasses, some Sugar, Rum, Cocoa Nutts Indigoe &c.^a soe that the Melasses which wee cheifly import from those forreign plantations, being of no use to them, and the freight to Holland and France so high, will nott admit of being by any shipped off, besides the prohibition of it in France, as alsoe if we consider the great Impositions they lay upon our Vessels tradeing to their ports, its more destructive than advantagious, unless a duty was laid upon such forreign Comoditys imported into our plantations, payable to His Majesty's Collectors, as allsoe that those Comoditys from forreign plantations, when unloaden be under the same restraints, as the produce of our plantations, which will be of great advantage to Trade, and raise a considerable revenue to the Crown.

But what we now proceed with humble Submission to acquaint your Lordshipps with is, That ye Severall Acts of Parliament made in Great Brittain, to render America more usefull and depending thereon by giving great premiums for raiseing Navall Stores, by which the lands may be improved, and the people enabled to keep a Correspondence with & to make Returns for their Trade to Great Brittain, are in a manner frustrated by a great omission of such improvements, and the Inhabitants are dayly running into the makeing of Brittish manufactures as Woollens &c^a by which they will in some time have no occasion to Correspond with Great Brittain for such Comoditys, and to which great Encouragement has been given of late Years by severall Acts which have passed in the respective Generall Assemblys of each Government in the said districts

And as allsoe we take leave most humbly to observe, That they very much encourage the circulation of province bills of Creditt, and letting them out to interest upon land security, and by the said Acts enforceing them to be received by all his Majesty's Subjects in all payments & Contracts (Specialties excepted) as equall to mony, though the Tenour of said bills say's only, shall be in all publick payments accepted by the Treasurer of each province and by reason of the great number of these bills which amount to Four hundred Thousand pounds or upwards in the severall Governments, and notwithstanding the publick Faith and Sanction to support them, and annually to sinke the Number of them, as by their Acts doe's more fully appear, and which they sometimes evade by which the Creditt of their said Bills is sunk so low that they have lost in their Value more than a Moiety.

This we must humbly conceive doth evidently shew to your Lordships That, we being obliged to receive them in all publick payments at the full vallue, how prejudiciall they are to his Majesty's Revenue, and of what dangerous consequence to Trade & Commerce, and how destructive to the Industry and property of the Subject, and those proceedings leading us to the source of such Evills, which we presume to take notice off in the following manner may open a Scene which will not a little surprize Your Lordshipps

The Gentlemen of this Country (Merch^{ts} and monyed men excepted) who possess most of the improved and waste lands, are the majority of Members in the severall Generall Assemblys, they for the most part take up those bills & circulate them upon the Creditt of their own lands, without any mony or treasure laid up in bank to support them, and by their laws obligeing them to be received in all payments by all persons; as lawfull tenders as hath been before observed by which they have taken in all moneyd Men's Estates, and are now in these bills, and the Merchants & Traders who are generally the possessors of the bills must take the Growth and Produce of the Country for them, which are risen to most extravagant prices; and the said Gentlemen are allso enabled by the said bills to carry on the Manufactures before mention'd, and to purchase more land, which is a great Engrossing thereof, so that poor people comeing from Great Brittain & Ireland upon the prospect of having lands to settle on, & are the great riches of this large and uncultivated Country, are in a great measure debarred, the land being in their possession, and raised to such great prices which is the greatest discouragement that can be to a farther improvement of these parts of his Majestys dominions.

And wee most humbly conceive it to be incumbent on us to make a Representation at this juncture, because these Evills being seen into by most of the Substantiall men in the Country, a Comittee of whom was appointed by the Generall Assembly at Boston, the Metropolis of North America, to consider of ways & means to redeem the Credit of the bills, & unanimously agreed upon the following propositions ~ 1st That no more bills of Creditt should be made. 2dly That what mony the Country should want upon publick Expences should be borrowed in these bills of Creditt allready made.

3dly That if those persons who had the bills upon Mortgage would pay them in should have Ten p cent Discount, which proposalls being so advantagious to those Men who had the bills upon Mortgage, and would pay them in, and now not being half the vallue, for which they received them. Yet notwithstanding these proposalls were rejected, & the said Men now in the Massachusetts bay have made an Act for emitting Thirty Thousand pounds more in these bills, without any alteration of Tenour or Form or Indenture or Escutcheon for carrying on an Indian warr, and postponed the cancelling or burning of Twenty seven Thousand pounds of bills of creditt, but continue them in currency, and obligeing all persons in all payments to receive, which with Submission is a manifest Breach of publick faith.

And the Government of Rhode Island in like manner, thô no way concerned in the Warr and not at all in Debt, and are not above Eight hundred pounds p annum charge for supporting the charges of Government yet at this time have passed an Act for continueing Eighty Thousand pounds at Interest in these bills, which is very destructive to Trade.

And wee thinke it our humble dutys to observe to your Lordshipps that, before the assemblies concluded on these Acts they received his Majesty's letter dated at the Court of Windsor the 31st of August last signified by his Grace the Duke of Newcastle to all the Governours of New England, comanding each of them not to pass any bills in their respective Assemblies there of an unusuall or extraordinary nature, and importance, wherein the kings prerogative or the propertie of the Subject might be prejudiced, or Trade any ways affected, untill the draught of such bill or bills had been transmitted home and the Royall approbation received thereupon, unless there was a Clause inserted therein, suspending the execution thereof untill it has the Royall Sanction; And notwithstanding such repeated comands these Acts have passed, and are putt in force without any such Clause which matter so tenderly affecting his Majesty's perogative & revenue (wee having no fare of mony but only in those bills) as likewise Trade in Generall and perticularly the Commerce of Great Brittain, and soe injurious to the Industry and property of the subject, these bills being sunk soe greatly in their Vallue, many of them being very often counterfeited, the Indenture worn out, and allmost quite defaced, that nothing can be foreseen but the uttmost Confusion even to the totall ruine of these his Majesty's dominions, unless the Royall Grace intervene for their preservation.

And wee most humbly propose it as absolutely necessary, That the bills of each Government may be called in, or that the possessors of them, upon paying them into the Treasury, may have Security from the Government for them, and lawfull Interest paid, untill the Government hath redeemed the principall, by which the Merchant, who doth not lett his Cash lye dead, may dispose of the bills he hath received, instead of being obliged to part with them at a great discount for the produce of the Country, which hath been raised to meet prodigious prices.

And wee further most humbly take leave to represent to Yo.r Lordshipps, That whereas this Continent carrys on a considerable Trade to the Bay of hundoras in the Spanish West Indies for Loggwood and great Quantitys being annually brought into these parts, and his Majesty haveing been most graciously pleas'd with advice and Consent of Parliament to take off the Duty from Loggwood and other Dying woods and Druggs to encourage the importation thereof to Great Brittain, as the Mart of Trade; That all the said Loggwood soe imported into the plantations, be subject to be bonded to be carried to Great Brittain, or if allowed and permitted to be transported to forreign Marketts, to pay the Duty of Twenty Shillings Sterling ℔ Tunn upon Exportation for the Use of his Majesty, which will consequently prevent Forreigners from haveing it at a cheaper Rate then the Brittish Merchants; as by the Act of the Eighth year of his Majesty it is paid at the Exporting thereof from Great Brittain.

All which is most humbly submitted to your Lordshipps consideration by

May it please Your Lordshipps Most humble ffaithfull and Most Obed^t Servants

Thos: Lechmere   Hilbert Newton
John Jekyll   Arch^d Cuming
Nath^{ll} Ray   Wm Lambert

Boston New England Aprill 30th 1725.

E: *New England*   *Plan^s Gen.*

Letter from M^r. Cuming with a Mem^l. from the officers of ye Customs Setting forth the great detriment the Plantation Trade suffers by Selling Horses to Forreign Plantations, by bills of Credit in New England & by a deficiency in the Act relating to the Importation of Logwood here Dated June 23^d 1725

         Rec^d July 28   }   *1725*
         Read Augt 11   }   *1726*

Add: On his Majesty's Service

To Allured Popple Esqr Secretary to the Right Honourable The Lords Commissioners for Trade & Plantations att White Hall

p Capt Barlow

Letter, Capt. John Gray to L^t. Gov. Wm Dummer

                           Falm^o May. The 4th 1725

May It Please Your Hon^r

The Inclosed is what I rec^d This day From the Minister of Black Point. and the Serg^t of the Garrison Their. This

I thought my duty To Acquaint your Hon.^r of. Cpt Bourn is Bound To Boston With some Lett^{rs} From Coll Westbrooke. Which prevents my Futher Inlargement.

   I am Hon^d S^r your most Hum^{ble} Ser^t Command

          John Gray ~

   [Superscribed]

The Honble William Dummer Esq, Liev^t Governour of the Massachusetts Bay &^c   Boston

Letter Col. T. Westbrook to L^t. Gov. Wm Dummer

          Falm° May ye 4th 1725

May it Please your Hon^r

  I rec^d your Hon^{rs} Orders p En^s. Triscott who coming by Cape Porpoise last Saturday with four men was fir'd on by a party of Nine or Ten Indians. Triscott is shott through the Thigh and through the Ankle, two of the men with him had the Stocks of their Guns shott. They immediately made up a party of about twenty four men some Soldiers some Inhabitants and some Fishermen from Cape Porpoise & follow'd them but could not come up with them.

  As to sending Capt Gyles thirty men just now I cannot possibly make them up, all the Marching Forces & sundry from the Garrisons being already Employ'd in your Hon^{rs} particular Orders as your Hon^r will plainly see by comparing the State of the Army, I now send with your Hon^{rs} Orders. As soon as I can call off such a part I shall immediately send them, the Enemy is certainly down on us in considerable Numbers, so that we have as much as we can do to keep the weak parts of our Frontiers from their Incursions. I have ask'd the Officers of Falm° the reason why they didnt make up a party and lye by the dead bodies of the Indians, their Answer is they did not hear of it till six days after it was done and not more than seven or eight hours before the Enemy was down wth them and kill'd two men and the place where ye dead bodies lay was sixty Miles from them, so considering the Enemys being amongst them judg'd it not safe to march so far from their several Garrisons, for a small scout at that Juncture drawn out wou'd have very much expos'd them their Number not being above five or six in a Garrison and the Garrisons very scattering. As to the marching Forces and sundry of the Garrisons they are constantly in the Woods in sundry small Scouts and are faithfull in their Duties by what I hear from them from time to time.

I shall Direct the Officers to prepare their Rolls as fast as they can.

Capt Bourn being indisposd and desirous to wait on your Hon^r I have permitted him to carry the Express for its more speedy Arrival. If your Hon^r should be at Newberry in a short time I would be glad to have leave to wait on You there for a few hours.

I am Your Hon^rs most Dutiful Servt
Thos Westbrook

Lt Gov. Dummer to Capt. Bourn.

11th May 1725

Sir

This Comes by Capt Holman & I hope this will finde you diligently Imployed in Enlisting & getting your Men ready for their Embarcation. Capt Holman Carried you £80. for bounty money for so many Men. & I desire you'l Exert your selfe so as to gett your ffull Number. thô. you should go as far as the Vineyard to make them up but I hope there will be no need of that. Gett them on Bord assoon as possible & when it shall please God you arrive safe with them at ffalmouth you are to take Coll° Westbrooks order for your further proceeding. See that the Men be well used & well disciplined. Shall bee well pleased to have Leu^t Dimock first Lieut. & you must have A second Leu^t wch will bee appointed you when you gett to your Rendezvous. I have nothing more at psent but to recomend to you all possible

Y

Letter Corp. Benj. Hassell to Lt Gov. Dummer

Dunstable May ye 11 1725

to his Honor ye Govener

An Information from Cap^{tt} Louewell Companey at Ossepye pond a man being Sick we Left nine men with him we made a forte thare And sent out scouts Discouerd tracks then we marched towards pigwackit we heard a gun then marched to Saweco River Discouerd more trackes then Coing to pigwacket found whare Some Indens went into Conowes then marched and See one indon kild him and Returning two milds thare we ware shot upon Cap^{tt} Lovewell wounded and non Returnd but I to ye teen men and we and no more are yet Come to Dunstable.

  Superscribed   Benjn Hassell Corp.
To His Honor the Left Gouner
William Dummer

Letter Eleazer Tyng to Lt Gov. Dummer May 12, 1725.

May it Please Your Hon^r
Upon my hearing of thee Newes Early This Morning This Twelfe Instant and Benj^a Hassel Gave me This account –

That on the Ninth of this Instant about Nine or Ten of The Clock in The Morning Capt Lovewell Saw an Indian on The Opposite Side of Sawco pond and Then Imediately Left Their packs and went about Two Miles before Thay Came To him Thay Coming Within about five or Six Rods Before Thay Saw The Indian and The Indian Made The first Shot at Them and Wounded Capt Lovewell & Sam^{ll} Whiting & Thay Imediately Killed The Indian and Returning back To Their packs Came Within forty or fifty Rods of Them The Indians Walaid Them under The bank of a Little Brook Capt Lovewells men being between The Brook and The pond it being a pine plain The Indians fired upon Them both in The front & The Rear Shouting and Runing Towards Them Capt Lovewell fell at The first Vollee The Indians Shot and Groan'd This man being Clost by him & Then he Saw Several of Capt Lovewells Men Gitt behind Trees; upon This he Seeing Such a Grate Number of Indians Thougt it best To Return To Some men Thay had Left With a Sick man at a fort Thay Made about Thirty Miles back By ossipe pond and he Got To the fort The Next Morning about Nine of the Clock. And if your Hon^r Thinks fitt I Will March up To The place

Your Hon^{rs} Most Hum^{ll} Ser^t

Eleazer Tyng

P: Sergent Nat^{ll} Woods Desiered me To acquaint Your Hon^r That he was Left with The Nine Men at The fort & upon hassels Coming To The fort The Men Would Stay No Longer. Woods both Desier'd & Comanded Them to Stay but Could Not prevail wth Them & Then he Made The Best of his Way home.

P: Lev^t Blanchard came home Last Night.

Letter L! Gov. Dummer to Col. Wentworth

May 13, 1725.

Sir

I have just Time to tell you That One of Cpt. Lovewells Men is run from him & left him engaged with the Indians at Pigwacket last Lords Day, & pretends that they were overpower'd by Numbers & that he saw Cpt Lovewell fall & heard him Groan, & that he him self was cutt off from the Comp^a by the Indians Pressing between them tho. Hee Cant Deny but our people were Chargeing ye Enemy briskly when he left I have Order'd out Coll^n Tyng with forty Men to make the best of his Way to Ossapy & Pigwacket in Quest of the Enemy, & Cp^t White to follow him with his Comp^a of Volunteirs; And I must pray that you would act in Concert with us in this Affair & send from N Hampshire a Party of Men upon the same Ground, For if the Enemy in that Ground are of such Strength as to defeat Lovewell They will thereupon be in great Security: It is of the utmost Importance that something be done vigorously & expeditiously on this Occasion.

Coll Wentworth

Letter L! Gov. Dummer to Col. Eleazer Tyng May 13, 1725.

Sir

This Morning I rec^d y^{rr} Acc^t of the Indians Engaging Cpt Lovewell at Pigwacket, I have not Time at present to make any Observations on the ill Managem^t of Hazzel & the ten Men at the Fort who have so cowardly deserted their Commander & Fellow Soldiers in their Danger.

Your Readiness to go out forthwith after the Enemy is well Accepted & Approved of by me & the Council, And

accordingly I direct you to a make up a Body of forty effective Men well arm'd & provided (if you think so many necessary) & proceed without Delay to Ossapy & Pigwacket & the Country thereabout, & make careful Search for y\ue Enemy in Order to kill & destroy such as may be found there And at the Place of their Engagem\ut with Cpt. Lovewell endeavour what you can to find the Bodies of the Indians or English that may have been slain there, You are hereby Impowered to draw out of Cpt. Willards Company twelve Men to join you, And he is accordingly Ordered to detach them & send them to your Rendezvouz forthwith: If you find it necessary, You are Directed & hereby Authorized & Impowered to Impress out of the nearest Towns in your Regim\ut twelve or fifteen Men for this Service, if you can not enlist y\um Cpt. White is Order'd to follow you as soon as he can possibly get his Men ready; And have written Lieut. Gov\ur Wentworth That a party may be sent from that Governm\ut to Pigwacket as soon as may be. I depend upon your Acting in this Affair with the utmost Diligence & Vigour. You must take your L\ut Blanchard with you in this March, Take one or two sufficient Pilots with you & (if it be necessary) Hassel who left the Comp\ua I would have you rather go without your full Complim\ut than make any Delay.
May 15. 1725.

Letter Eleazer Tyng to L\ut. Gov. W\um. Dummer

May it please your hon:
I Rec\ud your orders about Eleven of y\ue Clock today and I forthwith sent to Cap\ut Willard for twelve of his best men and to Robert Richardson Cap\ut of y\ue volunteere Shoe men

for fifteen who I Expect to morrow night so that I hope to be ready for them to march by Sabbath morning, I have also sent one of Capt Lovewells men the Bearer hereof who was in the whole Engagement a man who by the account the rest gave of him behaved himself couragiously to the last I should be very glad of this man or some other that Escaped to go with me for a guide.

there is five wounded men come in and Doc^r Prescot is with them and I hope none are Dangereusly wounded. Hassell says he is sick & cannot go with me.

I Remain Your Hon^{rs} humble servant
Eleazer Tyng

Dunstable. May 14. 1725.

Letter Lt Gov. Dummer to Col. Eleazer Tyng " May 14. 1725 "

S^r

This Comes with an Indian of note belonging to a Tribe of the ffrench Mohawks who with all the Nation are well affected to us. This Man Came downe with the Commiss^{rs} from Canada & being desirous to see Xtian I have sent Him to you, give directions if Hee getts to you before you are Marched that Hee bee very well used & that good care bee taken of Him & Lett Him bee sent to Me againe when Hee shall desire it. I have this Moment rec͡d your Express this Day with Blanchards Acc^{tt} of the action between Lovells men & the Indians, taken from Melven. & tho: the loss of so Many brave Men be great I am very much Comforted to finde they behaved with so Much bravery & Gallantry. I hopet it may please God to favour you with an opertunitye to take a Just revenge for the blood of your Country Men

I am Y^r humble S^r
Wm Dummer

Boston 14th May 1725

Send downe to me forthwith wth the Bearer hereof Mr Calef the most Inteligent pson Among Lovells Men returnd that I may have a pfect acc^t of that Action.

The Indian Seems Dispos'd to Go this March with you in Company with Christian, And You must by all means encourage it Pray make the best Search You can when You come into the Ground where the Action happened for the Dead and Wounded that none may perish for want of our Care.

Letter Col. T. Westbrook to Lt Gov. Wm Dummer

Falm° May 17th 1725

May it please y^r Honour

I receivd your letter of the fourth Currant on the 15th of the same wherein your Hon^r orders me to give a particular account of the black point Scout whom your Hon^r calls Eighteen men if so my Clark has made a mistake in Coppying, for there was but Eight men and most of them Inhabitants, so that there was no Officer with them, but a Soldier or two to go with them to look for their cattle. As to the men in Falmouth I immediately drew out all that I could Judge was proper which did not exceed Twenty and sent Capt Bourn & Liu^t Dominicus Jordan, I did not give them orders to pursue the Enemy let their numbers be what they would but left them to their own Judgments according to what discovery they should make knowing they had behav'd themselves very well when they had an oppertunity on the Enemy, and are reputed men of Courage and by the Acc^ts they had from Black Point people, and Mitchels and Spurwink Garrisons they were a considerable number as I acquainted your Hon^r before, and by what discovery they made by the Indian Tracks they could not Judge themselves to be a number sufficient to follow them.

I do assure your Hon.[r] I did not leave more then three men in a Garrison with the Inhabitants and Soldiers for their Defence which was as little as possible could be left In as much as the place where they were burning our houses and killing our Cattle, was not less then Eleven or Twelve Miles through the Woods the nighest way wee could get to them.

I Humbly subscribe my selfe your Hon[rs] most Dutifull Servant

Tho[s] Westbrook

Letter Col. T. Westbrook to L[t]. Gov. Dummer

Falmouth May 17th 1725

May it please your Honour

I rec'd your Hon[rs] orders of the Eleventh Currant and shall Endeavour when I have recd the recruits to Improve them in the best manner I can to Intercept and destroy the Enemy & follow your Hon[rs] Orders.

Cap[t] Bean arriv'd here from York the 15th Currant, I immediately dispatcht him to Capt. Gyles with directions that nothing may be neglected relateing the March on Amuscoggin haveing before sent the Quota of men Pursuant to your Hon[rs] orders. I have since that made up a Scout of Twenty Eight Men Soldiers and Inhabitants whom I sent out the Sixteenth at night under the Command of Lieu[t] Dominicus Jordan diligently to search the most likely places on the backs of the Towns from this place to Saco Salmon Falls, and intend to continue & strengthen them with more men as soon as possible if your Hon[rs] orders do not call them off, these being the places the Enemy cheifly aim'd at both last Summer & this

   I am your Hon^rs most Dutifull Humb^l Servt
           Thos Westbrook.

P S.
 I herewith send y^r Hon^r a Journal of our Proceedings Since I left Boston. _ I have not yet rec'd the recruits
           T W

Falm? May 20th 1725

Letter Lt Gov. Dummer to Capt. Bourn May 18, 1725

S^r I have Rec^d Your Letter of the 15th Curr^t by Mr Holman, And am Glad You have proceeded so far in Raising the Voluntiers I Ordered And that there is a Good prospect of Your Speedy Accomplishment of this Affair which I pray You would proceed in with all possible Expedition, It being of great Consequence to the Dispatch herein. According to Your proposal I have Sent a Warrant to Mr Young to remove his Sloop to Barnstable and have Sent an Impress Warr^t to Col? Otis Which may be Used to forward the Affair of the Indian Enlisting or to Supply the Deficiency with Such English Men as are So perverse as to Obstruct the Affair. I am Satisfied with Your Nomination of Messrs Bacon & Hawes and Shall Commissionate them Accordingly, If You can make Your Number of Voluntiers One hundred Men I Direct You so to do And Desire you would Advance the Bounty Money And it Shall be repaid You with other Necessary Charges — Put Maj^r Gorhain upon Expediting the Affair of the Whale Boats And if need be his Sloop must be Employed in Transporting the Boats & Men. Mr Holman Returns to You with these Dispatches And will Continue to Assist You in the Affair

I am Y^{rs}

W^m D⟶

Boston May 18 1725
Capt Bourn

Letter Lt Gov. Dummer to Col. Otis

Boston May 18th 1725

S^r

Mr Holman Informs Me that You Desire a Warr^t for Impressing Twenty Men Which You would make Use of in order to Awe those people that Instruct the Indians enlisting I have accordingly Enclos'd a Warrant which You will Use at Discretion for the End aforesaid If You Actually Impress any persons that Conceal the Indians or any ways hinder the proceedings, And they afterwards do their Duty by producing the Indians and assisting the Design, You may Dismiss them, Not accounting them as Men that have Served, But if they Obstinately Continue to give obstruction to his Majestys, You must not dismiss them but put them on Board the Transport as Recruits. I have Directed Capt Bourn to make up his Number of Indians, One hundred men, and Doubt not of Your Assisting in this Important affair to the Utmost of Your power, Mr Holman Returns to You with this Dispatch, And will Still assist in the Affair, All he is able.

I have Chosen this Method rather than Impressing but if there be any so evil Dispos'd to the Service as to Discourage Voluntiers from Enlisting, Such are very proper persons to be Impress'd —

I am Y^r Humble Servt

W: Dummer

Col^o Otis ⟶

Letter Col. Eleazar Tyng to Lt Gov. Dummer May 19, 1725.

May it please your Honour

This Day I marched from Amuskeag having 55 of my own Men & 32 of Capt Whites. The men are all well & proceed with a great Deal of Life & Courage – Yesterday I was forced to lie still by Reason of the Rain.

I would humbly offer something to your Honour on the behalf of our People who are left very Destitute & naked, that you woul^d be pleased to consider Their Circumstances & order what you shall think proper for Their Defence till we return.

    I am your Honours most Obed^t humble Servant
Amuskeag May 19, 1725   Eleazar Tyng.

Letter Col. T. Westbrook to Lt Gov. Dummer

        Falm? May 21st 1725

May it please your Hon^r

   Lieu^t Dominicus Jordan (who I inform'd of in mine of the Seventeenth) is returnd about three a Clock, and informs, that he Tract Two parties of Indians, that came out of the Country & returnd in two parties. the least of their paths much larger then what his Scout made who consisted of thirty two men, haveing added four to his Scout since my last, Wee Judge that the greatest part of the Enemy are drawn some Distance back on the great Rivers, this being their time to fish for Salmon & sundry other fish up the fresh Rivers on which the Indians yearly make a fishing voyage. Our winter scoutes discovered sundry of their fishing places on Saco, Pesomscott & Amuscoggin Rivers where they made large Quan^{ys} last Summer, The new recruits are not yet come notwithstanding we have had so many Westerly winds, as soon as they arrive if Arm'd, I will endeavour to visit some of their fishing places.

I have since my last examin'd Henery Mckenny relateing the Indians he saw when they burnt the Houses at Black Point and charg'd him to relate no more then he could give his Oath to. He attests that he told betwen Thirty & Forty on the plain Marsh from the Ferry Garrison where he was on his Guard in the Watch Box and at the same time there were others Scattered fireing the houses up and Down

I am your Hon^{rs} most Dutifull Humb!. Servant

Thos Westbrook

P. S.

I have permitted Ebenezer Nutting the Armourer to wait on y^r Hon^r he wanting sundry Tools, I think it of absolute necessity that he be sent down again as soon as possible Sundry of our Arms being out of repair.

T. W.

Letter, Lt Gov. J. Wentworth to Lt Gov. Dummer

Portsm° May 23^d 1725

Sir

Just now came Express to me from Capt Chesly who Commanded the men I sent to Osaby &c. they came into Cochecho this Morning.

On Thursday they came to Ossaby Pond (it rayning all Tuseday March^t but little but Sent out Sauvrall Scouts all that day in hopes of finding some of Capt Lovewells wounded Men) On thirdsday, before they came up with Oseby Pond they Discovered a Track of Indians much longer then theres, and then quickly found Lovewells Fort fast Shut up they soon got into the Fort where they found a Considerable Quantity of provisions and sundry other things, with a writeing on a bark, That the men that went out were all lost, the Day our people discovered Severill Indians and heard the Dogs bark, So found they were Discovered and Missing Your Men, They thot it advisable to return. least they met wth ye same fate Capt Lovewell did.

I finde thers agreate Uncertainty in our meeteing in the woods. so would propose that your Commanding Neer to us as Maj^r Hammond or Coll? Westbrook have fourthwith orders to Raise one hundred Men or More out of Your Eastern Forces or from the Melletia of Your Towns. You have Stout men in Berwick Kittry York &c^t and send up Emediatly I will not Disband these 53 that now came down Untill I heare from You, You may Depend Sir that they will be down on Some of Yours or Our Frontiers Uery Soon, and it may be boath, I will make our Number up Sixty On that March, I verryly beleive They will Stay in hopes of Our comeing up to bury Our Dead, and have a Considerable Number togeather thers fish Enough & Good other Huntting we may range all that Country as Pigwacket &c^t but this must be Don with all possible Dispach.

we can have no Dependance on The men You Sent from the Westward, wheather shall find em or not.

I am Dr Sir Your Most Obed^t Humb^l Ser^t

P. S. J Wentworth

I am of opinion that Capt Lovewell wounded many of the Indians and that thay can't Get them off, J W.

Liev^t Gover^n Dummer.

Letter Richard Davis to Lt *May 24, 1725.*

Much Honoured S^r I your Humble Petitioner belonging to Captain Samuel Hincks att Fort Mary in Biddiford Do Humbly Desire your Honours favour to Dissmis me from the

Fort because if it may be your Honours Pleasure I would get into Cap.[t] Jordans Company; I am Honoured S[r] Your Most Humble Dutifull and Obedient Servant;

Biddiford May: 24: 1725　　　　　　　　Richard Davis

Letter, L[t] Gov. to Capt. Cornwall, May 24, 1725

Sir,

It being highly probable that the Indians of Penobscot will speedily be out in the Vessels they took last Summer from the English, & will infest the Eastern Coast to the great Disturbance & Loss of those concerned in the Fishery;

I desire you to draw out of your Ships Comp[a] fifty of your ablest Men to proceed East so far as Passamaquody or the Mouth of S.[t] Croix River in two small Vessels provided for that Purpose to be under the Command of your Lieuten.[t] & such Officer (for the other Vessel) as you shall think fit to appoint: Let them keep near the Shoar, & look into the Harbours & Bays & among the Islands as they go along, more especially at Pemaquid, Penobscot Fox Island & Mount Desert Bays the Mouth of Petit River & Passamaquody, & Endeavour to get Intelligence of the Enemy & Decoy them by Sounding for Fish, Concealing their Men & such other Methods as are proper for that End, And by all possible Means to find out suppress & destroy the Indian Enemy as well as any Pirates that may haply be on the Coast at this Time. And for their Encouragem.[t] they will have One Hundred Pounds for each Scalp of a Male Indian above twelve Years old, & for other Scalps & Prisoners the highest Premium the Law Allows.

Notwithstanding the Direction before mentioned I don't limit you as to the Extent of Coast for this Cruize, But leave it to you & the Discretion of your Officer how far East he may proceed, In which he must govern him self according to the Intelligence he may meet.

If he shall hear of the Enemy on Shoar Let him Land such a Number of his Comp^a as he shall judge fit to ambush or psue them. And particularly I think it advisable that they ly some Time in Ambush on the Western Point of a small Island at the Mouth of Petit River within two Leagues of Machias & the usual Passage of the Indians from Passamaquody & St Johns River to Penobscot, For more particular Information in these Matters your Officer had best consult the Pilots.

This Cruize may be for fforty Days & if Circumstances shall be such as to give great Prospects of Doing Service Lett them Stay out longer. I am (Sir)

Boston May 24, 1725   Capt Cornwall

P S Lett your Lieut. Advise Coll. Dowcett Lt Govr of Annapolis of his Cruize If he meet with an Opportunity of Sending to him.

Letter Capt. Saml Hincks to Lt Gov. Dummer

Fort Mary 25: May 1725

May it Please y^r Hon^r

This Comes with Expresses to y^r Honour from Col^o Westbrook.

I cant inform Y^r Hon^r any Thing more but what offers here, one tarbox Lost a son by 9: indians on our plains 10 Dayes since & Carried of his Sculp we alarmed yesterday Know not ye occasion the Day before for Seing 3 indians and in Such parcels They appear at Every place they Discover themselves, I beleive in order to Know our Strength that we may issue out and as I informed y^r Honour before we want men to march, for now as well as other times I have ventered to Lend two or thre to Carry & forward Expresses which hope I dont offend in. I have heard y^r Hon^r is not so willing officers may come to make up their Rolls but Send.

I would Humbly acquaint y^r Hon^r I have no Clark neither any one within fort Knows anything about ye affairs ye Corporal I have, tho hes of late sickened is a man to fight but no man to send as I do not only victuall my men but look after my forces I have to send one of my Officers & if one on those does not go I must neglect my Role if yor Hon^r Doe oblige my tarry which I Depend yet not blame me if I do come since my fort is gone I try & strictly observe duty & all things and as before, so now ask Leave I may tho cant have a Return from y^r Hon^r before I humbly take leave to come I would not be so tedious but would inform your Hon^r my interest at portsm^o is partly Disposed of with Loss my wife left that place & is at Boston where she lately gone & my private affairs are in confusion thô I neglect no duty.

I hope y^r Hon^r will Consider these things and give Leave to y^r Humble Servant

Samuel Hincks

Col. Johnson Harmon to L^t. Gov. Dummer May 26, 1725

May it Plese your Hon^{or}

I have sent in my Role by Ensi^{gn} John Carleyle to attest he hath sarved y^r Hon^r &c his Country all most foure years A man of Good Report with us beloved by all I pray your Hon^{rs} faviour toward him.

S^r If you plese to Lett him have Liu^{tt} Jaques post its very a Greeable to me & my Compny Liu^{tt} Jaques hath devoted him selfe to the fishery at y^r Leve.

S^r My Compny by Dismissions &c Runaways Sum Turned into other Compenys &c Sum Scatred to the farthest part of y̆ᵉ Est I Can Make but Thirty & we are Scouting Continuely My Men at this time are up Saco River.

I should be Glad with a Sutable Number to visit the Indiens Hed qurters but wᵗ Submission.

pray Sʳ Give me Leve to visit Boston Sum time in June on My one privit Affairs if it be but two days Sʳ nothing new, your Honour I hope hath a Good Representative from York this year with Most Humble Duty am Sʳ

Yʳ Honʳˢ Most obedient Sarᵗᵗ

York May 26ᵗʰ 1725   Johnson Harmon
To yᵉ Honᵒᵇˡ William Dummer Esqʳ &c

Letter Lᵗ. Gov. J. Wentworth to

Portsmᵒ May 28ᵗʰ 1725

Sir

I have Yours p Express without date, Observe the cear you are and have taken, which must alarm̃ The Indians who are in pretty large Compˢ come Down Eastward as I hear if your 100 Indians are Sailed Eastward They may chance to come in a Good time.

I am greately concernᵈ for the misManagemᵗ of our Men in the March to the Pond, we all accounted them Stout men, what cheifely discorraged our men was there not marching Your Men, indeed I tho't Collº Ting was Two Dayes march before us, but when they came to Capᵗ Lovewells ffort and found no men there they were Discouraged.

I have as you hinted to me Passed a Note for paying our Quota towards building a Fort at the Pond, as allso the Vollentier Act One hundred pounds a Scalp and 2/6 p Day while on Duty and have given all possible Incorragemᵗ for Vollentiers.

I did not Discharge our men untill I Received your letter, which was Tuesday after noon we Thot then out of time, to

Send againe, on that Errand, before those Indians are gon off, and then you would have men enough to bury the Dead, its a strange thing our people should be so dispirited, There was in the 53 I sent out 40, as likely lusty Midle aged men as can be found in our hole Province but So it was.

Yesterday came into Berwick Ezek! Davis of Concord. one of Cap Lowuel' men, who was Eleven dayes wandring before he found the Fort.

I have him at Portsmouth where he is well Taken care of he is wounded in the belly and part of His Thomb Shot off & like to do well.

I have Sent you what was taken from his mouth Yesterday, I fear we shall have a hot Summer.

I am Dr Sir your Most Obed^t hum^l Servt
J Wentworth

Instructions to Capt. Sanders, June 1725.

You are directed to embrace the first favourable Season of Wind & Weath! & Proceed East with the Comp^a of Voluntiers under command in the Sloop Merry Meeting in Quest of the Enemy Indians who now infest the Eastern Coast in a Scooner by them taken from the English.

You must put into Falm? in Casco Bay & acquaint Coll. Westbrook with your Design & shew him ye Instructions, And there get what Intelligence you can of the said Indians,

And without Making any Delay at Falm? Proceed East according to your Intelligence Keeping near the Shoar & Sounding for Fish Concealing your Men & Appearing in all Respects in such a Manner as may most probably decoy the Enemy And Putting into the most likely Places to meet with the Indians or gain any Advice of them, And upon Meeting them Attack them with your best Courage & Conduct & do your utmost to take Kill & destroy them.

You must proceed East no further than Passammaquody & Return in thirty Days your Departure from Casco, Unless you have a very fair Prospect of Meeting the Enemy And in such Case you may extend your Cruize farther both as to Time & Place.

Send Coll. Dowcett Lt Govr of Nova Scotia an Acc^t of your Design & Proceedings with a Copy of y^{re} Instructions If you meet with any Conveyance.

Let me have Advice from you as often as you have Opportunity.

Letter Lt Gov. Wm Dummer to Col Johnson Harman

S^r

I have the Letters You lately wrote Me & Shall be Glad to hear of Your Success Upon Your Return You may Come to Boston to make up Your Roll which I understand labours upon a Complaint given into the house by or on behalf of Two of Your Men Sign'd by them pretending that You have detain'd their Wages from them & Rec^d the Wages of one of them without his Order which he Says he gave only to Capt Nowell I doubt not of Your Justifying Your self against these Charges & am Your Humble Servt

4th June 1725   W D ~

The Names of the Men are, Jos: Crosby & Hugh Holman Col? Harman

Letter Lt Gov. Wm Dummer to Col. T. Westbrook

Boston 4th June 1725

S^r

I have Rec^d many of Yours lately & perceive Your great Industry to obtain an opportunity of doing Some Service against the Enemy & the Reinforcem^t of Indians being as I hope 'ere this Arriv'd You, I doubt not of Your Employing them in Some Notable Enterprize, This Covers Doct^r Bacons Commiss^n under Capt Bourn & also Jerem^y House to be Lieu^t of the other Compan^y of Indians for They must be Divided into Two Companys Howes' Commission has a Blank for the Name of the Captain who must be Some Able Active Man I hope Capt Bourn will be with You in a Short time with More Indians & by Capt Franklyn You Shall have so Good Whale Boats, for the present You will Send those Indians out in a body or otherwise Employ them as You Shall upon the Best Intelligence find most proper for the Service. Two fellows of Col^o Harmons Company have put in a petition to the Genl Court to have him Sent for to Answer to their Complaints of Detaining their Wages from them, And the House have it Seems thought it worth while to Address Me that he may be sent for accordingly, And thô I don't think proper to Send for him Yet I would have You to tell him that he may have Liberty to Come to Town to Make up his Muster Roll which for the present is Demur'd as I am Inform'd. Mr Grant moves me for a Reinforcem^t of Two Men at the Garrison house of James Grey, Let him have them if it be Necessary & You can Spare them. Tell Capt Moulton that I expect if you have a prospect of any Eminent Service that he be Ready to March when You shall Direct him, If it be Consistent with the present occasion of Service let Capt Oliver Come to make up his Muster Roll

       I am Y^r Humble Servt
          W D

If it be necessary for You to come to the Court after You have Dispos'd the Troops in the best Manner You Can You May do it — After the present Exigency the Indians must be Employed according to my former Orders.
Deliver the Enclos'd to Col^o Harmon
Col^o Thos Westbrook

OF THE STATE OF MAINE 287

Letter L! Gov. Wm Dummer to L! Gov. J. Wentworth

June 21, 1725,

Sir

Upon Advice of the Motions of the Enemy I have Order'd two Troops from Ipswich & Newbury for Securing the County of York to have their Head Quarters at Berwick & Wells, And am Raising four Companies of Voluntiers, whom I intend to send a cross the Countrey from Dunstable to Berwick (which will be a great Defence to your Province) to be employed for the Annoyance of the Enemy according as they shall have Intelligence of their Motions after their Arrival in the County of York; I have likewise sent into the County of Bristol for thirty Indians, & Expect all the s^d Companies will be ready to March in a few Days.

I have likewise Order'd a Company of Voluntiers to be raised in the County of York for this Service.

And I hope you will Levy 100 men at least in your Governm^t upon this critical Juncture.

L! Gov! Wentworth

Instructions to Col^s Noyes & Appleton, June 21, 1725.

[In the hand-writing of Secretary Willard]

Instructions to the Commanders of the two Troops to be drawn out of the County of Essex & sent for the Defence of the Towns in the County of York.

You must march directly to the Towns of Wells & Berwick one of them must be posted at Berwick & the other at Wells as their Head Quarters;

They must generally be employ'd in passing through the Woods from the Heads of the said two Towns, unless more important business call them off & carefully look out for the

Tracks of the Enemy, & pursue them in all Places that are practicable, till they come up with them.

Upon Intelligence of the Enemies Assaulting any of the Places in the said County, Whether the Eastern or Western Towns, They must immediately Repair to the said Towns for their Defence & the Annoyance of the Enemy;

And in all Things they must act with the greatest Conduct & Vigour for the safeguard of the Inhabitants & Destruction of the Enemy: the Troopers must be assured for their Encouragem^t That the Governm^t will allow them 100 ℔ for each Scalp, besides their Wages for such Indians as they shall kill in their Marchings & Scoutings.

The said Commanders of the Troops must from Time to Time follow such Orders as y^y shall receive from T. W. Chief Commander of the Eastern Forces.

[Indorsed; in the hand-writing of Lt Gov. Wm Dummer,]

I supose you intend these instructions for Col^o Westbrook, there must be instruction to each Capt besides – agreeable hereto. begining wth an instruction to march forthwith to those Towns

        W D

Letter Col. T. Westbrook to Lt Gov. Wm Dummer

May it Please your Hon^r/

        In my last of the 17th Ins^t I informd that Capt Bourn and Capt Franklyn were not come, whom your Hon^r informd me in your's of the 4th Curr^t would be with me in a few days; We have not more than Six days Provision left. if Franklyn do not arrive in a few days I shall not be able to keep the Scouts out.

Jo: Nebon asserts that the Penobscot Tribe have planted a great Quantity of Corn at their old Town & at their new, but Saccaristis will not own they have planted any below their new Town. Saccaristis affirms that ye Indians fitted out two of the Scooners y^t they took last Summer & went a fishing & getting Seils off at Grand Menan and the Mouth of St Johns River some time in the latter end of May last, I am someth^g surpriz'd the Indians are so still at this Juncture —

I omitted to inform your Hon^r of Capt Moultons return on the 15th of this Ins^t from Pigwocket, he made little or no Discovery of the Enemy saving where Capt Lovewell had his fight there he found the place where the Bodies of twelve of our men and four of the Enemy were buried.

As they went up by the side of Ossaby River they found a dead body and judge it to be Capt Lovewell's Lieu^t I would have sent Capt Slocom with the Hostages before this had there been any Winds thó loth to part with the sloop till another Sloop arrivd, it being of absolute necessity to have one constantly here, we having frequent Occasion to remove Provision from place to place, according to our marches. If you Hon^r shou'd think fit, I believe it wou'd be best that all the Officers return to their Posts assoon as their Affairs will admitt of it, so that we may be in the best posture we can in all our Frontiers to receive the Enemy in case they shou'd make their Attempts on us.

      I am Your Hon^{rs} most Dutifull Servt
        Thos Westbrook
Falmouth 22^d June 1725

Letter Col. T. Westbrook to Lt Gov. Dummer

May it please your Hon^r
    I wrote the Enclos'd about ten a Clock in the forenoon, Capt Franklin arrived here about Eight a Clock in the evening by whom I rece'd your Honors orders

Dated the 16th Curr.t which I shall strictly observe, I have this morning landed the stores, and now wait for a fair wind to send Cap.t Penhallow with twenty men on board the Sloop to proceed to Arrowsick & S.t Georges to see wether the Indians have not attackt those garrisons in as much as I cannot learn any thing of them up this way.

I had forgot to inform in the enclosed that Sacaristy says that there was Sixty Indians at Black point when they burnt the houses and killd the Cattle there on the 29.th of last April and that it was the same Indians that fought Cap.t Lovewell at Ossiby which well agrees with Lovells fight that being the 7th of May following

Falm.o June 23.d 1725.

I am your Hon.rs most dutifull humble Servant

Tho.s Westbrook

P. S.

I would fain wait till Cap.t Bourn comes down that I may settle Indian Comp.ys so that they may be easy.

T. W.

Letter Col. John Appleton to L.t Gov. Dummer.

Ipsw̃ June 23.d 1725

May it Pleas Yō Hon.r/

You.r Hon.rs Order came to my hand on Tuesday y.e 22.th the 23th they March.d Cap.t Joseph Gold Comand.r w.th a full Troop to the Estward according to Yo.r Hon.r order ~

The Troops in y.e Reigment of Late do not consist more then 40. Men besides theire officers — considering the difficulty & dange.r of theire Marching in the Estward parts, I have taken out of Ipswich & Rowly Troop to make him a full Troop to y.e numb̄ of Six.ty Men, they are all likely Men & are well fitted, & goe out w.th good Courage (if I have transgressᵈ I pray that yoʳ Honʳ woold Signify it to me I had no ordʳˢ, to subsist the men; I ordered euery Man to take 3 or 4 days provition to carry them to Wells: & I Assured them it woold be allowᵈ as heretofore

 I am Yoʳ Honʳˢ Most Obdᵗ most Humble Servᵗ
John Appleton

A. Cumings Esqre to Mr Secretary Popple.
[Inclosing Memorial.]

S.ʳ

Inclosed I have sent you the Memoriall of the Officers of the Customes in these parts to the Right Honᵇˡᵉ board representing the trade of these Plantations for the Lordships Consideration.

 I wrote some time Since to the Honᵇˡᵉ Board about a Scheme for Saving the Nation £80000 pound p annum which if ther Lordships approve off shall be ready to obey ther commands.

The fishery att Canso this year is very great and like to be Successfull about 200 saill of Small vessels gone from these parts to fish on that coast and if have protection will prove very considerable and Beneficial to the British nations for returnes of the Commodities Imported here.

The Great Currency of Paper bills of Credite very hurtfull to Trade and the Expedient of Issuing them forth upon Loan has been very prejudicial thesse affairs of Trade require Serious consideration and a Speedy releif which I doubt not but ther Lordships will give ther ready Concurrence therto please Give my humble duty to ther Lordships and accept of my Sincere respects to your Self who am upon all occasions

    S.ʳ Your most Obedient Humble Serv.ᵗ
Arch.ᵈ Cumings

Boston June 23.ᵈ 1725
To Allured Popple Esq.ʳ

Letter L! Gov. Dummer to Col. Johnson Harman.

"Lett{r} to L! Colo Harman June 23 1725."

If you Can Inlist men to make up your Comp{e} It will bee very acceptable to Me wch I choose rather than Impressing & do hereby give you direction for what Able Men you Can gett for that purpose who are not of the County of Yorke

Y—/

To Collo Johnson Harman
  Boston 25th June 1725.

Letter Col. T. Westbrook to Lt Gov. Dummer

Falm{o} June 24th 1725

May it please your Hon{r}

  Some hours after I had Seal'd my last the wind came fair for Cap{tn} Penhallow to go East which he Embract, and the Sloop had not been out of sight more than an hour before I rec'd a verbal acct from Lt Dominicus Jordan (who was out with his Scout) that the Indians had kill'd a man at Spurwink garrison, and that he heard the Guns, and was on ye spott in less then two hours, I cannot give a further Acct at present, Capt Kenady will be able to inform your Hon{r} the posture wee are in at this time. If your Hon{r} should think fitt I will give Lieut Jordan the Command of the second Company of Indians.

  I am your Hon{rs} most dutifull Humb! Servant
        Thos Westbrook

To the Kings most Excellent Majesty

  The Memorial and address of the Lieutenant Governor, Council and Representatives of the Province of the

Massachusets Bay, in New England in General Court Assembled

Most Humbly Sheweth

That this Your Majesty's Government after many unjust and insufferable abuses, Depredations and Insults committed by the Indians; Instigated and excited by the French King's Subjects, and more especially by Monsieur Vaudreuil Governour of Canada, were obliged contrary to their own inclinations to enter into a War with them which has now continued these Three Years and is become almost insupportable to this Province, by reason of the Excessive Charge thereof, besides the great Loss Your Majesty's Subjects have Sustained both in their Husbandry and Fishery, and in their other Business by Sea and Land the Slaying and Captivating many of your Majesty's good Subjects w^h is owing to the Conduct of the said French Government and the wicked practices of the Jesuits, and other Romish Priests, although the s^d Monsieur Vaudreuil has often by your Majestys Governor and Lieutenant Governor been wrote to on that Head, and of late Commissioners were sent from this Your Majesty's Government to demand of him to withdraw that aid and assistance he has afforded to our Indian Enemys notwithstanding which, and all the measures that have been taken to induce him to desist, he still goes on, and even while the Commiss^{rs} were in Canada the last Winter, the said French Governor (as he had often done) was exciting and persuading, several other Tribes of Indians to the War against Your Majesty's Subjects of this Province, as the Indians themselves informed them, and after much expostulation on this head with the said Governor, he had the assurance in behalf of the Indian Enemy to insist upon it. That this Government should quit and abandon all the Forts and Towns for the Space of Thirty Leagues on the Sea Coasts within the Grant to this Province, from Your

Majesty's Royal Predecessors which has been settled and peopled more than Seventy Years. In which Tract of Land groweth most of the Timber fit for building Ships and Masting Your Majesty's Navy, and the Said French Governor countenanced the Indians, then in his presence in their Demand of the whole Country, or Territory of L'Accadie or Nova Scotia, excepting only Your Majesty's Fort of Annapolis Royal, and that the British Subjects should not Fish in and about the Sea Coasts, whereby they would be stript of the most valuable Branch of their Trade and an unspeakable Damage happen even unto Your Majestys Realm of Great Britain in both these Articles; and althô it was strenuously urged by the agents for this Government upon the French Governor, That his Conduct herein was a manifest Breach of the Friendship between the two Crowns, and the Treaty of Peace concluded at Utrecht, whereby all Nova Scotia or L'accadie was surrendred up according to its ancient bounds or Limits to Your Majesty, Your Heirs and Successors for ever, and the French King's Subjects to have nothing to do therein, yet the S.^d Governor has constantly a French officer in the Pay of the French King at the head of the Indians who resides in Your Majesty's Dominions and we are informed by some of our Captives, he hath been so inhuman as to suffer five of Your Majesty's Subjects to be murthered and burnt after they were taken, and upon this Government demanding by their Commissioners Your Majesty's Subjects Captivated by the Indians and in the hands of French at Canada, the Governor of that Country refused to deliver or return them, unless they were purchased, and that at an exorbitant price, so that it cost the Relatives of some of those distressed people upwards of Fifty pounds a piece for the Recovery of their friends who are bought and sold and treated more like Slaves than Christians.

We would with all humility represent to Your Majesty that

the plain design of the French Governor in this management is to deprive Your Majesty of Your just Sovereignty over these Tribes of Indians and to prevent Your Majesty's Subjects settling in those parts of the Country, and Supplying Your Royal Navy with Masts Planks and Timber of all Sorts and threatens the Destruction of the Fishery on the whole Coast of L'Accadie and as far Westward as Piscataqua River, all which would not only be an unjust Diminution of Your Majesty's Rightfull and extended Dominion in North America but also prejudicial to the Several Provinces and Governments therein, and even to the Trade and Commerce of Great Britain.

And in as much as your Majesty's Colonies of Rhode Island and Connecticut are covered by us and the Towns of this Province are a Barrier and Security to them, and Your Majesty's Commands have been heretofore given to Your Severall Governm^{ts} of the Massachusetts, New York Connecticut and Rhode Island for furnishing their respective Quotas to each other in Case of a War, and pursuant thereto we have made application to them for obtaining their Quotas in the present War, Yet we have not been able to prevail with them to furnish the same altho' this Government have heretofore supplied a Considerable number of Soldiers for the Defence of Albany, within the Government of New York when in Great Distress by the Enemy.

We therefore humbly Supplicate Your most Gracious Majesty that you will please to renew your Command to those Governments for that End, and that Your Majesty will direct your Governor at New York, to use his Interest with the Six Nations of Maquois bordering upon his Government to joyn with us against the Indian Enemy.

All which is most humbly offered and submitted to Your Majesty's just, Wise and most Gracious Consideration and Compassion by Your Majesty's Most Loyal Dutifull and

Obedient Servants and Subjects The Lieutenant Governour, Council and Representatives of the Province of the Massachusets Bay

By their Order
Boston June 25th 1725   Josiah Willard Secretary

E :) *Copy of a Memorial from the Lieutenant Governour of New England.*

E : *New England Lre from Mr Delafaye of ye 25th of Septr 1725 referring to ye Board by order of ye Lds Justices a Memorial & address from ye Lt Govr Council & Assembly of ye Massachusets Bay, relating to a Quota of assistanse from ye Neighbouring Colonies ag.^t ye Indians Recd. Septem.^r 27th   Read Septem.^r 30 : 1725.*

Letter Col. T. Westbrook to Lt Gov. Dummer

May it please your Hon^r

I rec^d your Hon^{rs} orders of the 19th and of the 21st on the 26th of this Ins.^t ab.^t nine or ten a Clock at night, I immediately dispacth repeated orders to all our fronteirs in the County of York to be strict on their gaurds, and orders to Capt Moulton to Assist the Cap^{ts} of the Troops with experienct and faithfull Pilots. — I constantly keep out Scouts some distance from the Towns endeavouring to make discovery. — I wrote some Letters p Cap^{tn} Kenady which will not be long before they come to your Hon^{rs} hands. — I diligently searcht to find out wch way y.^t Scout came y.^t killed ye man at Spurwink but cannot find out unless they came by water.

I am your Hon^{rs} most Dutiful Humb^l Servant
Falm.^o June 26th 1725   Thos Westbrook

Letter L! Gov. Wm Dummer to Col. T. Westbrook.

Sir,

I am inform'd that the Indians lately enlisted under Cpt. Bourne especially those 11. that Came last to you p Saunders have complained of great Injustice done them by Defrauding them of a Part of the Money allow'd by the Governm! for their Enlisting which was 20/. a Man. I would therefore have you take the first Opportunity, To enquire of the Indians if they can charge any of the Officers concern'd in Detaining from them their Money. And if any of them say they have not rec^d the whole of their Premium, Call the Officer that gave them their Money & the Indians that complain before you, And make the strictest Inquiry into the Truth of this Matter; For if I find the Indians have been any Ways oppress'd I shall take Care that full Satisfaction be given them, And such Officers shall have the utmost Marks of my Displeasure. Therefore I expect that you be very much in Earnest about this Inquiry.

I enclose An Acc? of intelligence I have from some that are acquainted wth the Indians affaires, which may be of use to you thô. I doubt not but you have taken Care to gett the best information in order to pforme some such service now When you shall have a good Number of Men with you I have two Deserters in Custody, one in Cambridge Goal & the other In Newbury, who being notorious offenders I shall by Advice of the Councill putt over into your Hands to be try'd by a Court Martial for an Example of Terrour to others It being of the highest Consequence to Check that Speritt amounghst the fforces. they shall both of them be Secured in Newbury Goal forthwith & I direct you send downe a faithfull Serjeant wth Seaven Men to take them into Custody & bring to Falmouth in order to their speedy tryal & you must take Care to have a sufficient number of officers to Make a Court. You shall have a more pticular Acc.t of these deserters in order to your proceedings lodged at Newbury to go along wth.

Letter J. Stoddard & J. Wainwright.

Portsmouth. June 28. 1725

S.r

The Sloop Merry-Meeting arrived at New-Castle yesterday about three of the Clock afternoon, and after the delivery of your Hon.rs Letter to Lieut.nt Gov.nr Wentworth he called his Council together, and by their advice did appoint Co.ll Shadrach Walton to Joyn with us in our Affair with the Eastern Indians, we hope he will be ready to goe on Board alittle after noon.

Lieut.nt Gov.nr Wentworth thinks that the Indians will not much encline to goe to Boston, but Choose rather to come to Casco-Bay, or Winter Harbour, which places he Judgeth more convenient for a Conference than Boston, where (he saith) those Indians did never meet on such an Occasion, and (accordingly) in his Instructions to Col.ll Walton, does allow him to agree to their coming to either of s.d places, if the Indians doe Insist upon it.

We are your Hon.rs most Humble Obedient Servants,

John Stoddard
John Wainwright

To His Hon.r Lieut.nt Gov.nr Dummer &c

Letter John Stoddard & John Wainwright to L.t Gov. W.m Dummer

from on board the Sloop Merry-Meeting at New-Castle, June 28 — 1725.

S.r

Since we wrote, Cap.t Slocum came into this Harbour with the two Indians, which are now on board with us. they tell us that the S^{nt} John^s and Cape Sable Indians have agreed to abide by what the Penobscott Indians have directed him to acquaint your Hon^r that they are willing to be at Peace, and that it lyeth with you whither there shall be Peace or not. they are desirous to treat in their own River which hath not been Stained with Blood. they further add that when we Come to S^{nt} George^s they can soon find some of the Penobscott Indians and bring them to us.

we are now weighing Anchour, and hope to be at Casco Bay before too Morrow Morning:

And are your Hon^{rs} Most Humble Servants

John Stoddard
John Wainwright

P. S.

This goes by Capt Slocum Who we desire may be dispatchd to Casco Bay as Soon as may be where we shall leave directions where we may be found —

Falmouth July 3^d 1725

May it Please your Hon^r/

I examin'd the undernamed Indians relating their Enlisting with Capt Bourn and they say they rec^d no more money than is Annex'd to each mans name. I immediately sent for Capt Bourn while they were present, and askt him the reason, his Answer was that he agreed with them for that sum and no more, which some of the Indians own'd and others made Excuses and said they did not so well understand it. Capt Bourns says that he Enlisted them in the Room of some that Deserted and inform'd them that they should receive wages from the time that the Deserters Enlisted & that they were well satisfy'd therewith.

I am Your Hon^{rs} most Dutifull Humble Servt
Thos Westbrook

John Comshite rec^d	£00, 11, 00	David Job	00, 10, 00
Jacob Paul	00, 10, 00	Aaron Wummock	00, 10, 00
Thomas Tarah	00, 10, 00	Joshua Hood	00, 10, 00
Tom Kennaway	00, 10, 00		

[Superscribed]
On his Maj^{ts} Service
To The Honble William Dummer Esqr Lieu^t Govr
& commander in cheif &c In Boston

Letter – Col. T. Westbrook to Lt Gov. Wm Dummer.

Falmouth July 3^d 1725.

May it Please your Hon^r/
I rec^d your Hon^{rs} Letters by Capt Bourn of the 24th and those pr Serj^t Parker of the 28th of last Month with the enclos'd Information relating–the Indians. I always make it my business to get the best Information relating–the Enemy I can, and Inform'd your Hon^r of the Indians living on the back of Mount Desert in my letter last September and that I was Inform'd they were supply'd from Annapolis by some man that married in that Country who supply'd one Bellisle, a frenchman who married with one of Casteen's Daughters and mostly lives thereabouts so that it well agrees with the Information Your Hon^r Enclos'd and likewise with what I inform'd in my Letter of the 17th of March 1724/5 that two Friars and several of them liv'd at Passimaquoddie and Adjacent to it; as to that part of the Information that they are up in the Countrey till the last of June about their Corn interfers with their yearly Customs in coming down the

last of May or not exceeding the first of June to gett Eggs and Fowl during wh^{ch} time they generally leave their old men & women to tend their Corn and then are down again the last of July or August Catching Sea Fowl and Seil. before I seald this I rec^d your Hon^{rs} p Coll^o Harmon the 3^d of July which was Dated the 25th of last Month. As to the Indians planting their Corn I wrote p Capt Kennedy the best Information I cou'd get at present. By your Hon^{rs} Orders to me I understand your Hon^r intends to visit the Penobscott Tribe. We have rec^d but four Whale boats since I wrote your Hon^r that we had few or none fit for service so that there is necessity of having them from the Castle and ten or twelve more. the Indians Capt Bourn Enlisted are most of them in the Woods, fourty are with Lt Jordan up Saco River whom I dont expect in this ten days and another party are with Capt Penhallow whom I have Directed to attend the Commissioners Orders so that I cant Settle them Comp^{ys} at present according to your Hon^{rs} Orders, I have therefore sent Capt Bourn with these Expresses to wait on your Hon^r hearing little of the Enemy and making no Discovery of them I woud desire to wait on your Hon^r a few days at Boston before I be put on any further Service. I shall take Care to leave the Frontiers on their Guard.

The Commissioners sail'd from this place ye 30th of last Month.

    I am Your Hon^{rs} most Dutifull Servt
        Thos Westbrook

Letter – Col. T. Westbrook to Lt Gov. Wm Dummer

        Falm^o July 3^d 1725

May it please your Hon^r /
    The Enclos'd is the Petitioners

Petition and his Acc.^t by wch your Hon.^r will see the little reason the poor fellow had to Complain.

I am your Hon^{rs} most dutiful Servant
Thos Westbrook

P. S.

    I rec.^d your Hon^{rs} letters p
Capt Bourn and Mr Parker the 2.^d Curr.^t

Letter Col. T. Westbrook to Lt Wm Dummer
Falm^o July 4th 1725

May it please your Hon^r

    As to the Two Deserters, wee have no manner of place at Falm^o to secure them, so that they will be a great clog to the service – neither have wee a sufficient number of Commission Officers to try them unless wee call them off from their several posts and Scouts so that the service will suffer the fronteirs being so long it is difficult getting them together. I would pray your Honour either to continue them where they are for the present till the Affaires are in a better posture, or that they be tryed by the Justices of the assises in the County where they were taken, as is explain'd in the Sixtht Article of the Martial Law However I submitt to your Hon^{rs} pleasure And am your Hon^{rs} most

Dutifull Humble Servant
Thos Westbrook

Petition of Robert Armstrong

    To the Right Honble the Lords Commissioners for Trade and Plantations.

    The humble' Petition of Robert Armstrong. Sheweth:

    That your Petitioner intends in a little Time to return to New England to do his Duty as Deputy Surveyor of his Majesty's Woods, which he has taken more Care to preserve (as he hopes sufficiently appears by the Papers before your Lordships) than any of his Predecessors have done.

That being Sensible how great an Injury he has received from Capt Ellis Huske, by his false accustations of your Petitioner, as being a Notorious Jacobite & a Person perjur'd on Record, He is resolved to do himself publick Justice in New England by bringing an Action of Damages against the Said Huske as soon as he arrives there.

That being advis'd by his Council here that he must Carry over sufficient Proofs to Support his Action & nothing less than an attested Copy from Your Lordpps Board of the said Huske's Information will do, He most humbly prays your Lordpps that such an authentick Copy may be Granted him.

And your Petitioner as in Duty bound shall every pray

Robert Armstrong.
6th July 1725.

Affidavit.

Falmouth July 6th 1725

Mr James March on his Arrival here informs y^t on Saturday last ye 3^d Curr^t in his coming from Kennebunk to Cape Porpoise he spake with a Sloop one Barns of Plymouth Master and informs y^t he came from Cape Neger that the Indians and French at that place had taken five Vessels that were his Consorts they being seven in Company and about an hundred Indians and French as near as they cou'd judge pursued after him another Vessel but they made their Escape.

Y S/.

The Bear^r Mr James March personally appear'd before me the Subscriber and Declares that the above mentioned Acc^t is what Barns the Master of s^d Sloop told him.

A true Coppy   John Gray Jus^t Pacis

Letter Col. T. Westbrook to Lt Gov. Wm Dummer
July 7, 1725.

May it please your Hon^r

The Lieu^t of the man of Warr arriv'd here the 6th Curr^t with a small Sloop they took from the Indians about Ten days ago, and one Samuel Trask whom he redeem'd from Casteen of whom I got the Enclosed Information and the other from Lieu^t James March, It seem to me as if the providence of God had sent him at this Juncture to do great service. I designe this night to follow Sanders & inform him of the Indian vessel for I question wether he be gone from St Georges, I hear nothing from Mr Grant if your Hon^r should draw my men from Berwick & Wells, I am of opinion that it would be best for the service to Draw the old Soldiers and let the new men gaurd the Inhabitants

Falm^o July 7th 1725

I am your Hon^{rs} most Dutiful Servt
Thos Westbrook

Letter – Col. T. Westbrook to Lt Gov. Wm Dummer
July 8. 1725

May it please your Hon^r

I have stopt Sam^{ll} Trask for the present by consent of Lieu^t Prichard for a Pilott, he has on board one Mr Bell that is a very good Pilott, I have talkt with him, he is willing to serve the Goverm^t if he can get his bread by it. if Capt Slocum be not saild it would be for the service to send him with Slocom and if he be to send him by the first, wee very much want Slocom

I am your Hon^{rs} most Dutifull servant

Falm^o July 8th 1725   Thos Westbrook

Letter – L! Gov. Wm Dummer to Gov. J. Wentworth

"Lett^r to Gov. Wentworth, July 9th 1725."

S^r

I must pray you to excuse me that I have not of late been more punctual in Acknowledging your Letters wch I don't use to be guilty of, but my time towards the End of the Sessions was a Little more than ordinarily taken up & has been Since. I Consulted the Council about your proposal for the Indians coming to Winter Harbour &c. but they were of opinion it was more honorable to Insist upon their Coming to Boston & I have sent orders Accordingly to our Commiss^{rs} & as I have Little faith of the Sinceritye of the Indians for a Peace at psent. & it seeming by Many Concurring Circumstances that they are Seeking an opertunitye to Surprise us & that they aime Cheifly at amusing us till they have gott in their Corne which wee have an Undoubted account that they have planted in Penobscott new Towne & Some Say in ye old Towne too, I have ordered About Two hundred & Twenty Men to March thether the Same Way that Capt Heath went the last Year & if you shall thinck fitt to Send a Company of your Men with them it will strengthen them & phaps Make the March More Chearful & I hope if it shall please God to Succeed us herein the Indians Will then be in earnest for a Peace & Come in whenever wee shall think it proper. I have order our fforces to March the 1^t of August. if you'l please to keep the Affair Secret as possible you may adjust the time of marching wth Coll^o Westbrook who is under order to be very Secret.

Letter – L! Gov. Wm Dummer to John Stoddard & John Wainwright.

"Letter to John Stoddard & John Wainwright, July 9th, 1725."

I hope ere this you^l receive my L^r by Capt Heath in answer to your last, who saild yesterday Morning with Capt Slocum, this incloses you Mr Winslows Acc.^o of the Indians proceeding at Sea & by this & Many other Accounts wee have of their Tracks by Land & they Killed at Spurwink You'l doubtless be of opinion that they have no honest intentions towards A peace as Yett & of the Necessity, (if it shall please God to favour us) of Making some other Impression on them. & of retaliating the Injuryes wee have rec.^d from the Penobscott Tribe & without that I doubt whether wee shall ever make a good & honorable Peace. I hope Sanders is seeking the Privaters before now. I have sent by ye same bearer to be Conveyed to Him this inteligence but if you have any opertunity of Communicating it more directly you'l do well to do it.

John Stoddard & John Wainwright Esq.^{rs} Comiss.^{rs} &c

Letter Lt Gov. Wm Dummer to Col. T. Westbrook.

"Letter to Coll Westbrook July 9th 1725

S.^r

I received Sundry of your Letters by Capt Bourne by whome you'l receive this. & I refer you to my L.^{rs} by Capt Heath who Saild with Slocum the 8.th instant by whome was sent you 29 Indians from Bristol County Command by Leif.^t Edwd Southworth.

I Cannot Consent to your Coming to Boston till the March for Penobscott bee proceeded on & then If you Should not go your Selfe, I shall be glad to See you in Towne but It would give me greater Satisfaction to have that Important Service Conducted by your selfe & desire nothing may hinder or delay that March but that the fforces May be well on their way by the 1.^t of August. the Gentlemen of the Councill to whome I have communicated It are in great Expectation of the Success of it & the Province being now at a Vast Charge & the People generaly well Spiritted for a Vigorous prosecution of the Warr It will become us to Strike while the Iron is hot.

You'l put 50 of the Indians under the Command of Capt Bourne forthwith and give orders to all the Officers & Commiss^r not to Lett them run in Debt for anything but mere Necessaryes, for otherwise it will impead the getting Indians in the Service an^r time

You'l have a Sloop Loaden with Stores of Provisions &c with you in a few Dayes. the Treasurer have taken one up already for that Service. Slocum brings 4 Whale boats & I shall order in a Little time.

If You have not sent to Newbury for those Deserters You may Defer that Matter till further Order.

> You Will always remember that this matter must be kept an Inviolable Secret And therefore You must make what Amusements You think proper for that end.

Letter – Lt Gov. Wm Dummer to Col. T. Westbrook.

"Letter to Coll^l Westbrook & Capt Sanders 9th July 1725."

This incloses you An Acc^t I just now rec^d of the Enterprises of the Indians upon your Coast I have sent one to be forwarded to Capt Sanders if you have any opertunity you'l do well to send Him a duplicate keep a good looke out The Indians will Certainely Surprise you if they Can if it were onely to introduce an honorable peace for them.

Y

Coll^l. Westbrook/

Letter – Lt Gov. Wm Dummer to Capt Sanders 9th July 1725.

This inclose You An Account I recev^d this Day of the Indian Enterprises at Sea. I make no doubt but youl do the utmost to finde & Surprise them you have now an opertunity by the favor of God to do Some good Service. I hav nothing more to ad but depend on your Industry Vigilance & Courage I shall bee in hope every Day to receive some good Acc^o from you & am Y^r ffriend to serve you
Capt Sanders.

Letter J. Stoddard Sha Walton & Jno Wainwright. Comm^{rs} to Wenemonet & other chiefs.

St Georges July 10th 1725

Sungamock,

We received Your Letter of the twentieth Instant New Stile, wherein You Complain of Unjust & Unchristian Treatment You have received from Liev^t Manoor.

We know of no Man of that Name, yet doubtless we shall be able when we arrive at Boston to understand who it is that hath perpetrated So Vile an Action, and shall readily use Our Interest that the Man may be brought to Justice.

The Action as Represented by you is detestable, and ought not to be Countenanced by any Government, especially by those that profess Christianity. Whether you are rightly informed of the Facts we shall not be able to judge until we hear what the Man can say for himself. We should more readily conclude that the Relation of the Action Made to You was reall, if We were assured that the French man from whom You had it was not a Gainer by the War, but if you can produce those Letters, Your Messengers inform us, were Sent on shoar by the officer You Mention, it will enable the Governments to convict him of his perfidious Dealing.

We do assure you that no Vessell hath been Sent by the Governments to Penobscot or thereabout with a flagg of Truice, and if any Man hath pretended to Set up such a Signal, he hath done it of his own mere Motion, which is an Abuse offered to the Governments, and tends to bring the publick Faith in Question.

We were Sent hither by the Governments of the Massachusetts Bay and New Hampshire, as we informed you in Our former Letter, and have with us Capt Bane and Capt Jordan who are known to You, and have been seen by divers of your people.

We have already given you Assurances of your Safety in Case You Come hither.

We are desirous to make a Speedy return, Yet shall make Our Selves easy Six days by which Time You may doubtless be here you being at little Distance, which Appears from your Letter's being dated yesterday, which was the twentieth New Stile.

In the Name & by Order of the Governments of the Massachusetts Bay and New Hampshire

Jno Stoddard
Sh$\tilde{a}$ Walton } Commission^{rs}
Jno Wainwright

To Wenemonet & the other Chiefs of the Indian Tribes.−

Copy

Letter Capt Joseph Heath to L^t. Gov. Wm Dummer

Falmouth July 12th 1725

Honorable

Sr The 11th Currant I came heither & Delivered to Colo^l Westbrook the Indians with y^e four whale Boats and Your Honours Letters.

I continue Exceeding week, & tho Heartily willing, fear I shall not be able to march as appointed; And least I should not have Strength to Travel, would Humbley Suggest to your Honour that Capt Wheelwright and Ensigne Bradbury who were with me last winter, are able to pilote the army through, whose Greatest Difficulty will be the length of ye way & want of water.

I am Your Honours Most Humble Obedient Servant

Joseph Heath

Colo^l Westbrook has (with a Suitable
Caution) acquainted me with your
Honours Last Orders to him, which
is ye Cause of my writing as above.

Letter ~ Col. T. Westbrook to L^t. Gov. Wm Dummer

May it Please your Hon^r /

I rec^d your Hon^{rs} Orders p Cp^t Heath Dated ye 6th Curr^t on the 11th Ins^t whereon I immediately Dispatcht Orders to Lieu^t Coll^o Harmon with what men of his Comp^y he had left to march immediately to this Place, and to draw ten men from Berwick out of Capt Olivers Company and eight out of Capt Wheelwrights Comp^y concluding them Towns would be well coverd with the Remainder and the Troops. At the same time sent Orders to Capt Grant to march in five or six days or I should stay for him. I doubt not but to have the Army on their March before ten days be out if I dont stay for some of the Forces from York and Berwick. I just now rec'^{d} your Hon^{rs} Orders and Express to Coll^o Stoddard and Capt Sanders p Capt Oliver about eleven of the Clock. Capt Oliver informs me that Capt Grant was to march the 12th Ins^t so I am oblig'd to draw 10 men more from Capt Oliver. Our People think it will be hard to march to the White hills at this time of the year the Weather being so hot. Capt Oliver heard one of the Troopers who had been at Boston say that he was in hopes the Troops would be dismist by the middle of this week. if so those towns will be very much Expos'd. My Express got to York on the 12th Curr^t

I doubt not but Capt Heath will be able to march altho' he seems to doubt it.

Falm? July 13th 1725

I am your Hon^{rs} Most dutifull Humb! Servant

Thos Westbrook

PS

I don't expect to sleep much night nor Day till I have gott the army on their march. I thankfully acknowledge your Hon^{rs} favour in leaveing it either for me to go or stay I hope I shall be ready on their return to head the next party and be able to satisfie your hon^r why I stay now.

Tho Westbrook

[Superscribed]

On his Maj^{ties} Special Service to The Honble William Dummer Esqr Lieu^t Govr and Commander in Cheif &c

In Boston

To be delivered to the Hon^{bl} Lieu^t Govr Wentworth so that there may be no delay.

I hope y^r Hon^r will not think I mistake your orders, for if y^{ll} please to refer to y^r last y^{ll} see I understand them

Letter Josiah Willard, Secretary, to Col. T. Westbrook

Boston July 14, 1725.

Sir,

His Honour the Lieut. Govr (who is now at the Castle) bids me tell you That upon Cpt. Bourns earnest Request, He has given him a Dismission from the Service, And therefore he Orders That Cpt. Dominicus Jordan (whose Commission will be sent in a few days) command one Comp.ª of Indians, And that Cpt. Kennedy have the Command of the other for this Expedition & that Lieut. Wright be Kennedys Lieutenant; That with the other Indians & a proper Number of English to be joined with them a Compª be made up for Cpt. Heath; It being necessary that a good Number of Officers should go upon this March, His Honour thinks it will not be needful for you to have the Command of a particular Compª.

I am likewise to inform you That his Honr. has dismiss'd the Troops at Berwick & Wells. I heartily wish you Success in yre Enterprize, And am with sincere Respects (Sir)

Your most humble Servt

J Willard

If you can project any particular Service by Sea wherein Mr Bell may be useful to you, his Honr. will very willingly encourage him

J W

*Letter Col. T. Westbrook to Lt. Gov. Wm Dummer
July 21, 1725*

May it Please your Honr

I rec^d your Honrs Orders p Capt Kennedy on the 20th Currt. About half the Army marcht for Richmond the 20th Inst. and this day the rest will march if the Weather will admitt and if something not now seen do not prevent they will march from Richmond on the Twenty fourth of this month. If there be any thing design'd against the Enemy on the return of the Army at St Johns Passimaquoddi and in Penobscott Bay, then Mr Bell would be of Service.

Falmouth July 21st 1725

I am your Honrs most Dutifull Servt

Thos Westbrook

P. S. This night since I wrote the above there is Run Twenty two Indians out of Capt Kenadys Company since I gave him the Command of it, notwithstanding I shall have the Army on their march as soon as the Weather permitts. I fear there has been some bad advise given them which I am endeavouring to find out ———

The bearer Ensign Williams has been in the service about a year and has behav'd himselfe very well of whom I shall endeavour to give y^r Hon^r a more perticular Acc^t

I am as above   T W

*Letter J. D de St Castin to Lt Gov. Wm Dummer
July 23, 1725.*

Sir

j have the honour to acquaint you that the 9th of this present month as j rode at anchor in a small harbour about three miles distant from Nesket, having with me but one jndian and one Englishman whom j had redeemed from the Salvages, as well as my vessel, j was attackt by an English vessel, the Commander of which called himself Lieutenant of the King's Ship, and told me also his name which j cannot remember. Seing my self thus attackt and not finding myself able to deffend myself j withdrew into the wood forsaking my vessel. The Commander of the vessel called me back promising me with an oath not to wrong me at all, saying that he was a merchant who had no dessein but to trade and was not fitted out for war, specially when there was a talk of peace and presently Set up a flag of truce, and even gave me tow safe-conducts by writing which j have unhappily lost in the fight—

Thus thinking my self safe enough j came back on board my vessel, with my jndian and my Englishman, whom j brought to Shew that j had no thoughts of fighting, and that j had redeemed him from the jndians as well as the vessel.

But as j was going to put on some cloathts to dress my self more handsomly the Commander who was com in my vessel with severall of his people would not permitt me to do it, telling me that j was no more master of any thing, he only granted me after many remonstrances to set me ashore. But after j came down and They held forth to me a bag full of bisket that was given to me as They said as a payment for my Englishman, They did catch hold of me and the jndian who accompanyed me. j got rid of him who was going to seize upon me, but my jndian not being able to do the same, j betook my self to my Arms, and after several voleys, j Kild the man who Kept him, and got him safe with me. This is the second time that I have been thus treacherously used, which proceedings, j do not suppose that you approve off, as being against the laws of Nations. Therefore j hope that you will do me justice, or at least you will cause me to be reimbursed of the loss j have sustained, namely,

For the vessel that costed me   80 french pistoles
For the English man   10 pistoles
51 pounds of beaver that were in the vessel with 20 otters 3 coats that costed me together 20 pistoles. 56 pounds of shot that costed twenty pence a pound. 20 pounds of powder at 4 livres a pound. 10 pounds of tobacco at 20 pence a pound. A pair of Scales 8^{tt} livres. Tow cloth blanketts each 23 livres Tow bear skins 8 livres apiece. 4 skins of sea-woolf 8 livres for the four. 3 axes. 15 livres for both. 2 Kettles 30 livres for both, and severall other matters which They would not grant me not so much as my cap. The retaken English man knoweth the truth of all this his name is Samuell Grass of the Town of Salem near Marblehead

         I have the honour to be Sir
             Your most humble & most Obedient Servant
                   joseph Debadis de St Castin
At Pentagous   23 july 1725.

Letter Capt. S. Wheelwright to Lt Gov. Wm Dummer
July 26, 1725.

May it pleas Your Hon^r

This day about Eleven of the Clock In the forenoon a man being on Some Occasion out att an old setlement about a mile distant above the garisons discover'd ten Indians being surprised hid himself untill they Passed not knowing whither they ware Enemys or Deseaters:

As soon as I had the acount Geathering my men with all Spead att the Severell Garisons My Enis^n with four men on Hors-back Coming to me discovred part of the Indians Coming out: In the scirts of the woods Rode Quick upon them and Requiered there Submistion Charging them with Desertion which they submited too and on Examination understood there was two more In the bushes he sent two of the men to Search for them who Endevered to make there Escape but the men being on hors back soon heded them and then they allso Submited and on Examination they all Say that they ware Incoriged by Liv^{tt} Bacon Liv^{tt} House and Ens^n Stanfort to deseart and that Enis^n Stanfort Promised that he would meet them att York: I heave Sent the ten Deserters vnder geard to Liv^{tt} Brown Att Arondall to be Convay'd too Co^{ll} Westbrook att Falmoth.

from your Hono^{rs} Most Hum^{ll} and Duitfull Servant
Sam^{ll} Wheelwright

Wells July: 26: 1725

Letter Capt. S. Wheelwright to Col. T. Westbrook
July 26, 1725

Hon^d Sir

This day about Eleven of the Clock one of my men being at Little River discovered ten Indians who run away from the Army and thinking they were Enemeis they came & made report thereof; I immediately sent for my men in ord.^r to Pursue them but while they were comeing together they were discovered by some of them near the highway, about a mile from my Fathers whom wee presently Secur'd and took their Arms from them. I askt them the reason why they Deserted from their Posts, they told me they were Encourag'd by Lieu.^t Bacon Lt Hows and En.^s Stanford which was the reason of their Desertion and further said that En.^s Stanford promisd to meet them at York I have sent the above said Deserters under a Gaurd to Lt Brown to be Convey'd along to your Hon^r

   from your Hon^{rs} most Humble servant
      Samuel Wheelwright

Wells July 26th 1725.
 a Coppy To Coll.^o Thomas Westbrook Esqr

Letter Col. T. Westbrook to Lt Gov. Wm Dummer July 28, 1725.

May it please your Hon.^r /

   The bearer En^s Noble is the Gentleman whom y^r Hon^{or} wrote to me of in the year 1723 to take notice of and to acquaint your Hon.^r of his behaviour. he has always readily observed Command and faithfully Complyed with all orders he has rec^d from time to time.

 Falm.^o July 28th 1725.
   I am your Hon^{rs} most Dutifull Servant
      Thos Westbrook

P S
 When I have settled the Army in order
 to gaurd the People, On your Hon^{rs}
 form^r ord'rs shall presume to visit my
 family for a few days   T W

Letter R. Waldron to L^t. Gov. J. Wentworth

Cochecho 31st July 1725

Hon^{rble} S^r

last night came in here Cap^{ts} Wyman & White & say that before they got to Penny Cook their men began to be taken sick, wth a bloody flux, soe that they were forc'd to Send Sundry back before they got to penycook & that the distemper Increased daily till they had not men enough to carry their own & Sick mens packs, & at last hardly 20 men in a Company were the Successive rains were very hurtfull & very much retarded their march by raising ye brooks & rivers, & by that time they got to the upper end of Winipiciauky pond they found their further March as was designed Impracticable so were forc'd to return bringing in one of their Sick men upon their Shoulders. The two Cap^{ts} came to me this morning & were very sollicitous that their Lt Govr might have an Acc^{tt} of their return assoon as possible, I told y^m. I w^d Imediately dispatch it to our Lt Govr who I was well assured w^d Expresse it to Lt Govr. assoon as if went hence direct, & this is the onely needfull at p^{r}s^t. from

Yo^r Hon^{rs}. most humble Servt

Richd Waldron

[Superscribed]
For his Maj^{ties} Service To the Hon^{rble}
John Wentworth Esq$_,$ Lt Govr. of N Hampshire
In Portsm^o

Letter — L^t. Gov. Wm Dummer to Col. T. Westbrook

Boston July 31, 1725.

Sir

This comes by Express to Acquaint you That I have Agreed with the Penobscot Indians on a Cessation of Arms every where to the Eastward of Kennebeck River, W^{ch} you must take Care to have strictly & exactly observed till my further Order And give Directions y^t ye Indians be well received at the Fort on St Georges River, and that what Messages they bring in from their Tribe be forwarded to me with all possible Dispatch: You must (the Hour you receive this) Order Cpt. Grant to disband his Company of Voluntiers: And for the Rest of the Forces, They must be employed in Guarding the Inhabitants in their Work in the several Towns that so they may be as beneficial as possible. If any other Companies of Voluntiers come in to your Posts, You must acquaint the Captains that I Order them forthwith to conduct their Companies Home in that they may there be ready for any further Directions.

Notwithstanding this Truce You must take Care that the Forts & Garrisons be carefully guarded to prevent any Surprise from the Indians.

"*Orders to Capt White & Wyman Augt 7th 1725*"

S^{rs}/

I received an Acc^o from Coll^o Westbrook of your returne to Cochecho I am very sorry for the Sickness & the difficultys of a Wet Season that has Attended your March, & make no dout but you have done the uttmost practicable under those pressures & Misfortunes, but Since It has Pleased God it should be so & that we have lately Concluded a Cessation of Arms wth the Penobscott Indians in order to bringing about a general peace. I Would have repair home & disband your Companyes & make up your Muster Roll forthwith allowing each man to stand untill his Arrival home.

Letter Capt. James Grant to Lt Gov. Wm Dummer
Aug. 7, 1725.

May it Please your Honour

I Have Rec^d a letter from Col^l Westbrook of the first Instant, Wherein he Says it is your Honours Order, That

Upon Sight Thereof I should disband my Company of Voluntiers.

These are therefore to pray your Honour to Allow me to Say That it looks very hard, if it be so. That we should be disbanded almost as soon as Enlisted.

We have put ourselves out of the way to serve the publick as Voluntiers, Upon the Encouragement given by the Genl. Assembly; And we had Never been at the Trouble and Charge we have to, to fit our Selves for this Service, were it Not that we Thought we had the publick Faith to Secure us, as I think we have in the late Act, which Says, That the Encouragment (therein mentioned) is to Continue from the Enlistment to the first of November.

We Expect the Benefit of this Act, the war Continuing and other Companys are Kept in the service, Else It will prove but a snare to us, & we shall not have Justice done us —

I pray y^r Honour to Countermand this Order for our Disbanding, And Allow us to make one Essay at least, if it may be, after the Enemy, according to the Act, for we are In Debt, and I have given Reciepts to the Comissarys for what my Men were Necessitated to take up when at ye Eastw^d to fit them for ye then Intended march und^r Col. Westbrook; And Unless my men Can Get somthing this way to pay me, I must loose it, as farr as I Know — Many of them being very poor men —

I pray y^r Honours favour in this matter as farr as is consistent with Justice and the publick Good —

    I am Y^r Honours most obedient humble Servt
Berw: Augst 7th 1725   James Grant
    [Superscribed]
   On his Maj^{tys} Service

To The Hon^{rble} William Dummer Esqr Lev^t Govern^r and Comand^r in chief in and over his Maj^{tys} Province of the Massachusetts Bay &c

Letter Col. T. Westbrook to Lt *Gov. W*^{m} *Dummer*
Aug. 12, 1725.

May it please your Hon^r
I receivd your Hon^{rs} orders on the Eighth Curr^t about Ten at Night and the next morning Dispatcht orders to the several Officers as p the Enclosed & am now sending through the fronteirs to get a pticular state of the Army psuant to your Honours orders & shall send them as soon as possible Leiu^t Col^o Harmon expects to get on his march by the 17th of this Month at furthest if something not yet known do not prevent

I am your Hon^{rs} most dutifull Servant
Thos Westbrook

York August 12th 1725

Letter Col. T. Westbrook to Lt *Col. J. Harmon Aug. 12. 1725.*

Sir
Pursuant to His Hon^r Leiu^t Govr Dummers orders to me to draw out one Hundred effective men for you to take the immediate command of and march them according to the Gov^{r}s Instructions to you delivered you by me on the Eleventh of this Ins^t the officers & their men are as follows Viz^t Yourselfe & Thirty one of your Company, Capt Heath & Twenty three of his Company Capt Sam^{ll} Jordan to send En^s Noble & Eleven men of his Company, Capt Dominicus Jordan & Thirty eight of his Company and I have sent ord^{rs} to the officers of each party on the 9th Currant to march to Falmouth & there equip their men for twenty two days march and wait further orders, excepting Capt Heath and he to be ready equipt at Brunswick, and I expect they will be all waiting by the 13th Curr^t to receive your Commands.

I have nothing further to add but to recommend it to you to make all the Dispatch with all the secrecy possible it being his Hon.^r the Leiu.^t Gov.^{rs} pticular orders.

I am S.^r yours to serve
T. W

P S

On your return direct each Officer and his party to their posts & Capt Heath to send Capt Kenadys men to him. Docter Bullman is to attend you

T W

York August 12.th 1725
Leiu.^t Col.^o Johnson Harmon

Letter Lt Gov. Wm Dummer to Col. Armstrong Aug. 16, 1725

Sir

I have the Hon.^r of y.^{re} Letter of the 29.th of June last, And cann't but be surprized at the Exceptions you take At y.^{re} not being Advised of the two Sloops fitted out here to cruize on the Eastern Coast of this Province, Since at the time of their Departure Your Arrival in these Parts was not known here, Nor have you since till on this Occasion thought fit to Notify me thereof, Or of y.^{re} having his Majesties Commission for Lt Govr of Nova Scotia, W.^{ch} I think would have been but agreable to the Practice amongst Gentlemen in our Station, & your Intentions express'd in your Letter such; W.^{ch} duly considered, would have left no Room for Censuring me as wanting in Complaisance & Friendship: And you may assure y.^{er}self Nothing shall be wanting on my Part to maintain a good Neighbourhood & for Acting in Concert with you in such Matters as concern his Majesties Service & the Mutual Advantages of the two Provinces, so long as I have the Hon.^r to serve his Majesty in this Station.

I have communicated y.^{re} Lett.^r to his Maj.^{ies} Council of this Prov. & have taken their Opinion as to those Articles in it that are of a more publick Concern, And with their Advice I nowe inform you That some Time in June last divers Indians of Penobscot came into the Fort at S:t Georges under a Flagg of Truce, had in their Discourse with the Officers there manifested their Inclination to Peace and their Desire that some Gent. might be sent from this Governm:t to confer further with them on that Subject. In Compliance with w^{ch} & at the Motion of the Gen:ll Assembly, I sent two Gent. to S:t Georges with Instructions (of which you have a Copy enclosed) They mett a considerable Number of Indians, who all express'd their Disposition to Peace, And sent two of their Chief Men to Boston to ask a Cessation of Arms till they could get all their People together & engage the Neighbouring Tribes to act in concurrence with them in Sending their Delegates to Boston to make their Submission to his Majesty, & agree upon Articles of Pacification: The Issue of our Conferences with these two Men was our Granting them a Cessation in all parts to the Eastw:d of Kennebeck River, for the Space of Forty Days from the Landing of these Messengers at their Return As you will see by the s:d Conferences wch I have also enclosed. What further Intelligence I may have of the Dispositions & Intentions of the Indians as to this Affair I shall communicate to you, as I have Opportunity. If you think it will be for his Majesties Service & for the Benefit of y^{re} Governm:t to send y^{re} Deputies to this Treaty We shall be very glad of their Assistance therein.

We thank you for the Regard you express for the Interests of this Prov. as well in the Protection & Encouragem:t given to our Fishery (W^{ch} will very much contribute to the growing and flourishing Estate of ye Province under your Governm:t & be for the Advantage of the Trade of G:t Britain (& therefore (without Doubt a Service very acceptable to his Majesty) As allso for y^{re} Suspending y^{re} Treaty with the Indians, That so Deputies from this Governm:t might act in

Concert with you for the Safeguard of the Subjects of both Provinces; But forasmuch as our Treaty with the Penob. Indians is (in all Probability) so near And y^{res} at Annapolis so distant & uncertain, We have not concluded to send any Deputies to appear for us at Annapolis, Confiding in your wise & successful Managem^t of that Affair, And that you will have a Regard to the Interests of his Majesties Subjects in Gen^{ll} as well as of your own Province at the same time We promise you to have the like Care of the Governm^t & People of Nova Scotia in our Treaty with the Indians here. As to your Proposal for our Sending 60 Indians to join with your Forces to stike a Terror into the Enemy, We should very cheerfully comply with this Motion, but for some invincible Difficulties that ly in the Way of it; For besides That our Charter absolutely forbids the Marching any of the Inhabitants out of the Limits of the Prov. without their free & voluntary Consent or the Consent of the General Assembly (who are not sitting at this Time) It will be esteem'd a Breach of our Truce with the Penob. Indians If we sh^d March an arm'd Force into any Part of Nova Scotia; as to the Supplys given to the French in y^{re} Neighbourhood, This Governm^t have it much at Heart & would be glad to come into any proper Measures to prevent that Trade, And I have not been wanting in my Endeavours to get an Act pass'd for that Purpose, but unless the Governm^{ts} of New Hampshire Rhode Island & Connecticut from whence the greatest part of the Supplyes go, will join with us in this Affair, Nothing that we can do will be effectual, And for the Members of his Majesties Council, I have no Reason to suspect that any of them are concern'd in this mischievous Trade. I have nothing further to offer at psent but with my hearty wishes for your Prosperity & the divine Protection over your pson & Government I am Sir Y^r Most Obed. & Most humble S^a

William Dummer

Letter John Bacon to L^t. Gov. Wm Dummer

Barnstable Augst 18th 1725.

May itt Please Y^r Honour S^r. These may inform Your Hon^r That On ye 12th of May Last my Son Solomon Bacon was here with us, And had Divers Patients under his hands. And Capt. Bourn then Coming Down to Our Town was very desireous that I should give my Consent that my said Son Should go Out with him into the Country^s Service, And Said he thought if my s^d Son would go itt would be a great incouragement unto the Indians to List. And that he had rather my Son should be his Second than Any Man And for his Incouragement he Doubted not but that Your Honour would give him A Commission therefor And that he should have a Warrant to be the Doctor of all the Indians And have both Doct^{rs} and Leif^{ts} pay. Whereupon My s^d Son did Assist in Listing the Indians and was in that Service from the s^d 12th of May until he came to Yourselfe riding from place to place the One way and Bourn the other to prevail with the Indians to List On the terms Your Honour proposed. And the Indians after they were inlisted were most of them with me and Importuned me to give Consent that my s^d Son should go with them, And especially those Indians that were with my son Att the fight att Norwichwak Last Year Whereupon by my consent he Left his imploy here And a Good Stock of Medicine which he had newly purchased in Order to Serve Your Honour, God & the Country And went Down to Your Honour And what Incouragement he had from Y^r Honour is best known to Your Selfe &c~. Yet notwithstanding I Rd A Letter from my s^d Son Dated June 23^d past wherein he Signifys that he had to that time faithfully Attended Your Honours orders & Directions but Capt Bourn was not then Come to him, whereupon I writ to him & Advised him to continue faithfull in the trust reposed in him, but On the 8th Instant I rec'd A Letter from him Dated the 23d of July Last And On Other this Day wherein he informs me that all the Indians were put under other Commanders And that he and Leift Hows had a forlow granted them to Come to Boston to your Honour, upon which he saith they did all they Could to perswade ye the Indians to be content with the officers they were put under but notwithstanding On the 21st of sd July 21 of sd Indians deserted And then forthwith the Coronall Confined my sd son & sd Hows Aboard the Country Sloop And ordered them to Richmonds fort. And in his Letters requests me to go to Your Honour to intercede for releif. And saith every word is true that he writes. And I should now come my Self to Your Honour but bodily Infirmitys prevent And Majr Gorham Informs me that he informed Your Honour how the case was And that Yr Honour would take Care that they should be dismist but fearing Lest Your Honr through a Multitude of business should forget their Case I make bold to send this to Yr Honour Humbly Intreating Yr Honours favour to the Young men And order them forthwith to be released And Consider ye imploy My son Left att home And the Danger And hardship he has & did Ingage in to Serve the Country, And the time & Moneys expended in Listing said Indians And will Use Your Indeavours that he as well as Leift Hows may Sutably be rewarded.

From Yr Honrs Most Humble and Obedient Servant
John Bacon

May it please yr Honr the above written being Shewn to my self there are two things mentioned therein that moves me to ask your Honrs favour in order to a Release of the sd Bacon first his indefatigable industry in Raising the indians. 2ly his Leaving so good & profitable a practice as he was in to Serve his Country: which if your honr shall Se Cause So far to

Regaurd as to grant him a Release & dismission in order to Return I shall Esteem it as a favor done to my self
 I am your hon^r Humble Ser^t always Redy at Comand
J^{no} Otis
[Superscribed]
To His Honour William Dummer Esqr
In Boston // These

"*Letter from Lt John Pritchard*" *to Lt Gov. Wm Dummer,*
"*denial of Monsr Casteens Complaints.*"

Boston Augt 18th 1725./

S^r

.He withdrew into the Woods before ever he was Attack'd or knew what we was. As to my Calling him back I could not, for he was too farr off. But sent the Pilot in our Boat to talk to him and Ordered him to Decoy them on Board (if possible) I believing they were Indians. As to my Hoisting a Flagg of Truce it was only for the time the Pilot was Talking to them, which was about a Quarter of an Hour, and when he came on Board it was Haul'd down, That Signifying that I had a Truce with them for the time the flagg was up and no Longer. This was Two hours before any thing of a Skirmage happened. We will State the Case thus. I am in a Ship of Warr and send my Boat on Shoar with a Flagg of Truce to the Enemy to Demand such or such things, (They Refusing my Demand,) When the Boat comes off I haul down the Flagg of Truce, and am at Warr with them again according to the Laws of Nations, and this was the Exact Case with us. We never fired under the Flagg of Truce; He says we promised him safe Conduct under Writing which I never did nor gave such Orders: He says thus thinking my self safe I came back on board my Vessell with my Indian &

English Man, I wish he had, for by that means we should have got something by the Cruise, but as It is we have got only our Labour for Our pains. The vessell Was Condemned and Apprized at One hundred pounds & Odd Money of this Currency, And was Delivered up to the Owners of her.

There was some Beavers, and Other Skins which was sold together for about 20 pound, which Money I Shared among the People which was but a Trifle among 60 Men, And Scarce enough to enable them to Drink Your Honours Health, as to the Other Trifles which He mentions: all of them were not worth Twenty Shillings.

I am Your Hon^{rs} most humble and Obed^t Servt
Jno Pritchard

Letter Lt Col. Johnson Harmon to Col. T. Westbrook Aug. 22, 1725

Sir

Not finding the Men So Ready at Falmouth as I expected & high wind has delay'd the Marching till this Morning I got to Casco ye 18th Cur^t – but to send as far as Black poynt & to fit on the 19 ye 20th high wind got to North Yarmouth 21 to Brunswick whare I found no heath he had ben thair But was gon home & so Send for him he Excuses by not being well but sent his Coto of men I have taken three from Cap^{tt} Gray & three from Capt Moody, but left Several of My one Not being able to March thare is not a Man in our armey that has ben on Ammuscogin River above the falls but I will march this Morning & dew as well as I can when I have Closed this Letter have nothing More to Dew but to take up our paks & walk with My harty wishes for your well fair Excuse hast am S^r your Humble Servt

Johnson Harmon

Brunswick ye 22^d August 1725
Cor^{ll} Westbrook

Letter Saml Jordan to Lt Gov. Dummer.

Beddeford August ye 23^d /1725

Honrd Sr After my duty to your Honour These may inform yor Honour that I Racd yor Honours order Dated ye Eleventh of August Instant wherein yor Honour orders me to Suply Mr Tarbox with a Suficient Guard not Exceding Twelve men to get in his hay these may inform yor Honour that Colon^{ll} Westbrook hath orderd Elevn of my men to go the march and I have but Two and Twenty men with me So that if I take a Suficient Guard to guard Mr Tarbox I shal Leave the Garisons wholy naked and now it is our only Season to get our hay and we are all of us in necessity to get our hay as well as Mr Tarbox and our Garisons are Such a Distance one from the other and not above two men in a Garison that Since Colon^{ll} Westbrook hath ordrd Elevn of my men to go the March I cannot Suply Mr Tarbox with a Suficient guard without I Leave the garisons wholly naked which is all from yor Honours most Dutyfull and Obedient Servant

Sam^{ll} Jordan

Letter Saml Cranston to Lt Gov. Wm Dummer

S^r

Yesterday arrived here a Sloop from New York, Wherein came John Hanson (belonging to Dover New Hampshire) Who has been to Canada after his Wife & Children & came away from Mont Real the 26th day of last Month for Albany & so to New York & has brought with him his Wife & three children & a Man & boy that were Captives there,   And is now going to take Passage for New Hampshire in one Thomas Millett belonging to that place: They have had a very great Fatigue in travelling which makes them Embrace this Oppertunity of going home by Water. Otherwise they would have gone thro'ugh Boston. I am informed by said Hanson That there was 150 Indians fitted out publickly at Mont Real & Supplyed with Provisions Ammunition &c And marched from thence the day before he came away for a place called Shamlee Where the Indians were detained 5 days / as s^d. Hanson was informed by a Frenchman he met with in his passage over the Lakes / to prevent them from meeting with any of s^d. Hanson's Company in their Return home, But he rather believes that they waited for more Men to joyn them, because he had heard at Mont Real That there was designed 400 Men on that Expedition for some part of New England: I thought proper to communicate this Information & Shall continue to be with the greatest Respect—

Your Hon^{rs} Most Obedient humble Servt

Sam^{ll} Cranston

Newport Rhode-Island 25th August 1725

Dr. Bacon has liberty to wait on His Hon^r the Lt Govr.

Sir

Upon your Parole of Honour you have liberty to go to Boston to wait on his Hon^r the Leiu^t Govr I haveing rec^d his orders to have all the fronteirs strict on their Guard so cannot have the Deserters and you face to face to make strict enquiery why they Deserted

Given under my hand this 27th Day of August 1725 To Doctor Bacon.

"Orders to Capt. Smith Aug. 27, 1725"

Sir,

These are to Desire & Direct you forthwth to embark on Board the Sloop Merry Meeting Cpt. Tho. Saunders Master,

& Proceed to Casco Bay, where you must stay no longer than to take on Board Cpt. Jos. Bane (or in Case of his Absence Cpt. Samll Jordan) who is hereby Order'd to go with you & assist as Interpreter, And then sail for St Georges River & Remain at the Fort there to receive ye Penobscot & other Indians that may come in in Order to be transported to Boston to the intended Treaty.

Cp{t} Saunders is hereby Order'd to attend you with his Sloop till the Indians are come in & declare their Readiness to embark & upon your Directions to him must return hither with you & the sd Indians with all possible dispatch.

You must acquaint the Indians That you are Impower'd by me to Receive the Chiefs & Delegates of the several Tribes & Conduct them to Boston there to treat of a Peace according to their own Motion & Desire, And that in the mean Time You will transmit whatsoever Advices & Messages they have to send to me.

If the Indians sh{d} enter into any Discourse of the War or the Terms & Conditions of Peace You must carefully advoid those Subjects & by no Means give them any Answer thereto, But assure them your Business is only to Accompany them to Boston to treat there & to receive & send forward any Messages to & from them as aforeds{d}, However you must note down in Writing any thing of Consequence that they shall deliver in their Discourse. You must by no means trade with the Indians y{re} self nor permit or suffer any other Persons to Traffick with them on any Acct And Inform against any such Persons that they may be prosecuted with the utmost severity of the Law, At the same time Acquainting ye Ind. that when a Peace is settled they will be well supplied.

Let the Indians be treated civilly & no Affront or Ill Usage offer'd them & especially be careful to prevent any Drunkenness among them.

The Officers & others at Fort at St Georges are hereby Required to observe your Directions in all Matters that may concern the Affair with wch you are charged.

Letter Col. T. Westbrook to Lt Gov. Wm Dummer

May it please your Hon{r}

I have got most of the Officers Lists, and am drawing fair Coppys of them to send your Honour. Capt Slocom arriv'd here last night from Falmouth but brings no news, I hear Colo Harmon marcht the 20th of this Ins{t} — wee have had an Acct of two or three Indians discovered at Berwick a few days ago, and of three at the head of Oyster River at a place called littleworth, on which I immediately gave orders to all the Fronteirs to renew their Care & be strict on their guard lest the Enemy surprise them. Capt Bean has been here a few days & says he had your Honours orders to visit his family, so that he returned to Georges in Twenty five days after the landing the Indians but lest he should be wanted I have advised him to get there before the time and he designes to set out to morrow morning.

I am your Hon{rs} most Dutifull Servt
Thos Westbrook

Letter Col. T. Westbrook to Lt Gov. Wm Dummer.

May it please your Hon{r}

I rec'd your Hon{rs} orders dated the 28th of last month on the 31st of the same about nine a Clock at night which I immediately observed & ordered men to attend Capt Smith— I am surpris'd that your Hon{r} has not rec'd any letters from me since the march ordered by your Hon{r} on Amuscoggin River.—I wrote one of ye 15th of August with a Copy of the Draught of Officers & men which I now enclose, and another by Cap.[t] Slocom of the 25th which I now enclose a Copy of. I should have had the state of the Army ready before now had I not rec'd your Hon.[rs] orders dated the 23.[d] of August that there were several parties of Indians comeing on us, whereon I immediately went to Wells & sent to all the rest of the Towns & garrisons on this side Kennebeck river to be strict on their guard ~

I shall use my utmost endeavours to get a Canoo, I wrote to Cap.[t] Bean to endeavour to get one at S.[t] Georges–and shall lay out every where else

      I am your Hon.[rs] most Dutifull Serv.[t]
York Sep.[t] 1.st 1725   Tho.[s] Westbrook
P S Col.[o] Harmons letter is Enclos'd which Informs when he marcht.

Letter Capt. Tho.[s] Smith to L.[t] Gov. Dummer

     Falmouth Casco Bay Septem.[r] 2.[d] 1725
S.[r] I gladly embrace this opportunity, by one Munrow of Dorchester, to pay my Duty to y.[r] Honour, tho' only to inform y.[t] I arrived here on Monday night y.[e] 30 of August & immediately Dispatcht a Whaleboat with your Honours Letter to Coll.[o] Westbrook of Wells, Also wrote to Cap.[t] Bean at Black Poynt w.[o] arrived here on Tuesday Night, I also forwarded your other Letters according to Direction; have been becalmed ever since we came in here and shall improve y.[e] first Wind to proceed to S.[t] Georges and now subscribe
    Your Honours most obedient hum.[l] Ser.[t]
       Tho.[s] Smith

   [Superscribed]
To the Honour.[ble] William Dummer Esq.[r] Leiu.[t] Governour And Command.[r] in Chief of y.[e] Province of y.[e] Massachus.[ts] Bay New England

Letter Johnson Harmon to Lt Gov. Dummer Sept. 5, 1725

May it please your Honour

Pursuant to your Honours Instructions I have been to Rockamagook & Six miles beyond & sent sundrys parties to Scout to the Pond near Amuscoggin & Beaver Damms adjacent but made no discovery of ye Enemy worth noteing I this day returnd to this place & shall as soon as possible send a more particular acc^t of the March. Col? Westbrook gives your Hon^r an Acc^t of the Enemys being on the Fronteir

I am your Honours most dutifull Humb! Servant
York Sep^t 5th 1725   Johnson Harmon

Letter Col. T. Westbrook to Lt Gov. Dummer Sept. 1725

May it please your Honour

Leiu^t Col^o Harmon is this Evening returned from his March up Amuscoggin River, but made no discovery of the Enemy worth noteing. on fryday last the 3^d of this Ins^t about Twenty Indians fought Scales garrison for some time & killd sundry cattle & carried them away, & the same day calld to Mr Parkers garrison, I just now receiv'd an Acc^t from Capt Wheelwright of an Alarm at Mowson whom I had ordered to march with about thirty men to Berwick which now designes to go that way to Inform more pticularly of said Alarm.

I am your Hon^{rs} most dutifull servant
Thos Westbrook

Albany 6th September 1725
Gentlemen

We can't express the concern we have for the unhappy Indian war your Governm^t is fallen into. and do heartily wish that it was brought to a happy Conclusion & Lasting peace with those unhumane Eastern Salvages, whom we hear are daly supported by the french Priests & people of Canada, and assisted by the neighbouring Indians to annoy the People of your Governm.^t we think we should not discharge our duty as Subjects of one King and neighbours not to Inform you of the Barbarous & Bloody designs of the Indians whom as we are Credibly Informd this day are with 150 men about three weeks Since on their March towards your fronteers, and probably are yet Skulking or hovering ab.^t to comitt barbarities, we are also told that 140 Indians were on their March above Chambly in one Body, 17 days ago, but it is thought this last party would turn back by ye perswasion of some from this tho' this is but uncertain. So that its adviceable to be on your Guard. we hope this advice may come timely and be of service to the publick and frustrate the designs of the Indians, this Express will Expect payment from you for his trouble or Journey. we hope youl satisfy him. if in any thing we can be serviceable to any in_ of your place or Governm.^t please to comand who are with Esteem & Respect.

    Gentlemen Your most humble servants
     Henry: Holland Pieter Van Brugh
     Evert Bancker Ph. Livingston
     Hend Van Rensselaer

Col. Thos Westbrook to Lt Gov. Dummer Sept. 9, 1725.

P. S. When I receivd your Hon^{rs} orders to be strict on our guard and that there was several parties of Indians comeing on our fronteirs I heard there was a letter on his Maj^{ts} service to Col^o Wheelwright which I was in hopes was from Your Hon^r to order the Inhabitants to be more carefull, I hear since that it never came to his hand.

My affairs at home more then ordinary wanting me for Ten or Twelve days I pray your Hon^{rs} leave in as much as Col° Harmon is on the Spott

    I am your Honours most dutifull Servant
York September 9th 1725   Thos Westbrook

Orders to Col. Harmon & Capt. Moulton Sept. 9, 1725

Sir

These are to direct you to march with thirty effective men to Saco Salmon Falls & to cross the Countrey from thence to North Yarmouth or Pesumpscot River Keeping out in the Woods at least ten or twelve Days, Passing & Repassing between the said Stations or Lying in Ambush in such Places where the Indians may probably pass, Taking the utmost Care of your Silence & good Order to prevent the Enemies Discovering you.
Coll. Harmon.

If you are too much fatigued with your last
March Let y^{re} Lieut: command this Party

Cpt. Molton to march from the Head of
Berwick to Saco Salmon Falls
Sep^t 9th 1725

Letter L^t. Gov. Dummer to Col. Westbrook Sept. 9, 1725

Sr These are to Direct You forthwith to deliver Col° Harmon & Capt Moulton, the enclos'd Orders & detach so many Able Men Indians & others to make up their number for the s^d Marches w^c I desire may bee pformed wth the utmost diligence

Boston 9th Sep^t 1725   Y^r Servt

Col° Westbrook

Letter H. Holland & others to Lt Gov. Dummer

Albany 10th Septem^r 1725

Honourable Sir

We should think it a neglect of our Duty as we have the honour to be appointed by his Excel^y Govr Burnet Esqr &^{c} to represent him here in relation to Ind^n Affairs, not to Inform you without Loss of time of a Message this day brought us by one of this place / who arriv'd last night in 13 days from Canada) who deliver'd us seven hands of Wampam from the part of the Cachnawages, Rendax and Skawinnadie Ind^{ns} living in Canada, desiring thereby to speak with you, or some deputed by you, his Excel^y our Govr & the Sachims of the six Nations at this City by the first of October next, but about what Subject this propos'd meeting is to be we cannot inform you tho its said that some Sachims of the Eastern Ind^{ns} were at Cachnawage so that its conjectur'd that there may be some proposals made of A Peace between you & them which we heartily wish may be brought to a happy & desired Issue. We hear the Ind^{ns} themselves are weary of this War but are vigorously sett on & supported by the Govr of Canada & their priests. We writt by this Express to the Justices of Westfield Informing them of the Motion of the Enemy, which we desire them to forward to you for your better Information, We intend to advise his Excel^y Govr Burnet of our proceedings in this affair which we flatter ourselves will be approved of by him We remain with Respect

    Sir your very Humble Servants
      Henry Holland Pieter Van Brugh
      Evert Bancker Ph: Livingston

Letter H. Holland & others to " Col⁸ Partridge & Stoddard."

Albany 10th Sept' 1725

Gentlemen
       Since our last of the 6th Instant we are assur'd by one of this place who arriv'd last night in 13 days from Canada that the 140 Ind^{ns} we Inform'd you lay Incamped near Chambly with a Design to go out against your fronteers are Actually returned home partly by the pswasion of the people of this place and partly by their Sachims, that the 150 Ind^{ns} said to be out are gone to the Eastward, yet we hear their Number is uncertain neither can we be inform'd whether they be in one Body or in parties, but we are told that one party of 9 & another of 14 Ind^{ns} are out who design to be skulking about your western fronteers of the last Graylock is Leader, We hope these two parties may be discovered & defeated by your out Skouts to pvent their further Attempts. We hear the Ind^{ns} are weary of the War and would long since have come to terms of peace & submission if the Govr of Canada & his priests did not encourage and Sett them on against the people of your Governm^t It will be a great Satisfaction to Us to hear that our advice be of Service to the publick as we heartily wish it may be The Inclos'd is for your Govr which we desire you to forward to him with all possible dispatch/ as also this Letter for his perusal/ it being as we suppose of Consequence with Respect We Remain
            Gentlemen Your most Humble Servants
                   Henry Holland   Pieter Van Brugh
                   Evert Bancker   Philip Livingston

Letter Col. T. Westbrook to L^t. Gov. Dummer

May it please your Hon^r
       The Lists now sent your Honour is as near as I can get it at this time, there may be some small Error, but I

know of none, some of the Officers have not given me an Account of their Dismist men or dead, since the last account given in, so I have not putt in any of them but shall get a particular list by itself

York Sep! 10th 1725

     I am your Hon^{rs} most Dutifull Servant
           Thos Westbrook

Letter Josiah Willard, Sec^y " to Henry Holland & others"
Sept. 13, 1725.

Gent.

 I am directed by the Honble the Lieut. Govr & Council of this Prov. To Acquaint you That they have received from Coll. Stoddard your Intelligence of the Fitting out & March of the Indians from Canada towards our Frontiers, And that they thankfully Acknowledge your Concern for the Interest of this Province express'd in your Letter & by your Advices from Time to Time of the Designs & Motions of the Enemy, And they desire you would please continue ye good Offices to give speedy & seasonable Intelligence of what ever may effect & concern this Governm^t as Occasi — shall require

             J Willard

 Boston Sep^t 13, 1725

Letter Col. T. Westbrook to Lt Gov. Dummer Sept. 16, 1725

May it please y^r Hon^r

 I rec^d y^r Hon^{rs} Order's about 8 of the Clock this night, dated the 9th Curr^t, & immidiatly gave Capt Moulton, the command of so many effective Men, who will be on that command, the 17th Curr't Col: Harmon, will take his own Men, & in case he wants, I shall immediatly Supply him ~

The inclosed, will confirm the Villany of y'e Penobscut Tribe ~ When time will allow, I doubt not, but there is such reason to be given, that will confirm it.

York Septemb'r 16th 1725

    I am Y'r Hon'rs most Dutiful humble Servant
            Tho's Westbrook

Letter L't Gov. Dummer to Col. Westbrook

         Boston Sep't 24, 1725

I have Yours of the 21st Instant which came to Me by Express whereas there was nothing in the Letter that required Such a Charge but it might have come as well by the Ordinary Post. I think well of the Disposition You have made of Your Men And I hope they will be Vigilant & faithful in their Duty otherwise they may Depend the Enemy will make Some Incursions upon Us. It was very Absurd for any Body to Spread Reports of 500 Indians being come from Canada, especially for such who pretend & ought to know the Indian Affairs, I observe the Soldiers make a handle of it for Cowardice by every Small party they meet with afterwards, I have a full Acc't of the Indians that are come out from Canada which I rec'd from Albany &c And they are in all 130 part of which made Directly to the Western frontiers where we have heard of them Divers times lately And the rest March'd East amongst You some of whom I am still in hopes You will give me some good Acc't of. Unless Your business be very Urgent it won't be proper to leave Your Command at this Juncture, but in that Case I Allow of it. You have never yet sent me any Acc't of the Examination of the Officers of the Indians pursuant to my Directions, it will be necessary to Set that Matter in a true light for they Complain of Great Injustice.

I am Sr Your Humble Servt
W. Dummer

Col° Westbrook

Mr Dalafaye to the Lords Commissioners for Trade and Plantations : (Inclosing Memorial from Lt Govr & Council of New England)

Whitehall Septem. 25.th 1725

My Lords

    The inclosed Memorial of the Lieu.^t Govr and Assembly of New England, Complaining, that the Indians in their Neighbourhood are instigated and assisted by the French to commit Hostilitys upon His Ma.^{tys} Subjects, and that the Neighbouring British Colonies do not give them any assistance, being laid before the Lord Justices; Their Ex.^{cys} have commanded me to refer it to yor Lo.^{ps} Consideration, that you may inquire into the Facts complained of, and report the State of the Case as it shall appear to you, with your opinion what is to be done in it. I am

My Lords Y.^r Lo.^{ps} most Obedient humble Servant

Ch : Delafaye

Letter – Col. Wm Pepperrell to L.^t. Gov. Dummer

May it Please y.^r Hon.^r

    Sum time past, I inform.^d y.^o that there was not an Ensign to ye company in ye Lower parte of ye Town of Kittery wch I have ye care off and at ye Same time mention.d M.r W.m Fernald Jun.r as a Suteable man for that place; Since dont understand that there is any commission Sent for any person — if y.r Hon.r Sees cause to send one for s.d Fernald I am of y.e opinion he will behave him Selfe well.

there is one James Breddeane Jun.r in the countorys Service belonging to Coll.o Harmons company and is indebt.d to me, he is able to pay but not willing because he thinks his being in y.e Service is a protection I pray y.e fav.r of y.o to Send his dismishon inclosed to me.

I ask pardon in being so troublesome ———
  I am with much Duty & respects Yo.r Hon.rs
   Most Hum.ble Serv.tt   W.m Pepperrell
Kittery Sept.r 29.th 1725

    [Superscribed]
  To The Honor.ble W.m Dumer Esq.r L.t Governour & command.r in Cheiff of his Maj.tys Province of the Massachusets bay —   Att   Boston———

Letter Col. T. Westbrook to L.t Gov. Dummer, Oct. 1, 1725.

May it Please your Hon.r/
   I rec.d your Hon.rs Letter of the 24.th on the 28.th of last month. How mine of y.e 21.st came to hand by Express I cannot tell unless Gov.r Wintworth made such a mistake in that as his Hon.r did in not sending Cap.t Canady's Letter with mine of the 16.th of last month to your Hon.r I sent it by a private hand and desir'd him to send a line or two to your Hon.r of his mistake which I hope your Hon.r has rec.d

 I never believ'd that there was 500 Indians come from Canada but inasmuch as it came from Cap.t Jordan to my hand, I look't on it as my Duty to forward it to your Hon.r

I always caution every body to make less rather than more of what they hear or see, relating the Enemy notwithstanding some make ye most of everything. If my Affairs did not more than ordinary want me at home I would not have desir'd it after I rec'd your Hon^rs Orders to have the Officers of the Indian company & the Witnesses face to face. I immediately sent for the Officers from Richmond in order to examine them but the Indians were out in the woods pursuant to your Hon^rs Orders so that I coud not bring them face to face. Doctor Bacon complaining that it woud be a great damage to stop him till the return of the Indians, I permitted him to wait on your Hon^r as your Hon^r will see by the Enclosd which is a true copy. Capt Moulton is returnd from his march a Journal of wh^ch is herewith sent your Hon^r The Indians are uneasy wanting to be dismiss'd and threaten if they are not to run away

I am Your Hon^rs most Dutifull Servt

York Octob^r 1st 1725   Thos Westbrook

P. S.   Lieu^t Markham wanting to go to Boston I have permitted him to wait on your Hon^r by whom I have sent an Indian Gun that was taken last year at Nerridgwock which I pray your Hon^r to accept.

T W

[Superscribed]
On his Maj^ties Service
To The Honble William Dummer Esqr Lieu^t Govern^r
& Command in Chief &c   p Lieu^t Markham

Letter John Minot to Col. Stephen Minot

Marblehead Oct^o 4 1725

Hon^d S^r

   Our not hearing of any late damages done by the Indians and Capt Smith being still detained by them after the limited time gives me some hopes, that we shall in a little time be so happy, as to have peace in our borders, that we may againe improve and injoye our Eastern Plantations, And that which I most build my hopes on is that I think the eyes of the Governm.^t seeme to be more open now then they have bin formerly, and are more inclin'd to taike those measures which may secure the honour and Interest of the province & the Indians have justice done them the latter of which without we have a Tender regard to we may not expeckt a lasting peace–I shall now give you my thoughts on some heads which I think very necessary to Establish our Interest with them Tribes And the first thing I shall speak to is the Affaire of the lands they claime, which I believe will be the only dificult point, that the Governm.^t will have to Treat with them on– I am very sensible it was the greatest handle the Jesuits made use of whereby they mov'd them to make Warr by telling them it was our intent to take away all their Countrey not only what we bought, of them, but what we had not bought, and to make them & their Children in time miserable, Its my Opinion if there were some measures taken to Assure them that some Considerable part of that Country should alwayes remaine to them & their Children to plant and Improve and that no man should be able to bye it, and if they did it should not be valid while they or any of their children were alive, As it is at Natick and some other parts of our Province where we have justly made reserves for them–if we put It to our selves & examine by ye golden rule of doeing as we would be done by, I think we should chearfully come into it, And as I remember at the last treaty they had no Assurance, that their planting fields at Nerigwalk and other planting grounds should be alwayes enjoyd by them many of them often tould me, that they Expeckted the English would in a little time endeavour to taike them away, as they had done by the Western Indians we should Consider they have a

Native right to all the lands they have not sould—I have often admired at the Weakness of many people when they have said if we should Confirme any land to them they would emediately sell it to the french, and they would settle it, but no man that is acquainted with that part of the Countrey can think so when there might be so many reasons given why the would not—besides there might be Exceptions made against it, no frenchman that is a man of any Consideration who is not under our Govermn.^t would venture to lay out his substance near so great a Province where they allwayes lye lyable to be Destroyd & We have an instance to Confirme this in the settlements the french made at St Johns River where the Indians gave them Liberty to plant & Improve who after they were Destroyd by Capt Southarick never made any more attempts notwithstanding we have had so long a Peace with france—

It must be Confest the Indians are barbarous & Cruell to us in time of Warr and God makes use of them as a rod in his hand, and its to be fear'd he uses it with more severity on us because we have not dealt justly by them in many things—

I can think of nothing that would sooner make them easy in the Affaire of y.^r Land then by letting them know what great care the Govermn.^t has taken to Confirme the lands to the Naticks & other Indians in our Province, and it would not be amiss that some of our Indians, that would make the best Appearance be at the Treaty & there assure them of the great proffit & advantage that they reap by it whereby they are enabled to raise Corn Sheep and Cattle & that many of them that are industrous live very well—If the Govermn.^t should ereckt Traiding houses (which I think very necessary to keep them in our Interest.) Its my Oppinion that it would give more satisfacktion not to Confine the traide to them houses only for they are a jealous people and love freedome.

& if they bought cheaper there than others could afford, & they had not liberty to trye they would not so apparantly see their Obligation & Dependance on ye Publick. As to letting them have rum I think it best it be not wholly restrain'd from them, for there are many amongst them, that maike a **Temperate** moderate use of it, and never Disguise themselves at all & many of them will not drinke any. I believe it best that matter be left to the prudence of the men that are entrusted with the stores, and that they be Exceeding cautious before they are well acquainted with the Indians that they dont let any of them have more than a dram at a time, but I need not say anything more on this head, the temptation of selling them for any proffit being wholly taiken of from them that have the caire of the Stores, if they be men of any prinsipalls of Honour & justice and have the good of their Countrey at heart ___ and I think few or none will sell them rum only for y^e Proffit they get on it the Indians giving them so much trouble after they are made drunck which made the most sober considerate indians tell me, that nothing would more suppress that base Custome then by erecting Publick Stores, for it was the temptation of getting proffit on other goods that causd many people to let them have rum and many of our quarrells with them arose from their drunken revills, I think it would be best also in my Oppinion that those Truck masters should have orders not to trust any Indian—for it might be a Temptation to them, as it was in South Carolina in the last Warr they had,/ After they are a great deale in debt to make Warr and then all is paid, besides its an Incouragm^t to Idleness. and I observ'd many quarrells with them arose from our demanding what was due from them. And yet there are some of the most Considerate influencing men amongst them. which I have Observ'd after they have bin hunting a great while have met with little or no success, and thereby their familyes brought to be very nessesitous. now if it were left to those that are intrusted with the stores at such times to give them a small matter of Corne or other nesesaryes that they stand in need of, the prudent timeing of those gifts would greatly ingaige them. As to bringing them over to our Religion I hope by Gods Blessing in time it might be Effeckted—And I hope the publick will be so happy in their Choice to have those men whose Conversation will be Exemplary and inofensive for the indians will be most with them.—

I Observ'd the Jesuits allwayes gain'd more on them by their blamless watchfull carrage to them then by any other of their artfull methods. Example is before preceipt wth them. their Religion being all superficiall they having but little internall sence of their duty when at their Devotions— if the Govermn^t would give those that have the caire of those houses some rules and methods to use with them, which they in their wisdome think proper to gaine them over to the protestant faith. I have great reason to think by Gods Blessing in time may have a good Effeckt, but at present they are so biggotted to the Romish faith that will require great patience & strength of Resolution in those endeavours. There might be many things concerted which at present does not Ocur to my minde which I hope the publick will not be wanting in if they should come into any termes with them— Ime sure if we look into Govern Burnets last speach, whereby he is laying downe the great and happy Consequence of their keeping in good termes with those Tribes of Indians bordering on him. And the french on the other side of us Assiduously & Artfully plotting and Contriving to keep them in their interest it highly conserns this Province to taike some methods to get them into our Interest who have suffered so much & which now groans under the burden of this unhappy Warr. S^r if you think my thoughts on these things may be of service desire they may be Communicated

    Yo^r Obed^t Son John Minot

 Superscribed
  To Coll. Stephen Minot Merch^t In Boston.

Letter Josiah Willard Sec^y to Col. Westbrook Oct. 4, 1725.

Sir, His Hon^r the Lt Gov (who is very ill of the Gout bid me tell you That you must dispatch the enclosed to Cpt. Smith without a Minutes Delay It being of great Consequence that he sh^d soon receive it.

His Hon^r having promised the Indians enlisted by Cpt. Bourn (being all those of the County of Barnstable) to dismiss them in the Fall that so they attend their Whale Fishing: directs you as soon as you have Opportunity to send them up to Boston in Order to their Return Home & let none of them be detain'd on any Pretence whatsoever. The thirty Indians of Bristol County must be Continued till further Order. Take special Care that the Garrisons be strengthen'd & protected & that Scouts be sent out as often as the Number of them will allow. His Hon^r has sent Orders to Cpt Grant to march to Norridgewock with his Comp^a of Voluntiers. You must take Care that the Design be conceal'd And give him what Assistance is necessary. In your last List you sent no acc^t of the Soldiers that were dead deserted killd or Dismiss'd. W^{ch} Honour expects as soon as may be

 Coll. Westbrook

Letter Josiah Willard, Sec^y to Capt Thos Smith - Oct. 4, 1725

Sir

 His Hon^r the Lieut. Govern^r (who is laid up with the Gout) bids me tell you That this Morning he rec^d your Letter of the 22ᵈ of September, That he is concern'd at the Indians Delay of Coming in, However Directs you to remain at Sᵗ Georges till further Order, The Indians having express'd their Doubts of being ready in Forty Days when they were here & the Lᵗ Govʳ declared his Readiness to lengthen out the time so far as should be necessary without any Limitation of Fourteen Days; And his Honour wonders whence the Discourse of fourteen Days Addition to the first Term shᵈ arise, There not being the least Foundation for it in the Transactions of the Governmᵗ with the Indians. His Honour expects that you express forward all Intelligence you have of any Moment with all possible Dispatch. And that when the Indians come in you bring them forward to Boston without delay

Cpt. Smith

Letter Josiah Willard Secʸ to Col. Wᵐ Pepperrell Oct. 4, 1725

Sir

His Honour the Lᵗ Govʳ (who is very ill of the Gout) directs me to acquaint you That he has recᵈ yʳ Lettʳ of the 29ᵗʰ pass'd & has according to your Desire sent a Commission for an Ensign wᶜʰ is herewith enclosed: As to Breddeanes Debt to you, You have not Said that it was contracted before he enter'd into the Service, Wᶜʰ is the only Case wherein the Law provides for the Dismission of Soldiers; However his Honʳ hopes he shall soon have Occasion to dismiss him with many others in the Service And in the Mean Time Advises you to secure your self out of the Mans Wages.

Coll Pepperil

Letter J. Willard Sec^y to Capt. Grant & Lt Bragdon.
Oct. 4, 1725

Gent.

His Hon^r the Lt Govr (who is very ill of the Gout) has rec^d your Letter of the first Instant, And bids me acquaint you that he approves of your Readiness for the publick Service & hereby Directs you with all possible Speed to March your Company of Voluntiers to Norridgewock in Quest of the Enemy, & to take kill & destroy all that you meet with there or in your March, Taking effectual Care that no Hostility be acted by you any where to the Eastw^d of Kennebeck River but at Norridgewock, And that Nothing be done on that Side the River contrary to the Cessation agreed on with the Penobscot Tribe. for the March must be perform'd with the utmost Secrecy & Silence. You must not divulge your Designs to any Persons whatsoever any further than is absolutely necessary. You must be very exact in your Journal in Noting down every thing that is worthy of your Observation; & send an Acc^t of your Proceedings.

Cpt. Grant & Lt Bragdon.

Letter Col. T. Westbrook to Lt Gov. Wm Dummer
Oct. 7, 1725

May it Please your Hon^r

I rec^d Hon^rs Orders from Secretary Willard Esqr Dated the 4th Curr^t at Portsmouth where I had been a day or two I immediately sent forward Capt Smith and the next morning came to Berwick to forward Capt Grant in his Orders pursuant to your Hon^rs Directions but he marched out four or five days before. I sent Orders to the respective Officers to deliver the Indians Arms & Ammunition to Mr Mountfort and then send them to Boston by the first Conveyance. Mr Secretary did not inform me that the Cessation of arms was out but by your Hon^{rs} Order§ to Capt Grant it seems to me it is over however not being certain I shall not give any Orders to ye Eastward of Kennebec River till I have your Hon^{rs} particular Directions. The Officers in general are very urgent to go to Boston to make up their Rolls particularly Capt Canady whom I have assur'd I wou'd ask your Hon^r for leave

I am Your Hon^{rs} most Dutifull Servt

Thos Westbrook

Berwick Octob^r 7th 1725.

P. S. I am not certain where Capt Grant is march't, but by what I understand from ye People here, he is onely ranging on ye heads of ye Towns, & will be in again, in four or five days I am rit supra

T. W

[Superscribed]
On his Maj^{ties} Service
To the Honble William Dummer Esqr
Lieu^t Govr & Commander in chief &c

Letter Saml Willard to Lt Gov. Dummer Oct. 14, 1725.

Saco October 14th 1725

May it Please your Honvor   pursuant to your Honvors Instructions Capt Blanchard and I marched up Marrimack About one Hundred and fiefty milles from Dunstable till we came to Head of it we saw some Signes of a Wigwarm where we suppose Some Indians had Been about Six weeks sinc and from Marrimack in about 3 milles we Came up on Saco River and came Down s^d River to Saco falls on wensday October 13 and in ye Evening came to winter harber to Capt Jordens and tooke some Stores of him for our Subsistinc for we had not any Provision Laeft, for in the moring we Before we came to Saco falls we fineched all our provisions so that we had not any Leaft And we are now coming Home as fast as we can we shall Give your Honvor amore particuler acovnt in our Journall.

Which is all in hast from your Honvors Humble Sarvent
Sam^{ll} Willard
for the Honble Wm Dummer Esqr

Letter Lt Gov. Dummer to Gov. Armstrong.

Sir

Since my last to you I have no other Advice from the Penobscot Indians but that they have sent to Canada to call in their People that are there to our Treaty at Boston. And that those of them that are come in to St Georges make strong professions of their Disposition to Peace, & they wait only for the Return of their Messengers from Canada.

If the War sh^d continue after all these Overtures I shall endeavour by the Help of God to push it on the next Winter with more Vigour than ever, and as the Penobs Indians retire in that Season to a Place near Menis & other Parts of Nova Scotia where they are entertain'd & subsisted by the French, I am thinking to send a Force there to dislodge them, But shall do Nothing in this Affair without your Privity & Approbation, As you have his Maj^{ties} Commission for ye Governm^t of that Countrey And I must pray you would take this Proposal into your Consideration & give your Answer to it as soon as possible.

Albany 5th November 1725

Sir

Mr Livingston being from home am order'd by the Com^{rs} of Indⁿ Affairs here, to acquaint you that they received without Date, acquainting them that your Lieu^t Govr and Council had received from Coll Stoddard their Intelligence of the sitting out & March of the Ind^{ns} from Canada towards your Frontiers, which they hope has prevented their Cruel Designs. This week arriv'd here some Gentlemen from Canada, but bring no News save that Govr Vaudreille is Dead. The Com.^{rs} assure you to Continue their Intelligence of the Motions of the Enemy from time to time with all care & Dilligence possible as Occasion Offers Am with much Respect Sir Your most humble Servant

James Stevenson

Letter – Sam^{ll} Stacy to Lt Gov. Dummer

May it please your Honour

Being inform'd of ye Arrival of ye Heads or Representatives of ye several Tribes of Indians, in Order for a Peace, I humbly take Leave to acquaint Your Hon^r That they have one of my Schooners in their Hands, wch they took from me some Time ye Summer before last.

The last Time ye Indians were at Boston I came up, hoping to have redeem'd my Vessel, and accordingly when your Hon^r met wth ye Counsel to have an Interview wth them, I prefer'd a Petition, Praying Liberty to purchase her of ye Indian who had her in his Keeping, who was then at Boston, but it was answer'd y^t it was not cosistent wth ye Honour of ye Governm^t to buy y^t of ye Indians wch they had unjustly taken away, especially when they were suing for a Peace wth us. And that it was hoped y^t I & every Body else y^t

had anything in their hands wch they had taken from us, should have it frankly restored to us without buying it of them, when they came to a Treaty wth us. and therefore I would humbly entreat y^t when ye Affair comes in Agitation I may not be forgot

My Neighbour John Chapman has ye like Request, who has a Vessel & Servant wth them.

I am your Hon^{rs} most Obedient & humble Servt
Sam^{ll} Stacey

Marb^lh^d Novr 15th 1725

Letter Lt Gov. Dummer to Col. T. Westbrook, Dec. 21, 1725.

Sir

The Peace being concluded with the Delegates of the Eastern Indians, I have determined upon a Reduction of the Forces on that Frontier, And therefore I desire you would repair to Falmouth in Casco Bay with all convenient Speed & reduce the Soldiers according to a List of the Numbers I shall allow to each respective Place wch you have herewith dd you; The Rest of Men must be forthwith dismiss'd; And in their Dismission you must have a just & impartial Regard to those that have been longest in the Service who are on that Acc^t first entituled to this Benefit, And more especially the Men contained in the other List, who must be immediately discharged; The Garrisons at Fort George & Fort Mary must stand according to their last Establishm^t And if there be wanting any Men at either of those Forts, You must supply them out of the Forces before their Reduction.

You must Notify the sev^{ll} Places in that the Peace is concluded, And give Directions in writing from me to the sev^{ll} Commanding Officers for the Observation of it & also That They see a faithful Duty perform'd, and that they be not off from their Guard, The Danger not being wholly over till the Ratification, But in the mean Time, If any Indians come in That they be well treated & a good Understanding cultivated with them & Friendship & After you have fully perform'd the sev[ll] Articles of this Instruction, and are return'd Home to your Family, you will look upon yourself Dismiss'd from his Majesties Service as Commander in Chief of the East[n] Forces, Thus giving you hearty Thanks for your Faithfulness, Diligence & Good Conduct in that important Trust: I am, W. D.

Resolve.

In the House of Representatives Jan[ry] 4th 1726 Resolved That no Settlements be made by any person or persons whatever in the County of York beyond North Yarmouth in Casco Bay without Leave therefor being first had and Obtained of the Great and General Court.

Sent up for Concurrence
W[m] Dudley Spk[r]

Letter Rev. Christopher Toppan to L[t] Gov. Dummer

Newbury Jan. 13, 1726.

Honourable S[r]

I have lately received Information that severall persons have gone this Winter from Casco Bay to Damiscotty (A place belonging to me) and Cut and Carried away abundance of Pipe Staves, and Capt. Moody has sent me Word, that there are Several more, fitting to goe down— Now the favour I would request of your Honour is, (if such a thing may be granted) that you'd please to send an order to Cap[t] Heath to send two or three men across the Woods, to Damiscotty, (wch is I suppose about ten or a dozen miles) and if any persons are cutting Timber in those Woods, to see who y.y are, and take an Account of their Names, and forbid y^m committing any further Trespass there—if yy. should need a Pilot the Cap.t may hire some Indian for that purpose, and 'ile repay w.t he gives him :—

If your Honour can gratifye me in w^t I request, it will very much oblige me who am your Honours most humble and Obedient Servant

my service to Madam/. Christopher Toppan

Letter Capt. John Gyles to L.t Gov. Dummer

1726/7   S.t Georges Riv^er
Feb^r 27   Gyleses Memorial

Lues   an Indian Cap^tn of the Penebscot tribe decleard y^t he had a Cecret to Deliver to me, that ye Government Might know of that at a Late Councell Concluded that if ye Cap^tns said War or Peace it must be so, which I had thoughts of hideing from you,

Gyles   Why should you & I hide from Each auther anithing of moment.

Lues   I Dont from you,

Gyles   hath made sum Inquiary of ye above & Informd that thier is no such Conclusion it is only the Pride of that Cap^tns hart &c

Lues   I aquaint you that the new Gouv^r of Canadey hath sent to ye Chieffs & authers y^t ar willing of our tribes to Give him a Vicett in ye Spring that he may Pay his Respext to them & Give them Presents as he is ordred by the King of france.

Lues   one thing more I must aquaint you of y^t is about ye 7th Currant or 10 Days Past 12 of our tribe wear ouer to Montinecous Islands to kill Sils but finding not any & being Detaind thier sun^d Days by wind & wether, they Lit of a Cow & hoggs belonging to the English which they Kild & must Pay for.

March 3

a Privat   Informar news from Caneday y^t ye Preson- taken by ye french in the Spring, & to be no more such actions Commited, tho' all is kept Privat at yet, and the Persons that Did ye mischief nameless, and at ye a Rival of our Messengors to Canedy they Demanded who was the a Casion of Killing after a Pece Concluded,

the new Govr s^d what was Don was Vnknown to him, for he was Com by order from france to Do Justies, and to have Pece & Love wth the English as it was at home, and what the blackcots had Don, thier must be no more such actions which was his Orders &c

Wowerena is Deracted to set Vp a mark in Keneback River above taconack, two men shaking hands and if Like to war, then to have a hatchet in Each hand, for those y^t Pass & Repass to View and be on their Guard, for Severall ar Expected wth thier families in ye Spring to Settle a Gain at Narrangawawock &c

Gyles   you Do well to Give me an accompt of all affears of moment, and you shall be well Rewarded from time to time for your Good Service and not be made Publick,

Informar,   the Messengars are Expected Daily from Canedy, and Connawol is supposd to be ariv^d thier by this Day, for they have been Gon about fourteen Days

p John Gyles Entepe^tr

The within newes Came from Canedy by ye way of Keneback River, it is Calld Privat, it is Likely your honour hath an account of all Redy, from, —— but Gyles is willing

[Superscribed]
On his Maj^tys Service

To the Honourd Wm Dummar ^esq Liu^tn Govr In Chieff of his Maj^tys Province Masachussetts Bay

Letter Col. T. Westbrook to L! Gov. Dummer

Portsm? Jan^{ry} 28th 1726

May it Please your Honour

I have been East as far as Falmouth and dismiss'd the forces agreeable to your Honours orders, and have given directions to the Commanders of Each party remaining, (Pursuant to y^r Honours order) to observe the Peace made with the Delegates of the Eastern Indians I am

Your Honours Most Dutifull Servant
Thos Westbrook

Letter Capt. Thos. Smith to L^t. Gov. Dummer.

St George March ye 6th 1726/7

Sr This (by way of Pascataqua) is ye Second Oportunity I have had since I came from Boston (In Obedience to your Hon^{rs} Comand) to write: & now have only, that the Indians (more or Less) Every day since my arrival have frequented the Garrison—They have not (as they say to their admiration) any news from Canada.; Capt Lewe was here the first of this Inst, and acquainted us, that about the begining of Last month Twel^v men of the Penobscot Tribe (Amongst whome was Victor and his son's) being by bad weather detained on ye Isle of Montenicus for some time; were by hunger Necessitated to Kill a Cow & a hogg they found there (which I understand belonged to Mr Vaughn of Pascataqua) and were ready to pay for them; on ye second of this Ins^t, Victor, his two sons were here. One of them owned he had killed three piggs there, tho at first they denyed it, & as I saide nothing to them about paying, so neither did they say anything about them, only that they were all so poore they would have dyed of themselves if they had not killed them: I shall carefully observe to Inform your Hono^r wth all occurrencyes, & further now only repeat my desires to yor Hono^r, for Liberty to come to Boston for a small time about the Latter end of May when the spring trade will be over here I am Yo^r Hono^rs most Obedient Humble Servant

Thos Smith

[Superscribed]
   To the Honou^ble William Dummer Esqr
   Lieu^t Govonour &c Comand^r in Cheif of His Majesties Province of ye Massachusets Bay &c att Boston Q D C

Letter from L^t. Gov. Dummer to Wenungennet
March 14, 1726/7

Good Friend,

I think it proper to acquaint you that I have rec^d Intimations That an Indian call'd Grey Lock has enticed a Party of Indians about Otter Creek & that they are preparing to come upon our Frontiers with mischievous Designs, And as by the late Treaty I promised to inform you of all Designs & Motions of such Indians as endeavour to disturb us, And you have by your repeated Repeated Assurrances undertook to perswade or Force the Western & other Tribes to be peaceable & come into the Treaty, & I in confidence of the Sincerity & good Disposition of the Indians have withdrawn the Forces from the Frontiers that so you might be assured of my Resolution strictly to maintain the Peace on my Part. It is therefore incumbent on you to enquire into this Matter & if you find the Matter as it is reported + that you forthwith take effectual Care to prevent these Indians from Acting their Ill Purposes & to oblige them to come in & ratify the Treaty as you have done, Let me have an Acc^t of your Proceedings as soon as may be.

Letter L! Gov. Dummer to Col? Stoddard & Partridge

Gent.,

Having considered the Report of Grey Locks Designs I think the best Way to prevent him will be to draw him by good Usage. I desire therefore that you would endeavour to get some private Intimations to him that may encourage him to come in, in order to ratify the Treaty; I suppose it will not be difficult for you to get a Message to him to this purpose; in wch you may assure him not only a Safety & Protection but Kindness & Good Usage, W^{ch} I leave entirely to y^{re} Good Conduct, and in Case of his Coming in with any other Indians of Note, & their Ratifying the Treaty It will be proper to give them some proper Presents, W^{ch} you must provide for them according to your own Discretion, and the Charge will be allowed you as well as what Expence will be otherwise occasion'd by the Managem^t of this Affair; In wch if you succeed you will do singular Service for the Province.

In the meantime you will take prudent Care to prevent a Surprize.

W. D.

Letter Capt. John Gyles to L! Gov. Dummer

March 17: May it Pleas your Honour
1726/7   This Day Moxses ye Chieff of Narangawock Received his Lettars & Present,
and he Desiars me to aquaint, that he heartily salutes your honour, and Councell wth his Cap of to ye Ground, and is thankefull for his Present and Lettar and Reioyces to see your well wishing to Loue, & wellfear of our People, on our Land, he Rackens him self weak, tho as God would Inable him, they shall not be wanting on thier Part, for the Same, hopeing this summar after his tribe

Coms ouer and settled – your honour will see thier Resolve for Love & Vnity

p John Gyles Enterpreter

March 17th
1726/7   Victor an Indian Desiars me to a quaint your honour Concerning ye Loss of his Canew & Goods Lost at awouck on his Return from ye trety at Casco bay his 2 Guns & Canew he sais he knows ye Value of, but ye 2 blankitts y^t wear Precented to them ye Value of it Vnknown, and as it was Done among ye English he should be Very thankfull to have sumthing to the Value of Made to him, he sais he has & will Labour heartily for the Continuance of Pece & Love in our Land,

And from his heart Salutes & to Serve your honour which Did not before

p John Gyles Enterpreter

S^r   this Victor is a Leding fellow & was a Malcontent to — & so was much made vse of by ye french Party I am of opinion y^t I have now much won him over to ye English Intrest by Reasons

I am your honours Most Dutyfull Ser^t
John Gyles

Letter Capt. Thos. Smith to L^t. Gov. Dummer

S^r

I am favoured wth yor Honours Letter of ye 6th Curr^{tt}, of the same date I wrote yor Honour via Pascataqua, & therein Informed, that Twelve men of the Penobscot Tribe at Montenicus killed a Cow & Several Swine belonging to Mr. Vaughn of Pascataqua, that the Indians Say (to their admiration) they have as yett no news from Canada, Also I repeated my desires for Liberty of your Honour, that I might returne to Boston (for a small time in May) when the Spring trade will be over.

And now yor Hono^r being pleased to Advise me, (from some Intimations you have had) that you thought a good agreement between Capt Giles & my selfe was absolutly necessary, to the well managing the Public Business &c at reading wch I was surprised, for here has not been the Least difference or angry word past between us since my Arrival, I know not the designes of any (unless Early to create a difference between us) that sent missinformations to this place, of my coming here with comand of the Garison twas whispered about among the Soldiers tho I heard nothing of it; And wch I think had Effect only to raise unreasonable Suspitions in Capt Giles, but soone after my arrival he asked me, whether I had any orders or Instructions for him, To which I answered I had no Instructions only relating to the Affair of Truck Master of which I had the Concern, and upon his repeating the Question (which I wondered at) I againe tould him I had nothing to do with the Garrison or men, nor was there so much as any mention of his name in my Instructions which I offered to shew him, but refused to see them, And that I had only brought a serv^t with me, wch yor Honour tould me, at the Castle, that you Intended when he came to Boston to direct him to putt into the Muster roll as my Servt without his dismissing any man, Neither have I so much as by way of Advice pretended to direct him, by word or wrighting to any person complained of, or faulted his Conduct in any respect, Neither have I given any one reason to gess what my thoughts are concerning him nor have I ordered any thing but in the truck house, or any man but my own serv^t there, Nor so much as desired any man without his Leave to do the Least matter for me, tho for the Service of the Province in the Truck house & then not without paying them somthing for it, thinking it most agreeable to Capt Giles so to do; Capt Giles also denyes that here is, or has been any disagreement or Difference between us. So that as I am not Conscious of any mismanagement or impudence (notwithstanding any wrong Intimations) I hope still to share in yor Hono^rs favourable thoughts___

I presume by this oportunity Capt Giles acquaints yor Hono^r that old Moxus has this day been here, rec^d the Letter & present for him with usual Expressions of thanks &c– Wenogonott Loron & most of the Indians are out hunting, no news from Canada.

I shall allwayes carefully observe yor Hono^rs Injunctions of writing what Ever Offers to Sr Yo^r Honours most Obedient Humble Servt

Thos Smith

Cinow here bring boards for Service of the Truck house &c If your Hono^r will please to give orders that the Carpenter here may be Imployed in doing whats of Necessity he'l readily do it without wch he is unwilling to Ingage in it I hope yor Hono^r will Excuse what you see amiss in my writing or Stile Sanders waiting to go off

T S

[Indorsed]

Orders to be given to ye Carpenter at St Georges, to repair ye Truck House.

[Superscribed]

To the Honou^ble William Dummer Esqr Lieu^t Governour & Comand^r in Cheif of His Majesties Province of the Massachusets Bay N E att Boston Q^d C

p^r Capt Sanders

Letter L^t. Gov. Dummer to Capt. John Giles March 21, 1726.

S^r

I Rec^d your Letter of the 27th of February last And am

Glad to hear of the safety of the Captives & doubt not, but by the Care of the Tribes I shall soon see them returned.

I am much Displeased at the Action of the Indians at Meintenicus in Killing the Creatures there; Upon which Occasion You must Inform the Sachem & other Chief men as well as the immediate Actors as follows.

" That I very much Resent this Liberty they have taken in Killing the Creatures which belong to the English, which is contrary to the Articles of Peace And that Common Justice which the English and Indians owe to one another, Not to Hurt one another in their Just Rights and Properties; Which Fault is much aggravated from the Constant Care I have taken to have them supplied with all manner of Necessaries at the Trading Houses: And as it was one View I had in this free & Generous Trade which I have carried on with them, To prevent such ill practices from them, So I flattered my self it would have that good Effect; And that as Justice & Honesty are the surest Methods to preserve the Peace, so, on the Contrary Violence & Robbery have a direct tendency To disturb ye friendship & good Agreement wch I have Endeavoured to maintain with the Indians & which I hope will subsist between us & them to the latest Posterity: That if they have not already made full satisfaction for the damage done, I expect "They do it without delay. And that I insist
" upon it that their Chiefs do frequently warn all the Young
" Men That They never Meddle with any of the English
" Cattle or other things belonging to them: And that I expect
" They will make strict inquiry whether this Action was done
" either through Rashness and Wantonness or by the Instiga-
" tion of Such as are both theirs and Our Enemies, who may
" have a wicked Design to make a Misunderstanding between
" us; And that in this and all other the like Cases They do
" Examplary Justice to the Offenders, in order to deter
" others from Doing the like Mischief. This is what you

are to say to them. No more at present from Your Humble Servt

Wm Dummer

Boston March 21, 1726.
Capt. John Gyles

Letter Col. Saml. Partridge to the Commissioners at Albany.

Hatfield, March 22th 1726/7

Gentlemen
Inclosed as you will see is a Coppy of a Letter from His Honn^{or} Lef^t Governer, to Co^{ll} Stoddard and my selfe and Co^{ll} Stoddard being Indisposed I tho^t Itt my duty, as Well as the Interest of ye Gourment to write to your selfe to Assist us In this Affair, And I would desire, and you will see also that tis our Left Governers Mind that Gray Lock, should be made a freind and Come Into ye Treaty of Peace, And also ye Chiefs of St. Francewa Indians: In Pursute of ye same I would desire that with all dispatch you Can, you would Send an Indian or two, or any other way you shall think Proper, to Invite Gray Lock, as also some of the Chiefe of ye St. Francewa Indians to Come unto us some Where In this County, In order to a Confirmation of Peace, and Gentlemen you seeing our Lef^t Gouerners Letter I make No doubt of your Frindshipp that you will not Scruple of being Garrantees for their Safety In Coming & Returning, and Well Treatment while Amoungst us= but if by No Means that Cant be obtained then that they be Prevayled with to Come to Albany Which they Know that they may doe with all Safty, And Please to advise mee by this Express, what is Probable to be done, and so I will acquaint his honor Our Left Governor with itt, that he may Imply some Meet Person,

or Persons to treat with y^m there to Ratifie And Confirm ye Peace ye Penobscott Tribes is Come Into, for if these Partys was Quiet I hope Wee should be all Easey—for Very Latly Our Left Governor had advise from one of ye Norridgwolk Indians that they and each of their tribes are Peaceably Inclined, And Intend to Continue so, And that in ye Spring they will doe their best Endevure either to Flatter or Force Any Ill Minded Indians In or about Cannada to Joyne with y^m In ye Ratification of Peace. Pray Gent^m Use your Prudence and Interest to Accomadat this matter. As for ye Charge In y^s Affaire you see by his honnors Letter itt will be Answered: Lett me hear by this bearer What Success there is Like to be In ye Affair In all which Gen^tmen very much Oblidg o^r Goverment and your most Hum^bl Ser^t

Sam^ll Paŗtridge

To ye Commissioners of ye Indian Affairs att Albany: Coppy:

Letter Wenungenit, Chief Sachem of Penobscot, to L^t. Gov. Dummer

St Georges Octob^r 4th 1726

Great Govr

I rec^d your Letters, as also the peice of Cloath & return you thanks y^r for as also for the Prisoners you sent to me. I can not send you any News from Canada as my Young men I sent their are not return'd and I Can't resolve on comeing to Boston untill they come & bring me News from Canada, & then I shall send you what News I have; & if I can conveniently I will wait on y^r Hon^r at Boston y^s winter. In asmutch as you sent me the Acc^tt of the Cape Sables men's Actions I shall likewise send to you if I hear of any such things. I have talk'd wth my people about the

Truck house being at St Georges Garrison but most of them choose it Should be mov'd to ye mouth of the River or any other place you think fitt Near ye Sea the reason is yt St Georges River is sometimes frozen so that they can't come to it in yr Canoes, I don't take on me to direct yr hon{r} only mention these things to you I have on ⁻ request to yr Hon{r}. wch is that you would be pleas'd to Order a Gunn Smith to mend our Locks &c I have nothing further to Add but remain Yr Good Freind

Wenungenit 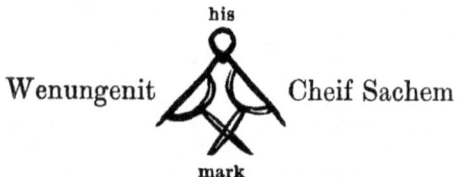 Cheif Sachem

At a Meeting of ye Cheifs of the Tribe they chang'd his Name from Wenemuit to Wenungenit who was their former Sagamore;

Letter Capt. Joseph Heath to Lt Gov. Dummer, Dec. 15, 1726.

Honourable

Sr Herewith is humbley presented An Acct of Disbursements for Building a Truck House & repairing the Garison at St Georges River, Agreeable to the Vote of the Honble Board Herewith Exhibited⸺
I have strove to recommend my selfe to your Honour & the Goverments favour in this affair (and the Difficulty of halling Timber with our Cattle Being Considered) am persuaded the Charge will not be thought to Exceed a Just proportion to the work.
About sixty feet more of the Old Stockado work is almost Rotten, but I let it alone, as thinking it soficient for this Year

which old work being made new (next Summer) like what I have now Done will (in my Humble Opinion) make the Garison Commodious & Defencable for many years to come without any other Repairs of y⁰ Out works—
When I built the Fort at Richmond I annimated the Labourers by working continually for y⁰ space of Eighty Days And have used the same method in the work at S.ᵗ Georges for Twenty Days. But did not (in the Richmond Acc.ᵗ nor do I at this Time) make any Charge for my Own labour. Neither do I mention it for any other reason then that your Honour & y⁰ Goverment may observe how freely I have Imploy'd my hands as well as thoughts, in the publick service On those Occasions.

   I am Your Honours Most obedient Hum.ᵇˡᵉ Serv.ᵗ
Dec.ʳ 15.ᵗʰ   Joseph Heath
   [Superscribed]
 To The Honourable William Dummer Esq.ʳ Lieut Gove.ʳ & Com̃ander in Chief of His Maj.ᵗⁱᵉˢ province of the Massach.ᵗᵗˢ Bay &c

Letter Capt Joseph Heath to L.ᵗ Gov. Dummer
        Richmond Fort March 24ᵗʰ 1727
Honourable
     S.ʳ Yours relating to M.ʳ Tappens Affair I rec'd, but y⁰ Trespassers were gon—
I supply'd Quinows & two Others with Necessarys for their Journey to Canada, who set out 17.ᵗʰ of Last moneth and said they should returne about the first of May Monsieur De la chass superior of y⁰ Jesuits in Canada & the Missionaries at y⁰ Indian Villages there Exert all their powers to prevent a General peace & y⁰ Missionary at Penobscut is their Echo on this side of y⁰ Continent nevertheless there is

nothing vissible in the face of these affairs that seems
soficient to remove the foundation which your Honour has
laid for peace ~ The Indians in these parts Desire a General
peace & Expect it And I percieve those of Neridgawalk &
Ammoscoggin Expect to Treat with Your Honour Some time
this Spring as the Penobscuts have done And I Desire to be
enstructed wheither their going Generally to Falmouth, Or
only some of their principal men to Boston, would be most
Acceptable to you I am Your Honours Most Obedient
Humble Servt

Joseph Heath

Letter L^t. Gov. Dummer to the Lords of Trade, &c.,
March 25, 1726.

My Lords,
   Some few Months after the Departure of
his Exc͞y Govern^r Shute for G^t. Britain I did my self the
Hono^r to write to y^r L^{dps} Giving you some Acc^t of the
Difficulties of this Province with Respect to the Ind. War
which has bin Excited by the Govern^r of Canada who has
supplied the Salvages with all Stores of War has shelter'd
them within his Governm^t from our Pursuits, & has received
them in Triumph with the Scalps of his Majesties subjects
slain by this barbarous Enemy: W^{ch} Conduct of the said
French Govr (as I suggested to your Lordships in my former Lett^r) seems to me to bee a Notorious Violation of the
Treaty of Utriecht and in some Respects makes the War
with the Indians more difficult than if the French were our
declared Enemies; For by our Successes in the last eight
Months We have driven them from their settlem^{ts} in our
Neighbourhood to the French Territories from whence they

make their Incursions upon us in small sculking Parties & after Mischief done retire thither again where I am cautious of allowing any of our Companies to pursue them till I can know his Majesties Pleasure in this Respect. And I must further inform your Lordships That notwithstanding the Advantages we have lately had over the Enemy, and the Distress'd Circumstances We suppose they are reduced to; The Expence of the War is so great & insupportable to this Province that Unless it shall please God to put a speedy End to it, It will inevitably ruine us; wch I humbly offer to your Lordships Consideration & that you would please to make such a Representation thereof to his Majesty as you shall think necessary for his Maj^s Service & the Safety & protection of these His Provinces. I should not trouble your L^{ds}ship any farther but that the ffrench Govern^r of Canada has given me to understand that he shall address a Complaint to His Master on the Acc^o of the Death of Been who was killed by our fforces in the ffight at Norrigewock of w^h please to take the following account.

In the Action at Norrigewock within this Province wch was in Augt last our Forces destroy'd a great Number of the Indians & broke up that Settlem^t amoung whome was Sebastian Ralle a Jesuit Missionary to that Tribe and the great Incendiary of this War who was slain in Fight Making actual Resistance to the Forces & at ye same time attempting to kill an English Captive in his Hands and refusing to give or take Quarter, To which Acc^t of ye Death of the s^d Ralle Coll. Harmon the Commander of the Forces at Norridgewock made solemn Oath before me in Council, As appears to y^r L^{dps} by the Minutes of Council transmitted to you by the Sec̃r̃y of the Prov.

:this Jesuit had all along push'd the Indians vpon their Rebellions Marching at the Head of Two Hundred armd Salvages through one of the Frontier Towns of this Province before the war was declared threatening Destruction to them If they did not speedily quit the said Town, of w.^{ch} & more to y.^t purpose His Ex^{cy} Govr Shute is well knowing This I thought proper to hint to y^r Lordships in Order to obviate any Complaints that may be made by the French Gov.^t whose Conduct in Exciting & Supporting the Indians in this War & Drawing down many remote Tribes with whom we have no Concern to their Assistance ye truth of which I have sufficient Testimonies to support I shall lay them before y^r Lordship If it be necessary for y^r Satisfaction. should rather have putt Him uppon offering at an Apoligy that a Complaint. All which I humbly submitt to your Lordship & am with the greatest respects y^r Lordship Most Obed.^t & humble S^t

Wm Dummer

Letter Capt. John Gyles to L^t. Gov. Dummer

March 27 : 1727   May It Pleas your honour

A Message this Day from Panobcut Sent by Wanoganet and Chieffs, to a quaint that their Messangers ar Returnd from Canadey to their Villages who wear about 20 Days Coming, & 2 Days since their arival, they ar much wearied & allmost Starved &c

Messangers   We ar to say to you, brother, tel Gevernor Dummar by ye first, that the Messangers ar returnd from Caneday wth Good news and ye Reason of thier tarring so Long, they wear Detained or taken, by ye Chiefs thier, to finish the Great worke they went upon, Which is Concluded on, to have Pece & Love Round our Land, So that the People may Now, go about thier affears without any Guard, for no Percon will Do them any harm, but ye People taken from Kenebunke wear kild on their Journey to Kenadey, Except one Little boy, they wear all^{a}most Starvd & ye English over took them was ye Reason of thier killing em they say.

those y^t Did us y^t mischief wear Indians from Ercegontagog nin in number Viz Wawhe & Peknabowet and Sakenelakud &c

the New Governor Monsieur Bornoway Gives Good advice y^t is to Live in Love & Pece wth ye English & sais he is Glad to hear y^t their is such a Good agreement Concluded between ye English & Indians

p John Gyles Enterpreter

May it Pleas your honour the formar account Concerning Raesonars Proovs Missinfurmation as to y^t articul of Captives, which I am ye authers seem to be well Confirmed,—and as to ye Chieffs say, Concerning ye Peoples Goin about thier affeair wth out Danger of any, in my humble Opinion they are Rale, by thier Coming over wth thier families In order to setle a Gain – Not y^t they ar a People to be Confide in, to fur, ye Jesuitts haveing Such Great Influence on them, I am your honours Most Dutifull Sar^t

Jn° Gyles

Letter Ph. Livingston & others Comm^{rs} to Col^s Stoddard & Partridge.

Albany 27 March 1727

Gentlemen

Yours of ye 22th Instant with copy to you from Govr Dummer rverec^d, desireing our Assistance that gray Lock Should be made a frind to come into the treaty of peace as also the Chiefs of St Francois Indians, we could wish that it was Effected to that end, we have not been wanting in sending a message ab^t ye 2^d Jan^ry Last by Malalemet Brother to s^d Gray Lock inviteing him, and other Chiefs who were hunting on our frontiers to come hither, but unfortunately missd him, being gone home but brought to this place on the first Instant three S^t francois Indians, to whom we thought fitt to Communicate that his hon^r Govr Dummer had confirmd & ratifyd the peace with the penabscut and Narrigewack tribes : that much blood had been Lost on both sides in this last war, and Expected that these indians, in behalf of S^t francois should Ractify & Confirm s^d treaty of peace, that for the future none of their tribe should go to molest or anoy any of our Brethren of N England or Elsewhere, which if they do faithfully pform, they should at all times be welcome to hunt on our frontiers, and be Civilly treated at this place on this we gave them a psent and a belt amounting to £11 : –they Promisd to use their uttmost Endeavor to prevaile on their Chiefs to come hither on our Invitation what Success we Shall have in our undertaking is uncertain & precarious, Assoon as an opportunity Shall Send Such a message to gray Lock & the Chiefs of S^t francois as you desire but have no belt as is Requird on Such occasion we think it more proper to do it, in our name, that your Goverm^t may not be seen in this message for fear it might miscarry And not to give the indians oppertunity to think it comes from you. we Shall not Scruple to make ourSelves garrantees for the Indians civill treatment with you and their safe return tho' Sucpect they will hardly be prevail on especially the gray Lock to go into your County, for the Latter has done much Mischief on your frontiers, and has doubtless a guilty consience we shall at all times be ready to do any thing which may Contribute towards Establishing afirm and Lasting peace between your Governm^t and the Indians, and could wish it was already accomplished, we fear that the french priests and their Govern.^r will if possible, oversett all amicable measures that may be Sett on/foot to Confirm or Conclude any treaty with you, these indians seem to be Sincere. they told us that Last fall on Invitation of some of our number while at Canada severall Sachims of s^d Indians were on their way hither as far as the Crown point, with an intent to make a treaty with your Goverm^t but were pvented by false Reports Spread among them, which made them desist from that design. the said Indians have faithfully promisd us to use their best Endeavours to prevent the indians from going to do mischief on your fronteers, tho there is but little dependance on what they Come to promise. is the needfull at psent from who are with Esteem Gentlemen Your very Humble Servants

    Philip Livingston   Myndert Schuÿler
    Hend^r van Rensselaer   Reÿer Gerritse
    Stevanv Groesbuk   Nicolaes Bleuker

Letter Wm Woodside to L^t. Gov. Dummer

Fort George March 31 : 1727

Hono^{ed} Sir

I Make bold to trouble you with these few Lines Begging the favour together with Maney other favours that is allredy granted that is your Hon^r would Grant the favour of Granting the Lev:^{ntsy} of Fort George to Samuel Eaton Son to Capt Eaton of Salsbury which Samuel Eaton was former Leu^{nt} at Fort George for som years The favour of your Honours granting this Request & sending the Commission by the bearer Capt Sanders Junr Noble being moving at this very time

Letter Col. Partridge to L! Gov. Dummer

Hatfield April 3d 1727.

May it Pleas your Honnor:

Sir I Recivd yours of ye: 14th of March Last: and Note ye Contents Am Very Much Pleased, with your desire, and designe yt ye Western Indian Should Ratifie ye Treaty of Peace, your Letter also being Communicated to Coll Stoddard, he declind Medling In ye Affaier, and I took such Measurs as advis Lead me to; for to Gett any Intimation to Gray Lock, Any way by us (att Present) itt was Impracticable and so I sent an Express to ye Comishoners Att Albany as Enclosed you may see a Coppy of ye Letter sent: With a coppy of your Honnr Letter Also: And here with is the Letter sent to us by the Commishoners: I being thot full Busins did not Require so much hast, I Waited an Opportunity to send itt, if I have done amiss In sending yt way I desire itt may either be Imputed to my Ignorance, or Elce to my Earnest desire or Zeal yt Gray Lock and other Chiefs of St Francois Indeins, should Ratifie the Treaty: Is any thing Further to be done I wait your Honours Directions: who am with due Regards & Submistion

Your Honours Most Humbl sertt

Saml Partridge

To ye Honble William Dummer Esqr Left Governor and Comandr In Chiefe:

Letter – Capt. Thos Smith to L! Gov. Dummer

St Georges Fort April 3d 1727

Sr

Its only in Obedience to Yor Honours Comands (laid on me at the Castle (Capt Giles also writes) That I trouble you with this, to Inform that on Saboth day ye 26th ffebry about Eleven at night, Two Messingers (ye same day) sent by

Wenegonett from Penobscott Arrived here, who say that nine Indians from St Francois, of whom Woahaway was Cheiefe, took & carryed away those persons Last fall from Kenebunk, and apprehending the_ were pursued by the English; killed all but a Little boy, who being carryed before the Others was Spared, further Say y^t no more Such Actions will be comitted by any Indians (Tho~ Mounse^r ye Younger being here ye next day who being treated wth Civility at my Lodgings, his discourse tended to Direct us to Look to ourselves & be on our Garde) They know nothing of Quenoiees being gon for Canada; but a more pirticular Acc^{tt} we may Expect, when those from Canada come hither which will be as soone as they are recruited being greatly Indisposed by a tedious Difficult Journy,

I am Yo^r Hono^{rs} most Obedient Humble Servt
Thos Smith

Letter. Capt. John Gyles to L^t. Gov. Dummer

May it Pleas your honour

I: Expect a more full account after the annuel Praying Meeting, which is on ye first or sacond Day of april,—I have Imploid on_ to be thier and if Lettars to ye Jesuitt & of moment to Let me know &c Canawas was not a Riued to Canedey when those Mescangest Came a way as they say the Inclosd I was a bliged to Detain, we haueing no boate, & not haueing Indians to Go to Casco it being thier Praying time So this Day I send by 2 Soldiers p Canow St Georges Riuer
April 3: 1727—

I am your honours Very humble Servant
John Gyles.

[Superscribed]
On his Maj^{tys} Saruice
To the Honourd Wm Dummar Esq Liu^{tn} Gournor
in Chieff of his Maj^{tys} Prouince "Masachusetts Bay"

Letter Capt. John Gyles to Lt Gov. Dummer April 8, 1727.

   May it Pleas your honour

   I Recivd yours wth the Inclosd of ye 21 of march Last p Exprece by ye hand of Liu^{tu} Wright, April 5th and on ye 7th hear a Riu^d Wenoggenet wth the 2 messangers that went to Canadey Viz Exexces & Franceivexsabe wth Sund auther Indians a bout 20 in numbar, & I Read & Intarpreted to them ye s^d Lettars & Delivrd ye fine Gun &c

Messangers We tel you now Gouernor Dummar, whereas we wear sent Last fall of a Messeg to Canedey, which you told vs to carry s^d Message in answer to ye Caneddeians, you also tould vs at Casco that we knew best what to say to our brother Indians, so at our a Riual thier, we s^d you Indians desiard a meeting to be at Morial, we tould them we Could not Comply wth their Proposall to meet thier, but much better to meet in our Parts in our Lands. thier we shall haue opportunity to discours all affears what may be for our fewter Good & better vnderstanding of Each auther, now we haue heard Each authers say.

Ercegentegog Indians, we have heard your Proposals, which we a prove of, and according as you Desiar, our meeting in your Land, we com according to your Request, Expecting to haue a faier Debate of affears & Good finnishing to &c this is ye fift time of your Inuiting vs to com by ye way of Olbeni & this way. which I now shall Com according to your Request ~ which I Present you wth this wampom belt in token of &c

Ercegentegog we now speak to wenoggenet & all ye Indian Chieffs in that Contenant, – hopeing & Desiar that we all may accomplish in our Debats a Good Vnderstanding & a Lasting Calm in our whole Land, which in token of, we Present to you these strings of wampom.

Messangers   the aboue mentioned belts & authers we Deliver to Gouernr Dummar & wenoggenet in Presents of our brother ye Enterpreter, in Pursuant to order, which is our answer & Return &c

hear is also another belt & a Letter to Gouar^n Dummar ye Contents of s^d Letter is Vnknown to Vs the belt is from twenty Dissadisfied Indians that are not yet Concluded in thier minds &c.

this is all y^t we ar knowing of y^t affear.

We 20 Indians say to you Wenoggenet & all chieffs we Desiar y^t you may make a Good finnishing of ye worke y^t we hear you ar a bout to haue a Good Vnderstanding & a Calm & faier wether in our whole Land, what we say to you we say to the ᴜhole tribes on ye Contenant, which we Present you wth a wampon belt in token of &c

Messangers after said Depets & those tribes Concluded on to send two of thier chieffs & sum authers in order to haue a meeting in our Land they sat out wth Vs, but ar hunting for food by ye way, & to be Expected hear in a few Days is ye whole truth from our hearts, & is ye whole burthen or Lode or Messag y^t was Put on our Shoulders & haue Delivered it to you C : Gyles our brether & fellow Labourer &c In order to send to Gouernor Dummar, we salute,-

p John Gyles Entarpreter

Wenoggenet   Good frend I Reed your Letters of C : Gyles & am heartyly theankfull for your mentioning of affears, and ye Present you sent to me, and what you mention as to any Doing vs harm I am not knowing of I hide nothing from you of moment, I speke from my heart for we ar both Labouring to haue Pece & Love in our Land, & we Promisd to a quaint Each auther of all affears of moment, as our Great God hears Vs spake, & if any Do Vs harm be it on thier own heds —

I Dont Vnderstand writing Letters & if any thing a miss
& nott a Greeable to you in ye Lettar y^t Goos wth y^e
Exprece I Desiar you to Mention to Me, for I know not
ye Contents of &c

as to what you mention to me Concerning Gray Lock I
nor my old men haue no knowledg of him for we ar not
aquainted wth ye Olbeni Indians, we will Endeuour to
know Concerning that affear &c we haue had fouer men
in actiul Seruice 2 of them Returnd Last fall, ye auther
2 ar now Returnd wth ye foregoin Messages your bounty
full thought for them, will be Incurridging for ye futer
&c. I salute you Gouernor Dummar & all ye Councell
hopeing if God willing we shall accomplish a Good
Vnderstand_ & a Calm in our whole Contenant,
St Georges april 8th 1727

p John Gyles Entarpreter

May it Pleas your honour
it is supposd by em that Sumthing mentioned in ye Letter
fromn Candeday will not be a Greeable to your honour
&c, is ye Reason of thier Say they Do not Vnderstand
Letters &c. it is surmised ye Jesuits haue ben Doing
they say they Expect ye 2 Chieffs of ye auther tribes in
short time Wenoggenet Desiars an answer by ye furst
Conuenient oppartunity, they much Plesd wth ye fine
Guns.

my Privat Informar is not Returned a Gain. I Inclose
and Send p Exprece to your honour by Leiv^{tt} Wright,
he being wth ye Last Packett

St Georges April 8th 1727

I am your honours Most Dutyfull Ser^t

John Gyles

[Superscribed]
On his Maj^{tys} Seruice
To the Honoured Wm Dummer Esq Liu^{tn} Gournor
in Chieff of his Maj^{tys} Prouince Masachussetts Bay

Letter Capt. John Gyles to L! Gov. Dummer.

April 8, 1727.

May it Pleas your honour

fraucewexcabe one of ye former Deligats, Desiars me to write to your honour, that you would be Plesd to feaveur him wth a Pass such a one as Loraant or Connawoses,

this Indian has & is much made Vse of in Going of Messages, he is one that Came now from Canedey, and Expects to be sent there a Gain when anything of moment, he tells me the new Goun^r of Canedey tould him if ye Goun^r of boston would Give him a Pass, he would Give him an auther, so y^t he might Pass & Repass on all occasions

this Indian seems to be a Serviceable man, and a well wisher To - if it might Pleas your honour to Grant his Request, &c

I am your honours most dutyfull Servant

John Gyles

St George River April 7: 1727

Letter Capt. Joseph Heath to L! Gov. Dummer.

Richmond April 13th, 1727

Honourable

S^r/ 25th of the Last I acquainted you of the Departure of Quinovis for Canada, his proposal to returne in May, the Assiduety of the French Missionaries to break your Honours Measures with the Indians, and the seeming good state of affairs, their Efforts notwithstanding

I shall now Humbly suggest to your Honour that about ye first of Jan^{ry} Last Finding in John Hegon and Sebacomon a Disposition to go to Canada & Endeavour to Mollify the

Disaffcted Indians there and thinking it for ye public service annimated them as much as possible to Engage in the affair which they did, and returned this day with ye following report viz That when they came to Canada they found the Indians of Wowenock in a peaceable Temper But those of St Francois for some time Inflexable to ye overtures of peace here also they met with Two Captains sent by the Penobscutts who were likewise mediating for a General peace And after a Conference of Twenty Days it was Concluded upon And that Three of the Chief men of St Francois and one from wowenock with such as the Neridgawalk Ammoscoggin and Pigwackets may Chuse to represent them, should wait upon and Confer with your Honour for that purpose assoon as they could Conveniently come together which they thought would be toward ye latter end of June.

they add that the Elder Indians of neridgawalk Ammoscoggin and pigwacket who fled with their famolies to, and resided at Canada during ye late war & untill this Spring, are now on ye way in order to people ye villages on this side ye Contenant as formerly. These men Intreat your Honour to give orders to ye frontiers. Especially near Connecticut River and Kennebunk that none of ye English fall upon their people while a Hunting. And they say that they them selves have neglected their winters Hunting by improving their Time & bending their thot's wholly to this bussenness; which if they have, and their report be True (as I believe) they seem to be worthy of your Honours perticuler favour. The report of the two Indians as above is further Confirmed by a Captain of the St Francois Indians who came with y^m

I am your Honours most Hum^ble Obedient Servant
Joseph Heath

P. S. I Believe that ye Indians who took ye people at Kenebunk apprehending that they were Closely persew'd by ye English Kill'd some of those Captives.

Letter Secretary Willard to Comm^rs for Indian Affairs in Albany April 13, 1727.

Gentlemen I am directed by the Honble the Lt Govr & this Prov. to acquaint you that They are Sorry to finde by a L^r d. 22 March last past from Coll^o Partridge to you that Hee has so greatly mistaken the orders Hee rec^d from him as trouble you with Sending a Message to Greylock & other Indians respecting a treaty with them whereas there was no such thing intended or desired by us (as you will judge by the Copy of ye Lett^r to Coll. Partridge wch he informs he has sent you thô without any Direction for so doing proper measures to bring those Indians in to Approbate the Peace lately Made But the good People of the County of Hampshire being more apprehensive phaps then was Needfull of the bad faith of Greylock they had direction privately to discourse & notifie Him to Come in then to Confirme them in his good intents. His Hon^r is however thankfull to you for your readines to do good offices to this Governm^t & desires this affair may be no further proceded in onely as you may Ocationely see any of those Indians to assure them of our ffriendship.

"*Secry^s Letters to Capt Heath & Gyles April 25, 1727.*"

Sir,

His Hon^r the Lieut. Govr going to Newbury soon after ye Rec^t of y^re Letter by Saunders directs me to write to you in Answer to it, That you acquaint Victor that by the first opportunity after his Hon^rs Return to Boston, He will send him the value of £5 in Consideration of the Guns he lost at Arrowsick & that Mr Trescot is Ordered to pay him what he sold the Canooe for; But that for the time to come he must keep himself sober, For he must not expect that the

Governm.^t will pay him for what he foolishly loses when he is in drink there being no Reason in that. I am further to acquaint you that His Hon^r has appointed the tenth of July next to ratify the Peace with the Norridgewocks & other Indians at Boston; and therefore he desires that you would acquaint ye Indians with this his Determination, & by all possible Means engage the Chiefs not only of the Norr. & Penob. & oth^r Eastern Indians but also of the St Francis Cagnawaga, Schohanadie & other Tribes of Canada Indians to appear at Boston, And that you will use all Means in y^re Power to bring them down to this meeting: His Honour consents to y^re Coming soon to Boston to the Court, Provided you take special Care that the Service be not hurt in y^re absence from y^re Post.

Sir,

His Honour the Lieut. Govern.^r going to Newbury soon after the Recepit of your Letter by Saunders, Directs me to write in answer to it, That he thinks it most convenient that the Indians should come to Boston to Ratify the Peace, & has appointed the tenth of July next as the most suitable Time to confer with them for that Purpose; And there He desires that you would acquaint the Indians with this his Determination ; And by all possible Means engage not only the Chiefs of the Penobscot & Norridgewock Indians, but also of the St Francis Cagnawaga, Schohanadie & other Tribes of Canada Indians to appear at Boston, And that you would use all the Means in your Power to bring them down to this meeting.

His Honour is surprized that he hears nothing of the Repairs of Brunswick Fort, and desires if you have not done it, that you would forthwith see the Matter effected.

Least you should have lost ye Coppy of ye Gen.^ll Assemb. Vote for ye Repairs, I herewith send you an other.

Letter Capt. John Gyles to L^t. Gov. Dummer

April 25th A Short Memorial to his honour ye Liu^{tn} Gouernour In Chief &c of Discours betwen a Machies Indian & Gyles at Georges.

Indian – I have a Good mind to tel you something

Gyles – So Do for I hide nothing from you of Moment.

Indian – I dont Cear to tell it, but I will to you, for ye Caneback Indians tel us y^t ye English have taken one Indian & keep 2 or 3 more Reconars and if they Dont send them to us, it will be best this summar to kill & take sum of ye English

Gyles – you know ye English have sent thier Preconers accordingly to Promis at ye Confurrance.

Indeed thier may be one or 2 behind as you say, that might be then at sum Distance.

but you have not sent in any, one you have at St Johns, and authers your People say at Caneday sold to ye french, and 3 young women Maried to Indians thier & have Children, and authers you say ye Indians have taken for their own, but Let them be brought in & Discours wth thier frinds, & then if they wont tary, they wont be compeld,

as to ye yong Indian you spake of Last fall, he was tendred as a hostig, of your Peoples faithfullness in finding out those that kild us, at Kenebunk and when Connawos Returns from Caneday & is faithfull according to Promis Governour Dummar will Do you no Rong you may Depend on it &c

Indian – I tould ye Canebacks that they wear forward in killing & makeing war, but they Must Remember that they Run away, & Left thier Country & ye Penobscut Indians tow, and we stud by, and now we Desiar Peace &c.

Gyles – you tould them wright which is the truth &c.

Indian – the Jesuitt & I am at Differance, he tels me I Love ye English but ye English, will Do by us as they have Don by ye southern Indians to take away our Lands & Privilidges and then Compell us to Pray as ye English Do, and not to be aloude to use the Cross.

Gyles – I should be Plesd if I wear to travil a mong those Southern Indians you spake of, and to see how they live, & the Cear our Government takes of them that they have Justies Dun them, and y^t they Dont tell thier Drunken fitts but to have ye Governments approbation &c and as for Compelling any to Pray as we English Do, is a mistake, for they Compel non, but Parswad & Invite Ani that will Com & Pray as we Do, and that is according to Gods word which is our Guide & ye true Path, Christ Left for those y^t lieve in him, & their is but one God, & one Rite Path y^t Leads to happiness, but Many Rong ones, & ye french have Compeld People so far as to burn em at ye Stake, to make them Pray as they Do, which is not according to Gods word &c

Indian – I tould ye Jesuitt that I believed the English kept the Sabbath best for they Praied all Day, but the french Shott Guns and Go to Play, but ye Jesuitt tels me I am above ye English which are not Good.

Gyles – I find in Gods word, (in his Book) whear God Commands us to keep ye Sabbath Day holy which is ye Seventh Part of time, Set a Part to worship ye only true & Liveing God, that made ye heavens ye Earth ye Sea & all Creaturs, and man in six days, and on ye seventh Day he Rested, and ordred man to keep holy ye Seventh Day (which is the Sabbath) to his service to Praise him, and to have no Regaurd to other Gods which are Images & ye worke of mens hands, they Can neither hear See nor smell nor Do us any Good, but that only true & Liveing God, Knows all our thoughts & actions & tis of him we Live move & have our being, our health breath meet Drink & Clothing & all we Enioy is from him &c

Indian – I like your Discourse & shall not hide anything from you of moment, farewell,–

Gyles – I shall Do for you & your People the best I Can (as our true God Enable me,) which is my Instructions from Government, farewel,

p John Gyles Enterprter.

May it please your honour
if it might Pleas ye Government to apoint Sum Good Grave teacher to Reside in those Parts it might be a means to bring Over Sum of those Poor Deluded People to Worship ye true God.

St Georges River April 25 : 1727 :

I am your honours most Dutyfull Servant
John Gyles

Cpt Gyles Conference April 25, 1727.

Orders to be sent to the Officers in ye Frontiers to treat well the Indians that may be Hunting.

Indians to be inform'd of it.

Cpt. Gyles & Cpt. Heath to stay till the Indians come.

To endeavour to bring the Indians to Boston, but if they finally insist on treating in the East^n Parts that they immediately send Express

Cpt. Gyles to tell Lorone that the Insinuations of ye English Designs are false &c & that the intended Treaty is not to be separate but a Confirmation of the last Treaty.

Cpt. Heath to countenance the Indians Settlem^t of Norridgewock.

Whale Boat.

Letter Capt. John Giles to Lieut. Gov. Dummer.

April ye 28th 1727. A Memorial to his honour ye Liu^{tn} Governour in Chieff Discourse betwen an Informar & Gyles.

Informar— At the a Rival of ye two Messengars from Caneday We had 2 great Meetings & sundry Debats on the Letter they brought, & others &c the Lettar was Red by ye Jesuitt & Casteens and not well a Proved of by Casteens nor the Chief of Panobcut, sum wear for sending it back to old Wawenorawot and tel him to treat for him self, for they had Dun what they thought Proper wth thier brother English but on ye sacond Concediration they thought it Most Proper to send s^d Lettar to Governour Dummar as Diracted &c

Informar the Messengars say that many things Conserning the English & Indians treaty, ar Endvered to be Stivefled and not made known to those other nations, (not Stifled by ye New Governour) at their furst a Rival to Caneday the Messengars had a wompom belt Presented to them to stop their Eyes & Ears & mouths but they Returnd s^d belt back, & said they Came to Make Known ye truths to all, then they had a Great Meeting, and then ye Praying Mohawks & Mountain Indians and sinecours, wear Parmitted & they all approved well of what was Don at ye Confurance Except ye old Whithed Wawenorrawot (he is half french) and old Onedahauet (his old name is Com hommon thier ar 16 in number of ye Malcontents the two named, ar chiefs, of Excegontegog, thier is sidings tho but few of ye malcontents Party, that sent the Letter, the auther Party y^t ar for Peace, have sent old Adamhegon & Amanequened as Messengars to know the truths &c thier will be several more as Specttaters. the Chiefs of Panobcut at their Last Great meeting have Concluded to send Messengars to Caneback St Johns Cap Seples, To Invite two of each Tribe to be at thier Great Annual Meeting at Panobcut which is about fourty Days hence, and those from Canaday ar then Expected thier at s^d meeting.

tho ye Canedeians sat out wth the Panobcut Messengars, but ar to hunt by ye way &c

p̱ John Gyles Enterpreter

Informar — this is ye truth of what I know at Present, thier is nothing of moment in our Jesuitts Letter, what is, is Relateing, ye friar affears, when I hear Enithing more, of moment, I will inform you according to Promis.

Gyles — you will Do well, & I will be to my word to you, So farewell.

Memorial of Capt. John Gyles to L^t. Gov. Dummer
May 4, 1727.

May it Pleas your honour

on ye 4th Currant Capt Loron a Riv^d hear from ye westward from hunting, & Rec^d his Present ye Superfine Gun & his Letter wth Great thankfullness

he mentioned to me y^t he heard t^t ye Canebeck Indians had sum Expectation of your honours Meeting them to have a Seprate Peace, if so it would as it wear Season the Panobcuts formar Proceedings as they acted for ye whole

Desiaring my opinion, I tould him I would Give him my opinion, but he must not take it as any Diracttions from ye Government, for I had non Concerning that affear I tould him I Did not Supose your honour would meet them in any of these Parts this Summar, I Did not know, but if Desiard Sum of the Council might be apointed to meet them, but to have a separate Peace I Did not believe any such thing, only to Ratifie ye articols alredy Concluded on &c

he further said that he heard your honour this winter had been treating wth ye Mohawks to Com & Distroy them for they wear now much weakend &c

I tould him he might ashuer him self thier was no such thing on action, it was only sum Devil seruars that would a Mues them wth such Notions. for it was altogether Contrery to ye English Profession to Use treachery, I Desiard him to Look back (for I had been aquainted in affears near 30 years Past) and if he could mention to me one trecherous action Don by ye English in s^d time &c

St Georges May 4th 1727

    I am your honours Most Dutyfull Servant
            John Gyles

   Memorandom

this 4th Currant Connawos a Riv^d from Ritchmond and s^d he had tould thier, & was Com to aquaint hear, that he Proseeded Part of ye way to Caneday & their meeting with sum of ye Caneday Indians, who tould him it would be of no service, of his Going to Caneday for it was a Greed on, that thier Chieffs should Com over hear, to treat on ye affear he was Going on, & authers, and it was well known who Did that Mischief at Kenebunk, & thier was but one Presonar a Live, which upon he went no further, but Returnd.

I Gave s^d Connawos my advice, & Put him In mind of his Engagements, & that, auther serviceses was Expected of him then what he had Don, & that to Prove him Self an honest man, & Do what he Promised ye Government Concerning Presonars &c

      p John Gyles Enterp^rtr

St Georges River May 4: 1727:

Letter Capt Thos. Smith to L^t. Gov. Wm Dummer

        S^t. Georges May ye 15th 1727

S^r

  I am favour'd wth Mr Secretary's Letter of ye 25th Last in & (by y^r Hono^rs direction, as he sayes) signifying

Your being willing I should come up to Boston, wch I should not desire were I in the Least Suspitious, that the Governm^ts business Comitted to my Care would suffer by it, but all the Indians here, have been for Six weeks or more Aprised of and Expect it, and in a few dayes more I Expect that they will all be here supplyed, with what they shall need for some time, I have also Mr Treasu^r Allen's Letter intimating the fall in the price of Beaver & directing me to give but 7/6^d p h, which Occations great dissatisfaction, but as I have Don, so shall continue to do my utmost Endeavo^rs to make them sensible that they are justly dealt with, and may be assured of having all Possible Justice don them, An unhappy accident falling out at this juncture, a Caske of Rum on board Capt Sanders (coming to me) Leaking out on the Passage, wch would, if he had come to hand, most of any thing have shewn the fall also in the price of what they are supplyed wth from us, which makes the Indians seam suspitious of the reallity of its being so follen in price, therefore I must desire that without delay a hh^d may be sent, with some Other things according to Mem^o sent to Mr Treaso^r to whome I have now also sent five hh^ds of Beaver small furrs feathers &c amounting to £705 : 14 : 2 : wch being the pres^t offers

I Subscribe Yo^r Hono^rs Most Obedient Humble Servt

Thos Smith

Letter Capt John Gyles to L^t. Gov. Dummer May 15, 16 1727

May it Pleas your honour

I Rec^d a Letter from Mr Secretary, p Cap^tn Sand^rs and have Communicated ye same to Wenoggenet & shall Notifie ye auther Chieffs by ye furst, as to time & Place, according to your honours appointment to Ratifie the Peace &c

Wenoggenet seems to be hearty in ye afear, I have nothing of moment to acquaint p Canow to Casco Bay

St Georges Garrison May ye 15th 1727

I am your honours most Dutifull Ser^t

John Gyles

I hope to weight on your honour next trip in order to make up my Mustar Roll &c for my Liu^{tn} is Returnd who is a Good Cearfull hand, & I Can Leve Charge wth him.

May 16, 1727. Wenoggenet Desiars me to aquaint that he heartily Salutes your honour & ye honorable Council, & wieshes you Long Life, & that nothing shall be wanting on his Part In order to have a Good Understanding & Calm Round ye Continant & y^t he hath Sent in behalf of Govern^r Dummar & for him self to ye Caneday Indians a belt of 13 Wampom Peges breath to a quaint them that they must make no more breaches on us, if they Do he will Resent it, and Consult wth Govr Dummar and have Satisfacttion of them &c

p John Gyles Enterp^{tr}

[Endorsed]

Capt John Gyles L^r

Georges Garrison May 15 & 16, 1727

Capt. Gyles to acquaint Wennogenet that His Hon^r is satisfied with his Message to the Indians Mess^a to be repeated wch he has expected, It being agreable to the Treaty."

Sir

I have had your Honours Order to Capt John Gyles to dismisse my Servant after the Enlisting an other man—

which is a Very hard thing to D? there unlesse he can contrive to make a man & to Enlist him &c

A day or two since I Mett with Capt Penhallow & Lt Benj^a Wright, who say y^t My Servant hath ben in ye Service (Come fall of ye year) four years, & have given y^r attestation to it, ye one by wrighting, & ye other sighning of A Certificate of it, as also y^t he hath ben Confined to ye fort two years – I hope your Hon^r will Reconsider ye Matter & ye hard ship y^t ye young man lays und^r Especially, being a Volunteer as he was – & favor me with a New ord^r to Capt John Gyles to Deliver him on Sight; for I shall otherwise be a great sufferer, & be at ye Charge of Sending for ye man & be disap^{td}

S.^r for fear of your Hon.^{rs} forgetting ye natere of your Ord^r have Enclosed it, & hope y^t you'll oblige me with an other, with out any Conditions or Reserves in it, w^c is ye Needfull from

Your Hon^{rs} Obed^t hum^{ble} Servant
Wm Vaughan

Portsm? May 20th 1727

To ye Hon^{abl} Wm Dummer Esqr
Lt Governour

May 19th, 1727.

May it Pleas your honour

an Informar from Keneback River to a quaint, that ten of the Malcontant Indians sat out this Spring In order to Kill & take English, and when ye Peacble Party heard of it, they sent a Party affter them & over took them, & Reasoned ye Case wth em, and told them if they wear Resolved to Go on, they wold go wth them, & if they Did any harm to ye English, they should Neiver Return to Caneday a Livef, for they would Inform ye English & Rais men to am bush Every Carring Place throw ye Continant, & if any made thier Escape to Ercegontagog they would fetch them out, or if they had a mind to tri thier Manhood they would see them on a Pond that was hard by, but on Concideration of these & auther arguements, they Desisted, & have Don no harm to any.

 thier ar several Indians from Caneday, a bout 50 or 60 men they Reside Chiefly at taconnock, Sum ar of ye Praying Mohawks & of Ercegontagog som of Wowenog & sum of those y^t wear Drove from Norangowock & those Parts, they ar a Mixt Crew, many of them Dont Pray and sum ar Wisards a mong them, thō they Generally Seem to Inclin to Peace wth ye English, & ar Calld English Indians, on y^t account

    p John Gyles Enterpet^r

This Certifys all Concern'd That James Blaggdon or Braggdon now a Soldier at St Georges under the Command of Capt John Gyles was inlisted into the service sometime in Novr 1723

as attests   Benjn Wright

The s^d Braggdon has been posted at St Georges Two Year Last January.

 Portsm° May 19th 1727

Capt John Gyles

    Mr William Vaughan having represented to Me That James Bragdon (his servant) now a soldier in your Garrison, has been in ye service of this Province a long time Desiring that he may be Dismiss'd.

 These are to direct you to Enlist another able bodied man

in his stead, and then to dismiss the said James Bragdon accordingly.

Given under my hand at Boston the 29th day of May, 1727.
In the Thirteenth Year of his Maj^{tis} Reign
Wm Dummer

Letter Lt Gov. Dummer to Capt. Heath & Capt. Gyles
May 23, 1727.

Sir

I rec^d your Letter of the 13th April while I was in the Countrey. I am extreamly pleased with the accurate & useful Accounts & Observations you give us upon the State of Affairs with the Eastern Indians, & have great Dependance on your Diligence & prudent Conduct as a considerable Means to confirm their good Disposition. I have shall send you by Sanders the Value of £10 in Goods wch you must deliver in my name & in the most proper manner to John Hegon & Sebacomon in Consideration of their Time & Service in the Journey to Canada wch you mention in your Letter, and as a further Testimony of my Favour to them you must present them with the Value of 40. each in Provisions. I would have you do all you can to countenance & encourage the Indians Resettling at Norridgewock & those Parts.

You must acquaint Loron that you have my Orders alwaies to treat him as a particular Friend to the English.

& must tell them that I have given Orders that no. Body shall molest them in their Fishing & Hunting, more especially on Connecticut & Kennebunk Rivers as they have desire.

Letter Lt Gov. Dummer to   *May 23, 1727.*

Sir

I rec^d your sev^{ll} Letters sent by Lt Wright & since that those of the Latter End of the Last & Beginning of this month, & am well pleased with y^{re} Diligence getting the best Intelligence you can of the Temper & Designs of the Indians.

The Secr̃y by my Order informd you that I had appointed the tenth Day of July for Ratifying the Peace with the Norridgwocks & other Indians at Boston, & directed you to endeavour that the Chiefs of the Indians repair hither accordingly; W^{ch} Instructions you must observe & use all proper Argum^{ts} to induce them to make Boston the place of their Meeting for that affair, But in case you shall find them finally averse to treat here you must immediately send me an Acc^t of it by Express, that I may take measures accordingly; And althô I gave you Leave to come up to Court to pass y^{re} Muster Roll at the next Session, I think it absolutely necessary that you stay to receive the Indians & conduct them to the Place of Meeting; & send an^{er} Officer up with your Roll.

As to what Loron tells you of a Rumour of our Engaging the Mohawks agst the Eastern Indians you must assure him that It is a false & malicious Story invented by our Enemies with a mischievous Intention, and that I wonder he will open his Ears to such a vile Sugestion after the Indians have had so many Marks of my Sincerity.

And as to the other Matter he mentions of a Design for a separate Peace with the Norr. Indians, You may tell him there is no Foundation for it. My Intention being to meet the Indians in Order to ratify the Peace already made & I shall come into Nothing but what is entirely conformable to that Treaty. &

In answer to what you have written by the Desire of Wenungenet & the other Indians & in their Name, You must say to them as follows;

That I rec^d y^r Letter of the 8th of April last some time since, but being then at my Countrey House at a considerable Distance from Boston I had no Opportunity to send y^m an answer.

that I observe y^{rr} Messengers are return'd from Canada with Success, & that the Tribe of Indians at Arrasaguntacock are entirely satisfied with the Peace you have made with me on their Behalf as well & that they have sent two of their Chiefs & others to meet me in Order to ratify the s^d Peace: and that althô twenty Indians of that Tribe were something dissatisfied yet they did at last approve of our Proceedings & express themselves well pleased that there is now a Calm in our whole Land, that I have likewise rec^d the two Belts you sent me one from the s^d Arrasaguntacook Tribe & the other from the twenty Indians above mention'd. I am well satisfied with y^{re} success on that Message, and hope that the English & Indians throughout the Continet will live in perfect Friendship & Goodwill for the time to come & will promote each others Welfare all that is in their Power; It being alwaies my Desire & Endeavour to accomplish such a Peace as would prove for the great & lasting Benefit of the Indians as well as the English. I desire that the Chiefs & others Messengers from the Arrasaguntacook Indians would proceed to Boston as soon as they can, in Order to meet & confer with me upon those important Affairs, & that Wenungenet & Moxus & other Chiefs of the Penobscot & Norridgewock Tribes would accompany y^m. And they may depend upon my Receiving them very kindly; And I hope our Interview will be for the better Establishm^t of the Peace between us: That as to the twenty Men y^y say were dissatisfied but are now brought over to join with you in the Peace, I doubt not but y^r Account of them is true; But the French Letter sent me wch y^y say is from those Indians does entirely contradict y^r Representation of the Temper & Designs of those Indians, For that Letter says they keep the Hatchet still well up & makes unreasonable Demands contrary to ye Treaty at Casco from wch I am resolved never to depart, Pretending that they twenty are the Chiefs of the Norr. Indians & Act for y^m, wch I know to be false having rec^d sev^{ll} friendly Letters from Moxus & others who are the undoubted Chiefs of that Tribe, & that Letter casts very unjust Reflections upon me & the English W^{ch} I sh^d much resent, But that I entirely rely on the other Acc^t of those Indians as true, & that French Letter being without date & not sign'd by any Person what soever, I take it to be a villanous Design of some evil minded Men that mortally hate both the English & Indians & are desireous to involve us in new Troubles; And therefore I shall reject the Paper as nothing else but a scandalous Libel; However if those or any other Indians may be so far prevail'd upon by the Artifices of any ill minded Persons as to attempt any thing upon the English contrary to our Treaty & wch may lead to break the Peace I shall depend upon y^{or} Solemn Engagem^{ts} y^y will effectually bind them to Peace & hinder them from offering the least Injury to the English. I have sent to Cp^t Gyles a Reward to Alexis & Francis Xavier for their Time & faithful Service in the Message sent to Arrasaguntacook & as a Token of my further Respect I shall Order then a Supply_Provision.

That Upon Inquiry into what Victor mentions of the Loss of his Canoe & Guns, I find Ensign Trescot has taken up a Canoe & two Hatchets wch is supposed to be Victors & he has p^d £3.10 for them W^{ch} with £5 I shall give him in consideration of y^e Loss of his two Guns will be sent to him in Goods by Saunders.

that I have rec^d Advice from Annapolis that a Body of Indians being assembled near Menis & Secanecto some ill minded Men among them were meditating Mischief agst our Fisher Men in Revenge of ye Justice done to ye French & Indian Pirates the last Fall. I think it proper to communicate this to y^m Agreable to ye Treaty Expecting that they may inquire into this matter, And, if it be so that y^y oppose these Indians & Reduce them to a Peaceable Behaviour, W^{ch} is conformable to ye Engagem^{ts} in ye s^d Treaty.

In answer to what Loron says

Letter L^t. Gov. Dummer to Col. Wheelwright.

Sir

I have rec^d from the Eastern Indians very full Testimonies of their peaceable Temper & Intentions and as a Mark of their entire Confidence in our Friendship, Many of them (who have been driven by the late War into the Governm^t of Canada are now Returning back with their Families to their old Habitations near our Borders, and they have desired I would take the proper Methods for their Safety in their Hunting near us; more particularly at Connecticut and Kennebunk River.

These are therefore to disire & direct you to take effectual Care that the Inhabitants of the Frontier Towns in your County be notified hereof, & that they give no Molestation to the s^d Indians in their Hunting & Fishing, but treat them with Kindness & Friendship, and that they avoid all Occasions of Quarrelling with them, W^{ch} is absolutely necesssary In Order to preserve the Peace. You must more especially restrain the People on Kennebunk River from any Resentm^t of the Injury done to our People there, For I have taken Proper Measures for Satisfaction.

May ye 26 : 1727

May it Pleas your honour

This Day Espequead ye sacond Chief of ye Panobcut tribe, wth sum authers Desiard me to a quaint your honour that he Desiars that ye yong Indian boy y^t was Left as a hostig Last fall, may be Returnd to them by ye furst, autherways he is thoughtfull whether it will not Create Mischief to befall us by sum,

he further Desiars y^t whereas he in ye time of war, Lent a vessell to three Maruelhed men that wear Preconars, to go to thier home, & to Return in a set time wth ye Ransom for themselves, and scoonar, but he sais as it is now Peace, he hath Nothing to say to ye mens Ransom, but Expectes his Vessel to be Returnd by ye furst, or satisfaction for her or he shall think he is not Justly Delth wth

Wth Respect Salutes Governor Dummer
p Jno Gyles Enter^{pt}

May 27th 1727

this Day ye 2 Indian Messengers y^t brought ye Messuage or Letter from ye Ercegontegog Malcontent Party, Say that they Expect an answar to their Letter by ye furst & s^d Messengars further say they ar of Opinion if they have no answer sent them, they may be Incurridged to Do Us sum Privat Mischief, for they ar not without Councelors to Do it. the s^d Messengars heartily salute your honour & ye honorable Council & say they will Do to thier Uttermost for Peace & a Good Understanding Round ye Contenant.

p John Gyles Enter^r

Letter L^t. Gov. Dummer to Capt. Heath & Capt Smith May 27, 1727.

Sir

I rec^d your Letter by Cpt. Saunders, & observe what you mention of the Uneasiness of ye Indians upon the Fall of the Price of the Bever; To satisfy them in this matter, You must shew them by your Invoice that our Goods are likewise fallen especially Rum (wch is much lower in Proportion than Bever) That It was Agreed at ye Treaty that they sh^d have the utmost for thier Furrs that they would fetch in the market at Boston. That we then told them that the Prices of Goods were not fix'd but would frequently change according to the Circumstances of Trade, And when they Come to Boston They will have Liberty to try the Merchants & Shop Keepers here they will find that we have allowed them the full Price of every thing We have brought & sold our Goods to them at very easy & moderate Rates. And they will certainly find that no other People will give them so much for their Furrs nor sell Goods so cheap to them as we do.

Capt Heath and Smith.

Letter L^t. Gov. Dummer to Capt. John Gyles May 27, 1727

Sir

The Letter herewith enclosed was design'd to go in a Sloop bound for Falm^o. but Cpt. Saunders being come in I have stop'd it till his Return to you: By him I have sent the Goods mention'd in the other letter, W^ch you must deliver to the several Indians in my Name in the most proper Manner you can.

I have rec^d your Letter by Saunders; In answer to it You must acquaint Wenungenet That I take it well of him That he has sent a Message to the Canada Indians (with his Belt of Wampam) " That they must make no more Breaches " on the English, & if they do, that he will resent it & con- " sult with me & have satisfaction of them. And that is what " I have expected he would do. He being obliged to by " Treaty.

May 27th, 1727
Capt Gyles.

Letter Samuel Jordan to L! Gov. Dummer.

Beddiford June 8th 1727

May it please yo' Honour

Having this Opportunity I thought it my Duty as it concernes the Publick Interest, especially at this Juncture Affairs, to inform your Honour, of what happened of Late in this Town; There being several Irish Men settled in and about this Place, and more perticularly at Saco Falls, they prictice ye catching of all Sorts of Fish with Scains, began last Spring, and continue the same Practice Still: By wch means prevent the Fish going up the Falls, into the fresh ponds, as usual, which has been found of great Prejudice to the Indians, insomuch, that many of them have come and made their Complaint to me, & desired that the Governmt might be inform'd thereof, that proper Measures might be taken effectually to prevent the same. Otherwise ye Consequence will terminate to ye Disservice of ye Province, as I conceive. Since ye Indians have made their Application to me, as I was a Town Officer, and a Well Wisher to the Province's Wellfare, I, with the rest of the Town Officers, thought it our Duty to forbid the aforesd Practice, notwithstanding which, they continue to go on, & will do so, without some immediate Command from ye Governmt So I leave the whole to yor Honrs wise Consideration & Determination in ye affair and remain

Yor Honre Obedient Faithful Servt at Command
Samll Jordan

Letter Chiefs of Norridgewock Woweenock & Arressegontoogook to L! Gov. Dummer.

Richmond Fort, June 12th 1727

Great Governour

We wrtie in love to Informe you that its Fifty seven dayes since we came to Teconnock and we

Desire to Know your Intentions concerning us. The Penobscut Indians also Invited us to come over from Canada, but have not Told us your mind.

The Messengers Sent to us at Canada, Said nothing of our meeting you at Boston, nor can we come there:

We have come a great way, waited long, and begin to want victuals. Those who sent for their neighbours us'd to find them provision.

Tho: wee are a poor people it's our custom when wee send for any to find them victuals while they stay with us.

We desire you not to think our words Strange, For wee have (heitherto) waited in Silence Expecting Our Brethen of Penobscut (who were first in making peace) had long agoe told you ye Time of our Coming and buisseness, as they promised to do.

We Ernistly Desire to meet you at this Fort as soon as may be, it being very difficult for Our people to live altogether. We Deliver this message to Capt Heath by order of the Sagamores & Captains at Taconnock in whose name and behalf also, we Salute you & y^e great Council

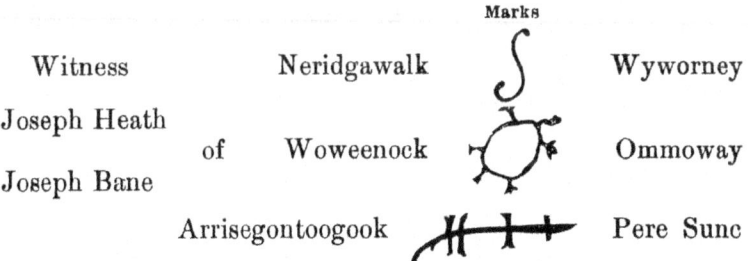

		Marks	
Witness	Neridgawalk		Wyworney
Joseph Heath	of Woweenock		Ommoway
Joseph Bane			
	Arrisegontoogook		Pere Sunc

Letter Capt. Joseph Heath to Lt Gov. Dummer June 12, 1727.

Honourable

Sr This covers a letter from the Sachems and Captains of the Indians, Assembled at Taconnock in this River.

The Indians of Noridgawalk & St Francois were made to feal the frowns of Heaven in a more distinguishing manner then any others Engeaged in the Late war. Yet being a people to a great Degree Stubborn and Insolent, have been dilatory: And the Emissaries of ye Jesuits amongst them, to gether with the alteration of ye price of Beavour caused a Demurr. They hoped also by their delay to move your Honour to make the first Overtures of a Treaty; nevertheless (so far as I am able to desirn) the result of all their Councils is a general peace.

It's probable they'l be no less Exobitant in their Demands about Land then they are Respecting provision For it has even been their custom to be Extravagantly wild in their first proposals and afterwards submit to reason. Nor is it contrary to former usuage for them to be sustained with provision at a Conference; hence it's likely that ye Treaty once Opened, those affairs will soon be Accomodated.

It must be granted in their favour, that (their furrs being Exhosted) they cannot long subsist in great Companies, And if the Affairs of ye Government should not admit of your Honours meeting them in a little time they seem to be under a necessity either to prey upon the Cattle in these parts, or Disperce their Company, which at present consists of 80 or an hundred men whose famelies are Generally with them.

The Canada Indians Stifly Opposed going to Boston & prevailed.

The messengers who signed the Indian letter proposed to Insist upon An Answer from your Honour in Ten dayes, which I resisted & persuaded them to leave it to you with out seting any Time.

And when they Insisted upon having ye Congress at this Fort, I laboured to have them submit that also, but they would by no means Conceed to it. It appears to me that the noridgawalk Indians being Disgusted at some former Treatment at Falmouth are resolved not to goe their they also complain of Ill usuage at their last meeting at Arrowsick, but if it be more acceptable to your Honour to Treat with them at Arrowsick then in this place believe they will meet you their if you Insist upon it.

And an answer to their letter with ye Time you propose for ye s^d meeting being speedily Dispatched heither will be amighty satisfaction to them.

The Indians have been very urgent with me to goe to Boston on this Occasion And apprehending ye Service would not suffer by it did at least presume to promise them that I would goe with Capt Saunders whome I have Several Dayes Expected from St Georges to Take from this Truck House about a Thousand pounds worth of Furrs. But that no Time should be lost have sent these letters p^r Express

& am with all my heart Your Honours
most Dutifull Obedient Hum^{ble} Servt
Richmond Fort June 12th 1727   Joseph Heath
P. S. Lieu^t Clark ye bearer hereof seems to be the most likely person to bring your Honours letter to ye Indians as being an Expeditious man & well acquainted with ye way.

Letter Capt. John Gyles to Lieut. Gov. Dummer June 14, 1727.

May it Pleas your Honour I Rec^d your Letters p Cap^{tn} Sanders on ye 4th Currant a bout a 11 of the clock at night & then we haveing not any Indians wth us it being their annual time of meeting for Prayer, &c which upon I Ordred 2 Guns to be fired Daily to notifie them, which was according to my a Greement wth Wenogenet when any Exprece Came from Govr Dummar,

on ye 8th Currant hear a Rived sum Indians tho no Message, but say y^t they have had a Great Meeting of 2 or 3

Days Debate of a fears, & y^t a Canow from ye Canebacks wth a Message to them and a Canow of ye Penobcuts Returnd wth ye Canebacks to taconnock wth a nother message to them in answer which ar not yet Returnd, and ye a bove s^d messages ar not as yet made known, only Many Debates Concerning ye moveing ye truckhousen & haveing new articuls & to have a Line Run betwen ye Lands, and Concerning ye french & Indian Pirotrs y^t wear hanged Last fall, in my opinion they ar set on by.

On ye 9th Currant I sent a Messag to Wenogenet & Chiefs to Com & hear your honours Letter Red &c
on ye 12th Currant hear a Riv^d ye Caneback & Penobcut Messengers from taconnock Returning to Penobcut AcCompaned wth a 11 yong Indians, I advis^d s^d Messengers to stop wth me, for I had sent for ye Chiefs of Penobcut to Com & hear Govr Dummars Lettar & answar, Red and Enterpreted to them, In pursuant to my orders And I Expected them in a Day or two &c
which they Concented to, Desiaring Provision &c
which after 2 Days waiting & the Penobcuts not a Riveing, they went on for Penobcut but meeting wth Sum of ye Penobcut tribe Returnd hether a Gain &c

June 14, 1727

p a Privat Informar sais y^t many of ye yong men that Came from Canadey ar wery of waiting for Gou^r Dummars Coming to meet them in these Parts and ar Returnd (they say y^t Govr Dummar & ye Panobcut Chiefs sent for them) tho ye Chief men ar all yet waiting at taconnock, and Expect Gou^r Dummar to Com to them, the Informar further saith y^t a bout half of those y^t Came from Caneday will be unsadisfied if y^e truckhousen & authers be not moved further to y^e westward, not y^t they will fall on to Do Us any Mischieff but will not be asy about the Lands, (Jesuitt for that) the nams of those Chief men now waiting at taconnock, is Moxses,

Chief of Narangewock: Ya=ha=ham=ma=wit a Chief at Ercegontecock: We=na=muggen: A Chief at Wowenog: Arsar: rabarot: Wowerena: Pearis: & John hegon: is y.

June 16th 1727

this morning hear a Riv^d a Canow from y^e Chiefs of Penobcut wth a Messag, to Desiar me not to be out of patience, for they wear holding a Council wth the Canebacks & St John Indians, & then they would be wth me wth all speed to hear Gou^r Dummars Lettar &c

June 19th

this Day hear a Rived ye Chief of St Johns son, and aquainted me, that sum Indians from Cape Saples, this summar had a meeting wth them at thier Chief Plantation & well a Proved of ye a Greement y^t the English & the Penobcut tribe had made &c

ye 20th

this Eving I Recud a Messeg from ye Chiefs of Penobcut to aquaint y^t ye Chiefs Propose to be hear tomorrow a bout 12 of ye Clock, & ye reson of thier not Coming soonar was ye Death of ye Chiefs Child, which they tarried to bury her &c

June 22

A Messeg from ye Indian Camp to a quaint y^t thier Chiefs & Jesuitt wear a Riv^d this Evening & Saluted ye officers, & the Chiefs s^d the Reson of his Long stay was ye Death of his Child & auther affears of moment

p John Gyles Enterpretr.

*Letter L^t. Gov. Dummer to the Penobscot Sachem
June 17, 1727.*

Wenungenet & his Chiefs

I have a Message from the Indians of Norridgawack, Woowenock, & Arraseguntecook (who are now to the number of 4 Score Men & upward at Taconeck that they Come so far upon your invitation in your own & my name in order to know my intentions Concerning them, w^h they say you have not inform'd them of. My answer to their Message you have a Copy of herewith, by wch you'l see that I have determin'd to Meet them the 10th of July next in order to ratifie & Establish the peace p & in the same Manner as that Concluded with you at Casco. from w^h I shall not depart, & being resolved to Acquaint you our good ffriends with everything I transact with the other Indians I desire youl meet me at Falm° at the time appointed where care will bee taken to provide for you in order to be psent at the ratification & Capt Gyles will provide you a Passage.

Letter L^t. Gov. Dummer to Capt. John Gyles June 17, 1727

Capt Gyles

You'l see by the inclosed Letter to the Sachem & Chiefs of Penobscots of my appointment to the Norrigawaks &c. for ratifying the Peace. You will send for them & Interpret the s^d Letter to them forthwith assuring & explaining to them at the same time my great regards to them on all Occasions as the first who Came in to a good agreement & a happy peace with us. After wch you are to meet me at Falm? for wch purpose & the passage of the Penobscot Cheifs the vessell wch Carrys Provision to Richmond was Ordered to Call for you. I desire you'l acquaint ye Indians hereof & Encourage them by all means to Come.

Letter Lt. Gov. Dummer to Lieut. Clark, June 17, 1727.

Leift^t Clark

You are with the greatest speed to repair to the Fort at Richmond with my Message to the Norregawack Woowenock & Arrasaguntacook Indians, & arriving there you are in ye absence of Capt Heath to deliver the same to Capt Jos: Bean in order to be Communicated to the Cheifs of the Indians whome you are forthwith to Notifie to Come in to you for that purpose & you are to deliver to such Indians as appear Provissions daily according to the Souldiers allowance. & I shall take Care to send you a ffresh supply forthwith for them & the Garrison You must take the utmost Care to keep all in Peace & quietness & that the Indians have no Cause of Complaint.

Letter L^t. Gov. Dummer to Indians at Richmond, June 17, 1727.

Good Friends

I rec^d your Letter of ye 12th Instant from Richmond, W^{ch} is the first Message I have rec^d from you since your being in these parts, & Accordingly to y^r Desire I am Determined (God willing) to meet you on the tenth of July wch is the time I desired the Penobscots to acquaint you of. Cpt. Heath will Lett you know the Place I shall judge most proper. In the mean Time I have given Orders for y^{re} Support till my Arrival When I doubt not but by ye favour & blessing of God We shall establish a happy & lasting Friendship between us agreeable to what has been already Settled with the Penobscot Indians at Casco in their own & your behalfe.

June 17, 1727.

To Wyworna, Ommaway & Pere Sune to be communicated to ye Rest of the Indians at Richmond.

Letter L^t. Gov. Dummer to Capt. Jordan. June 17, 1727.

Capt. Jordan

I have determined to Meet the Eastern Indians on the Tenth of July next, in Order to Ratify the Peace with them: and therefore desire That You would not fail of Meeting Me at Falmouth at that time in Order to Serve as Interpreter

I am Sir Your Humble Servant
Boston June 17th, 1727.

W^m. Dummer

June 22, 1727.
May it Pleas your honour

On this Day p a Privet Informar from Ercegontacook being Improved by Gyles on y^t service a bove 20 years

he sais y^t Great Disputs this spring Concerning Affears, have been betwen ye Indians of ye several tribes from Cape Saples to ye mountain Indians, & ye french, & at thier Great Debats & Councils was whether thier should be a treaty wth ye English or not, the several tribes s^d it was Proper to hear what ye English said before any breach made on them, but Arobree ye Jesuitt and Anadahouitt his Decon, & Amareguened, & Wewonorawed: Indian Chiefs, usd all Possible mens to force on to Slay the English, before they heard what they had to say & the new Gou^r s^d he was in frindship wth ye English & would be well Plesd y^t ye English & Indians have a Meetting, but ye Jesuitt Utterly Declard against it, and Pusht on for war, & sent out 10 Indians to Give a stroke on ye English, before they had any Discours further, &c which upon ye Chiefs, y^t were well wishers to Peace sent a Party & overtook them & Debeted Affears, as I find ye formar, Informar Gave me an account of which this is a further Confurmation &c the Informar further saith y^t ye new Govr is over born & swaid by ye Jesuitts.

June 24th

p an Informar that ye tribes have sent a Messag of two Wompom belts to ye furren tribes beyond Ercegontecook to bury ye hatchet and not to offer any hurt to any for y^e **futer** for they ar in Good frindship wth the English &c

p̱ John Gyles Enterp^r

Letter Capt. John Gyles to Lt Gov. Dummer June 26, 1727.

May it Pleas your honour

I Rec^d your Letters to ye Indian Chiefs yesterday a bout 2 of ye Clock by ye way of Ritchmond by ye hand of Liu^{tn} Clarke and have notified ye Chiefs of s^d Letter, they not being Gon from thier Camp to thier Plantation.

June 26, 1727

the Chiefs Came & I Red s^d Letter and they Like it well, and Desiard me to write thier answar, which gos in Closd, and I also Inclose (to the best of my skill) the motions & tempars of the several tribes, in my opinion is Chiefly Realities, if worthy your honours Perrusing, it may be of service to ye officar, on ye whole &c

St Georges River June 26: 1727

I am your honours most Dutifull Servant

John Gyles

I send your Canow & 2 Padles p̱ Capt Sanders.

My affears my wife Rites me word wants me much at home.

Letter Wenogent to Lt Gov. Dummer

St. Georges June 26: 1727.

Loven Govr Dummar I Rec^d your Letter of ye hand of Cap^{tn} Gyles, you say to meet you on ye 10th of July at Casco, I Like well, & shall Endever to Comply wth ye Place & time & you will hear what I Wenogeenet & our tribe say to ye auther tribes for we could not finish by Reason of ye auther tribes being absent, which now I hope we shall finnish to Ratifie ye Peace &c is what I have to say & heartily salute you Govr Dummar & Concil & hope we shall have a Good meeting if God willing.

Letter

Richmond June 30th 1727.

Sr The Express p Lieut Clark I rec'd 23d Currant, and the same day Dispatch.d the other letters to Cap. Gyles at S. Georges. The day following Toxas & Sosep of Noridgawalk, Jummoway of St Francois and Nemmageen of Woweenock Accompanied wth men women & Children to ye number of 120 came heither, Recd His Honour the Lieut Governours Letter and a Supply of Provision and Desired me in their behalf to Thank him for his said Letter to, & care of them.

Some of their young men are gon to penobscutt & pigwacket & on ye 13th Instant 15 of them went to Canada to bring over their famolies.

In his Honour the Lieut Govers letter to these Indians I observe It's said that I am to Informe them what place he thinks most proper for ye Conference which Instructions have not rec.d as yet But apprehending (by his honours Letter to the Penobscutts) that Falmouth is Intended have acquainted these Sachems of it who seem mightily sattisfied that he is coming but don't speak of meeting him there, which together with what they said when they wrote to him maketh me doubt they'l be somewhat stiff about it They intend to be all together at merry meeting bay in 6 Dayes (and) upon his Honours arrival at Falmouth) I think a message to them would be for the service—

I observe also in his honours Letter to Capn Gyles that its proposed ye sloop which brought ye provision here should bring him & yᵉ penobscot Indians to Falmouth by yᵉ 10th of July which Time being at hand & mʳ Tarr (master of yᵉ said sloop) having no Orders in that respect have presumed to Direct him to attend that service, as knowing yᵉ said Indians being Disappointed of a Conveyance (as his Honour proposed, would be Disgusted.

The Indians are very Gealous that the Missionary at Sᵗ Francois has wrote a letter to his Honour reflecting upon them and Intreat (if it be so) they may Know it. And I should greatly rejoyce if such a letter could be produced at this Juncture

    I am Sʳ Your Most Humᵇˡᵉ Servᵗ

            Joseph Heath

Governor's Message June 27, 1727.

Gent. of the House of Representatives

  In answer to your Message to Me this morning

  I now acquaint you that besides a Guard of fifty or sixty men (which I shall Order to be Raised in the County of York to save the Charge of Transportation whose pay ought now to be Stated. I Expect that a Number of Gent: of both Houses Accompany Me to the Eastward, that so I may see the Indians in such a manner as may be Convenient & for the Honʳ of yᵉ Governmᵗ & I desire you would make provision accordingly.

  June 27: 1727"

       Portsmᵒ. N. England Augˢᵗ 7ᵗʰ 1727.

May it please Your Lordships

  My last bears date Aprill ye 8th past Duplicates of which I forwarded by yᵉ Industry William Shepardson

Comander which hope came safe to hand; since which I received a letter from Mr Popple by your Lordships command bearing date Jany ye 3d, last which letter came to my hand about ye Middle of Aprill following with Mr Attorney & Sollicitor Generals opinion concerning His Majesty's right to ye Woods. A Coppy gave to the Deputy Surveyor for His better Government. I dont know but this will strengthen the Surveyor something in this Province; but in ye Massachusets they will not mind it. Since Mr Attorney & Sollicitor General are of Opinion that it is His Majesty's just right that all such trees should be reserved. humbly am of Opinion that an additional Clause be to that Act, of the 6th of His present Majestys Reighn (Vizt) in Townships as well as out without respect to either; for if the Act be not Severe the people will break in upon it. I shall say no more Relating the Kings Woods, least I should be thot troublesome, but shall do my utmost to preserve the trees from being destroyed. Those that are imployed, as Agents; to the Contracter for Masts. (Vizt) Mr Gulston they have great Oppertunitys to make waste of pine trees here. by falling more then they want and those people that are Imployed in that Service are generally concerned in Saw Mills that what they dont make use of for Masts are free for ye Mill men. having been told that great quantities have been cut down formerly for that End. I dont know that it is so now. Neither do I mention this by way of complaint. I only humbly offer that a letter may be wrote by your Lordships Command to the Deputy Surveyor or to whom your Lordships may think proper which may prevent the Destruction of many a good mast.

This Government Joyned with the Massachusets & Nova Scotia in ratifying the peace made with the Eastern Indians. When Lieutennant Governour Dummer myself & Major Maskarene on the part of Nova Scotia was present at Falmouth in Casco Bay the 31ˢᵗ July last past were three tribes present (viz! Arresaguntecooks, Norridgewocks & Wowenocks that borders near Cannada made their Subjection to King George and Confirmed the peace we made with the Penobscots last Summer. a perticular account your Lordships will receive from Lieutennant Governour Dummer. That Goverment being cheifly concern'd in making this last war. I hope we shall have a lasting peace with the Indians which will very much contribute to the Settlement of this Province.

According to your Lordships Order, I have given directions to the Naval Officer to be careful in sending home the Account of all Negroes here Imported within this month we have had more Negroes imported then for many years before Viz! Twelve from Antiqua, Eleven from the Island of Tercera one of yᵉ Western Islands & two from Nevis most of them new sent here for sale in our trade Vessels.

I have herewith inclosed the Journals of Councill with what Acts I have passed from November 1726 to May 1727 together with the remaining Stores & Expence of Gun powder to the 28ᵗʰ May 1727. I hope your Lordships will be pleased to be put in mind how verry bare we are of Stores of all sorts at Fort William & Mary so I found it, at first when I had the Honour of Commanding it, our agent had Instructions to Sollicit, am in hopes we shall succeed thô we wait long. Mʳ Bacon our Collector of this Port accounts will come by the next.

The trade of the Country which is almost at a Stand, partly Occasioned by the Warr with Spain its thot two hundred thousand Quentols ffish now remains in yᵉ Country for want of the usual number of Shipping to carry it of, one thing more that has greatly crampt our trade which is calling in our bills of Credit With the greatest Submission to His Majestys Instructions that was of late sent, to these Goverments. Humbly taking leave to say a word or two; I

Designe it for the good of Trade & the Incouragement of the Manufactures in England. The trade of this Country has been four times more within these last ten years then before (This reason) that we have had a medium which has Increased the trade & Incouraged people to run more into it; so that the makeing their own cloathing has Decreased by reason of the Currency of paper Credit; by this means we have had more merchandise, perticularly woolens from England within these Seven Years past then in twenty or twenty-five years before and I am perswaded that the Custom Houses in London & the Several Ports in England will Evidence the Verity of it. I dont conceive that this great trade has been so advantageous to this Country but Chiefly to Support our Ambition. The common people are come to that pitch that they will wear nothing but the best of Cloaths and so in proportion now the calling in the bills of Credit put every body upon thôts. for if the Merchants has not money, then the trademen, not Country men cant have it. so that they will be obliged to spin their own Cloathing; or wear none; & live within themselves. The Contrary a Sufficiency of bills of Credit makes them live in great plenty & trade Circulates quick. but when no medium then it stagnated to that Degree that the grass in Boston streets will soon appear. its hardly possible to conceive the Difference that the calling in the last hundred thousand pounds has made; neither gold nor Silver remains with us. The ballance of trade is verry much in favour of Great Brittain. but as fast as it comes in, so soon is it stript off. and there our whole trade naturally Centers. if no paper Credit then the People will be Obliged to keep the Silver here. I suppose three hundred thousand pounds would answer the End their's not in boath Goverments (not Exceeding forty) but would gladly petition the King for striking bills of Credit and those forty are the great Usurers of the Country who layes wait for his

neighbours land &c as for my Own part I want it as little as any, I'm no trading man my Farms brings me victuals & Drink and for Cloathing I must do as I can, I beg your Lordships will forgive the freedom I have taken with my most dutifull respects, I take leave to Subscribe myself
My Lords Your Lordships most Obed! Humble Servant
Jn? Wentworth

Portsm? N. Engl. August y? 24th 1727
My Lords
Since the within we have the surprizing News of the Death of His Majesty King George which has filled our hearts with a Dutifull Sorrow, in proportion to the Great Joy we had upon His Majestys Accession to the Throne. I pray God that King George the Second, may long live to reign Over us. on Thursday the 17th Day of August the Funeral Solemnities for King George the first was Observed at Castle William & Mary by fireing half minute Guns, attended by myself and His Majestys Councill with the Representatives and a Considerable Number of Gentlemen & others. This Afternoon the flag was hoisted & the Cannon discharged three times with great Huzzas and acclamations of Joy (Let King George the Second long live) A Regiment of Foot & Throop of Horss also attended I have Summonds all the officers (Civill & Millitary) to attend the next week to take the Oaths appointed by Act of Parliament to King George the Second whom God preserve.
I shall alwayes be ready & willing to Obey your Lordships Commands in Every thing in my power thats for the Kings Interest

I am with great respect Your Lordships most Obedient & Most Humble Servant

    Jn̊ Wentworth

e :   *New Hampshire*
  Lre from Mr Wentworth Lieu^t Govr of N. Hampshire, dated the 7 of Augt last.
  Recd. Oct. 2 : 1727. Read Febry 16 : 1727/8

Message from the House.

In the House of Representatives Oct° 10th 1727–

 Voted That a Message be sent to His Honour the Liev^t Governour to acquaint him that it is the earnest Desire of this House that his Honour would please to give His orders for the Dismission of Capt James Woodside from the Command of His Majesties ffort Mary at Winter Harbour, inasmuch as the Indians have desired another person to have the Care of the Trade and be Truck Master there, whom His Honour as we apprehend in some measure promised the Indians at the late Conference.

 And the House would observe that it will save the Charge of the pay of the Commanding there to have the Truck Master the same person besides the Difficulty if not Impossibility that will arise (if that officer should any longer be continued in that Command) in procuring a proper person to have the Care and Management of that Branch of the Indian Trade, which the House are very willing and desirous should be carried on apprehending it for the Interest of the province, and agreeable to the Indians Inclinations.

          Wm Dudley Sp^r

In Council, Oct 11, 1727. Read.

Message from the Lieut. Gov.ʳ Oct. 10, 1727.

Gentlemen of the House of Represent:

I look upon it to be of great Importance at this juncture to have a Supply made for the Arraseguntacook Indians, either at winter Harbour or rather at Saco River, if it be Considered that its not only in a manner necessary for the Support of those Indians; but the only favour they insisted on at the Treaty & wch they were also incouraged to Expect from my Answer to them, with the Approbation of his Maj^ties Council, & in the presence of a number of the Represent^ves sent down to attend Me on that Treaty; And I am of Opinion that the refusing of it will appear to them very partial whilst its granted to the other Indians; And I can't but very much Apprehend that such a distinction will greatly disaffect them, & give the French an Advantage, to Recover these Indians, who have not without great difficulty been gained to the English Interest, the Consequence of wch I leave to y^r serious Consideration.

Wm Dummer

Octo^r 10. 1727
    Read

Vote.

In Council Oct. 11. 1727.

Voted that a Message be sent down to the Honble House of Represent^ves To desire they would pass on the Councils vote upon the Committees Report respecting a supply for the Indian Trade to be sent to Fort Mary; The Board apprehending it to be of very great Consequence for the Strengthening & Confirming the present Peace That a suitable Supply of Goods be sent there without Delay, And the Countreys Sloop being now ready to proceed thither.

Message from the L! Gov!

Boston 11th Octo" 1727

Gentlemen of the House of Representatives

In answer to your Message to me this Morning desiring the dismissing Cap' James Woodsides from the Command of the Fort at Winter Harbour, I must Acquaint the House that I never made any promise to the Indians respecting the pson proposd for a Truckmaster, nor do apprehend any difficulty in procuring a proper pson for that Service, notwithstanding the psent officers Continuance there, or that His Continuance Can any Wayes interfere with the good Management of the Trade: I must also observe to the House that they did not esteem the saving of a greater Charge for the pay of an Officer of any Consequence in their Choice of a Truckmaster for the Blockhouse at Georges River.

Upon the whole as I Would be glad at all times in every Way to Express the Esteem & regard I have for the Sentiments & desires of Y' Hon[ble] House so I am also determin'd to give no Example of any Violent or arbitrary proceeding during my Government but shall endeavour that all the officers of My Appointing may be assured of My protection whilest they behave well: therefore as this affair now stands I cannot as I Conceive with Honour & Justice Consent to Cap' Woodside's dismission before Hee have a Hearing upon what has been objected to Him in y° Sundry Votes & Messages of y' House

Wm Dummer

To the Honorable William Dummer Esq' Lieu! Governour and Commander in Cheif the Honourable the Council and House of Representatives in General

Court a sembled at Boston the 4th Day of October Anno Dõ 1727

The Petition of Samuel Jones of Boston Humbly Sheweth

That Whereas your Petitioner went as a Tender on Board the Ship Martha to Casco Bay at the late Treaty with the Indians there and the Petitioner not only performed that Service but Acted as a Drummer on board and kept one of the Storehouses at Casco Bay, for which Extraordinary Service the Petitioner was told he Should have an Allowance, And Whereas your Petitioner at the former Treaty with the Indians the last Year when he Acted only as Drummer was Allowed Six Shillings p Diem, But So it happens that in the Muster Roll of the said ship lately made up the Petitioner is Allowed only four Shillings p Day being Thirty one Days he was in the Service which is one Third Less than he has heretofore had paid him by the Government: Wherefore the Petitioner humbly prays your Honours Consideration of such his services, And that he may have Such further Allowance for the Same as the Wisdom of this Great and General Court shall seem meet.

And as in Duty bound shall ever pray &c

Sam Jones

In the House of Representatives Oct? 11th 1727

Read and in Answer to this Petition

Resolved That the Sum of Thirty one shillings be allowed and paid out of the publick Treasury to the petitioner in full of the Services within mentioned

Sent up for Concurrence

Wm Dudley Sp^r

In Council, Oct. 11, 1727 Read & Concur'd

J. Willard Secry

Consented to

Message from the Governor, Oct. 14, 1727.

Gentlemen of the House of Representatives

I shall be sorry to have this Court rise, untill a provision be made for the supply of the Arraseguntacook Indians, & those living about that Country, there being such frequent Accounts & Instances of the indefatigable labour of the ffrench Popish Missionary's to stir up the Indians every where to Warr upon us: And it cant be strange if they should find amongst those poor people some Instrum^{ts} for their wicked purposes, And I look upon it next to impossible by anything we can do to Oblige or restrain those Priests from their Outrage. Wherefore I think the only Method left us is to Cultivate, & Improve the friendship, good Esteem & Affection wch those Indians have at present for us, who have signed the Peace, & which I make no doubt will with prudent managemt render our Frontiers safe in all time to come; And therefore I now once more earnestly recommend the aforesaid Supply to You.

Wm Dummer

Oct? 14, 1727.

Read

Falmth June 28. 1728.

We the Subscribers Resident Proprietors in the Town Falmth being Deeply Sensible of ye Necessity of Preferring A Petition to ye Gen^{ll} Court at ye next Sessions to Represent ye Unhappy Circumstances we are now labouring under perticularly with resp^t to the Irregular proceeding of Our Select men & Comittee in laying out & granting Away ye Undoubted Rights of ye Antient Proprietors wch we humbly conceive is contrary to ye Act of ye Gen^{ll} Court in y^r Grant made to sundry Petitioners for resettling s^d Township do therefore desire y^t our Names may be Sett to such a Petition as shall be thought propper for ye Informing ye Honble Court of our present Unhappy Circumstances in order to our quiet & peaceable settlem^t ---

    Domini Jordan   John Robison
    Jeremah Jordan   Nathaneal Jordan
    Robard Jordan   John Jordan
    Thomas Jordan   Samvall Jordan
    John Sawyer   Bengamin York
    Samuel Bucknam   Benj: Skillen

May it please this Honble Court

 To Inforce & Maintain the Petition Now before this Honble Court

We Would Humbly Observe

    That Falmouth was setled Anciently by Lawfull Proprietors & their right confirmed by the Honble President Danforth & No Man Invaded their rights till the Heathen Beat them off.

That upon their resettlement in 1718 the Generall Assembly from their Consciousness of this Ancient right Justly provided that their Order shall in no wise prejudice & Infringe any just right & title that any person have to Lands there.

Therefore when the same Court then Order, that the Inhabitants of the Town be Invested with Town priviledges, And that fifty ffamilys more be Admitted as soon as may be and Setled in the most Defencible Manner it can't be Meant that all the Inhabitants that were Not before Proprietors were thereby made Prop^{r}s: or that the Inhabitants in a Town Meeting were thereby enabled to Vote in and settle ffifty Proprietors of the Common & undivided Lands throughout the Town because with humble submission We believe No One Member of a Gen¹ Court could have thought so, within five years after the Province Act made to Order & direct Proprietors meeting, distinct from all Town Priviledges : But the plain sense is as We Most humbly conceive, that, The Inhabitants shall have Town meetings & Act as a Town, And the Proprietors shall have their Meetings & provide that ffifty more ffamilys whether of the old Proprietors their Heirs or Assignes or of Such persons as they shall give Proprietys to, shall be there setled as aforesaid

But Notwithstanding the Inhabitants thinking or Desireing to think, this Power was all given to them, have at their Town Meetings taken all the Lands into their Own hands, gone on Admitting Inhabitants and Making them Proprietors to the Number of Above a hundred Instead of ffifty, given Among them Not only the Common Lands but the Proper Estates of Ancient Proprietors whose Titles Were Above fourscore years old, & some where their Fathers, Uncles & Grandfathers have been killed by the Indians upon the spot, & Voted to Defend them against the Proprietors And Make good their Losses, that it seems they are resolved Whether the Indians or English have the Land, the right Owners shall be Nothing the better for it.

Wherefore Upon the whole We humbly think it Necessary in Order to Justice And a peaceable Issue of these Contentions that a Coṁittee of Good & Prudent Men be Appointed to Attend their Proprietors Meeting to receive the Claims of the Old Proprietors & Allow them, that a fair list may be Made of Such as may be come at; What they can't supply out of themselves, of the ffifty ffamilys, may be by the good liking as well of the Proprietors as of the Committee made up, out of the best of those persons that have been Irregularly introduced into the Town, & the Same Committee may report to this Honble Court their Opinion concerning any others that May have been Innocently introduced into the Town by the aforementioned Mistakes of the Town & Also that sufficient provision may be made for any Ancient Proprietors that may come hereafter & are Not yet Known : This is What is Humbly Prayed or such other & better provission as this Honble Court shall think fitt, Which is Most humbly submitted by us.

   John Higginson for self & Mr James Lindall
   Samuel Bucknam Edmund Mountfort
   John Smith   Benj Walker
   John Walker   Corn^s Waldo for
   Thomas Westbrook Esqr & Samuel Waldo
   Peres Bradford

Petition of Heirs &c. of Ancient Proprietors, &c. of Falmouth.

To His Excellency William Burnett Esqr Capt General and Governour in Cheif in & over his Majesties Province of the Massachusetts bay in New England, And the Honble the Council & Representatives in General Court Assembled August 14, 1728

The Petition of the Subscribers the heirs or Assignes of the Ancient Proprietors of the town of Falmouth in Casco bay, for Ourselves, and at the Desire, and in behalf of the other Proprietors of said town

Most Humbly Sheweth That Whereas the Honble The Governour & Company of the late Colony of the Massachusetts Bay Proprietors of the Province of Maine Appointed & specially impowered their Committee to Regulate & bring forward the Settlements of the Eastern part of Country, as may Appear of Record, And Whereas The Honble Thomas Danforth Esqr, Commissioner & President of said Province, by power and Authority derived from the Honble The Governour & Company of the said late Colony of the Massachusetts bay on the twenty sixth Day of July One thousand six hundred & Eighty four, did give Grant Convey & Confirm The Lands in Falmouth Township unto Capt Edward Tyng, Capt Silvanus Davise Mr Walter Gendall, Mr Thaddeus Clark, Capt Anthony Brackett, Mr Dominicus Jordan, Mr George Brimhall, & Mr Robert Lawrence their heirs and Assignes forever as trustees, for & in behalf of the inhabitants of Falmouth as Appears of Record, And the said Trustees or Committee of said Town by Vertue of the power and Authority so delegated to them did proceed to lay out many lotts of land, & Gave Granted & Confirmed the Same to sundry Persons, who builded thereon & made improvement of until the late terrible Indian War, when the town was almost destroyed entierely, they haveing taken the Fort & laid most of the houses in Ashes, and what was As fatal to the true Interest of your Petitioners the town book was then destroyed for it Cannot since be found. So that it is A difficult matter to find out the whole number that were admitted Settlers & Proprietors by the Trustees aforenamed Your Petitioners would further humbly Sett forth that they have at Sundry times made Application to this Great & Honourable Court Viz^t in the year 1715, 1717 & 1718 for their protection & authority in bringing forward An Honest & Regular Settlement, that in the year 1715 the Court was pleased to Appoint the Honble Coll^o Wheelwright & others A Committee to prosecute the Reguler Settlement of the Eastern frontiers, That upon the Petitioners Renewed Application in the Year 1718 the Court were pleased to Revive the said Committee & fill up the Vacancy of those that were deceased, the said Committee on the 11th of November 1718, reported that it was Absolutely Necessary that we Should be vested with the power of A town by the Mets & bounds

therein Sett forth & described in order for the Establishing
A Methodical proceeding in a fair & reguler Settlement of
the said town, which Report was Accepted & Confirmed, And
it was then further Ordered that the Inhabitants of said
town, for the time being Should have power to Act in all
town Affairs but with a Proviso so as not to prejudice or
infringe on any Just right or title that any persons have to
lands there, & that fifty familys att least more than now are
be Admitted as Soon as may be & Settled in a reguler and
Defensible manner as by the said Report and order thereon
herewith humbly exhibited more fully & perticulerly Appears,
Now Your Petitioners would with all humility Remonstrate
their Lamentable, and deplorable Case, to Your Excellency
& this Great and Hon[ble] Court, and doubt not but you will of
your Consummate Wisdom and wonted Goodness find out
Some way to Save our Rights and Estates, which we hold by
force & Vertue of our (former) & honest purchases of the
Assignes of Sir Fardinando Gorges And the Grant of the
Hon[ble] Thomas Danforth Esq[r] Aforementioned, President of
the Province of Maine, by Order & Authority of the late
Colony of the Massachusetts who purchased that Province
of the Assignes of Sir Fardinando Gorges; Since the late
peace So happily Established with the Eastern Indians there
are Numbers of people from almost all parts of the Province
and many others from beyond Sea, have rolled in on your
Petitioners Estates. like a flood, and under pretence of the
authority of the vote of Court of the 11th of November 1718
aforesaid for admitting fifty familys att least to Settle in the
said town, which your Petitioners Humbly Conceive must
undeniably be done by their Consent only who were & are
the true proprietors of said town, And they have without
the least Consent or Approbation of your Suppliants the
Proprietors in a most unjust and disorderly manner Sett
down on and possessed themselves of their known Estates

and Settlements which have been defended att the Expence of the lives and blood of many of your Petitioners Ancestors and predecessors, and they are dayly in the practice of these their unjust proceedings, for they now set themselves up not only as town Inhabitants but even proprietors of the lands, & admit such persons as they See Cause into town, & Also allow Others that are Neither Proprietors nor Inhabitants to Vote in thier Meetings for Town Officers (&c) And by these means get their Votes And Obtaine thier Ends And then Grant away Such Parcells of your Petitioners Lands And known rights, and Ancient Settlements as they see Cause; Also without any Reservations or Proviso's Altho' the Same was Specially pointed att and so wisely guarded and preserved to us by the Vote of November 11th 1718 Aforesaid, passd by this Court, Wherefore Your Petitioners take leave to make known this their Sad & unfortunate Case to Your Excellency and Honours, And Pray you would of your wonted Goodness, Clemency & Justice interpose your authority in Preserving our Estates to us, and order that Mr Danforths Deed may be deemed Good to the Trustees, therein named for the Use Specified and to those that hold under them, or that you would Revive the said Committee Vizt The Honble Collo Wheelwright and others, or Raise another with power to do what may be thought Equal and Just, as to the bringing forward A fair & honest Settlement in said town, as it was your pleasure in the Case at North Yarmouth our next neighbouring town, whose Case would have been as miserable as ours, had it not been for the happy Effects, of the power and Prudence of that Committee, which is Acknowledged by the proprietors And those that knows the Case of that town, and that you would over rule the orders & acts of (those) people who pretend to Act in town Affairs Choosing Select men, Creatures of their own who will in a little time if not prevented Grant away the whole township.

Your Petitioners need not put you in mind of your Exercising your Paternal Authority in Such Extraordinary Cases, of Superceeding town Votes, as of the town of Sherbourn, Haverhill &c. On the whole your Petitioners Pray and Earnestly Intreat they may find a Speedy Releif & Redress in the premises from the authority of this Great and General Court, nothing less then which will Save us from Ruin and Destruction, And your Petitioners as in duty bound Shall ever pray &c

Edwd Tyng	John Tyler	Thomas Westbrook
Willm Thomas	Saml Sewall	William Cooper
John Robrson		Jon^a Sewall
Joseph Otis		Jos. Calef
Samuel Buckm		

Joseph Maylem } In behalfe of the heirs of Micaell
Eliner Pvllen } Mitten And Anthony Brackett
Saml Pousland
Thomas Fayrweather=
= in behalfe of Mr Saml Waldo
Grace Marshall for y^e heirs of George Brimhall

Dom^s Jordan	
Jno Robinson	John Sawyer
Jeremiah Jordan	Benj: York
Nat^{thl} Jordan	Sam^{ll} Bucknam
Robt Jordan	Benj: Skillin
Thom^s Jordan	
John Jordan	

House of Representatives August 16th 1728/
Read and Ordered That the further Consideration of this petition be referred to the next Session of the Court and that the petitioners Serve the Select Men of the said Town of Falmouth with a copy of the petition twenty days before

the Second Friday of the said Session that they then shew Cause why the prayer thereof should not be granted

     Sent up for Concurrence
         Wm Dudley Sp^r

In Council Aug. 16. 1728.
  Read & Concurd   J Willard Secr̃y
    Consented to,
       W Burnet

In Council April 18, 1729:

Ordered that this Petition & the former Order thereon be revived, And that the Adverse Party give in their Answer on the first Tuesday in June next. The Petitioners seasonably to notify them of this Order.

    Sent down for Concurrence
       J Willard Secr̃y

In the House of Representatives, April 18th 1729
  Read & Concur'd
       Wm Dudley Sp^r
    Consented to,
      W Burnet

Copy of a Letter from Mr Ralph Gulston the Contractor for New England Masts. Dated the 2^d of October 1728.

Sometime ago I laid before you, that by reason of the great Waste of late Years made of white Pine Trees, in the Province of Newhampshire in New England (from whence the Royall Navy was formerly Supplyed with Masts) I found it impracticable now to get them there, which obliged me to Send a Number of Men, Cattle & Materialls, further along the Coast to the Eastward to a place called Casco Bay, but my Agent there and likewise the Capt. of my Mast Ship who lately came from thence, informs me, that for want of a Fort to protect the Men they are very much exposed to the Indians, who have already once annoyed them, so that they were forced to retire and Quitt their Work, and they further add, that unless a Fort is built there, the Ships may in Case of Warr be taken out of the very Harbour of Casco, and if the War should be with France, as they possess all that part of the Country in the River Canada, which lays on the back of the Continent of Casco, and not very farr distant, it is to be presumed, that they would not only encourage, but join with the Indians on their Side, who are Numerous, as they formerly have done to molest and destroy the Inhabitants at Casco, as much as possibly they could; the apprehension and fear of which is chiefly the Occasion of that part of the Country being so thin peopled, whereas the Security of a Fort would draw and Encourage the Inhabitants to go and Settle there, and be a Means of Enabling them to Secure and defend themselves in their said Settlements which in former times they have been forced to abandon, and as to the charge of such a Fort as will be requisite, My agent says it will not exceed Five hundred pounds Sterling besides the Guns, and as in Case of a War either here, in Europe, or with the Indians in New England, the supply of the Navy for Masts may depend thereon. I thought it my Duty to lay the Affair before you

         I am &c.ª
         Ralph Gulston,

A Copy
 Thos: Pearse

E: *New Hampshire*
 Order in Council dated the 5. Inst. referring to yᵉ Board a Lre from yᵉ Admty. one from the Navy & another from Mʳ Gulston in relation to yᵉ Destruction of White Pines in New Hampshire & to yᵉ building a Fort at Casco Bay
Recᵈ Novʳ 9.   Read Novʳ 26 : 1728

Capt. John Gyles to Gov. W^m. Burnett, Nov. 2, 1728

May it Pleas your Excellency

this Day M^o Casteen Gave me a Vicett, & says he Came Diractly from Menos town, wth a Messeg from the Jesuitts to the Indians Concerning a Jesuitt not being a Loued to Carre on his service at Wanopolos Rial, and he thought it his Duty to a quaint the Chieffs of Panobcut wth such a Weighty affear &c that they Might a quaint your Exellency wth it,

In my humble opinion it is a Jesuitt^s Contrivance to move ye Indians in that affear, but it being such a Distance from this place, they ar not much Concernd at Present Not but y^t ye Jesuitts & will make ye Indians Vnasy if they Can on this Affear at Wenopolos.

I Desiard of M^o Casteen whether s^d Jesuitt Did offer to Cary on his Service in or near ye Garricon he s^d Just by ye fort, I tould him if any Jesuitt should Presume to Carry on his Service in this Garricon I Commanded, they might Depend that I should also forbid him &c the indians s^d they believed it, they Could not Say to ye Contrary.

St Georges fort
No^{br} 2nd 1728

    I am your Excellencys Most Dutyfull Servant
            John Gyles

Mr Sam^{ll} Wainwright the Truckmaster Gives his Duty to your Excellency.

Letter Saml Wainwright to Gov. Burnett

        St Georges No^v 18th 1728

May it Please Yo^r Excellency

S^r / This I hope will wait on Your Excellency in Safety and in Good Health, and Serves only to Pay my Duty to

Your Excellency in the first Place and to pray your favour, that I may make a vissitt to the Westward to See my ffamily and the rest of my ffriends, when Your Excellency thinks most convenient. As to the Affairs relating to the Indians Cap^{ta} Gyles Informs me he has Acquainted Your Excellency therewith, soe that I have nothing of my own to Acquaint off, only this to Begg Leave to Tell Yo^r Excellency My Opinion, That the Peace concluded on with the Indians seem's to look with a good Prospect. I conclude with heartily begging Yo^r Excellency's Pardon for the Trouble of this Letter, and with this Assurance to Yo^r Excellency that I shall, as I have been alwayes ffaithfull in my Duty to Yo^r Excellency and ye discharge of the Trust reposed in me – I am

Yo^r Excellencys Most Humble and Most Obedient Servt
Saml Wainwright

Colonel Dummer to David Dunbar Esqre

Boston N: England March 26th 1729

Dear Sir

Since my Last to you of ye 14th of Jan^{ry} I have been to the Eastward as far as Kennebeck River wch is about 150 Miles from this Town; in my way I went thro' the greatest part of the Massachusetts Gover^{mt} on this side the River Merrimack, and from thence cross'd over into New Hampshire as far as Piscataqua River, wch is divided at ye Top into 5 Large Branches all wch I went round and then rid thrō all ye woods in the Townships of Exeter, Nottingham, Chester and Dover, and from thence cross'd over the great Salmon Falls wch divides New Hampshire from ye Province of Maine on ye other side I entered the Township of Berwick in ye County of York, and Rid all thro' ye woods to Cascoe Bay, and from thence to Kennebeck in the whole I travell'd above

800 Miles the most part of it up to the Horses Belly in Snow. Mr Haley has given you an Acco.^t by the Last Ship in my absence that Mr Slade and I had Seiz'd 200 Large Trees in New Hampshire, wch I since Libell'd and they were Condemned (no body appearing to claim them) for the Kings use: they were at that time so cover'd with Snow y.^t we cou'd not examine them, but Since y.^t we have; and there was 60 of them very fine and sound from 26 to 33 inches Diameter; but while I was down at Cascoe the Country fellows cut 40 of them into Loggs and carry'd them away, this provok'd me so much that I went again to all their Saw Mills wch are above a hundred in Number, where, and in the Woods adjacent I seiz'd 1300 Loggs Some of which are 40 Inches Diameter, and 280 fine white Pines wch are not as yet cut into Loggs; I left Mr Slade at Piscataqua to Libell them, and they were to be tryed yesterday, but I have had no acc.^t of ye Success as yett. the greatest Difficulty y.^t I apprehend we shall meet with will be in ye Province of Maine, where the people are (by ye instigation of one Mr Elisha Cook of ye Town who has a large interest there) of opinion that the King has no Right in y.^t Province; however, I have seiz'd 94 Loggs in the Township of Berwick wch will be enough to try the Title and then I shall be better able to tell you what we may expect to do there, it would grieve you to see what Distruction has been made in the Woods, there is Scarse a Tree Standing anywhere within 6 or 7 miles, of the waterside between this and Kennebeck that is worth halling to the Bank; Coll.^o Westbrook who is Agent here for the Contractor is forced to go 9 or 10 miles into the Woods for Masts, for the carriage of which he is at a great Expence every year, in Cutting Stay Roads thro' the Woods to the water side, he has got very near as many Trees fit for Masts Yards and Bow Sprits, as will load 2 Ships, but they not being as yet Squared he cant tell what Dimentions some of them will be

of. I have hired a Man to look after 20 very fine Trees y.^t are Left of those y.^t were condemn'd wch I beg to know your orders about; in my opinion the Contractor should be Obliged to take them from ye King at a reasonable price, otherways it will not answer the Expence of trying them; for by Order of the Court of Admiralty here some of the Refuse of these that were condemn'd were put up to publick Sale in order to pay ye fees of the Court, but no Body wou'd bid one farthing for them, So that as yet I am at the whole expence of the Tryall out of my own Pockett. There is a great deal of fine white Oake in this Country, and some very good Ash, but without the government think proper to make some further provision for the preservation of it, we shall not be able to prevent its being distroyed, I hope what we have done this Winter will be approved of at home I am very sure we have prevented the cutting down Sev.^{ll} Thousand pounds worth of Trees more than would pay our Sallaryes wch will never bear ye charges of any Body in ye Office, that will do his Duty. I have been forced to draw upon you for fifty pounds Sterl wch I must intreat you to advance for me, I shall go with Mr Haley, Hamilton and Oldershaw, in the very first Vessel for Annapolis in obedience to our Instructions and will leave Mr Slade here to look after the Woods in these parts, but it will be near 2 Months before any Vessel goes that way, without we Hire one on purpose, and the people here ask us 200£ this Currency to Sett us down there. I have no more to add but to beg of you to represent this where 'tis most proper; and be assur'd y.^t nothing shall be wanting on our parts to fullfill ye trust reposed in us. I have shew'd the directions for raising Hemp, and making Pitch and Tarr, to a great many of the People here, but whilst they can cut the Pine Trees, and Steal them away, wch I hope we shall in a great measure prevent by proper care next Winter, they think it less labour to Logg, than do anything else, So that as yet they dont seem inclined to make ye Least Step that way, but laugh at us for proposeing it to them, however, I design as soon as ye Governour calls the Assembly together to give in a Memorial to pass an Act upon that head, I shall sett out tomorrow morning for the Narraganset Country where I am told there is some very fine Timber, of wch you shall have an Acc^t pr next Ship Mr Slade and I have Mark'd upwards of a Thousand Trees with the broad arrow in New Hampshire, and the Province of Maine, all upwards of 24 Inches Diameter, but sev^{ll} of them grow 16 : 18 : or 20 miles from the heads of Rivers

       I am Dear Sir Your most affectionate and
           obed^t humble Servt Jer : Dummer

P. S. There is one Reason in my opinion Sufficient for laying a Restriction upon cutting of white Oak, and ash, which is, that sev^{ll} of the Merchants in this Country send great Quantityes of them every year to Spaine; as they likewise do small Masts under 24 Inches Diameter, wch I think care shou'd be taken to prevent, and our Instructions dont empower us to Seize them wch I hope is only an Omission in them.

Directed to David Dunbar.

Copy of a Grant from ye Council of Plymouth to John Beauchamp and Thos. Leverett of a piece of Land in New England to the North and North East of Penobscot River containing tenn Leagues square paying only a fifth part of all Gold and Silver oar found therein Recd. wth Co^{ll} Dunbar's L^r of 9 : Octo^r 1729

    To All to whom these Presents shall come greeting Know Ye that the Councell established at Plimouth in the County of Devon for the planting ruling ordering and governing of New England in America for divers good Causes & Considerations them thereunto especially moving Have given granted bargained sold enfeoffed allotted & set over and by these presents do duely and absolutely give grant bargain sell alien enfeoffe allott assigne and Confirm unto John Beauchampe of London Gentleman and Thomas Leverett of Boston in the County of Lincolne Gentle[n] their Heirs associates & assignes all & singular those Lands Tenements & hereditaments whatsoever with the appurtenances thereof in New Engl[d] aforesaid which are situate lying & being within or between a place there commonly called or known by the Name of Muscongus toward the south or south west & a streight Line extending from thence directly Ten Leagues up into the main Land and Continent thence towards the great Sea commonly called the south sea & the uttmost Limitts of the space of Ten Leagues on the north East of a River in New Engl[d] aforesaid Commonly called Penobscott towards the north & north East & the Great Sea commonly called the Western Ocean towards the East and a streight and direct Line extending from the most western part and point of the said streight Line which extends from Muscongus aforesaid towards the south Sea to the uttermost Northern Limitts of the said ten Leagues on the north side of the said River of Penobscott towards the west and all Lands Grounds soiles Rivers Waters fishings hereditaments profitts Commodities priviledges franchises and emoluments whatsoever scituate lying & being arising hapening or renewing or which shall arise happen or renue within the Limitts & bounds aforesaid or any of them together with all Islands that lie and be within the space of three miles of the said Lands & premises or any of them To have & to hold all and singular the said Lands Tenements & hereditaments & premises whatsoever with the appurtenances & every part & parcel thereof unto the said John Beauchampe and Thomas Leverett their heirs Associates & assignes for ever to their only proper & absolute use & behoof of the said John Beauchampe & Thomas Leverett their heirs Associates & Assigns for ever more To be holden of the Kings most excellent Majesty his heirs & Successors as of his Mannor of East Greenwich by ffealtie only and not in Capite nor by Knight^s Service Yeilding and Paying unto his Maj^{tes} heirs & Successors the fifth part of all such oar of Gold and Silver as shall be gotten & obtained in or upon the premises or any part thereof In Witness whereof the said Councell established at Plimouth in the County of Devon for the planting ruling ordering and Governing of New Engl^d in America have hereunto put their Common seal the thirteenth day of March in the fifth Year of the Reign of our Sovereign Lord Charles by the grace of God King of Engl^d Scotland France and Ireland Defender of the Faith &c Anno Domini 1629.

Thomas Coram Esqre to the Lords Commissioners for Trade and Plantations.

May it please your Lordships

Pursuant to your late Comands Concerning That Large Tract of Country laying Wast and uninhabited Between the Province of Maine in New England, and Nova Scotia Bounded by the River Kenebeck and the River St Croix Which said Tract of Country was given up without Resistance, by the New Englanders of the Massachusets Bay, In the Reign of K. William, Anno 1696, To the French who annexed it to their Government of Nova Scotia, and it remaind to them at the Treaty of Riswick and many years after the Peace Concluded there, In which Time the Jesuits of Canada built a great Church at Noridgwok near the River Kenebek as a Standing Proof of the French Right and Possession of the said Tract of Country Which was Anno 1710 taken by Conquest with Nova Scotia at the Crowns Expence with British Forces sent from England under Gen.ll Nicholson for that Purpose; By her late Majesty Queen Anne, To Whome the said Tract of Country together with Nova Scotia was Surrenderd by Articles by Monsieur Subrecass, the French Kings Governor there, as may fully appear as well by the said Articles as by the said French Governors Commission and the same was Confirmed to the Crowne of Great Britain by the Peace of Eutrecht.

As your Lordships were pleased to Require my opinion In what part would be most proper to begin to make Settlem.ts in Case the King should think fitt to Settle Inhabitants on the North East side of the River Penobscot towards Nova Scotia and to leave that part of the said Tract on the south west side of the said river Penobscot, Towards New England to be Settled hereafter, or for some other purpose; I must here beg leave to say again as I have heretofore to your Lordships on like occation, That I humbly conceive If any part of the said Trust should be Sufferd to go under the Government of the Massachusets, It would Infalabley be the Destruction of the whole thereof, by the provoked Native Indians there (let whosoever Settle on any other part of it) they having in time past received so many Injurious provakations by the Base & fraudelent practices of the Massachusets in making them drunk, then enticing them to Execute Deeds of Conveyance for large Quantities of their Land, when they knew not the meaning of those Deeds, and other base practices which has already been the Cause of Long warrs, and of sheding the Blood of Many of His Majesties Subjects, and those Insenced Indians will never whilst any of their Blood remain be Truely reconciled to the Massachusets, or any Els who shall Settle on the said Tract whilst they have any pretensions to it or any part thereof.

But if His Majesty will never the Less have Settlements began on the North East side of the River Penobscot I humbly Conceive the Nearer that River and the Bay befor it the Better on many acc^{tts}, More Especially for that Penobscot Bay will between the River & the Sea, hold a good fleet of Ships Comodeously, and I conceive it highly Necessary That the said Tract of Country (which is very valuable) should be Settled, planted and Peopled under His Majesties Government, The same having laid Derelect a long Time by Default of the New Englanders, Who after having given it up as aforesaid, They absolutely neglected and Refused to be at any Expence for regaining or resettling thereof altho pressd to it very Strenously by the Governours, The Lord Bellemont and Coll Dudley in the Reigns of King William and Queen Anne, by their said Majesties Orders.

Wherefore it is not Improbable but that the French King may Claime it as his Right, and soon take Possession thereof as belonging to France, with as good pretence as he did the Iland of Lucia a few years past when he Dispossessed His Grace the D of Montegua of it, Which in Truth belongd to the Crowne of Great Britain as fully & amply as I humbly Conceive, To all intents & purposes, as the fore said Tract of Country now laying Wast & uninhabited.

Moreover it would be vastly advantageous to the French to do so, For that tho the River Penobscot has one or more falls in it, it is Navigable for the Indian Cano^s a vast way up into the Country and within forty miles of the River Canada at their Cheife City Quebeck, from whence they may easily have Communication with France at all Times of the Year by the Atlantick Osean at & near Penobscot in Case they take Possession of the said Tract of Country, and might thereby have Supplys from France all the year round Whereas they cannot have it now but by the River Canada a little in the latter part of the Summer not 1/4 part of the year, That

River being Frozen up all their Long Winters, and the Great Freshes from out of the Great Lakes runing very Strongly downe in the Spring & all the fore part of the Somer renders the Navigation thereof Impracticable for Shiping. Wherefore it would be Greatly for the French Intrest to have possession of the said uninhabited Tract of Country. All which is most humbly Submited to yor Lordships by

  My Lords Your Lordships Most Obedient & most
    humble Servt   Thomas Coram
London 28th Novem.^{br} 1729
To the R.^t Honble The Lords Com^{rs} for Trade & Plantations.

Petition of Robert Boyes and David Cargill.

To the Honourable Colon: Dunbar Esqr
 The Humble Petition of Robt Buoyes and David Cargill In Behalf of one hundred and fivety families whereof your Hon^{rs} Petitioners when you were in England were a part
May it please y.^r Honour that whereas y.^r Honours Petitioners have Design upon your Hon^{rs} Encouragement to go and settle at that place Comonly called Penmaquid and their being such a number of us we Pray that the Lands from the old part of Penmaquid Extending three miles Westwards and four miles Eastwards and so Equivalent to that Extending Backwards into the Countrey with the Islands adjacent to It and y.^r Honours Petitioners will Settle it as soon as it Can be laid out and y.^r Petitioners as in Duty Bound Shall Ever Pray &c

        Robert Boyes
        D. Cargill
Boston 8^{br} 1st 1729.

Colonel Dunbar to the Lords Commissioners for Trade and Plantation

Boston, New England Octr 9th 1729.

My Lords,

I Landed here the 23.^d of Last Month, since which a great many hundred men of those who came lately from Ireland as well as some English & Irish familys many Years settled here, & likewise many Natives of this Country who are uneasy under this form of Government, applyed to me that they might Settle to the Eastward of Kennebeck River, haveing heard from England that a New province was Erected between the Rivers of Kennebeck & St Croix by the name of Georgia & under my Government, and as the greatest part of those who lately came from Ireland had removed themselves to Pensilvania upon the ill treatment they received here, where a very Numerous Mobb threatend and insulted them as foreigners, I have presumed upon your Lordships Report to the Lords of the Council in favour of this New Settlement to promise all those people that they should have grants of Lands from 50 to a hundred Acres pr head in Each family, paying one penny sterl^g pr acre quit rent to his Majesty after 10 Years, subject to one penny more whenever his Maj^{ty} should demand it to defray the expence of the Governm.^t this gave such general Satisfaction that I have been exceedingly pressed to begin the settlement without loss of time, so that I goe hence by sea in 4 or 5 days with about 250 Men, wth their own armes, in behalf of themselves and many other familys who will follow in the spring to make a beginning at a place called pemequid; as soon as they have got a Covering they intend to clear land, make staves of all sizes & cutt timber for small Vessels, all these they can do in the frost & Snow, and as soon as the spring opens, they will open grownd & putt in garden seeds, grain & a little hemp each; the soil has formerly been tryed & is very good, so that I hope within 18 months to send samples of hemp for the Navy and to give a good account of the other produce of the lands; I intend to call the first town St Georges and doubt not it will in some Measure deserve that Name I am told there are 5 fathoms depth of water close to the Bank at this intended Situation, wch will encourage trade and ship building:

Several people have been with me claiming large tracts of land in this province by virtue of Antient grants from King James & K. Charles the first, and from the Council of Plymouth, and some Indian titles among them Doct^r Cook at the head of a Company of Gentlemen & Merchants who call themselves the Muscongos Company, the name of a river a little to the Eastward of pemaquid, these Gent^n shew a grant from the Council of plymouth for thirty Miles square dated in 1629, thô never improved, they had since another grant under the late Duke of York (since K. James ye 2^d) but they would not claim under it because it was a reservation of one penny p acre chief rent, least the arrears should be demanded; I told them that ye title to those lands had been often changed since their first grant & that it was now absolutely in the Crowne, but that his Majesty intended it should be given to such of his good Subjects as would go upon ye immediate Settlement & improvement thereof upon ye same Considerations as before mentioned, wch they positively refuse to accept or to allow any consideration or acknowledgement to the King thô ever so small; Doctor Cook sayd they were in possession and would see who w^d dispute it, for his part he would as soon go to law with the King as any private man, his character is so well known at the Council Board, & Board of Trade, that I need not dwell upon it but can't omit saying that he is here at the Head of the Obstinate faction who oppose all the Kings Measures, and was lately the instrument of procureing their Memorable act against dwelling to putt all upon a level, so that a man is lyable to comon affronts to wear a sword or to be distinquished like a Gentleman, for by that Act, to draw a sword upon any pretence, without reserve, ye punishm^t is no less than to be drawn in a cart with a rope round ones neck to ye gallows & there to sitt upon it 12 hours they have been remarkably insolent since this law, & if their Acts are thought worthy of consideration at home I should hope this one might be returned repealed wth resentment, it would Mortify theme extreamly and they richly deserve it.

to the Eastward of Pemaquid a few miles, there is a fine Navigable river called shepscott, where two different setts of people claime large tracts, one sett are 50 in Number the other 32, they have the like old titles, but upon my telling them as I did the first Company, they seem very well pleased and are resolved to settle 2 towns compact, & to improve each of them small tracts contiguous to the towns, some few of them are of the stiff neckd generation here, and talk like their Oracle Dr Cook.

It is very probable that from the Doc^{rs} party there may go orders for application at home in behalf of their claim wch contains more than halfe a million of acres, it is impossible they can say anymore of me than what I Have here owned to wch I added that any man y^t has made any improvements or cleard ground should have such included in their grant provided they would goe upon the immediate Settlement. I could wish that this famous Doct^r could be stigmatized in being particularly excepted from haveing any part or grant.

there are some small tribes of Indians near these intended Settlements, who will expect some presents as those near New York, a small Matter wth the good usage I will allways give them, will keep them in peace & friendship and this with a few guns, small armes & amunition is all the Expence I w^d propose to the publique.

I Have received much Civility since my landing here, but it has been I have observed generally from such as are well affected to his Majesty & heartily wish for a thorough reforme in this Government by Act of Parliament, I sayd they might wth reason expect it if it could not be done by ye comon course of Law, and I added, for Joke sake, y^t I did not doubt but a Governour would be sent over in the Spring wth a Commission for a Kingly Governm^t and a Charter of incorporation for this great towne, with Blanks to name a Mayor Aldermen & Recorder in lieu of their boasted Charter, this gave great pleasure, and one of the Gentlemen saying he would give a great deal to see that joyfull day took a guinea from me to give me 30 when he should be in that Number this may be made a usefull Collony to England if it be brought under a good regulation & in my humble Opinion it is high time, it is very populous & ye people generally deem themselves independent, as is their religion for they hate the Church of England & presbiterians alike, and are a selfish dogmatical people; the town or Citty of New York is not near so large as this; & has a Charter wth a Mayor &c. but if his Majesty should be advised to give one to this town I should humbly propose y^t it be not too- Extensive at first, but putt ye people upon their good behaviour to deserve further favour in another.

the Church of England labours under some discouragen^{ts} here there being no allowance but to one Clergyman, and there are 2 Churches, but the clergy depending on ye Courtesy of the people wch is very precarious; thô these 2 Churches are large they are not well filled, and I am informed that wherever churches have been built, people have allways resorted; this Continent may deserve a Bishop resideing, his Residence may be in Georgia, where provision may be made for him out of the quit rents & reserved penny p̱ acre. I am firmly persuaded y^t a good man who would take pains this way & encourage schools might in time work a reformation among these independents, I could wish that

Dean Berkeley's Colledge may go on, & that Georgia might be thought a proper place for it.

It will be Spring before I can have any answer to this letter and by that time I shall have a thousand familys settled at pemaquid and Shepscott; upon Kennebeck up some leagues there is a large forest of fine masts, wch will be part of what I am to reserve for his Majesty, My Deputys are out upon their duty, in ye Spring I shall send 2 of them to Nova Scotia, and to Anapolis and one to Canso to Execute my instructions, by y^t time I hope to have the order for ye 40 men from Coll^o Philips's Regim^t sent me to cover ye Surveyors in their duty.

before I conclude I beg leave to offer to Your Lordships consideration whether as this New Colony is proposed to be planted at little or no expence to the Crown, & to be wholy governed by the laws of England until they are permitted to form a Council & Assembly as in other provinces they may not deserve the indulgence of a free trade for their own use & consumption for 7 years, this would be noe small encouragement, & dureing my time I will take care such indulgence shall not be Abused.

I am now afraid to be thought too impertinent and teadious, & in matters y^t do not belong to me, if any thing I Have sayd may be of use it will be a vast pleasure to me, or if any part of it can be induceing to give me discretionary power in going on wth the New Settlement where particular instructions cannot be thought on, my best Endeavours shall not be wanting, if I dare promise that the fruits of it shall soon appear, particularly in Naval stores to the advantage of England.

I am with great duty, My Lords, Your Lordships Most Humble & Obed^t Servant,

David Dunbar

Lords Com^{rs} for Trade &c.

Rec^d & Read Novem^r 20th 1729.

The Claims of Christopher Toppan to Lands in the Eastern Country.

The Claims of Christopher Toppan to Lands at Munsneegs Bay—Lying on Munsneegs Great River and Little River, & at Sheepscott, and at Damasscotty.

Att Munsneegs up the River as farr as Consegon, and four miles due North from ye main River with the Priviledges of both Rivers

At Sheepscott, all the Great Neck to Conefixit beginning next Willm Cole, and so up to Conefixit falls, with five miles in length of the Great Neck as high as Wincittico falls and thence down the River to the house where dwelt Elizabeth Ghent.

At Damasscotty, on the west side of ye River from the fresh falls over to Conefixit River and three Leagues upwards above s^d falls and downwards on the River to the house where Walter Phillips first dwelt.

on the East side of the River 500 acres on the fresh falls and all the Land thence extending upwards to the head of the fresh pond or one branch thereof, and six miles in breadth.

down the River next to one Kimbolt six miles in length, and six in breadth.

Rec^d & Read Novem^r 20th 1729.

America and West Indies.

John Gyles to Colonel Dunbar.
May it Pleas your honour.

On ye furst Currant wenogenet ye Chief of ye Penobscot tribe & other Princable Indians Gave me a Visett, & daily

Messuages from yᵉ Chief Viliag & a recent Party, & I Reherst sum part of your honour's Letter to them, & assured them yᵗ I had itt from your mouth, yᵗ you did not propose to Plant further then Sᵗ Georges River at Present, only ye timber for Mast &c as far as Pasmaquady which King George had mead a Returne for his Vse in all this Continent, & I expected if they knew of any Particuler trees to Give me an account of them, which they promised to do, and at ye Rehersing your Letter & what you say yᵉ Indians Seem to Look with new faces, they being Informed before (as I Perceive) by sum whitts & others that your Enimies to yᵉ Planning these Parts, have Informed ye Indians that your honour was com to hinther them of all their Privileges to Pasmaquady &c.

My humble Opinion is yᵗ your honour & others yᵗ are well wishers to ye settling this Continant wᵗʰ a Protistant People, will meet with sum opposers, it is a Great work your honour has Vndertaken (but God is all sufficient) and affears Look wᵗʰ a faier Prospect for Settlements & I shall as I have at all times Dun Vse ye Little Influance I have on ye Indians to Passifie & Deliver to them ye truthes, & to promote ye Planning of those Parts in what I may.

     I am your honours very humble Serᵗ
          John Gyles

Sᵗ Georges River Noʳ 14: 1729

The Chiefs of the Indians of Penobscot to Col. Dunbar

         St. Georges Noʳ 14: 1729
  Great
Sir   we heard your Lettar, it was Red and Interpreted to Vs by Capᵗⁿ Gyles & we Like it well & we hear you ar Planted at Pemaquid, it was Vnknown to Vs but

since you ar Settling ye old Settlements that was formaly we Consent to it, and not to Excead ye old boundarys of Pemaqu?d we are well Plesd to hear of your Observing the articles of Peace made between Vs & y.e Province of ye Masachussetts Bay.

Good frind you say you ar Imploid by his Maj.ty King George, if you Pass S.t Georges River we shall be Vnasy we mention this to you Bleiving you are Imploid from his Maj.ty & that you will be our frind

We say no more at Present & what we have s.d is from our hearts, & what we concluded on at our Chief Village at Penobscot, and if any Pass S.t Georges River to Plant we shall not thinke them to be our frinds,

We salute you Col. Dunbar

p John Gyles Interpreter

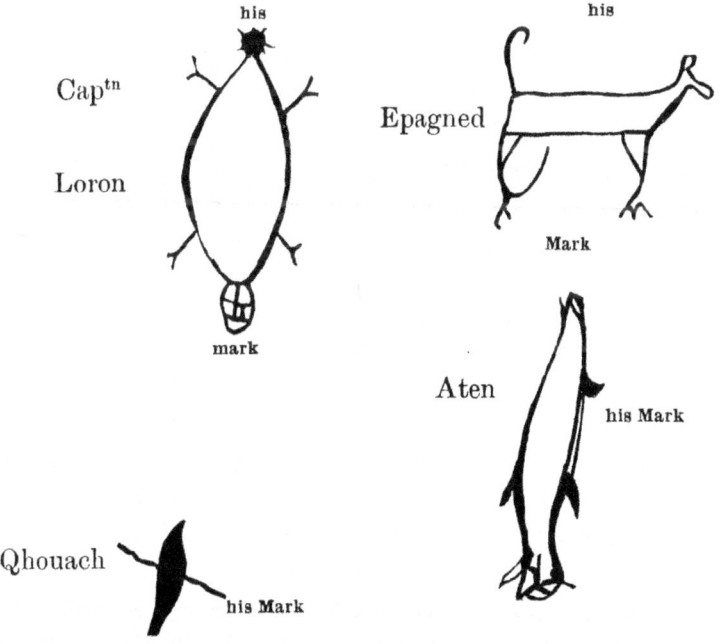

E: We wright to you Coll.o Dunbar The New Gen.t Man att Pemaquid

In the House of Representatives Sepr 26th 1729

The within Petition Read and Ordered that the same be Revived and Referred to the Consideration of the Next session of this Court and that the Petitioners serve the select men of said Town of Falmouth with a Copy thereof thirty days before the Second Tuesday of said session that they then shew cause why the prayer of the Petition should not be granted.

 Sent up for Concurrence
      J Quincy Sp^kr
In Council Sept. 26. 1729
 Read & Concur'd
      J Willard Secry
 Consented to.
      Wm Dummer

In the House of Represent^es July 3, 1730.

Read and referred for further Consideration to the Second Tuesday of the next sitting of this Court.

 Sent up for Concurrence
      J Quincy Sp^kr

Lieut. Gov. Wentworth to the Lords Commissioners for Trade and Plantations.

      Portsm?. N. England Nov. 15th 1729
May it please your Lordships

  The following is a Coppy of my last wch I hope came safe to your hands, This serves to inclose the Minuts of Council & General Assembly in our late Governour Burnett's time to the 15th of May 1729. with the Expence of Gun powder and the remaining Stores for Fort William & Mary at Newcastle the of May 1729, I am still Complaining for want of Stores, our stock being very small, I yet live in hopes a good peice with Spain &c will give us Some, I hope our Agent Mr Newman will apply himself properly to the Ministry at home.

I have the Hon^r of your Lordships Letters of the 28th May Signed by Mr Secretary Popple wth advice of the rec^{tt} of my Several Letters and Papers therein inclosed, shall do everything in my power to assist Coll° Dunbar Surveyer of his Maj^{ts}. Woods, I have had two Letters from him, tho not as yet seen him, he being gone to ye Eastward, and Sett down at a place called Pennequid, where we formerly had a strong Fortification, but the Country to save Charges gave the Command of the Fort to a Scrub fellow, who in the late War (ab^t the year 1702) had for Some years been Sargent, & a French Man of War of 40 gunns Engaging vith s^d Fort took it & Demolished it, and I vell Remember the Reason why it was not rebuilt was, The Massachusetts suppos'd it belonged to the Crown of Great Brittain. So it was layn wast ever since.

I very well approve of Coll° Dunbar settling first at Pennequid, & Rebuilding that Fort, it may be means of keeping the Indians at peace & thereby giving him an Opportunity of Settling downward as he sees fitt. This Land Ten Miles or more up the river is fine Land & Good Harbour. I hear Coll° Dunbar is very Expeditious, and in case the Season proves moderate, he will soon be Strong Enough to Defend himself from the Indians, its a very fine Country down as far as Mount Desert, on the bay of Funda, and provided the Coll° Settle Strong on that Coast, The Indians in a few years will be obliged to quitt that Country, or come into their Living as the English do, for the Settlements will drive all the Hunting far from them, and I don't know but a just Treatment of them in all our Trade will bring them to be our friends.

I hope Coll° Dunbar's coming, and alteration of former Act, may pritty well answer, in Case the officers do their duty, there has been no Complaint as yet, I have by Coll° Dunbar's desire issued forth Proclamation forbiding all persons going into the woods to fell any Pine trees until further orders.

The officers have been diligent Since their Arrival, & I hope things will be founded on a better footing than before, & if I should at any time See any mismanagement in respect to the woods, if I can't prevent it, I shall alwayes think it my Duty to acquaint your Lordships therewith, with my most Dutifull Respects I conclude

May it please your Lordships, your Lordships Most obed.t & Humb Serv.t

Jno Wentworth.

Reced Jan.ry 29 th 1729/30: Read June the 9.th 1731

Lieutenant Gov.r Dummer to Colonel Dunbar

& Copy of a Letter dated Dec.r 3.d 1729 to the Honb.le David Dunbar Esq.r

S.r

Having some time Since Shewed you a Clause in His Majestys Commission for the Governement of this Province, whereof I have at present the Honour to be Commander in Chief, wherein the Lands lying between the Territory of Nova Scotia and the Province of Main are expresly mentioned and Included; and having then & lately at your own House desir'd you to shew me if you had any later Commission or authority for the Governm.t of that Country from His Maj.ty that I might duly conform my Self to His Maj.tys Pleasure, you were pleas'd to assure me that you would in two or three Days give me entire Satisfaction therein; and since you have lately had an Interview with the Eastern Indians, and have been building the Fort at Pemmaquid, I find my Self obliged to remind you thereof, that His Maj^ty Service, especially relating to the Indians inhabitating there, may meet with no Obstruction or Detriment.

And I am &c.
(Signed) Willm Dummer

E: N. England.   N. Scotia
Copy of a Letter from Lieu^t Govr Dummer to Col^o Dunbar. Dat. 3^d December 1729.
Rec^d   Read 2^d Septem^r 1730

Colonel Dunbar to Govr Dummer

Boston Decr 4th 1729,

Sir

In answer to your letter wch I had ye Honour to receive this Morning I beg leave to acquaint you that when it was proposed to his Majesty to settle ye lands you mention, between the province of Maine and the Territory of Nova Scotia, all ye lands to ye Eastward of the River of Kennebeck were deemed to be Nova Scotia & were included in Mr Philips's Commission as Governour of that Province, & was for Many years in the possession of the French King, until given up to England upon the peace made, Anno 1712; Moreover when his Majesty was pleased to Constitute me Surveyor General of the Lands of Nova Scotia (wch Comission I shewed you) I desired to be informed at the Board of Trade of ye bounds of that Province, and was given to understand that it extended from Kennebeck River Eastward; if any part of it had been looked upon to belong to this Governm^t I should have had no power over it as Surveyor of the lands, because there is a Surveyor to every Government.

I Desire farther to Acquaint You that when his Maj^ty in Council was pleased to referr the Consideration of ye Settlem^t of this new Collony to the Lords Commissioners for

Trade and Plantations, their Lordships (who are not asett of broken Merchants as some people have taken the liberty to say, but Men of Quallity character & fortune, & members of either House of Parliament) in their Report were pleased to say That the Tract of Land extending from the River Kennebeck to the River S.t Croix, should be Separated from the Goverment of Nova Scotia, and erected into a New province by the name of Georgia, and that a district Government be Established there.

In the Instructions given me and signed with y.e Kings Own hand & Countersigned by the Lords Commissioners of y.e Treasury as Surveyor Gen.ll of the Woods I was directed to Survey and lay aside not less than two hundred thousand acres of land bearing Timber in the province of Nova Scotia as Contiguous as may be to the Sea Coast or Navigable River to be reserved as a Nursery of trees for the use of the Royal Navy. And in the Report before mentioned, the Lords Commissioners for Trade say that as this new Government is near one Moyety of the province of Nova Scotia, I am (by name) to lay out One hundred thousand of the said two hundred thousand acres in this New province.

This Sir, are the express words as I quote them & are Sufficient for me that the Masachusets province have no jurisdiction beyond, or to the Eastward of Kenebeck, if any, their complaint at home against me will be heard, but I can't help observing y.e motive for demanding my power Viz.t that I have been rebuilding a Fort at Pemaquid; that ffort, Sir, was destroyed 33 years agoe by the french and Indians, & has layn in rubbish ever since, notwithstanding the repeated Orders from England to this Government to rebuild it, until it was included in Governour Philips's Commission which is now devided as before; it will be thought not a little extraordinery at Court That any Servant of his Majesty should be found fault with for rebuilding the Kings Fortifications by a people who have often disobeyed Orders for soe doeing, it looks like y® dog in y?. Manger (I beg pardon for the Comparison) that would not let the Horse eat hay or eat it himself, I could have wished That y! objection against me had been made by some body else, it would have looked more of a peice with disowning the Fortress in this Harbour to belong to his Majesty, when in some late proceedings the words = His Majestys fort, were left out, and onely called Castle William.

I am in Hopes Matters will suddainly be put upon a New footing here, being persuaded that his Majesty thinks it high time to exert his Sovereignty where many are so audacious as to disown it (of which I can prove some instances) & make this a happy Collony in despight of them.

I would have Acquainted with what is herein related by word of Mouth, & have shewn you the proper papers, but I waited to have it demanded in writeing, that there should be no mistake in what Might pass thereupon, & y? rather because I heard it was intended by the assembly or House of Representatives of this Province.

If what I have sayd, be not satisfactory you'l pleas to Signyfy any orders to me, which I will obey so far as I can be justifyed thereby I am with respect, Sir,

Your most Humble & most Obedient Servant
David Dunbar

E: *Boston Dec. 4th 1729*

Colonel Dunbar to M^r. Secretary Popple,

Boston December y? 10th **1729**

Sir

Since my last about the middle of October directed to the Lords Commissioners for Trade & plantations I have been thro the provinces of New Hampshire & Main and am glad to tell their Lordships that the publishing the new Act of Parliment seems already to have a good Effect upon the Generality of the Loggers, who applyed to me in Numbers to know whether they might cutt trees of any dimensions, because there is a penalty for all trees of 12 inches diameter & under, which includes all without any exception; but as I humbly Conceived it was not so intended, I have ventured for this winter to indulge them so far as by the inclosed Copy of what I have published, I consulted the Governours of this Province & Main & of New Hampshire, who sayd the the liberty given hereby was sufficient, & Mr Slade, one of my Deputys, who was bred in the Kings Yards, told me that his Majesty could not be prejudiced thereby; the winter is yet open and as long as it continues soe there will be no working in the Woods, I beg Sir, to have ye opinion of my Lords Commissioners thereupon, & whether I may continue the same from Year to Year. Notwithstanding this, there is yet a sett of people who neither regard acts of Parliment or any prosecutions upon them, the famous Incendiary Doctor Cook, proclaims in the province of Main that the King has no right there, he has built Saw Mills in the heart of ye Mast trees one of which will saw eight thousand feet of boards in 24 hours, he says they are upon his private property, & should a tryal be comenced against him, the people he imploys would be his Jury, however, I am resolved to see what they will do in that case.

the Agent for the Contractor for Masts &c. for the Royal Navy has also lately built 4 saw Mills but pretends they are upon his private property, wch was a new acquisition on purpose under his Lycence for cutting trees to supply his Mills; of this I have given a full account to the Lords of the Admiralty, as the contract is more immediately under their Lordships Cognizance.

I have been in several parts of the new Province of Georgia and have began to settle the people who last year petitioned his Matie from hence for leave to settle to ye Eastward of Kennebeck River, most part of that Country is claimed by people of this Province under old grants from the Council of Plymouth in 1629 and Indian deeds of later dates, some for 30 miles square and for ye consideration of a few skins, I told all these claimants that it was judged in England that the property to all those lands, wch are included in Nova Scotia, was intirely in the Crowne, and that his Majesty being now desireous to have them settled, improved, & made useful to England would give them to such of his good subjects as would goe upon the immediate settlem^t thereof, reserveing only one penny sterl^g p acre quit rent, many seemed thankfully willing to accept the Kings favour, but Dr. Cook and others of his turbulent kidny refused to pay any the least Acknowledgement to his Majesty, of this I believe in my former letter I gave an Account & of the answer I gave to all, Viz^t That until I should receive farther instructions I would not concern myself with any lands thus claimed, and Since there are so many of them that if they are allowed, the King will have no more there than here, & the Country as hitherto may lye for Ever a wilderness.

I made choice to plant the people I carried wth me at Pemaquid about 7 Leagues to the Eastward of Kennebeck River, there was formerly a stone fort at that place but destroyed by the French before the peace of Reswick, I rais'd a dry stone wall upon the old foundation, & built barracks wth in side for 200 people, as soon as that was done I hoisted the Union fflag under discharge of a few ship guns & 3 vollies of small armes, and with all the people drank to his Majesty's health, the Entrance into this Harbour is easy and open & very safe anchoridge within, it was formerly much frequented by fishing vessels, but since ye demolition of ye ffort, they have not gone there fearing the Indians, whenever it is rebuilt, it will be of great advantage to the shipping who trade hither, and instead of being blown from off this Coast in Winters as often happens, they can put in there & ley safe until a favourable opportunity to put to sea again, when in a little more than one day they may reach Boston; the land contiguous to it is good but covered with small Spruce; some Oak and brick, the people are this winter employ'd in clearing the land for gardens, pasture & corn. I have ordered a few acres to be prepared for hemp which I intend to putt into the ground in Aprill if the seed I now write for arrives in time, there is very little of that useful Commodity raised in this Country to ye Eternal shame of the Inhabitants, who are the worst at improvements of any people in ye world, even their bread corn comes from other provinces, & the pitch and tarr wch they export, is first imported from the 2 Carolinas.

I did intend to have honour'd the first Settlem^t with the name of St Georges, but there being a fine River by that name 10 leagues to ye Eastw^d of Pemaquid I have called it ffredericksburg, I am afraid it may be thought I have been too forward & have gone beyond my power; here I found such a spirit and Earnest desire in many people to make the settlement, that to have delay'd it would have baulked it, this I humbly hope will plead my Excuse.

within this New Province are many forests of large white pine trees, so that the Royal Navy can never want a supply, but even the lands whereon they stand are claimed with all trees, woods, and a hundred et cetera's, as I have seen in long lawyers deeds, if such are allowed his Majesty has done there, it may lye waste for ever, but if one common answer is given to all & that the sole property is in the Crowne, I dare answer that the Province of Georgia will soon recommend itselfe to the Royal favour, & rival its Neighbours, in ye Spring a Great Many hundred familys of substance and the best of the fishermen of this Country will go thither if not Countermanded, the Scituation was designed by Nature for the fish trade, ye fish being taken now in great abundance near ye shore, and made & cured in better time, is preferable at Market to fish brought farther to the shore.

It gives me great concern to hear by letters from England of the 3^d of October that Mr Hinty was not then set out for Germany to Conduct ye Pallatins I hope he did soon after because I would willingly have them before I am to meet the Indian Tribes in May or June next, not y^t Numbers of people will be wanting, but I am persuaded ye pallatines will be very usefull: I Have wrote a very long Miscellany to His Grace the Duke of Newcastle wch I believe will in course be referred to ye Board of Trade, in it I have mentioned of w^t importance the Scituation of Pemaquid was for many years thought to be in England, when from the year 1702, the rebuilding of it has been strenuously recommended from Court, without any regard had by the People of this province to Royal letters and instructions relateing thereunto, & so far are they at this time from shame or remorse on that account, that they have even now printed an Abstract of all their proceedings upon that Subject, and their obstinate withstanding fixing the Governours sallary in so many years, it has so harden'd them that they are now firmly of Opinion that if the Legislature at home could have touched their charter, so many letters would not have been sent from Court, I send you one of these New books for ye perusal of my Lords Commissioners, and after dipping into a few pages their Lordships will be much Surprised at a dispute between the Governour & me for my rebuilding (as he calls it) that ffort; I have sent 2 of his Original letters & Copys of my answers to him to my Lord Duke of Newcastle, I intended sending Copys to You but am prevented that as well as enlargeing my letter (thô I fear in the latter I am easily pardond) but that the Sarah Gally, Capt Irwyn, sails hence sooner than I expected, so y^t if Mr Dummer writes to the Board before their Lordships see my letter to my Lord Duke,

I beg the favour not to be judged until his Originals and my Answers appear.

I will not longer trouble you at this time but to desire you will please to lay all this before their Lordships with my most humble duty, & to beg that in any references to them relateing to this New Settlement they will think a few small armes, artillery & Amunition Necessary to ye undertaking in hand. I am with respect Your Most Humble & Most Obed.^{t} Servant

David Dunbar

P. S. He has not time to send ye same account as he did to ye D. of Newcastle ab.^{t} ye Indians. I intended sending the same acc.^{t} as in my Lord Dukes Letter of my interview with the Indians but for a Surprize in time, ye ship sailing sooner than expected, & haveing no help nor hand but my own, wch puts me to some hardship.

Sir,

Since finishing my letter I am informed there has been a meeting of Several of the claimants in Georgia and mony raised by Subscription to imploy Agents in England to Sollicit a Confirmation of their claims, some of them are for whole Islands, 10 or 15 miles in length, where chiefly are the forests of Masts, in short all the lands that are Valluable are claimed by one or another, and now there is an appearance of makeing settlements, those people would hinder them, who from the beginning never made any themselves.

D. D.

Recd Janry 30th 1729/30
Read May the 6.th 1730.

Colonel Dunbar to the Duke of Newcastle.

Boston, New England, Decr 10.th 1729.

My Lord

Since I has the Honour of writeing last to y^r Grace I have been as far as Pemaquid in the New intended province of Georgia having Landed there ye 20th of October with about One Hundred men of those who last year sent home a petition to his Majesty for leave to settle to the Eastward of Kennebeck River, We made Hutts of Spruce trees for our lodging: Pemaquid was formerly a Settlement and there was a Stone fort built there about 50 yards Square, with 2 Bastions, each Commanding or Covering 2 sides, that Fort was taken and entirely demolished by the ffrench before the Peace in 1697, and the whole Settlement destroyed; I imployed the men with me, to raise a dry stone wall upon the old foundation to 9 feet high, and in building Barracks wth in side, as soone as the Wells were finished I hoisted the Union fflag under a discharge of 7 small ship guns wch I carried with me & 3 Vollies of small armes & we all drank to his Majestyes health, I called in at Piscatua in the province of New Hampshire, & at Winter Harbour & Casco bay in the province of Main in my Voyage, at the latter I went on board the New Hampshire Mast ship then ready to sail to England for the use of the Royal Navy. So soon as I raised the Walls of the old ffort and hoisted the Kings Colours I called ye place Fredericksburg, I would have called it St. Georges, but that there is a large navigable River already of that name 10 leagues farther East; Pemaquid was formerly a noted place it has a fine harbour & good entrance immediately from the Sea, I find since my return hither y^t frequent orders have been sent from Court, since the year 1702, to the Government of the Massachusets province to rebuild that fort wth some additions, particularly in the Year 1705, when on the 24th of October in y^t Year the Council and Assembly addressed her late Majesty against rebuilding it, it has frequently been recommended to them since, from Court without any regard had thereunto, as may fully appear from a book wch I herewith take the liberty to transmit to y^r Grace, the design of printing this book at this time is expressed in the first page; and appears to me to keep the same spirit in this people who do not, for the most part, stand in need of such help; it may be worth persual thô hardly to be read with any temper; there are 100 instances of refuseing the recommendation of the Crown to fix a sallary on the Governours.

I was ffollowed to Fredericksburg by two other Vessels full of people, and every day ye sight of the Kings Colours brought in fishing Sconners & boats, crossing the bay, to see w^t was the occasion of it, their joy was very great, many of them haveing formerly known the Conveniency of shelter there, it being near the fishing places & has not for many years been frequented for fear of the Indians; I had Visits from many of them at different times, and on the 12 of November about 25 of them came in a body with the chiefs of the tribes of Penobscot and Narihwack at their head, they sent to acquaint me that they were near & desired to see me, upon invitation they came and I received them with much Civility. I told them I was come from the King of Engl^d to settle some of his Subjects there & to renew settlements wch were began 100 years agoe they told me King George was welcome & I was welcome. One of their old men asked me how little King William did & explained himself, by saying King George's little son, when I told he was very well, he sayd they were glad of it, for they had heard from Canada that King George gave their country to his little son, I sayd his Majesty might do so, but it was not declared when I left England; they seemed extreamly well pleased to have settlements near them where they may be supplied with blankets and provisions in exchange for their furrs wch they often carry to Canada, about 200 miles by land When I entertaind them all together (for there's no distinction but in War & Council between the king and any other) some were merry, and One of the Sagamores (wch is noble among them) sayd that the Land about Pemaquid was his, & he would sell it to me for what I pleased to give him, I told him I did not come here to buy Land, no body had aright to sell any for it all belongd to the King My Master, & had for many years, the man seemed satisfyed, laughed & sayd, then King George was welcome, he freely gave it to him and would lay no other claim to it, but to desire he might have the liberty of comeing thither as his Occasions should require, I sayd, he and all of them should be free at all times to come and goe when they pleased without interruption, Wynongonet (wch is the name of the King of the penobscot tribe, awell looking man, more like a frenchman than an Indian, seeming grave & reserved, I asked ye reason of it, he answered that it was in great respect to me that he was so, and when he was better acquainted, he would be as Merry as I pleased, they stayed aweek with me in the day time, but retired every Evening to their Camp or Wigwam's made with boughs of trees, covered with birch bark, at a small distance from the ffort, I always gave them provision with them; When they came to take leave, Wynongonet, told me they had dispatched 2 Months before a Messenger to the french Governour at Quebeck to know his Opinion of an English Settlement among them, they believed he would be against it, & would by the Jesuits, stir up the Canada Indians against it, but as for himself & the Indians on the Sea Coast, they desired to live in peace, and would do so & keep friendship with the English as long as they were well used, they never made War but to resent an affront or revenge ill treatment, they sayd y^t Governour Dummer was a good man but he had not power like the Governour of Canada to performe what he promised, all they desired of me was to suffer them to follow their hunting & fishing without Molestation, & to keep truck houses where they might trade with their furrs wth. out being cheated, and they hoped I would give them some few presents & Commissions as the Govr of Cannada does, I promised them ye liberty as they desired and that nobody should be suffered to abuse or wrong any of them, I then gave them a few laced Hatts, blankets, pipes, tobacco & a little powder & small shot for their hunting, We parted on very good terms, they were very thankfull and desired they might meet me in their Tribes in May or June next, to come to an understanding with each other.

They are a poor Miserable people in comparison with others, haveing no settled habitations, & even their food uncertain, their dress is frightfull and upon extraordinary Occasions they make themselves hideous with red paint, they clean their hands in their hair & make large holes thrô their Ears in which they put scutts of hares, long feathers & long tobacco pipes.

All the Expence I was at by them was wthin thirty Seven pounds sterl^g which I do not mention with design to ask it, a small Matter so bestowed may keep allways quiet, and so prevent a large Expence & much trouble.

During my stay in Georgia I went up three of the great Rivers wch are Navigable for large ships 25 Miles into ye Country, they are wide and deep but in most places rocky shores, the Names of them are Johns River Damarescotty River, & Shepscot River, they all lye between Kennebeck and ffredricksburg, wch is about 7 leagues in all, so that they must be very near one another, the land is neither mountainous nor level, but in Easy Hills, where a plough may goe, all is covered with trees mostly spruce, but there are good white pines and large Oaks, nobody y^t had care of the Woods on this Continent ever was in these parts before me, and 'tis pitty, for the people from this Province have made it a practice for many years to send thither to make cannoos and Shingles of the largest Mast trees & staves of Oak fitt for ship building, leaving the crooked parts to rott on the ground; as those rivers w^(th) others are wide & long it will be difficult to prevent this practice, my best endeavours shall not be wanting, but really it will be impossible without a small sloop & six men to attend me, I burnt in one of the Rivers above 60 Cannoos made this Summer out of trees fitt for large Masts, & a parcel of shingles, I just in time prevented a tree of 39 inches, w^(th) ye bark, in diameter, and a proportionable length, from being Cutt by a Shingle maker, & have left two Deputations in those parts to guard ye woods this winter: I Have accounts of fine forests of Masts in that province, on ye East side up Kennebeck River, besides many w^(ch) I saw myself, so that His Majestys Royal Navy can never be in danger of wanting Masts yards & bowspritts, thô in my humble Opinion as all the land, at least one hundred thousand acres best wooded & nearest navigable water, are to be reserved as a Nursery for the Royal Navy in this new province, the Masts there should be preserved until new Hampshire & province of Main are exhausted, which w^(th) care may yet supply England for several years, althô vast destruction has been made among the woods, where many Saw Mills are Erected to cutt them into plank & boards; Here it may not be improper for me to refer to an Original letter inclosed from Coll^o Wentworth Leiu^t Govr of New Hampshire before my voyage Eastward, my deputys here have told me the same before, and when I was at Casco the like was confirmed to me Coll^o Wentworth is a Gentleman well affected to his Majesty, but being a Native here he may be prejudiced by this kind information, should it be knowne.

Upon my returne hither I took occasion to speak to Mr Walove the Agent here for ye Contractor in England with the Navy office, upon the subject of those saw Mills, his answer was that he built them upon his private property and was at liberty as other owners of Mills, I told him this private property was not very new and that it did not look well, because he, under the Lycence of cutting trees for the Kings use might abuse that power, he insists upon it as his right to use his Mills & I onely sayd I would represent it at home.

Since I have mentioned this claim of private property I beg leave to add to what I sayd in my former letter to your Grace of the claims & titles to Lands in Georgia, that soe Many of the like Nature were made to me that if they are allowed, his Majesty has none there. I have seen some pretended Indian deeds of different dates wherein 30 miles square were sold for 50 skins, & even several deeds to different people for the very same tracts of land, & many of the Indians say that the people pretending to sell those lands had no claim or right to them; most of these claimants are willing & thank full to take new titles or grants from his Majesty as proposed at One penny stirl$ quit rent p acre, and would go upon the immediate Settlem! and improvement of the Lands, but they desire 3, 4, 500 and some thousand acres according to their familys and abilitys, wch is more than was proposed by the Lords Commissioners for Trade and Plantations to be in one Grant, the spirit to make this new Settlement is now so strong in these parts that if it be not baulked, a more Considerable progress will be made in 3 or 4 years, than ever was in any Collony in 40 years, and I flatter myselfe be more usefull to England than some of its neighbouring plantations, the land is extraordinary good in many places, and will produce grain as in England. I have opened some acres in wch I intend to putt hemp seed in Aprill next if the seed arrives in time wch I now send for, and I shall hope to send some of the produce next year to the Navy for a sample & tryal, If the pallatines come soon after, they are skilled in dressing it, & are good husbandmen and artificers.

As it was proposed to make this Settlem! without expence to his Majesty, everything in my power shall not be wanting, but if it be thought expedient at home that the ffortifications should be rebuilt, and that a few pioneers tools be sent me from the Ordinance Office & any sum of Mony payd as the Lords Commiss[rs] of Trade shall appoint, I will husband it to y[e] best advantage, their Lordships will see what Fortifications were ordered at & near this place by her late Majesty about the year 1705, the Guns w[ch] were at Pemaquid when taken by the ffrench were carried to S[t] Johns in y[e] bay of Fundy afterwards to Annapolis, where I am credibly informed, 24 of them lay last year in the Earth, useless; at this town of Boston are a great number of Cannon, some of them well mounted in a fort, entring this Harbour, but close to the towne are 34 large iron guns ab[t] 30 to 34 hundred weight, mostly buried in rubbish & useless, thô they are called ye North & South Batterys, I mention these to save expence of sending from home if his Majesty pleases to order them, and Carriages may be made, costing onely workmanship. If those I mention are ordered with a few smaller from home I will endeavour to dispose them to the best advantage, & in expectation of it, I have Ordered a great quantity of Lime to be burnt from a vast ridge of Oyster shells near y[e] place and I shall have Oak plank ready for the carriages, all w[ch] may be devoted to other purposes if what I propose be not approved, w[ch] I most humbly beg to know as soon as May be. I am very fearfull, My Lord, that I trespass too farr upon your Graces time & patience but as I am at a great distance I hope to be pardond for laying before you at Once what Occurs to me relateing to this undertaking, there is one thing w[ch] I mention wth reluctancy and this is this new Country being in y[e] state as Nature left it, wild and unimproved, it will be some time before corn and provisions will be plenty, there are many able labouring men that will want bread until then if not supplyed by some means, it has been proposed to me y[t] if they could be supported that they would repay the expence in Hemp the 3[d] 4th & 5th year. What I most covet at present is a few Small armes and ammunition, I wish I could have some before I meet the Indians in May next, that y̌ᵉ people May appear in Armes, there are none to be brought here so that I have not been able to leave about 80 guns or firelocks among all yᵉ Men. If this Affair does recommend itself I have not the assurance to hope for any Consideration on my own Account. The Indians all along this Continent haveing Jesuit Missionarys among them are much influenced by the french Governour at Quebeck. I Have been thinking that if a letter was asked from the french Court to their Govʳ at Cananda to command him not to stirr up yᵉ Indians against the English, it might easyly be obtaind & would be of good Consequence to us, and if a Copy was sent to me I could convey it thro ye Country to him.

Since my return to Boston Mʳ Dummer the present Governour has seemed highly dissatisfyed that I have been to make any foundation for a Settlement in Georgia, saying that all the lands as far as Nova Scotia is under the Governmᵗ of this province, he asked me if I had any Comⁿ or Authority for what I did there, I answered that in a few days he shᵈ be satisfyed in that point, hoping I might have received farther orders from home & not careing to shew him the report of the Lords Comissionʳˢ for Trade relateing thereunto, made yᵉ 14ᵗʰ of May last, if it had been known that I had not an Absolute Comission it would have spoiled yᵉ undertaking; What passed hereupon between Mʳ Dummer and me will best appear from his Original letters herewᵗʰ sent to your Grace and my answers to them, the behaviour of Many of the people here has often ruffled me, some do publiquely say his Majesty has no right to the Woods here, others have asked me what right the King had to any land here, & how he came by such right, some have claimed by Indian titles so late as dated in 1719, & in their deeds they have warrantees to defend the prossession against all persons whatsoever, the people of this province now sitting here in Council & Assembly are upon laying out a line of towns before they have a new Governour, the upper & lower Houses do not agree, ye former wth the late Governour haveing nominated an Attorny General, the latter lately upon ye annual day of Election insisted to have aright of Nomination, wch the upper refuseing, it was Moved in the House of Representatives by the famous Dr Cook That there should be an Order of the House to the Grand jury to regard any indictement or presentment of the Attorny General onely as Wast paper.

they are upon some Methods how to raise ye vallue of their bills of Credit, wch are now so low as 20^sh pounce for silver there is about 3 hund^d thous^d pounds of these bills from this province, they were at parr at first & some people who then lent out Mony to interest, if they were now rep^d principal & interest, would not get back one half of the vallue of what they lost at first. It is wonderfull to see how little this province has been improved, & chiefly occasioned by too great Tracts of land in few hands, some haveing several hundred thousand Acres & the improved lands sells very dear, th whole y^t is layd out into townships does not yield 3 pence p acre one with Another. I have been thinking that if ye Charter here be declared voyd or forfeited by Parliament, and in the new form of Goverm^t all new stragling towns excluded from sending Representatives, their Number w^d be diminished to one third, and those for the principal towns, might be men of some Substance, whereas at present to see such as are sent from the New towns looks like Mockery, if then a small tax of one penny sterl^g was proposed to be raised upon all lands layd out into townships & granted to private people p acre, to pay off the debt & cancel their bills of Credit, many w^d relinquish their remote grants not yet improved (wch would thereupon fall to his Majesty) and remove nearer the Sea shore so that the Settlements would be more compact, and ye lands much better improved, I dare say some Millions of Acres would be disclaimed rather than pay this trifle especially for lands remote.

this Province of Main, wch is annexed to the Masachusets, is divided from it by ye province of New Hampshire, wch is a distinct Governm^t & a very small one, it would certainly be more for the Ease of the people either that Main & Hampshire, were annexed or New Hampshire to the Masachusets & Main to Georgia, to wch it now joyns, onely Kennebeck River between them.

I shall be excused for not entertaining your Grace longer at this time, but must humbly beg it for what I have sayd extra officio, it is My Zeal for his Majesty's Service wch prompts me to do it, I am with all possible respect and duty

My Lord Your Graces Most Obedient & Most Humble Servant

David Dunbar.

Lieu^t. Govr. Dummer to the Duke of Newcastle. Extract of a Letter from Lieutenant Governor Dummer to his Grace the Duke of Newcastle dated Boston December 26th 1729.

Colonel Dunbar, His Majesty's Surveyor General of the Woods in these Parts, having (as I am informed, tho' not by himself) given your Grace the trouble of perusing the Letters I lately wrote him, which were intended for His Majesty's Service: I beg leave to inclose Copies of his Letters as well as my own, & submit it to your Grace to determine, whether I have proceeded agreeable to the Commission I have the honour to sustain. I have endeavoured to cultivate a good Understanding with Colonel Dunbar, that I might be able to give him my best assistance, as there should be occasion for it, in the Execution of his Majesty's Commands relateing to the Preservation of the Pine Trees in this Province; and if I have not had the Success I wished for, I cannot impute it to any neglect or want of Inclination in my self. The principal occasion of my desiring to see his Commission was, (as is intimated in my first Letter) on account of the Indians inhabiting those Parts, who, as I was informed by my Officers in the Forts there were under some Discontents and Jealousys that the late Treaty made with them might be infracted by new comers; and it seems necessary that the Indians should know to whom they were to apply themselves for their Satisfaction therein. It may not be amiss to put your Grace in mind, that His Majesty has a Fort in that Country between Kennebeck & Nova Scotia, where there is a Garrison of Soldiers supported at the Charge of this Province, and a Trade carry'd on with the Indians from thence, according to the Treaty made with them at Casco, at some considerable Expence, any Interruption whereof may be a great Detriment to His Majesty's Service.

Rec̃ed.

Read 2ᵈ. Septr 1730.

INDEX.

A

ABOMHOMEN, 95.
Acadia, a portion of sold to Temple, 16, 17; the rights of England to, 16, 18, 20, 34; restoration of, 22, 87; the French claim the right to fish on the coast of, 34, 38, 104; former boundary of, 47, 87, 177; French and Indians demand the whole of except Annapolis, 294; the French will prevent the English fishing on the coast of, 294; mentioned, 21, 35, 96, 103.
Account of Penobscot, 25, 30.
Adamhegon, 386.
Addington, Isaac, letter of, 73, 74; mentioned, 11, 33, 54, 95, 97, 104.
Address of Governor, Council and Representatives of New Hampshire, 54; of Lieutenant Governor, Council and Representatives of Massachusetts, 292, 296.
Adeawanadon, 95.
Affidavit, of March, James, 303.
Agemogen Reach, 238, 239, 240.
Ahanquil, 11.
Ahasombamet, 10.
Albany, 69, 88, 100, 108, 109, 157, 227, 234, 240, 241, 295, 328, 333, 336, 337, 339, 352, 364, 365, 371, 374, 376, 378, 381, 396.
County of, 42.
Alden, Capt. John, relations of, 57, 59, 60, 62, 67; attempted bribery, 61, 62; interested in a matrimonial affair, 61, 62; his property, 61, 66; bargains of, 66; traded with St. Castine, 58.
Alexander, Sir William, Earl of Sterling and Lord of Menstrie, 16, 17, 25, 26, 74, 75.
Allen, ——, killed, 231.
Lieut., 162.
Mr., 150, 151.
Jeremiah, treasurer of the Province, 147, 149, 389.
Amanequened, 386.

Amarascogin ⎫
Ameriscoggin ⎪
Ammuscoggin ⎬ Indians, the, 368, 380.
Amoscoggin ⎪
Amuscoggin ⎭
Falls, 327.
River, 327, 331, 333.
Amassakantic ⎱ 91, 95.
Amassakuntic ⎰
Ammunition in trade, 1; lack of ends a war, 1; needed, 3, 102; wanted at Wells, 43; in the towns, 64; at Nova Scotia and Penobscot, 80, 81; to be brought from Winter Harbor, 149; needed at Georgetown, 151; general need of in Maine, 152, 156, 221; sent to Spurwink, 212; of the Indians delivered, 349; for Fort William and Mary, 448, 449; needed in the Province of Georgia, 458, 465, 466.
Amoskeag, 277.
Anadahouitt, 408.
Anderson, ——, 191.
Andrews Point, 95.
Andros, Sir Edmund, 20.
Androscoggin, see under Amarascogin.
Annapolis, 110, 123, 124, 125, 176, 219, 281, 323, 396, 430, 433, 444, 465; Fort at, 294.
Anne, Queen, 176, 437, 483.
Answer to the Earl of Limerick's petition, 57.
Antiqua, 107, 112, 413.
Appleton, Col. John, instructions to, 287; letter of, 290, 291.
Armourer, an, among the Indians, 91; detained at Falmouth, 195; desired tools, 278; gunsmith wanted at St. Georges, 366.
Armstrong, Lawrence, Lieut.-Gov. of Nova Scotia, 321.
Robert, defence of, 166, 174; petition of, 302, 303; mentioned, 121, 126, 157, 158, 159, 167, 168.
Simon, killed, 212.
Arobree, a Jesuit, 408.
Arondall, 315; see Arundel.
Arresaguntecook ⎱ 396, 405.
Arresegontoogook ⎰
Indians, 395, 406, 413, 417, 420.
Letter from the chief of, 400, 401.

472   DOCUMENTARY HISTORY

Arrowsic, 153, 155, 183, 185, 199, 200, 201, 204, 381, 403.
 Garrison at, 290.
 Island, 144.
 River, 204.
Arsar, 405.
Arundel, 152, 182, 201, 315.
Ashhurst, Henry, 34, 72, 102.
Ash trees, 433, 434.
Aten, 466.
Attkinson, Theodore, 56, 123.
Autograph, see Marks.
Aver'll, Corp., 188.
Awansomeck, 11.
Awouch, 360.
Azores, the, 115.

B

BACON, LIEUT. ——, of Barnstable, 315, 316.
 Mr. ——, Collector at Portsmouth, 167, 413.
 Sir Edmund, 167.
 John, letter of, 324, 325.
 Dr. Solomon, 286, 324, 325, 329, 342.
Bamet, Kahton, 44.
Bancker, Evert, 334, 336, 337.
Bane ⎫
Bean ⎬ ——, killed at Norridgewock, 369.
Been ⎭
 Lieut. ——, 202, 203, 209, 212, 215, 239, 249.
 Mr. ——, 215.
 Jeremiah, 120.
 Jona., 191.
 Capt. Joseph, 181, 182, 256, 257, 274, 309, 330, 331, 332, 401, 407.
Barbadoes, the, 112.
Barbekin Point, 47.
Barillen, 22; see also Brouillan.
Barington, Mr. ——, 142.
Barlow, Capt. ——, 265.
Barnes, Capt. ——, of Plymouth, 303.
Barnstable, 324.
 County, Indians enlisted from, 347.
Baronets of Nova Scotia, 75, 79.
Barony of La Tour, 75.
 of St. Denniscourt, 75.
Barrillon, Mons. de, 38; see also Brouillan.
Bass, 156.
Bassett, David, 30, 31.
Bay François, same as Bay of Fundy, 18.
Bay of Fundy, 18, 449, 465.
Bay of Mexico, 69.

Bean, see under Bane.
Beauchamp, John, 434, 435, 436.
Beauharnois, Charles, Marquis de, Governor of Canada, 371.
Beaver trade, 28, 113, 389, 398, 399, 402.
Belfast, Ireland, 106, 107.
Bell, Mr. ——, 304, 312.
Bellisle, Mons. ——, 300.
Bellomont, Earl of, letters of, 65, 67, 68, 71; mentioned, 36, 45, 52, 54, 55, 56, 57, 59, 62, 85, 88, 90, 95, 97, 103, 175, 438.
Belts of Peace, see Wampum Belts.
Berkeley, Rev. George, 444.
Bermudas, the, 2.
Berwick, people of in garrison at, 152; Col. Westbrook to go to, 160, 185, 189; Oliver deserted from, 161; garrison at not to be lessened, 186; Lieut. Lane sent to, 203; Capt. Harmons company sent to, 204; men logging near, 238; Ezek. Davis arrived at, 284; men to be drawn from, 304; men from march to Falmouth, 310; troops at dismissed, 312; soldiers to rendezvous at to equip, 320; Indians at, 331; men ordered to, 333, 335; Col. Westbrook at, 349, 350; Col. Dummer at, 431; logs seized at, 432; mentioned, 161, 279, 287.
Betting, one guinea against thirty, 443.
Biddeford, 152, 279, 280, 328, 400.
Bills of Credit, 110, 261, 262, 263, 264, 265, 291, 413, 414, 467.
Blackcoats, 356.
Black Point, 193, 246, 259, 265, 273, 278, 290, 327, 332.
Blanchard, Capt., 350.
 Lieut., 269, 271, 272.
Blankets in trade, 1.
Blathwayt, Wm., 57, 66, 87.
Blechynden, Chas., letter of, 142, 143.
Bleuker, Nicholas, 373.
Blockhouse at St. Georges River, 418; see also Garrisons.
Block Island, 123.
Bolam, Capt. ——, 168, 173.
Bomazeen, signed treaty, 11; his squaw a prisoner, 215; his squaw examined, 216.
Bondet, Mons. ——, 59.
Book, a, printed without licence, 105, 106.

INDEX 473

Bornoway, Mons., *see* Beauharnois.
Boston, 2, 4, 20, 33, 37, 39, 41, 43, 45, 52, 54, 61, 62, 65, 67, 71, 76, 80, 81, 86, 92, 97, 99, 100, 102, 104, 108, 119, 125, 126, 128, 136, 149, 150. 151, 152, 153, 154, 156, 163, 164, 166, 167, 175, 179, 180, 184, 189, 190, 192, 193, 195, 197, 198, 202, 203, 205, 206, 207, 208, 213, 216, 217, 219, 224, 225, 227, 229, 230, 232, 237, 238, 240, 242, 254, 255, 262, 265, 266, 272, 275, 276, 281, 282, 283, 285, 291, 292, 296, 298, 300, 301, 306, 308, 311, 317, 322, 326, 329, 330, 335, 338, 339, 341, 342, 347, 349, 351, 352, 357, 358, 361, 362, 364, 365, 379, 381, 382, 385, 389, 393, 394, 399, 401, 402, 408, 418, 419, 431, 435, 439, 440, 451, 453, 456, 465, 466, 468.
   Harbor, 144, 465.
   North Battery, 465.
   South Battery, 465.
   Streets, 414.
Bounty for scalps, 230, 280, 283, 288.
Money, 267, 275.
Bourn, Capt. ——, 188, 196, 201, 225, 227, 232, 243, 266, 267, 273, 275, 276, 286, 288, 290, 297, 299, 300, 301, 302, 306, 307, 311, 324, 347.
Boyes, Robert, petition of, 439.
Brackett, Capt. Anthony, 424, 427.
Bradbury, Ensign, ——, 310.
Bradford, 190.
   Peres, 423.
Bragdon, Lieut. ——, 349.
   James, 392, 393.
Brandy, 158.
Bread Corn, 456.
Breddeane, James Jr., 341, 348.
Brenton, Jahleel, too long in Europe, 71; surveyor of woods, 98.
Brick, 456.
Bridger, J., letters of, 119, 125, 126, 128, 129, 130, 134, 142; vote of thanks to, 125; mentioned, 134, 172.
Brimhall, George, 424, 427.
Bristol County, Mass., Indians of joined the Provincial forces, 287, 306, and did garrison duty, 347.
   England, servants imported from, 107.

Brouillan, Jacques François de, Governor of Acadia, letter of, 96, 97; mentioned, 22, 28, 104.
Brown } Sergt. ——, 187, 188, 199,
Browne } 201.
   Lieut. Allison, letter of, 182; mentioned, 233, 315, 316.
   Benjamin, 33, 102.
   Robert, of Plymouth, 212.
Brunswick, 108, 163, 327.
Buckminster, Lieut. ——, 147.
Bucknam, Samuel, 421, 423, 427.
Bullman, Dr. ——, 183, 184, 185, 217, 321.
Burinston, Mr. ——, deputy, 121, 126.
Burnet, Gov. William, letter of, 234, 235; mentioned, 336, 346. 423, 428, 430, 448.
Byfield, Col. Nathaniel, 87, 95, 102.

C

CABEC, 157.
Cachnawages } the, 241, 336, 382.
Cagnawaga }
Calais, 169.
Calef, Mr.——, 273.
   Jos., 427.
Calendar, the, new style, 308, 309.
Camblette, 142.
Cambridge, goal, 297.
Came, Samuel, 191.
Canada, 3, 9, 21, 23, 44, 58, 65, 72, 75, 90, 91, 100, 108, 109, 113, 117, 144, 155, 156, 165, 215, 227, 233, 235, 236, 246, 247, 272, 293, 294, 328, 334, 336, 339, 341, 351, 352, 355, 356, 357, 360, 362, 365, 367, 368, 370, 371, 373, 375, 376, 378, 379, 380, 383, 386, 388, 391, 393, 395, 397, 399, 401, 404, 410, 413, 460, 461, 462, 466.
   Indians, 402, 461.
Canady } Capt. William, letter of,
Canedy } 240; mentioned, 244, 341, 350; *see* also Kanady.
Canebec, *see* Kennebec.
Cannawoses, the, 367, 375, 379, 383, 388.
Cannebick, *see* Kennebec.
Canso, 110, 160, 291, 444.
Cape Ann, 61.
   Breton, 110, 113, 114, 117.
   Cod, 122.
   Elizabeth, 179.
   La Héve, 83.
   Neddick, 193.
   Neger, 303; *see* also Negue.
   Newagin, 49.

Cape, *continued.*
  Porpois, 179, 186, 212, 233, 266, 303.
  Sable, 15, 18, 32, 365, 386, 405.
  Sable Indians, 299, 405, 408.
  Seples, 386.
Capon, ——, not an envoy but a comissary, 176.
Captives, given to soldiers, 3; to be delivered without ransom, 9; Indians forced them to return home, 93; released by Indians, 154; as pilots, 155; taken at Kennebec River, 165; escape of Peter Tallcot, 232; Hanson family reach New York, 328; in safety, 363; returned to Wenungenit, 365; killed by Indians, 371, 375, 380, 383; misinformation concerning, 371; not all returned, 383.
Carbass, Mr. ——, Secretary, 167.
Cargill, David, petition of, 439.
Carkesse, Cha., letters of, 114, 115, 116.
Carleyle } Ensign John, 248, 282.
Carlile
Carolinas, the two, 456.
Casco Bay, noblest in New England, 49; trading-house at, 74, 85; colony to be erected at, 163; prisoner escaped from, 192; men to cruise in, 204; a soldier posted at, killed, 231; Saunders to report to, 284, 285; Indians to hold a conference at, 298; Slocum wanted at, 299; Harmon at, 327; Smith ordered to, 329, 330; Indians to make treaty at, 409; the treaty of, 412, 413; mentioned, 87, 95, 179, 209, 257, 258, 259, 332, 353, 354, 375, 376, 390, 406, 407, 419, 423, 428, 429, 431, 432, 459.
  Fort at, burned, 49, 51; new one erected, 74, 85, 99; one needed at, 429; mentioned, 93, 207.
  Harbor, 429.
Casteen, *see* St. Castine.
Castle Island, 42, 99.
Cattle Mills, 260.
Chamblé, 109, 337.
Chapman, John, 353.
Charles I, 25, 26, 74, 130, 436, 441.
Charles II, 17, 28, 29, 30, 79, 80, 81, 82.
Charlestown, 7, 150.
Charters, *see* Patents.
Chebecto, 32.

Chesly, Capt. ——, 278.
Chester, 431.
Choate, Samuel, 190.
Christian, 272, 273.
Chub, Capt. ——, 252.
Church of England in Boston, 443.
Cinow, 362.
Claims of Toppan, Christopher, 445.
Clark, Ensign ——, 194.
  Lieut. ——, 403, 406, 409, 410.
  Thaddeus, 424.
Clergymen sent to the Indians, 59, 69, 85; allowance for only one in Boston, 443; *see also* Ministers.
Clothing in trade, 1; imported, 111; of home manufacture, 122.
Cloven Cape, 83.
Cochecho, 252, 278, 318.
Cochron, James, 247, 255.
Cocoa Nuts, 260.
Cod Fish, 112.
Coffin, Peter, 56.
Coinage, needed, 110, 414.
Cole, William. 445.
Coleby, Mr. ——, 162.
College of Dean Berkeley, 444.
Collossians, 63, 65.
Comeso Quantic, fort at, 49.
Comshite, John, 300.
Concord, 284.
Conefixit, 445.
  Falls, 445.
  River, 445.
Conference of Capt. John Gyles with the Indians, 385.
Connecticut, 107, 109, 209, 210, 211, 228, 241, 295, 323.
  River, 380, 393, 397.
Connawol, 356.
Connawoses, 379.
Conscience, liberty of, 134.
Consegon, 445.
Convin, Jonathan, 102.
Cooke, Elisha, report of, 149; mentioned, 102, 126, 127, 129, 134, 135, 136, 137, 138, 148, 150, 432, 441, 442, 454, 455, 467.
Cooper, William, 427.
Coram, Mr. ——, 121.
  Thomas, letter of, 436, 438.
Corn in trade, 1; poor in Canada, 113; imported, 456.
Cornwell, Capt. ——, 280, 281.
Cotton, 143.
  Rev. ——, 62.
  Wool, 122.
Cox, Capt. ——, 201.
  Messrs., 208, 209.

INDEX 475

Craggs, James, 116, 117.
Cranston, Samuel, letter of, 328 329.
Cromwell, Oliver, 26, 27, 78, 79, 83.
Crosby, Jos., 285.
Crosses of silver given to Indians, 59.
Crown Point, N. Y.
Crowne, John, his title to Penobscot, 25, 29, 30, 74; petition of, 74, 82, 83; report on his petition, 86.
  Point, Maine, 27, 29, 79.
  William, 27, 28, 29, 78, 79, 80, 81, 82, 84.
Cuckhold's Point, 48.
Cumings } Arch'd, letter of, 291;
Cummins } mentioned, 265.
  Mr. ——, 164.
Currency, 110, 112, 261, 414; *see* Bills of Credit,
Cutt, Richard, 191.
  Robert, 190.

D

DAQUIELL, MONS., 233.
Damariscotta } 354, 355, 445.
Damasscotta }
  Fresh Pond, 445.
  River, 47, 204, 445, 462.
  River, Fresh Falls, 445.
Damariscove Island, fort on, 49.
Danforth, Thomas, 149, 423, 425, 426.
Dartmouth, England, 12, 107.
D'Aulney, Charles de Menon, 75, 76, 77, 81, 177.
Davenport, Richard, letter of, 184; mentioned, 185.
Davis, Elisha, 119.
  Ezek., 284.
  Richard, letter of, 279, 280.
Deal boards, 15.
Dearing, Clement, 191.
  Roger, 191.
De Bonaventure, Capt. ——, 31.
Defence of Armstrong, Robert, 166.
Delafaye, Ch., letter of, 340; mentioned, 296.
Derry Lough, 163.
Deserters, place to try them, 297, 302.
Devon, Council of, 102.
  County of, 434.
Diaper, 143.
Dimock, Lieut. ——, 268.
Disowning a fortress, 453.
Doctor, a Quack, 167; needed in the army, 183, 184, 185, 187, 218; for Indians, 324.

Dokes, Mr. ——, 216.
Dondomkegon, 95.
Doney, Robin, 11.
Dorchester, 332.
Doucett } John, Lieut.-Gov. of
Dowcett } Nova Scotia, 281, 285.
Dover, N. H., 328, 431.
Dow, Elisha, 160.
  Henry, 56.
Downer, Benjamin, 179.
Druggets, 142.
Drugs, 264.
Dublin, Ireland, 106, 107.
Dudley, Gov. Joseph, 252, 438.
  Sir Matthew, 173.
  William, letter of, 241, 242; message of to House of Representatives, 416; mentioned, 136, 156, 157, 178, 211, 428.
Dueling, law against, 441, 442.
Dummer Island, Fish Market, 221.
  Island, Grape Street, 221.
  Jeremiah, letter of, 143; mentioned, 149, 167.
  Samuel, 167.
  William, letters of, 165, 166, 175, 178, 180, 201, 202, 218, 223, 224, 225, 232, 244, 246, 249, 256, 257, 267, 270, 272, 275, 276, 285, 287, 292, 297, 305, 306, 307, 308, 317, 321, 323, 335, 351, 353, 358, 359, 362, 364, 368, 370, 392, 393, 398, 399, 405, 406, 407, 408, 431, 434, 450, 451, 468, 469; message of, 417, 418, 420; mentioned, 134, 143, 146, 161, 162, 168, 179, 181, 182, 183, 184, 185, 189, 190, 191, 192, 193, 194, 195, 196, 197, 198, 199, 201, 202, 203, 204, 205, 206, 207, 208, 209, 213, 215, 220, 224, 229, 230, 232, 233, 234, 235, 237, 238, 241, 243, 246, 254, 265, 266, 268, 271, 273, 274, 277, 279, 281, 282, 288, 289, 290, 298, 299, 300, 301, 302, 304, 308, 311, 312, 313, 315, 316, 319, 320, 324, 326, 328, 331, 332, 333, 334, 336, 337, 338, 339, 340, 341, 342, 349, 350, 351, 352, 354, 355, 356, 358, 359, 360, 362, 366, 367, 370, 371, 372, 373, 374, 375, 376, 377, 378, 379, 383, 385, 386, 388, 390, 391, 400, 401, 403, 404, 405, 409, 410, 412, 413, 418, 448, 451, 457, 461, 466.
Dunbar, Col. David, letters of, 440, 444, 451, 453, 458, 468; mentioned, 431, 434, 445, 446, 447, 449, 450, 468.
Dunsmore, John, 154, 156.
Dunstable, 268, 272, 287, 350.

Dunston, 186.
Durrell, Capt. ——, 214.
Dutch, the, 29, 30, 77, 81, 260.
Duties on shipping, 114, 115, 116, 117.

E

EAST GREENWICH, 436.
East India, 158.
Eaton, Capt. ——, of Salisbury, 373.
  Moses, 246.
  Samuel, 373.
Edgar, an Indian, 157.
  Henry, 175.
Edgeremet, 10.
Eels, 156.
Elliot, Capt. ——, 160.
  Robert, 56.
Emerson, the Rev. Mr. ——, 167.
England, 4, 5, 6, 8, 16, 18, 26, 64, 66, 71, 78, 79, 82, 90, 96, 101, 108, 109, 119, 122, 123, 158, 167, 169, 176, 414, 437, 439, 440, 443, 444, 451, 452, 455, 457, 458, 459, 460, 463, 464.
English, the, trade with Indians, 1; Indian war broke out with, 1; chiefs sue for peace and continue the war, 1, 2; the conquest of Canada of value to, 3; the French instigated the war with, 8; regulations between the Indians and, 9, 91; expelled from St. Johns, N. F., 12; Acadia regained by, 17; discovered Nova Scotia, 26; St. Estienne desired the protection of, 27; discovered Penobscot, 30, 75, 81; not allowed to fish or trade on French territory, 31, 33, 104; Jesuits stir up the Indians against, 58; St. Castine a friend of, 58; those at Woodstock and New Oxford alarmed, 68, 69; the French determined to hold lands belonging to, 72; the Estiennes had been in the service of, 75; to besiege New York (1654), 77; French priests and missionaries to be expelled from the territory of, 85; the Indians to be supplied by, 90; Indian boys not to be sent to learn of, 92; Indians desire a banner of, 93, 94; captives still with Indians, 95; Indians to

English, the, *continued*.
  be fixed in the interests of, 99; to seek the Mohawks in time of war, 153; boundary between the French and, 176; Indians in a rage because hostages had died with, 207, 208; boys retaken, 215; Mohawks kill cattle of, 246; Indians desire peace and just methods with, 251; many truces broken with, 252; bodies of those killed in Lovewell's fight sought, 271; Penobscots seize vessels of and become pirates, 280, 284, 289; attack St. Castine, 313, 314; story denied, 326, 327; Indians expected to be defrauded by, 343; Indians must pay for creatures they killed belonging to, 355, 356; Indians must live in peace with, 356; further depredations of the Indians, 363; the French endeavor to prevent the peace between the Indians and the, 367, 373, 386, 408; their religion compared to that of the Jesuits, 384; not treacherous, 388; Indians prevented from killing, 391, 392; Loron to be treated as a friend of, 393; attacked while the treaty was being discussed, 408; Indians will quit the country or live like, 449; the French will not like the planting of a colony at Fredericksburg, 461; Indians desire to be at peace with, 461; mentioned, 9, 19, 35, 44, 52, 53, 63, 95, 99, 112, 115, 275, 360, 371, 383, 386, 395, 396, 405, 422, 440, 466.
English Grass, not grown in Canada, 113.
Espagned } 397, 447.
Espequead
Ercegontagog, 371, 392, 398, 405, 408.
  Indians, 376, 386, 392.
Essex County, 6, 33, 119, 237, 287.
Estienne } *see* La Tour.
Etienne
Eveleth, Mr. ——, 213.
Exeter, 120, 431.

F

FALMOUTH, burned, 50, 51; messenger came to for a doctor,

INDEX 477

Falmouth, *continued.*
183; Nutting the armourer at, 195, 278; Westbrook at, 202; the Mohawks at, 230; officers at neglectful, 258; Capt. Bourne to go to for orders, 268; scouts sent from, 273; three men left in the garrison at, 274; scouts returned to, 277; Capt. Saunders to report for orders at, 284; proposal to try the deserters at, 297, 302; March arrived at, 303; captured sloop at, 304; Trask at, 304; deserters sent to, 315; soldiers to go to, to equip, 320; soldiers delayed at, 327; Smith arrived at, 332; the number of soldiers at to be reduced, 353, 357; Indians will not go there to settle the treaty, 403; Dummer desires to meet Indians at, 406, 410; Gyles to furnish passage of Indians to, 406, 411; Jordan to act as interpreter at, 408; petitions of, 420, 421; irregular proceedings of the selectmen of, 420; second petition of, 421; petition of heirs of, 423; lands are granted to Tyng and others, 424; almost entirely destroyed, 424; petitions to be served on the selectmen of, 427, 428; mentioned, 153, 181, 184, 185, 200, 203, 216, 219, 220, 225, 231, 240, 244, 255, 265, 266, 273, 274, 275, 289, 290, 296, 299, 300, 301, 302, 303, 304, 309, 311, 316, 331, 368, 399, 412, 413.
Ferry Place, 243.
Garrison, 240, 274.
Fayal, 169.
Fayrweather, Thomas, 427.
Fernald, William, 191.
William Jr., 341.
Finns, 112.
Fisheries, 15, 19, 22, 23, 31, 32, 33, 34, 26, 38, 39, 40, 46, 50, 51, 71, 86, 97, 104, 110, 111, 114, 115, 118, 162, 197, 214, 225, 249, 277, 280, 282, 291, 294, 395, 322, 396, 400, 455, 456, 457, 459.
Fitch, Col. ——, 219.
Five Nations, the, 55, 69, 70, 101, 144, 153, 227, 228.
Flanders, 38.
Fletcher, ——, 66.
Forts, to be built and repaired, 13; sold to Temple, 16; built by

Forts, *continued.*
Temple, 17, 22; tools needed to build, 71, 72, 73; the French slighted theirs at St. Johns, 86; places at which they are needed, 100; New Hampshire able to build, 100; many required because of long extent of territory; ammunition needed, 102; desired at Canso, 110; the English will build on their own territory and not ask permission, 178; men would not remain at the, 269, 270; the French demanded the English to quit those on the sea coast, 293; needed at Casco, 429; orders to build not fulfilled, 452, 457, 459; "disowning a fortress," 453.
Fort at Ammassakuntick, 91.
at Annapolis, 294, 295.
at Augusta, 144.
at Berwick, 186, 284.
at Brunswick, 108, 144, 382.
at Casco Bay, 49, 50, 74, 85, 93, 99, 146, 207, 429.
at Castle Island, 99.
at Comeso Quantic, 47.
at Georgia, the Province of, 449, 450, 452, 455, 459.
at Great Island, 45, 46.
at Damarascove Island, 49.
at Marblehead, 108.
at Mechisipi, 69.
at Mississippi, 69.
at Narracomecock, 51, 91.
at Newagin, 49.
at Norridgewock, 49, 91, 108.
at Nova Scotia, 80.
at Onondage's Castle, 70.
at Orange, 42.
at Ossipee Pond, 283.
at Pemaquid, 3, 12, 13, 42, 47, 48, 99, 449, 450, 452, 455, 457, 459, 461, 464, 465, 469.
at Penobscot, 26, 28, 29, 81, 154, 155, 156.
at Piscataqua, 42.
at Port Royal, 97.
at Quebec, 109.
at Richmond, 206, 243, 325, 367, 400, 403.
at Saco, 13, 85.
at St. Georges, 146, 154, 156, 181, 244, 245, 250, 290, 318, 322, 330, 331, 374, 430.
at St. John's River, 77, 83, 86.
at Salem, 108.
at Schenectady, 42.

Forts at, *continued.*
  at Wells, 144, 186.
  at Winter Harbor, 50, 51, 108, 144, 148, 149, 416, 418.
  at York, 186.
  Castle William, 108, 144, 311, 361, 374, 453, 465.
  George, Maine, 163, 247, 256, 353, 373.
  George, N. Y., 152.
  Lovewell's, 278, 283.
  Mary, 148, 179, 182, 212, 232, 279, 281, 282, 353, 416, 417.
  North Battery, 465.
  South Battery, 465.
  William and Mary, 221, 413, 415, 448.
  William Henry, 7.
  see also Garrisons.
Foster, John, 102.
  Thomas, 154.
Fox Islands, 224, 280.
France, 13, 17, 18, 19, 26, 29, 36, 37, 38, 58, 64, 74, 77, 78, 81, 92, 100, 101, 107, 108, 109, 177, 208, 223, 228, 260, 355, 356, 429, 438, 466.
Franklyn, Capt. ——, 191, 202, 204, 205, 286, 288, 289.
Francewexcabe, 379.
Fredericksburg, name of Dunbar's province, 456, 459; two vessels filled with new settlers come to, 460; fishing vessels at, 460; Indians visit, 460, 461, 462; the French may not like to have the English there, 461; the rivers of, 462; *see* also Georgia, Province of.
French, the, assisted and influenced the Indians, 1, 8, 15, 40, 41, 55, 60, 63, 69, 72, 73, 85, 86, 90, 94, 108, 109, 154, 155, 165, 175, 178, 223, 228, 229, 236, 239, 294, 300, 323, 329, 336, 337, 340, 346, 351, 355, 360, 368, 370, 373, 408, 420, 461, 466; illicit trade with, 2; beaten by Phipps, 3; attack the frontier, 5; the Indians must forsake, 9, 176; danger feared from, 12; at Pemaquid, 12, 449, 452, 455, 459, 465; encroachments of, 14, 31, 34, 35, 36, 37, 38, 40, 41, 71, 72, 85, 176, 177, 295, 436, 438; designed to hold control of Indians, 14, 96; the original boundary of the territory of, 15, 58; obstructed the fisheries, 15, 19, 22, 31, 34, 37, 38,

French, the, *continued.*
71, 97, 294, 295; claim to the shore of the Bay of Fundy, 18; renewals of the submission of, 19, 20; the English lost by the rendition to, 19; still holding English territory, 20; disturb trade, 23, 31; had no claim to Nova Scotia, 26, 81; disturb the people at Penobscot, 26; Nova Scotia surrendered to, 29, 75, 80; Penobscot delivered to, 29, 76, 83, 87; had no claim to Penobscot, 30, 81, 82, 87, 176, 177; threatened to seize English vessels, 31, 40; seized fishermen, 32, 33, 34; designs of, 38, 40; have the best part of St. Georges' River, 46, 47; destroyed fort at Pemaquid, 47; burned fort at Casco Bay, 49; besieged Wells, 51; revenge of, 52; cruelty of, 52; St. Castine exposed the designs of, 59; captured by the Dutch at Penobscot, 81, 82; have a large part of the trade with the Indians, 85; slighted the fort at St. John's, 86; improving garrisons at Port Royal and St. Georges, 86; seduced the English, 90; Indians not to trade with, 90, 99; Indians not to assist in the wars of, 91; a potent enemy, 102, 110; had no fortification at Cape Breton, 110; as hunters, 113; fishery at Cape Breton, 114; to swear allegiance to King George, 123; still hold English prisoners, 165, 207, 294; fermented war, 229, 293; cause not supported, 236; privileges ariving to their plantations, 260; demand Acadia and Nova Scotia, 294; aim to hold jurisdiction over the Indians, 294, 295, 346, 367, 373, 379; seize vessels at Cape Neger, 303; endeavor to prevent treaty between the English and the Indians, 367, 373, 386, 408; meditate mischief against fishermen, 396; sent out Indians to attack the English while the treaty was being discussed, 408; the territory of the Penobscot advantageous to, 438, 439; the Indians sent to know about the English at Fredericksburg,

INDEX 479

French, the, *continued.*
461; mentioned, 67, 68, 70, 117, 118, 123, 344, 384, 396, 404, 417.
French Indians, 109, 272, 336, 382.
Mohawks, 272.
Friars, the, 76, 146, 154, 215, 246, 300; see also Jesuits.
Frontenac, Louis de Baude, Count de, 51.
Frost, Major ——, 195.
Fryer's Island, 46.
Fryor, Nath., 56.
Fuller, John, 56.
Fulling Mills, 142.
Furs, 112, 113, 399, 402, 403, 460.

G

GARRISONS, to be repaired, 152; men needed in the, 186; fears that they will be surprised, 192, 195; people ordered to the, 197; attacked at Arrowsic, 199, 200, 201; at St. Georges attacked, 205, 206; Indians near the one at Winter Harbor, 231; forces at can't be reduced, 266, 267, 328; to be guarded against a surprise, 318; to be strengthened and protected, 347; Indians frequented, 357; Jesuits forbidden to hold services in, or near, 430.
  at Annapolis, 176.
  at Arrowsic, 144, 199, 200, 201, 290.
  at Black Point, 265.
  at Casco Bay, 85, 99.
  at Crowne's Point, 29.
  at Falmouth, 240, 274, 278.
  at Georgetown, 151.
  at Negue, 29.
  at North Yarmouth, 212.
  at Pejepscot, 163, 164.
  at Pemaquid, 99.
  at Perpooduck, 202.
  at Port Royal, 86.
  at Richmond, 148, 195, 225.
  at St. Georges, 86, 156, 205, 206, 290, 366, 367, 390, 418.
  at Small Point, 197.
  at Spurwinck, 212, 273, 292.
  at Wells, 152.
  Bucknam's, 212.
  Cutts, 190.
  Ferry, 278.
  Frost's, 195.
  Grey's, 286.
  Heath's, 225.
  Jordan's, 212.

Garrisons, *continued.*
  Parker's, 333.
  Sawyer's, 243.
  Scales', 333.
  Woodside's, 163, 164.
  Yorke's, 202.
  see also Forts.
Gendall, Walter, 149, 424.
George I, 123, 139, 154, 176, 413, 415.
George II, 415, 446, 447, 460, 461.
Georgetown, 150, 161, 196, 199, 224.
Georgia, Province of, named, 440, 452, 456; may have a resident bishop, 443; a place for Dean Berkeley's college, 444; should have free trade, 444; Dummer doubted Dunbar's right to exercise authority in, 450, 451, 457, 466; a distinct government to be established there, 452; Massachusetts had no jurisdiction over, 452; settlement begun, 454, 455, 459; conditions and rent proposed to settlers, 455; name changed to Fredericksburg, 456, 459; land claimed by others, 456, 460, 464; prosperous outlook of, 456, 457, 458, 464, 465, 466; fort at rebuilt, 459; claimants hold a meeting and decide to send an agent to England, 458; rivers of explored, 462, 463; country of, described, 462; Dunbar burned thirty canoes, 463; a nursery for the navy, 463; the future value of the province to England, 464; should be annexed to Maine, 468; *see* also Fredericksburg.
Germans, 158.
Germany, 457.
Gerrish, John, 56.
  Paul, 137.
  Timothy, 137.
Gerritse, Roger, 373.
Ghent, Elizabeth, 445.
Gibbons, Maj. ——, 77.
Gibson, the Rev. ——, 146, 147.
Gillis, Thomas, 200.
Glasgow, 107.
Gold, Capt. Joseph, 290.
Gooch, Capt. James, 44.
Gorges, Sir Ferdinando, 149, 425.
Gorham }
Gorhain } Maj. ——, 275, 325.
Grand Menan, 289.

Grandfontaine, Chevalier Hubert d'Andigny, 17.
Grant, Mr. ——, 286, 304.
   Capt. James, letter of, 318, 319; mentioned, 310, 318, 319, 347, 349, 350.
Grants, *see* under Patents.
Grape Street, 221.
Grass, English, not grown in Canada, 113.
   Samuel, 314.
Gray, Capt. John, letters of, 219, 255, 265, 266; mentioned, 185, 220, 259, 303, 327.
Graylock, 337, 358, 359, 364, 371, 372, 374, 378, 381.
Great Island, 42, 45, 46.
   Fort, 46.
Great Lakes, the, 113.
Great River of Canada, *see* St. Lawrence River.
Green Island, 206, 212.
Greenland, 183.
Grey, James, 286.
Groesbuk, Stevans, 373.
Gruett, Joseph, 56.
Gulf of St. Lawrence, 57.
Gulston, Ralph, letter of, 428, 429; mentioned, 412.
Guns, in trade, 1.
Gunsmith, *see* Armourer.
Gyles, Capt. John, conference of, 383, 384, 385, 386; letters of, 245, 246, 247, 255, 256, 359, 360, 370, 371, 375, 376, 379, 383. 385, 387, 389, 390, 397, 398, 403, 405, 408, 409, 430, 445, 446; memorandum of, 388; memorial of, 387; mentioned, 195, 230, 240, 256, 257, 266, 274, 361, 362, 364, 374, 377, 378, 381, 391, 392, 393, 396, 399, 406, 409, 410, 431, 446, 447.

H

HALEY, MR. ——, 433.
Hall, Edward, 172.
Hamelton. 157.
Hamilton, Mr. ——, 433.
Hammond, Maj. ——, 433.
   Jonathan, 45.
   Jos., 191.
Hampshire County, 207, 227, 381.
Hampton Court, 145.
Hansard, 157.
Hanson, John, 328, 329.
   Thomas, 137.
Harden, Stephen, 204, 232.

Harman } Capt. and Lieut.-Col.
Harmon } Johnson, letters of, 188, 282, 283, 327, 333; mentioned, 147, 160, 162, 179, 187, 189, 191, 192, 193, 194, 199, 202, 203, 204, 205, 206, 216, 217, 219, 222, 226, 229, 232, 238, 248, 249, 258, 259, 285, 286, 292, 301, 310, 320, 321, 331, 332, 335, 339, 341, 369.
Harvard College, 72.
Harvey, Sergt. ——, 205.
Hassel, Benj., brought news of the death of Lovewell, 268, 269; ill management of, 269, 270; to go with Tyng against the Indians, 271; ill, 272; letter of, 268.
Hatfield, 364, 374.
Hathorne, John, 102.
Hatters, 112.
Heath, Capt. Joseph, letter of, 194, 195, 206, 207, 229, 230, 309, 310, 366, 367, 368, 379, 380, 401, 403, 410, 411; mentioned, 148, 162, 179, 182, 205, 217, 225, 226, 246, 250, 305, 310, 311, 312, 320, 321, 327, 354, 381, 385, 393, 398, 399, 401, 407.
——, a brother of Capt. Joseph, 185.
Hegon, John, 379, 393, 405.
Hemp, 123, 124, 433, 440, 441, 456, 464, 465.
Henry, Hugh, 259.
Higginson, John, 33, 102, 433.
Hill, Abr., 57, 87.
   Nath., 56.
Hilliard, David, 33.
Hilton, Lieut. ——, 147.
Hinckes, John, 56.
   Capt Samuel, letters of, 179, 180, 212, 213, 231, 232, 281, 283; mentioned, 279.
Hinty, Mr. ——, 457.
Holland, 29, 77, 81, 260.
   Henry, 334, 336, 337, 338.
Holman, Capt. ——, 267.
   Mr. ——, 275, 276.
   Hugh, 285.
Homespun, 143.
Hood, Joseph, 300.
Hopkins, Samuel, 196.
Hornebrook, John, 11.
Horses, 112, 115, 260, 265.
Houghton, Mr. ——, 69.
   Wm., 37.
House, Lieut. Jeremy, 286, 315, 316, 325.
Hudson Bay, 35, 113.
Hull, 100.

INDEX 481

Hunt, Capt. ——, 2.
  Hannah, letter of, 243.
  Jacob, 243.
  John, letter of, 243.
Hunter, Col. ——, 168.
Hurons, the, 144, 227.
Huske, Capt. Ellis, 158, 169, 170, 171, 172. 303.
Hutchinson, Elisha, 102.
  Em., 102.
Hyde, Edward, Lord Chancellor, 79.

I

IBERVILLE, MONS. DE, led forces against Pemaquid, 12; master of Newfoundland, 12; in New York, 69.
Illinois, the, 144.
Importations, laws concerning, 111, 114, 115, 116.
Independency, 123, 127, 443.
Independent Congregation of Boston, the, 80.
Indians, touching the trade with the, 1, 23, 99; assisted and influenced by the French, 1, 8, 15, 40, 41, 55, 58, 60, 63, 69, 73, 85, 86, 90, 94, 108, 109, 154, 155, 165, 175, 178, 223, 228, 229, 236, 239, 293, 294, 300, 323, 329, 336, 337, 340, 343, 346, 351, 355, 367, 368, 369, 370, 371, 373, 408, 420, 461, 466; the war of 1638, 1; illicit trade with the, 2; attacked the frontier towns, 5; the submission of Aug. 11, 1693, 7, 11, 176, 177; to forsake the French, 9, 91, 99, 176; not to disturb the English, 9; to be ruled by English justice, 9, 10; led by the French against Pemaquid, 12, 450, 452; the French mean to control, 14, 96, 294, 295; will scorn the English, 14; cause of their trouble with the English, 14; should assist neither the English nor French in war, 24; still held as prisoners by the English, 31; on the Kennebec claims of the French, 31; a war prevented by Bamet, 44, 53; never occupied lands at the mouth of the Piscataqua, 46; burned fort at Casco Bay, 49, 50, 51; their forts a means of correspondence, 51; besieged Wells and burnt Fal-

Indians, *continued.*
mouth, 51; cruelty of, 52, 55; those from Natick stir up war, 53; in need, 53; to be subdued or exterminated, 55; to go to Pennycook, 59, 68; ministers sent to, 59, 69, 85, 94, 133, 385; crosses given to, 59, 60; treated as slaves or soldiers, 60; must be driven from the towns, 63; they withdrew, 64, 65; to make war against the Mohawks, 65, 72; the English fear an outbreak, 69, 73, 85, 192, 195, 210, 211; Bellomont's encouragement to the, 69, 70; a fort wanted for them, 71; in mischief at Kennebec, 72; told to shun the English, 72; trading house built for, 74, 85, 99; treaty of 1701, 88; want to trade, 89, 91; and rum, 89, 345; to induce their neighbors to join the English, 91, 92; an armourer to settle with the, 91; will not send boys to the English for an education, 92, 93; forced captives to return home, 93; want a trading house at Merry Meeting, 93; used French colors, 93; desire an English flag, 94; raised a pyramid on treaty-ground, 95; to release captives, 95; cruelties to be avoided, 96, 103; may join in war with the French, 100, 101; had little difficulty in attacking the frontier, 100; the Five Nations a barrier, 101; have advantage over the English, 102; number of civilized, 106; number of enslaved, 106; Jesuits should not be allowed among the, 110; bring furs from the far west and north, 113; the aim of the planters is to convert, 144; shot a man at Richmond, 148; not hindered by fort at Winter Harbor, 148; attacked St. Georges, 150, 154; attacked a party at Merry Meeting, 150; at Long Reach, 150, 151; robbed the whites, 151; at Wells, 151, 152, 189; Mohawks as deputies, 153, 272; at Arrowsic, 153, 201; to be waylaid, 153, 281; led by a friar, 154; released captives, 154; rebuilt fort at Penobscot, 155; eat seals, 156; at Pejep-

32

Indians, *continued.*
scot, 163, 164; killed the Rev. Joseph Willard, 175, 176; sold land to the English, 177; at Arundel, 182; about the garrisons, 185; the Maquas to protect the whites, 192, 193; at Spurwink, 193; at Winick's Neck, 193; at Kennebunk, 193; Lieut. Harmon marched after, 193, 194, 199; to be ambushed, 194; house for the Mohawks finished, 194; at Georgetown, 199, 200; to be watched on the Islands and rivers, 199, 201, 202, 204, 206, 277, 278, 280, 281, 284; all along the frontiers, 201, 225, 241, 258, 259, 266, 279; at Pernooduck, 202; supposed to be gathering, 203, 208, 210; at St. Georges' River, 205, 251; in a rage because a hostage died, 207, 208; to march upon the frontiers, 208; fears for prisoners in their hands, 208; war against the Eastern, 209; their manner of attacking, 211; at Spurwink, 212; at North Yarmouth, Saco River and Cape Porpois, 212; volunteers sent after, 212; on a privateer, 212, 213, 214, 280, 284; to be prosecuted vigorously, 214; coming from Canada, 215, 352; killed at Norridgewock, 222, 228; under English jurisdiction, 223; in the whale fishery, 225; at Winter Harbor, 231, 232; held at Albany, 233; their envoys depend on Vaudreuil, 236; brought an express to St. Georges, 240; designs of the, 241; desire peace, 242, 249, 251; resolved on war, 256; conference with, 250, 254; Bane and Gyles to lead a party in search of, 256, 257, 258, 274: should have been waylaid, 258, 266; at Black Point, 259, 265, 278, 290; near Cape Porpois, 266; near Pequakett, 268, 269, 270, 272, 278; Tyng sent against, 270, 271, 277; a Mohawk to go with Tyng, 272, 273; to enlist, 275, 276, 286, 309, 324; their enlisting obstructed, 276; tracked by Jordan, 277; the fishing time of, 277; tracked by Chesly, 278, 279; Lovewell wounded some, 279; seize

Indians, *continued.*
English vessels, 280, 284; near Fort Mary, 281; collected at the eastward, 283; infest the coast as pirates, 284; recruits to be divided into two companies, 286, 290; how to be employed later, 286; enlisted from Bristol County, 286, 306, 347; go fishing in stolen vessels, 289; their stillness surprising, 289; supposed to have been at Arrowsic and St. Georges, 290; killed a man at Spurwink, 292, 296, 306; the French mean to manage those on English territory, 295; complain of injustice, 297, 339, 340, 342; defrauded of their pay, 297, 299, 300; Walton to join in the affair with Eastern, 298; concerning the conference at Boston, 298, 305, 332, 351, 382, 385, 394, 401, 402; they prefer to meet at some other place, 298, 299; two more tribes desire to treat, 298, 299; steal vessels at Cape Neger, 303; Dummer has little faith in their sincerity, 305, 307, 318; commanders of the companies of, 307, 311, 312, 347; desert, 312, 315, 316, 325; cessation of arms, 318, 319, 322; to be well received at fort on St. Georges River, 318; Dummer will not send them to assist Armstrong, 323; a doctor for the, 324; commanders of changed, 325; planned an expedition into New England, 329, 334, 338, 352; to be transported to Boston, 330; seen on the frontiers, 331, 332, 334, 337; at Scales' and Parker's Garrisons, 333; Harmon and Moulton to ambush for, 335; sent wampum belts, 336, 376, 377, 386, 390, 395, 399; started to attack frontier, but returned home, 337; still skulking about, 337; false report of intended raid, 339, 341; those in the army desire to be dismissed, 342; reservation for, 343, 344; a rod in God's hand, 344; not to be entirely deprived of rum, 345; concerning the conversion of the, 346; dismissed from the army, 347; delay in their com-

INDEX

Indians, *continued.*
ing, 348; their arms and ammunition delivered, 349; probably at the head of the Merrimac River, 350; called in to make a treaty, 351; capture vessels of Stacy and Chapman, 352, 353; one to be hired as a pilot, 355; secret in regard to the peace, 355; depredations at Montinecous Islands, 355, 356, 357, 360, 363; frequented the garrisons, 357; Gray Lock prepared to attack the frontiers, 358, 359; want a truck-house and gunsmith, 366; the French endeavor to prevent the treaty with the English, 367, 373, 386, 408; those of the east desire a general peace, 368; small skulking parties still out, 369, 372; supplied at the trading-houses, 363; raid on Kennebunk, 370, 371, 375, 380, 383, 388; civil treatment promised those who signed the treaty, 372; the dissatisfied would not make peace, 377, 380, 395, 398; return from Canada to re-occupy their villages, 380, 393, 397; word sent to, to come and settle the peace, 382; conference of Capt. Gyles with, 383, 384, 385, 386; still holding captives, 383; desire a minister, 385; hold a great meeting at Penobscot, 386; supplied at St. Georges, 389; the malcontents started on a raid, but returned, 392; settled at Taconnet, 392; to be encouraged to settle at Norridgewock, 393; Mohawks not to fight the eastern, 394; the dissatisfied will make peace, 395; assembled near Minas, 396; to be protected, 397; hostage to be returned to the, 397; their fishing interrupted by the Irish, 400; assembled at Taconnet, 400, 401, 404; desire food, 401, 402, 404; the tribes most injured by the war, 402; desire Capt. Heath to go to Boston on their behalf, 403; to be notified of messenger's arrival by a gun, 403; have debates on several questions, 404, 405, 408; Dummer's letter to be read to the,

Indians, *continued.*
404, 406, 407, 409, 410, 446; desire the removal of a trading house, 404; names of the chiefs at Taconnet, 404, 405, 406; a child's death causes delay, 405; Dummer's letter to, 405; to ratify the treaty of Casco, 406, 409; passage to be supplied to Falmouth, 406; provisions sent to, 407, 410; instigated by the French to attack the English while the treaty was being made, 408; jealous of the missionary at St. François, 411; the governor to be accompanied by a retinue to meet them, 411; desire a new master at trading house, 416, 418; supplies for the, 417, 420; disturb men cutting masts, 428, 429; Jesuits desire to have one of their number among the, 430; provoked by Massachusetts, 437; a few near the proposed eastern settlement, 442; visit St. Georges, 445; not to be disturbed at Passamaquoddy, 446, 451; may be kept at peace by a fort at Pemaquid, 449, 455; will quit the country or live as the English do, 449; if treated justly in trade they will be friendly with the English, 449; Dunbar had an interview with the, 450; visit Fredericksburg, 460, 461; sent to Quebec about new settlers, 461; beg for presents, 461; presents given them, 462; described by Dunbar, 462; expense of entertaining them, 462; jealous of new comers, 469; mentioned, 12, 22, 40, 43, 50, 55, 66, 99, 108, 109, 117, 157, 160, 176, 180, 181, 190, 192, 209, 210, 217, 224, 226, 227, 228, 232, 233, 234, 235, 237, 238, 239, 240, 241, 244, 245, 250, 255, 284, 296, 309, 313, 324, 326, 334, 342, 343, 346, 353, 354, 355, 357, 365, 375, 376, 379, 380, 390, 394, 395, 396, 399, 403, 413, 419, 422, 431, 437, 457, 458, 464, 466.

civilized, number of, 106.

friendly, 275, 276, 286, 292, 297, 299, 300, 301, 309, 312, 343, 392.

the Mountain, 386, 408.

the Southern, 383, 384.

Indians, *continued.*
see also Canadian and French and the names of the tribes.
Indigo, 260.
Ingogen Cape, 83.
River, 83.
Inhabitants of Massachusetts, number of, 106.
Instructions for Noyes and Appleton, 287.
Saunders, Capt. Thomas, 284.
Shute, Gov. Samuel, 145.
Ipswich, 213, 287, 290.
Ireland, 106, 111, 115, 163, 262, 440.
Irish, 440.
Jacobite, an, 159, 166, 168, 303.
settlers, 409.
Iron in trade, 112.
Irwyn, Capt. ——, 457.
Isle of Orleans, 109.
Shoales, 212.

J

JACKSON, BENJAMIN, letter of, 41; mentioned, 11.
Geo., 191.
Jacobite, An Irish, 159, 166, 168, 303.
Jaffrey, George, 158.
Jaques, Col. ——, 258.
Lieut. ——, 248, 282.
James I., 16, 25, 26, 31, 83, 84, 441.
James II., 30, 56, 82, 441.
Jaquesh, *see* Jaques.
Jefferies, David, 38, 136, 172.
Jeffers, Capt. ——, 66, 67, 70, 71.
Jeffery, Lord. 22.
Jeggels, Capt. William, testimony of, 32, 33.
Jekyll, John, 265.
Jenkins, Thos., 191.
Jersey, the Earl of, 57, 66.
Island of, 106, 107,
Jesuits, the, an injury to the public, 49; at Narracomecock, 51; stir up the Indians, 58, 69, 72, 73, 85, 94, 108, 110, 175, 239, 242, 293, 334, 336, 337, 343, 346, 367, 369, 371, 373, 383, 384, 402, 420, 430, 461, 466; tell of the designs of the French government, 72; to be expelled, 85; letter of, read at the peace conference, 386, 387; endeavor to prevent the peace between Indians and the English, 408; desire to have one of their number at Wanopolos Rial, 430; not permitted to

Jesuits, *continued.*
hold service in or near the garrisons, 430; built a church at Norridgewock, 430; mentioned, 375, 378, 404, 405, 461; also called Black Coats, and Friars.
Jewett, Nehemiah, 106.
Jimmison, Elihu, 191.
Job, David, 300.
John, an Indian, 92, 93.
John Negon, 379, 393, 405.
John Sheepscot, 10, 11.
John "Signum," 11.
John's Island, 48.
River, 462.
Jones, Samuel, petition of, 419.
Jordan } Mr. ——, 179.
Jordon }
Lieut. Dominicus, 242, 243, 273, 277, 280, 292, 301, 309, 311, 320, 421, 424, 427.
Jeremiah, 421, 427.
John, 421, 427.
Nathaniel, 421, 427.
Robard, 421.
Robart, 427.
Capt. Samuel, letters of, 328, 400; mentioned, 242, 320, 330, 341, 351, 407, 421.
Solomon, killed, 212.
Thomas, 421, 427.
Journal of House of Representatives, 152.
Jummoway, 410.

K

KAHTON, BAMET, 44.
Katerramogis, of Norridgwock, 10.
Keensotuk, 65.
Kembal, ——, 190.
Kenady } Capt., 180, 205, 215,
Kennedy } 292, 296, 301, 312, 321; *see* also Canady.
Kennaway, Tom, 300.
Kennebec, 316, 386, 431, 432.
Indians, 53, 108, 110, 383, 387, 404, 405.
River, the French claim it as a boundary, 14, 31, 34, 40, 72, 86; of value because of the lumber near, 15; safe for large ships, 48; Indians at in mischief, 72; Westbrook at, 161, 221; prisoners taken at, 165; scouts at, 199, 256, 257; cessation of arms at, 317, 322; no hostility beyond the, 349, 350;

INDEX 485

Kennebec River, *continued.*
  a marker to be set up at, 356; the Indians hunting near not to be disturbed, 380, 393; Dummer at, 431; mentioned, 47, 49, 51, 81, 182, 204, 216, 217, 221, 225, 332, 391, 436, 440, 444, 451, 452, 455, 459, 462, 463, 468, 469.
Kennebunk, 188, 193, 303, 370, 375, 380, 383, 388.
  River, 204.
Kent, Capt. ——, 180.
Kettler in trade, 1.
Kimbolt, ——, 445.
Kingston, 201.
Kittery, ammunition needed at, 152; value of Cutt's house at, 190; soldiers wanted at, 196; stout men to be sent from, 279; has no ensign, 340, 341; mentioned, 341.
Knight, John, letter of, 259.
  Nathan, letter of, 193.

L

Laborie, J., letter of, 59; mentioned 69.
La Chassaigne, M. de, Governor of Montreal, 233.
La Chasse, Père, 211, 367.
Laffevre, ——, 176, 177.
La Néve, 83.
Lambert, Wm., 265.
Lane, Lieut. John, 191, 203.
La Tour, Charles St. Estienne, 16, 25, 26, 27, 74, 75, 77, 78, 84.
  Claud, 25, 26, 74, 75, 77, 78.
  Port of, 83.
Lawrence, Robert, 424.
Lead in trade, 1.
Leather, home manufacture of, 112.
Lechmere, Thomas, memorial of, 260, 265.
Legon ⎫
Leagon ⎬ Jno., 247.
Samson, 247.
Ledgel, Col. ——. memorial of, 1.
Leighton, John, 191.
Letters of,
  Addington, Isaac, 73, 74, 103, 104.
  Appleton, Col. John, 290.
  Arressegontoogook, 400.
  Bacon, John, 324.
  Bellomont, the Earl of, 65, 67, 68, 71.

Letters of, *continued.*
  Blechynden, Chas., 142, 143.
  Bridger, J., 119, 125, 128, 129, 134, 142.
  Brouillan, Gov. J. F., 96, 97; answer to the same, 103, 104.
  Brown, Allison, 182.
  Burnet, Gov. William, 234.
  Canedy, William, 240.
  Carkesse, Cha., 114, 115, 116.
  Coram, Thomas, 436.
  Council and Representatives, 103, 104.
  Cranston, Samuel, 328.
  Cumings, Archd, 291.
  Davis, Richard, 279.
  Delfaye, Ch:, 340.
  Dummer, J., 143.
  Dummer, William, 165, 175, 180, 201, 209, 218, 223, 225, 244, 246, 249, 256, 257, 270, 272, 275, 276, 285, 287, 292, 297, 300, 306, 307, 308, 317, 321, 335, 351, 353, 358, 359, 362, 364, 368, 392, 393, 397, 398, 399, 405, 406, 407, 431, 450, 468.
  Dunbar, Col. David, 440, 451, 453, 458.
  Grant, Capt. James, 318.
  Gray, John, 219, 255, 265.
  Gulston, Ralph, 428.
  Gyles, Capt. John, 245, 246, 355, 370, 375, 376, 379, 383, 385, 389, 397, 398, 403, 408, 409, 430, 445.
  Harmon, Capt. Johnson, 188, 282, 327, 333.
  Hassell, Capt. Benj., 268.
  Heath, Capt. Joseph, 194, 206, 229, 309, 310, 366, 367, 379, 401, 410, 411.
  Hincks, Capt. Samuel, 179, 212, 231, 281.
  Holland, Henry, and others, 333, 336, 337.
  Hunt, John and Hannah, 243.
  Jackson, Benjamin, 40, 41.
  Jordan, Samuel, 328, 400.
  Knight, Nathan, 193, 259.
  Laborie, J., 59.
  Livingston, Philip, and others, 371.
  Minot, John, 208, 250, 254, 342, 347.
  Moulton, Jeremiah, 198.
  Mountfort, Edmund, 239.
  Nelson, John, 13, 16, 37.
  Parker, James, 230.
  Partridge, Capt. Samuel, 364, 374.

Letters of, *continued.*
  Penhallow, John, 150, 196, 199, 224.
  Penobscot Chiefs, 446.
  Pepperell, William, and others, 190, 340.
  Phipps, Sir William, 2, 4.
  St. Castine, Joseph Debadis de, 313, 314.
  Saunders, Thomas, 238.
  Schuyler, John, 233, 240.
  Sharpe, Richard, 159.
  Shute, Samuel, 104, 105, 108.
  Smith, Capt. Thomas, 357, 360, 374, 388.
  Stacy, Samuel, 352.
  Stevenson, James, 352.
  Stoddard, John, 298, 299, 309.
  Stoughton, William, 34, 84, 86.
  Thaxter, S., and Dudley, W., 241.
  Toppan, the Rev. Christopher, 354.
  Trescott, Zach., 156, 157, 207.
  Tyng, Eleazer, 268, 271, 277.
  Vaughan, Wm., 390, 391.
  Villebon, Chevalier de, 30.
  Wainwright, John, 213, 298, 299, 308, 309.
  Walton, Sha., 308, 309.
  Wells, 43.
  Wenogent } 365, 409.
  Wenungenet }
  Wentworth, Gov. John, 255, 278, 283, 411, 415, 448.
  Westbrook, Col. Thomas, 146, 147, 153, 156, 159, 160, 161, 181, 182, 183, 184, 185, 187, 188, 189, 190, 191, 192, 193, 195, 197, 199, 201, 202, 203, 204, 205, 206, 207, 215, 216, 220, 221, 226, 238, 243, 248, 259, 266, 273, 274, 277, 288, 289, 290, 292, 296, 299, 300, 304, 310, 311, 312, 316, 320, 331, 333, 334, 337, 338, 339, 341, 349, 350, 353, 357.
  Wheelwright, John, 151.
  Wheelwright, Capt. Samuel, 315.
  Willard, Josiah, 311, 312, 338, 347, 349, 350, 351, 381.
  Woodside, William, 373.
  Woweenock, 400.
  Wyllys, Hez., 235.
    to Massachusetts Agent in London, 227.
Leverett, Thos., 434, 435, 436.
Lewe, Capt. ——, 357.
Lewis, Moses, 56.
Lexington, ——, 87.
Ligett, William, 154.

Limerick, Thomas, Earl of, petition of, 56; answer to, 57; referred to, 102.
Lincoln, County of, 435.
Lindall, James, 423.
Linens, 111, 115, 122, 142, 143.
Liquors in trade, 1; permit to sell, 230, 231.
Lisbon, 173.
Little River, 315.
Littleworth, 331.
Liverpool, England, 107.
Livingston, Philip, letters of, 371, 373; mentioned, 334, 336, 337, 352.
Lock, Gray, *see* Graylock.
Loggers, 140.
Logwood, 264, 265.
L'Omery, 83.
London, 16, 37, 66, 67, 70, 93, 106, 107, 159, 167, 227, 435.
  Custom House, 116, 414.
  Royal Exchange, 66, 70.
  Sun Coffee House, 66, 67, 70, 74.
  Tower, 80.
  Whitehall, 4, 7, 41, 57, 87, 116, 130, 143, 265, 340.
Long Reach, 150.
Loraant } 362, 379, 385, 387, 393,
Lorone } 394, 396, 447.
Lorie, Mr. ——, 207.
Lothrop, Barnabas, 102.
Lone, 157.
Lovell } Fight.
Lovewell }
  Capt. John, 268, 269, 270, 271, 272, 273, 278, 279, 283, 284, 289, 290.
Lowder, Henry, 73.
Lucia, Island of, 438.
Lues, 355.
Lumber, 113, 119, 120, 124, 126, 127, 128, 168, 172, 173, 183, 203.
  see also Timber.
Lynde, Joseph, 102.

M

MACHIAS, 281.
  Indians, 383.
  River, 27, 79, 82, 84.
McKenney, Henry, 278.
Macphedris, Capt. ——, 173.
Madockawando } cousin to Wenon-
Madochawando } gakewet, 10; signed treaty of Aug. 11, 1693, 10.
Madagwunesseak, 95.
Madaumbis, 11.

INDEX

Madeira Wines, 115.
Madumbessuck, 181.
Maherimet, Jno., 95.
Maine, Province of, 3, 57, 127, 129, 135, 136, 149, 423, 425, 431, 432, 434, 436, 450, 451, 453, 454, 455, 459, 463, 468.
Malalemet, 372.
Manahadas, 77.
Manning, Nicho., 11.
Manoor, Lieut. ——, 308.
Manufactures, 111, 112, 122, 123, 142, 143, 261, 414.
Maquas, the, 64, 65, 95, 185, 192, 295.
Marblehead, 100, 208, 209, 212, 314, 342, 353, 397.
  Fort at, 108.
March, Lieut James, affidavit of, 303; mentioned, 304.
  Lieut. John, 147.
Markham, Lieut. Moses, 246, 342.
Marks of,
  Ahanquil, 11.
  Arressegontoogook, 401.
  Aten, 447.
  Awansomech, 11.
  Bomageen, 11.
  Doney, Robin, 11.
  Edgeremet, 10.
  Epagned, 447.
  Katerramogis, 10.
  Loron, 447.
  Madackawando, 10.
  Madaumbis, 11.
  Moxist, 10.
  Nathaniel, 11.
  Nitamemet, 11.
  Phil-Ousa, 11.
  Quonach, 447.
  Sunc, 401.
  Webenes, 11.
  Weenokson, 10.
  Wenungenit, 366.
  Wessembomet, 10.
  Woweenock, 401.
  Wyworney, 401.
Marquoit, 245, 246, 247, 248, 255.
Marshall, Grace, 427.
Mary, Queen, 8, 131.
Mascarene ⎫ Paul, Governor of
Maskarene ⎭ Nova Scotia, 412.
Massachusetts, 7, 8, 9, 17, 19, 33, 34, 42, 45, 52, 55, 57, 87, 88, 98, 104, 106, 111, 114, 116, 117, 119, 123, 143, 144, 149, 151, 152, 156, 163, 166, 195, 209, 222, 237, 263, 293, 295, 296, 309, 319, 332, 341, 356, 358, 362, 367, 375, 378, 412, 423,

Massachusetts, *continued*.
  424, 425, 431, 436, 437, 447, 449, 459, 468.
Masts, 15, 40, 41, 120, 125, 136, 137, 158, 169, 171, 172, 173, 294, 295, 412, 428, 429, 432, 434, 444, 446, 454, 458, 462, 463.
  men, 136.
  ships, 428, 459.
Mather, the Rev. Increase, 6.
  the Doctors, 165.
Maylem, Joseph, 427.
Meadows, Ph., 57, 87.
Mechisipi, fort at, 69.
Mediterranean Sea, 112.
Meeting, a praying, 375, 403.
Memorandum of Gyles, Capt. John, 388.
Memorials of,
  Council and Representatives of Massachusetts, 98, 102.
  Gyles, Capt. John, 358, 359, 387.
  Lechmere, Thomas and others, 260, 265.
  Massachusetts in regard to religion, 130.
  Nelson, John, 20, 21, 25.
  Rayment, Lieut. William, 52, 54.
  Romer, Wolfgang Wilhelm, 45, 52.
  Touching the trade with Indians, 1.
Mendon, 64.
Menis, 351, 396.
Mentrie, 25, 75.
  Lord of, *see* Alexander, Sir William.
Mereliquish ⎫
Merlequash ⎭ 18, 83, 84.
Merrimac River, 8, 241, 350, 431.
Merry Meeting, 93, 150, 410.
Messages of,
  the Governor, 411.
  Dummer, 417, 418, 420.
Metropolis of America, the, 262, 443.
Michel, Mr. ——, of Spurwinck killed, 193.
Miles, Morgan, 200.
Militia, the, 106, 279.
Millett, Thomas, 328.
Minas, 18, 19, 124, 351, 356.
Ministers for Indians, 59, 69, 85, 94, 133, 385; *see also* Clergymen.
Minot, John, letters of, 208, 209, 250, 254, 342, 347; mentioned, 249.
  Stephen, 342, 347.

Minzier, Mr. ——, 171.
Mississsippi, fort at, 69.
 River, 109, 113.
Mitchell's, 186.
 Mr. of Spurwink, 193.
Modochawando, 10.
Mohawks, the, 153, 157, 194, 195, 207, 209, 230, 246, 272, 394.
 the French, 272.
 the Praying, 386, 387, 392.
Mohegans, the, 65, 72.
Moidores, 158.
Molasses, 112, 260.
Monhegan, 203.
 Indians, 72.
Montegue, the Duke of, 438.
Montinecous Islands, the, 355, 357, 360, 365.
Montreal, 109, 113, 157, 207, 233, 242, 328, 329, 376.
Moody, Capt. ——, 327, 354.
 Dr. ——, 184.
 Maj. ——, 152.
Moore, Ebenr, 191.
Morril, Nicho., 191.
Moulton, Lieut. ——, 163.
 Capt. Jeremiah, letter of, 198; mentioned, 188, 189, 191, 194, 202, 226, 227, 286, 289, 296, 335, 338, 342.
 Joseph, 191.
Mount Desert, 160, 239, 280, 300, 449.
Mountfort, Mr. ——, 349.
 Edmund, letter of, 239; mentioned, 423.
Mount Hope, 65.
Mountsweeg Bay, 204.
Mowson, 333.
Moxes, 10, 72, 92, 95, 359, 362, 395, 396, 404.
Munrow, ——, 332.
Munsneegs Bay, 445.
 Great River, 445.
 Little River, 445.
Muscongus, 26, 27, 83, 84, 204, 435.
 Company, 441.
 River, 78, 79, 82, 441.
Muslins, 158.
Muster Rolls, 203, 258, 267, 285, 286, 318, 350, 361, 390, 394, 419.

N

NANTUCKET, 122.
Narihwacks, the, 460.
Narrackamagog } 91, 95; fort at,
Narracomecock } 51.

Narragansett, 123, 434.
Narrangawawock, 356, 359, 405.
Nathaniel, 11.
Natick, 53, 343.
 Indians, 344.
Nebon, Jo., 289.
Negroes, 106, 107, 413.
Negue, 27, 28, 29, 79, 303.
Negus, Dr. ——, 183, 184.
Nelson, John, letter of, 13, 16, 37, 39; memorial of, 20, 21, 25; petition of, 16, 18, 20; mentioned, 33, 35, 87, 95.
Nemmageen, 410.
Nenequabben, 63, 64.
Nesket, 313.
Nevis, 413.
New Castle, 45, 46, 123, 222, 298, 448.
 Horse Ferry, 46.
New England, 1, 4, 7, 12, 13, 14, 16, 17, 18, 21, 26, 28, 29, 30, 31, 33, 37, 39, 41, 47, 49, 51, 52, 56, 58, 61, 74, 77, 79, 80, 81, 87, 88, 97, 98, 117, 127, 128, 130, 135, 142, 143, 145, 152, 156, 157, 159, 163, 164, 165, 169, 173, 195, 208, 233, 236, 260, 263, 265, 293, 296, 302, 303, 332, 340, 372, 411, 415, 423, 428, 429, 431, 434, 435, 436, 437, 440, 448, 451.
 Council of, 340.
New Hampshire, 18, 45, 54, 55, 61, 62, 66, 100, 101, 105, 120, 137, 143, 144, 145, 157, 159, 166, 167, 168, 170, 173, 174, 179, 222, 228, 309, 317, 323, 328, 416, 429, 431, 432, 434.
New Jersey, 235.
New Oxford, 59, 68, 69.
New Plymouth, see Plymouth, Mass.
New Roxbury, 59.
New Scotland, 84.
New York, 20, 21, 23, 29, 36, 42, 45, 55, 56, 66, 67, 68, 69, 70, 71, 77, 81, 82, 85, 100, 101, 108, 109, 144, 152, 234, 295, 328, 442.
Newberry, 180, 267, 287, 297, 298, 307, 354, 381, 382.
Newcastle, the Duke of, 263, 457, 458, 468.
Newfoundland, 12, 19, 107.
Newman, Henry, agent for N. H., 145, 168.
Newport, 329.
Newton, Hilbert, 265.
Newtown, 48, 49, 305.
Nicholson, Gen. Francis, 437.

INDEX 489

Nitamemet, 11.
Noble, Ensign ——, 316, 320, 373.
Norridgewock, 10, 72, 95, 157, 175, 215, 218, 222, 225, 226, 228, 229, 230, 246, 324, 342, 343, 347, 349, 356, 359, 369, 385, 392, 400, 401, 402, 405, 410, 436; fort at, 49, 91, 108.
   Indians, 157, 176, 223, 365, 368, 372, 380, 382, 394, 395, 400, 402, 406, 413.
North Carolina, 456.
North Yarmouth, 149, 150, 212, 327, 335, 354, 426.
Northfield, 211.
Norwich, 179, 180.
Nottingham, 431.
   the Earl of, 2, 4, 7.
Nova Scotia, 14, 16, 18, 20, 21, 23, 25, 26, 27, 28, 29, 32, 33, 34, 35, 38, 47, 57, 77, 78, 80, 81, 82, 83, 84, 86, 87, 108, 110, 118, 144, 177, 285, 294, 321, 323, 351, 412, 436, 437, 444, 450, 451, 452, 454, 455, 466, 469.
   Barons of, 25, 28, 75.
Nowell, Capt. ——, 285.
   Peter, 197, 198.
Noyce ⎫ Col. ——, instructions to,
Noyes ⎭ 287; mentioned, 161.
Nutting, Ebenezer; 195, 278.

O

OAKS, 433, 434, 456.
Oil, Whale, 112.
Olbeni, see Albany.
Oldershaw, Mr. ——, 433.
Oliver, Capt. ——, 286, 310, 311.
   Lieut. ——, 161.
Ommaway, 401, 407.
Onedahauet, 386.
Onondage's Castle, 70.
Omery, L', 83.
Orange, 42.
Orders to,
   Harmon, Col., and Moulton, Capt., 335.
   Smith, Capt. Thomas, 329.
   White, Capt., and Wyman, Capt., 318.
Ossipee Pond, 268, 269, 271, 278, 283, 290.
   River, 193, 289.
Otis, Col. ——, 275, 276.
   Jno., 326.
   Joseph, 427.
Otter Creek, 358.
Ousa, Phil, 11.

Owaneco, 65.
Oyster River, 331.

P

PALATINES, the, 457, 464.
Paper money issued, 110; see Bills of Credit.
Paris, 13, 16, 35.
Parker, Mr. ——, 232.
   Sergt. ——, 300, 302.
   James, letter of, 230, 231.
Partridge, Col. Samuel, letters of, 364, 365, 374; mentioned, 359, 371, 381.
   William, 56.
Pass, a desired by Davenport, Richard, 184, 185.
   for Saccamakten, 180.
   Corns, 200.
Passamaquoddy, 244, 280, 281, 285, 300, 312, 446.
Patents, Charters and Grants,
   Alden, Capt. John, 61.
   Alexander, Sir William, 25, 74, 75, 83, 84.
   Beauchamp and Leverett, 434.
   Boston, 443.
   Charles I, 130.
   Cromwell, Oliver, 83, 84.
   D'Aulnay, Charles de Menon, 177.
   Georgia, Province of, 443.
   La Tour, Charles de St. Etienne, 27.
   Limerick, the Earl of, 56, 57, 102.
   Massachusetts Bay, 3, 17, 127, 467.
   Muscongus, 441.
   New England, 134.
   Nova Scotia, 82.
   Temple, Sir Thomas, 15, 40.
   William and Mary, 131.
   York, Duke of, 20.
Paul, Jacob, 300.
Peace, see Treaties.
Pearis, 405.
Peas, 113.
Pegnohket, 44.
Pegwoket, 108.
Pejepscot, 163.
Peknabowet, 371.
Pell, Mr. ——, 179.
Peltries, 1, 2, 15, 78.
Pemaquid, treaty of 1693 at, 7; surrendered, 12, 449, 452, 455; 459, 465; Iberville at, 12; fort at to be rebuilt, 13, 449, 457; a boundary, 15, 26, 27, 78, 79,

Pemaquid, *continued*.
82, 84; would have of importance, 47; why surrendered, 47, 48; fort needed at, 48; Earl of Limerick desired grant of, 56, 102; already granted, 57; Capt. Harmon ordered to the neighborhood of, 204; Capt. Cromwell ordered to cruise near, 280; Boyes and Cargill petition for land in, 439; settlement to begin at, 440, 444, 446, 449, 451; boundary of, not to be extended, 447; Dunbar, the new Gentleman of, 447; Dunbar rebuilt fort at, 449, 450, 452, 455, 457, 459, 464, 465; Dunbar settled people at, 455; of an important situation, 457; formally of note, 459; a sagamore offered to sell it to Dunbar, 461; but gave it to the king, 461; mentioned, 441, 442, 456, 458; fort at, 3, 7, 12, 13, 42, 47, 48, 99, 449, 450, 452.
River, 47.
Penhallow, Justice, ——, 192.
Capt. John, letters of, 150, 196, 197, 199, 200, 224; mentioned, 147, 162, 185, 205, 290, 292, 301, 391.
Samuel, 56.
Pennecook } 44, 53, 59, 65, 68, 108.
Pennycook }
Indians, 44, 53, 64, 65, 68, 72.
Pennsylvania, 440.
Penobscot, title to, 25, 30; an English plantation, 26, 30, 75, 81; La Tour built a fort at, 26; resigned to the English, 26, 78; made over to Temple and Crowne, 27, 78, 84; Temple sold his interest to Crowne, 27, 79, 84; Temple captured the fort at, 28; restored to Crown, 28; Temple governor of, 28, 79; leased, 28, 29, 79; delivered to the French, 29, 76, 80, 81, 83, 87; the Dutch at, 29, 78, 81; under the jurisdiction of New York, 29, 81; John Crowne petitioned for, 29, 30; by right it belonged to the English, 30; John Crowne's title to, 74, 82, 87; Willet sent to, 75; D'Aulney bound for, 75, 76; given to La Tour, 77; La Tour governor of, 78; William Crown dwelt at, 79; to be planted, 81; basis of the

Penobscot, *continued*.
claims of the French, 87, 176, 177; Indians at, 110, 144, 215; soldiers march to, 162, 218, 222; Le fevre has no right there, 176, 177; expedition against, 215, 221, 250; sloops ordered to, 221; new route to, 222; Indians may infest the coast of, 280; Indians at, to be watched, 280, 281, 305, 306; Indians planted corn, 305; the government sent to vessel, with flag of truce to, 309; Wenungenit, sachem at, 365, 366, 375, 386; a missionary at endeavored to prevent the proposed treaty, 367; Indians hold a meeting at, 386, 404, 410; mentioned, 11, 20, 25, 83, 84, 155, 181, 216, 218, 230, 245, 311, 370, 438, 447; fort at, 154, 155, 156.
Bay, 154, 244, 312, 438.
Indians, letters of the chiefs, 446; mentioned, 58, 92, 108, 176, 216, 223, 289, 299, 301, 306, 317, 318, 322, 323, 330, 339, 349, 351, 355, 357, 360, 365, 372, 380, 382, 383, 387, 395, 397, 401, 404, 405, 406, 407, 410, 411, 413, 430, 445, 460, 461.
River, 8, 27, 47, 57, 58, 108, 146, 217, 226, 280, 281, 434, 435, 437, 438.
Pentagöet, 20, 83, 311.
Pepperell, Col. William, letters of, 190, 340, 341; mentioned, 348.
William Jr., 191.
Pequaharet, 11.
Pequakett, 108, 182, 232, 268, 270, 271, 279, 289, 410.
Indians, 380.
Perkins, Mr. ——, 182.
Pernooduck, 202.
Perot, ——, an interpreter, 33.
Perpooduck, *see* Purpooduck.
Perry, ——, of Spurwink, house burned, 212.
Pesomscott, *see* Presumpscot.
Petitions of,
Armstrong, Robert, 302.
Boyes and Cargill, 439.
Crowne, John, 82, 86.
Falmouth, 420, 421.
Heirs of the Proprietors of Falmouth, 423.
Jones, Samuel, 419.
Limerick, the Earl of, 56.
Nelson, John, 16, 18, 20.

INDEX 491

Petitions of, *continued*.
  Woodside, James, 163.
Petit River, 280, 281.
Philip, King, 65.
Phillips, Col. John, 87, 95, 158, 166, 444.
  Richard, Governor of Nova Scotia, 110, 111, 451, 452.
  Walter, 445.
Phipps, Capt. Samuel, 150.
  Sir William, 2, 3, 4, 5, 6, 7, 8, 10, 19, 34, 176.
Physicians, need in army, *see* Doctors.
Piggwacot } *see* Pequakett.
Pigwoket }
Pines, 119, 135, 138, 412, 428, 429, 432, 433, 450, 456, 462, 469.
Pinkerin, John, 56.
Pipe Staves, 354.
Piracy, 101.
Pirates, 214, 280, 396, 404; *see* also under Privateers.
Piscataqua, 12, 60, 61, 62, 153, 192, 212, 242, 357, 360, 432, 459; fort at, 42.
  River, 15, 45, 46, 295, 431.
Pitch, 433, 456.
Plaisted, Capt. Elisha, 172.
Plymouth, Mass., 26, 75, 81, 100, 212, 303.
  Council, 434, 436, 441, 455.
Point Barbekin, 47.
Pollexfen, J., 57, 87.
Popple, Allured, 291.
  William, 21, 105, 114, 125, 128, 129, 143, 412, 449.
Population of Massachusetts, 106, 117.
Port Royal, 3, 18, 19, 20, 21, 77, 83, 86; fort at, 97.
Portsmouth, 46, 159, 183, 187, 222, 250, 255, 278, 282, 283, 284, 298, 349, 391, 392, 411, 415, 448.
  Goal, 192.
Portugal, 112.
Pousland, Saml., 427.
Powder in trade, 1.
  Money, 145.
Praying Meeting, a, 375.
Prescott, Dr. ——, 272.
Press, the restricted, 105, 106.
Presumpscott River, 181, 238, 277, 335.
Prichard } Lieut. John, 304, 326.
Pritchard }
Priests, *see* Jesuits.
Prior, Mr. ——, 87.

Privateers with Indians on board, 212, 213, 214, 280, 284, 306; *see* also pirates.
Proone, Nathaniel, printed a book without a licence, 105.
Pullen, Eliner, 427.
Purpooduck, 202.
  Point, 216.
Pyke, Ensign ——, 188.

Q

QHOUACH, 447.
Quack Doctor, a, 167.
Quakers, 132, 133.
Quebec, 58, 90, 109, 113, 114, 157, 165, 175, 176, 438, 461, 466.
Queries, 106, 108, 109, 110, 111, 112, 113, 114, 117, 118, 119, 143, 144.
Quincy, J., 448.
Quinovis, 367, 375, 379, 383, 388.

R

RABAROT, 405.
Ragatewawongan, 10, 11.
Rallé, Sebastian, 175, 178, 223, 369.
Ramesay, Claude de, Governor of Montreal, 113.
Rawson, Rev. ——, 69.
Ray, John, 170.
  Nathl., 265.
Rayment, Lieut. William, Memorial of, 52, 54.
Recancourt, 242.
Relation of Alden, Col. John, 57, 60, 62.
Religion, Memorial of Massachusetts in Regard to, 130.
Rendax, the, 336.
Render, James, 56.
Report of Cook, Elisha, 149.
  on Crowne's Petition, 86.
Resolutions in regard to settling the Eastern parts, 354.
Revenue Commission, 30.
Rhode Island, 122, 123, 263, 295, 323, 329.
Richardson, Capt. Robert, 271.
Richmond, 148, 150, 183, 184, 188, 194, 198, 204, 206, 207, 217, 218, 225, 226, 247, 256, 312, 342, 388, 400, 406, 407, 409, 410; fort at, 206, 243, 406, 407.
River of Canada, *see* St. Lawrence River.
Robin, an Indian, 92, 93.

Robinson ⎫ Capt. David, 66, 67, 70,
Robison ⎬ 71, 73, 74.
Robeson ⎭
   John, 421, 427.
   Jno., 427.
Rockamagook, 333.
Romer, Wolfgang Wilhelm, his considerations concerning forts, 42, 43; memorial of, 45, 52; forts built under his directions, 100.
Rose, Joshua, 154, 155, 156.
Rowley, 290.
Rowsick Island, 48.
Rum, Indians want none sold, 89; in trade, 260; not to be kept entirely from the Indians, 345; a cask of, lost, 389.
Russell, Ja., 102.
Rutland, 175.
Ryswick, 25, 37, 97, 104, 436, 455.

S

SABIN, EBEN, 64.
   John, 63, 64, 65, 69.
Saccamakten ⎫ 180, 181, 249.
Sackamaten ⎭
Saccaristis, 249, 289, 290.
Saco, 51, 169, 192, 204, 350; fort at, 13, 85.
   Falls, 51, 181, 194, 199, 203, 232, 274, 335, 351, 400.
   Mills, 244.
   Pond, 269.
   River, 8, 50, 181, 186, 193, 203, 204, 212, 238, 268, 277, 283, 350, 351, 417.
Safransway, 156, 157.
Sagadahoc, 57, 203, 205.
St. Castine, Jean Vincent, Baron de, refused submission to England, 20; his house pillaged, 20; instigated Indian war, 21; traded with Alden, 58; hoped to become an English subject, 58; feared to write to the governor of New England, 58; family of, 58; married an Indian, 58; a chief of the Indians, 58; would not visit the French governor, 58; exposed the designs of the French, 59.
   Joseph Debadis de, his vessel taken by the English, 313, 314, 326, 327; used treacherously, 314, 326; desired to be paid for his loss, 314; his story denied, 326, 327; a letter of his read at the conference, 386;

St. Castine, Joseph Debadis de, continued.
   brought message to Capt. Gyles, 430; mentioned 300, 304.
St. Croix River, 20, 40, 47, 58, 78, 84, 87, 280, 436, 440, 452.
St. Denniscourt, 74, 75.
St. Estienne, see La Tour.
St. François, 242, 410, 411.
   Indians, 241, 364, 371, 372, 375, 380, 382, 402.
St. Georges, 146, 150, 154, 161, 182, 186, 204, 215, 217, 218, 219, 239, 240, 299, 304, 308, 318, 322, 331, 332, 348, 351, 357, 362, 365, 374, 378, 383, 388, 392, 403, 409, 410, 430, 440, 456; fort at, 146, 154, 156, 181, 244, 245, 250, 290, 318, 322, 330, 331, 374, 430.
   River, 15, 35, 40, 41, 46, 47, 80, 86, 154, 176, 181, 205, 245, 318, 322, 355, 366, 375, 379, 385, 409, 418, 446, 447, 456, 459.
St. Johns, 12, 40, 58, 312, 383, 386, 465; fort at, 77, 83, 86.
   Indians, 405.
   River, 32, 40, 77, 281, 289, 299, 344.
St. Lawrence River, 14, 113, 114, 429, 438.
Sakenelakud, 371.
Salem, 6, 33, 61, 100, 142, 143, 314; fort at, 108.
Salisbury, 373.
Salmon Falls, 194, 199, 274, 275, 431.
   Fishing, 50.
Salt, 114.
Salter, Capt. ——, of Isle of Shoales, 212.
Saltonstall, Gov. Gurdon, 209, 237.
Salutation of Wenoggenet, 390.
Saunders, Capt. Thomas, instructions to, 285; letter of, 238, 229; mentioned, 215, 217, 238, 240, 297, 304, 306, 307, 308, 310, 329, 330, 373, 381, 389, 393, 396, 398, 399, 403, 409.
Savages, see Indians.
Saw Mills, 124, 412, 432, 454, 463.
Sawyer, ——, 243, 244.
   John, 421, 427.
Sayes, Col. ——, 179.
Sayward, Joseph, 191.
Scales, 186.
Scalps, 230, 280, 283, 288.
Scarborough, 152.
Schenectady, 42.
Schohanadie Indians, the, 382.

INDEX

Schuyler, John, letters of, 233, 234, 240, 241; mentioned, 256.
Myndert, 373.
Scotland, 16, 17, 74.
Scouts, *see* under Soldiers.
Seals eaten by Indians, 156.
Sebacomon, 379, 393.
Sebago Pond, 181.
Secanecto, 124, 396.
Sedgewick, Maj. ——, 26.
Sergeant, Peter, 102.
Serges, 142.
Servants, white sold in the Province, 106, 107.
Sewall, Jno., 427.
Saml., 102, 427.
Shapley, Nicho., 191.
Sharp, Richard, letter of, 157, 159; mentioned, 166, 167, 169.
Sheconneto, 124, 396.
Sheep, 122, 123.
Sheepscot, 444.
Great Neck, 445.
River, 47, 204, 442, 462.
Shepardson, William, 411.
Sherburn, Capt. Henry, 158, 173.
Ships, *see* Vessels.
Shot in trade, 1.
Shute, Gov. Samuel, letter of, 148; mentioned, 117, 119, 128, 145, 150, 151, 153, 156, 165, 168, 171, 251, 368, 370.
Siganectoe, 18, 20.
Signums, *see* Marks.
Silks, 158.
Sincler, John, 120.
Six Nations, the, 295, 336.
Skawinnadie, the, 336.
Skillen, Benj., 421, 427.
Slade, Mr. ——, Deputy, 432, 433, 434.
Slaves, number of in the Province, 106.
Slopers, Capt. Henry, 158,
Slocum, Capt. ——, 182, 220, 289, 298, 299, 304, 306, 307, 331, 332.
Small Point, 197.
Smith, James, (Judge), 128, 129, 130.
John, of Falmouth, 423.
John, of New Hampshire, 56.
John, of North Yarmouth, 149.
Samuel (serjeant) 182.
Capt. Thomas, letters of, 357, 358, 360, 374, 375, 388, 389; orders to, 329; mentioned, 331, 342, 347, 348, 349, 398, 399.
Soldiers receive captives and plunder, 3; Wells supplied with, 43; Indians as, 60; go to Nova

Soldiers, *continued.*
Scotia and Penobscot, 78; paid by La Tour, 78; number of the militia, 106; number in Canada, 113, 118; none on pay in eastern forts, 144; to be released or retained, 159, 160; desert, 161, 179, 186, 307, 329; army in poor condition, 161, marched to Penobscot, 162; must keep a strict watch, 183; dismissed, 190, 195, 196, 201; 203, 283; few impressed, 192; to range the woods for Indians, 194; recruits, 195; at Frost's garrison, 195, 196; desire to go home, 197, 198; to be sent in a fishing vessel, 201; behave gallantly in the west, 201, 202; number of in the service, in 1724, 203; needed at Richmond, 206, 207; to scout with Mohawks, 207; needed from Connecticut, 209, 211; to go against Penobscot, 215; to be sent to surprise the enemy, 225, 226; to go to Piggwacot, 232, 233; well trained, 249; should have been sent to waylay the Indians, 258, 266, 267, 274; muster rolls to be made out, 203, 258, 267, 285, 286, 318, 361, 390, 394; start for Cape Porpois, 266; bounty for, 267, 275; at Ossipee, 268, 278; refused to remain in fort, 269, 270; men to be impressed for, 271, 275, 276; men from the east, wanted as, 279; trouble concerning the wages of, 285, 286; volunteers for the east, 287, 290; Harmon to enlist men, 292; sent to Albany, 295; deserters to be tried, 297, 302; to be drawn from Berwick and Wells, 304, 310; desire to be dismissed, 311; dismissed, 312; Grant's volunteers to be disbanded, 318, 319; to go to Berwick to equip, 320; not to be marched out of the Province, 323; delay at Falmouth, 327; to march to Berwick, 333, 335; under Grant to go to Norridgewock, 347; a list of dead and missing wanted, 347; forces to be reduced, 353; released, 392, 393.
Solomon, 64.
Sosep, 410.

South Carolina, 345, 436.
South Hampton, 107.
Southack, Capt. Cyprian, 46, 72, 344.
Southwell, Edward, 117.
Southworth, Lieut. Edward, 306.
Spain, 112, 158, 173, 413, 434, 449.
Spruce 456, 462.
Spurwinck, 193, 212, 243, 296, 306. Garrison at, 292.
Stacy, Samuel, letter of, 352.
Stage Gut Point, 51.
Stamford, Lord, 57, 87.
Stanford, Ensign ——, 315, 316.
Steel, in trade, 1.
Stepney, George, 57, 87.
Sterling, Earl of, *see* Alexander, Sir William.
Stevenson, James, letter of, 352.
Stoddard, Col. John, letter of, 298, 299; mentioned 236, 305, 306, 308, 309, 310, 338, 352, 359, 364, 371, 374.
Stoodly, *see* Studley.
Storehouse at Casco Bay, 419.
Storer, Joseph, 45.
Storey, Mr. ——, of Portsmouth, 167.
Stoughton, Lieut. Gov. William, refused to sit on the bench at Charlestown, 6, 7; letters of, 34; 84, 86; mentioned, 30, 32, 87.
Studley, Capt. James, 158, 169, 170, 171.
Sturgeon, 156.
Subercase } Daniel Auger de, 437.
Subrecase
Submission of Eastern Indians, 7.
Suffolk County, 42.
Sugar, 260.
Sunc, Pere, 401, 407.
Surinam, 112.
Swasey, Capt. John, testimony of, 32.

T

TACONNET } 10, 356, 392, 400, 401,
TACONNOCK } 404, 406.
Tailer, William, 211.
Talbert, Mr. ——, 161.
Tallcott, Peter, 232.
Tappan, *see* Toppan.
Tar, 120, 124, 433, 456.
Tarah, Thomas, 300.
Tarbox. Mr. ——, 281, 328.
Tarr, Mr. ——, master of the sloop, 411.
Taylor, John, 136.
Teas, 158.

Teconet, 10; *see* also Taconnet.
Temple, Capt. ——, 163.
Sir William, 15, 16, 17, 18, 20, 22, 27, 28, 29, 30, 40, 47, 78, 79, 80, 81, 83, 84.
Terceira, 413.
Testimony of, Swasey, Capt. John, and Jeggels, Capt. William, 32, 33.
Thacher, John, 102.
Thames River, 70.
Thaxter, Col. Samuel, letter of, 241, 242; mentioned, 178.
Thomas, William, 427.
Tilton, Capt. ——, 200.
Timber, 15, 40, 46, 98, 158, 294, 295, 354, 355, 434, 440, 452; *see* also Lumber.
Title to Penobscot, 25, 30.
Titmouse Island, 160.
Tom, Capt. ——, 53.
Toppan, the Rev. Christopher, claims of, 445; letter of, 354, 355; mentioned, 367.
Topsham, Eng., 106.
Totems, *see* Marks.
Townsend, Col. Penn, 87, 95, 102.
Toxas, 410.
Trade, memorial concerning with Indians, 1; commodities used in, 1; Hunt's illicit, 2; to be governed by the English, 9; locality of New England's chief, 18; hindered, 22, 23, 295; the French threaten concerning, 31; design of the French, 38; value of the Piscataqua River for, 46; value of Pemaquid for, 47; the fishing the principal of New England, 51; with Indians desired, 75, 85, 99, 323, 344, 345; treaty concerning, 89, 90; at Quebec, 109; at Montréal, 109; on the Mississippi, 109; a fort at Canso would assist, 110; discouraged by lack of coinage, 110; paper money issued, 110; to prevent illicit, 111; commodities issued, 112; of Canada, 113; laws concerning, 114, 115, 116; questions concerning, 118; a pernicious material in, 122; wool, 123; with Indians, 239; concerning duties and freighting, 260; with Great Britain, 261; injured by Bills of Credit, 261, 262, 263, 264, 265, 291, 467; value of the fisheries of New England, 294;

INDEX 495

Trade, *continued.*
between the French and Indians, 323; none with Indians till after the peace, 330; at a stand still, 413; Bills of Credit and the, 413, 414; balance in favor of England, 414; the Indians', 417; should be free in the Province of Georgia, 444; if just with the Indians they will be friendly with the English, 449; will improve when a fort is built at Pemaquid, 455.
Lords Commissioners of, 18, 21, 25, 37, 41, 66, 67, 72, 82, 86, 104, 114, 130, 142, 143, 157, 165, 166, 221, 260, 291, 296, 302, 303, 340, 368, 436, 439, 440, 441, 444, 448, 451, 452, 453, 454, 457, 464, 465, 466.
Trading Houses, at Casco Bay, 74, 85, 99, 419; wanted at Merry Meeting, 93; for the Maquas, 185; the keeper of one a rogue, 254; will keep the Indians in the interest of the English, 344; Indians supplied with all necessaries at the, 363; amount of furs at, 403; talk of moving one, 404; new master desired at Winter Harbor, 416; mentioned, 361, 362, 363, 366, 461.
Trask, Samuel, redeemed, 304; to be a pilot, 304.
Treaties of,
Albany, (Oct., 1700), 88.
Breda, (July 31, 1667), 14, 17, 19, 29, 35, 40, 87.
Casco, (June, 1701), 87, 95, 395, 406, 469.
Neutrality, (1686), 22, 31, 37.
Pemaquid (Aug. 11, 1693), 7, 10, 13, 176.
Ryswick, (Sept. 10, 20, 1697), 21, 25, 37, 97, 104, 436, 455, 459.
Utrecht, (April 11, 1713), 177, 178, 294, 368, 437.
Treaties with,
Eastern Indians, (1725), 250, 353.
Maquas, (Oct., 1700), 95.
Mohawks, (1724), 209.
Norridgewocks, (July 10, 1727), 382, 394, 406, 407, 409, 410, 419.
Penobscots, St. Johns and Cape Sable Indians, (1725), 298, 299, 323, 351, 385, 413.
St. François Indians, (1725), 241, 371, 380.

Trees, 98, 119, 120, 134, 136, 137, 140, 158, 172, 432, 433, 434, 446, 450, 454, 456, 462, 469.
Trescot, Ensign ——, 257, 266, 396.
Mr. ——, 381.
Zech., letters of, 156, 157, 207, 208.
Trois Rivieres, 109.
Truck Houses, *see* Trading Houses.
Master, 361, 418.
Turpentine, 112, 124.
Tyler, John, 427.
Tyng, Edward, 427.
Capt. Edward, 424.
Eleazer, letters of, 268, 269, 271, 272, 277; mentioned, 270, 283.

U

UTRECHT, 177, 178, 294, 368, 437.

V

VAN BRUGH, PETER, 334, 336, 337.
Van Rensselaer, Henrich, 334, 373.
Vaudreuil, Philip de Rignaud, Marquis de, 175, 207, 223, 233, 234, 236, 293, 352.
Vaughan, Mr. ——, of Piscataqua, 357, 360.
William, letter of, 390, 391.
Vernon, James, 18, 65, 67.
Vessels, number of and tonnage of those belonging to Massachusetts, 111, 114; duties on, 115, 116, 117; number of the French in the fisheries, 114; the Penobscots seize some belonging to the English, 280; Indians use them to infest the shore, 284; stolen to use in fishing, 289; seized at Cape Neger, 303; taken from Indians, 304; Indians stole those belonging to Stacy and Chapman, 352, 353; mast ship of New Hampshire, 459.
Dolphin, 32.
Endeavor, 169.
Elizabeth, 73.
Envieux, 31.
Industry, 411.
Lancaster, 172.
Martha, 419.
Merry Meeting, 284, 298, 329.
Renomée, 69.
Samuel and Mary, 4.
Sarah, 457.
Sea Flower, 473.
Sparrow, 32.
Stratton's, 148.

Vessels, *continued.*
  Victor, 357, 360, 381, 396.
Villebon, Chevalier de, letter of, 30, 32; mentioned, 34, 40.
Vineyard, the, 267.
Vo, Capt. ——, 245.
Volunteers, *see* under Soldiers.
Vuarre, 74.

W

WAGER, one guinea against thirty, 443.
Wainwright, John, letters of, 213, 298, 299; mentioned, 305, 306, 308, 309.
  Samuel, truckmaster, letter of, 430, 431; mentioned, 430.
Waldo, Cornelius, 423.
  Samuel, 422, 427.
Waldron, Richard, 56, 60, 61, 125.
Walker, Benj., 423.
  John, 423.
Walove, Mr. ——, agent for mast contractor, 454, 463.
Walton, Col. Shadrach, 153, 155, 156, 190, 252, 298, 308.
Wampum Belts, 336, 376, 377, 386, 390, 395, 399, 408.
Wandol, Jacob, 157.
Wanopolas Rial } 430.
Wenopolas }
Wasahombomet, 95.
Water Mills, 260.
Wawenorawot, 386.
Wawhe, 371.
Weaver, Mr. ——, 66, 67, 68, 70, 71.
Webenes, 11.
Weeks, Nicholas, 191.
Weenokson, 10.
Wells, suitably supplied with soldiers, 43; desired ammunition, 43; Indians about, 51, 52, 53, 151, 152, 189; soldiers to be drawn from, 232, 304; a headquarters for troops, 287; Noyes ordered to, 287; men to go to, 291; troops at dismissed, 312; to be guarded, 332; mentioned, 315, 316, 332; fort at, 186.
We-na-muggen, 405.
Wenegonett } letters of, 365,
Wenoggenet } 366, 409; men-
Wenogonet   } tioned, 10, 358,
Wenongahewet } 362, 370, 375, 376,
Wenungenit } 377, 378, 389, 394,
Wenungennet } 395, 399, 403, 404, 405.
Wenemonet, 308, 309.
Wenongahewet, 10.
Wentworth, Capt. Benj., 172, 226
  Lieut. Gov. John, letters of, 255, 256, 278, 279, 283, 284, 411, 415, 416, 448, 450; mentioned, 167, 171, 271, 287, 298, 305, 311, 317, 341, 463.
Wessembomet, 10.
Westbrook, Col. Thomas, letters of, 146, 147, 153, 155, 156, 159, 161, 181, 182, 183, 184, 185, 187, 188, 189, 190, 191, 192, 193, 194, 195, 196, 197, 198, 199, 201, 202, 203, 204, 205, 206, 207, 215, 216, 218, 220, 221, 222, 226, 227, 238, 243, 244, 248, 249, 259, 266, 267, 273, 274, 275, 277, 278, 288, 289, 290, 292, 296, 299, 300, 301, 304, 310, 311, 312, 316, 320, 331, 332, 333, 334, 337, 338, 339, 341, 349, 350, 357; mentioned, 150, 179, 182, 184, 187, 188, 190, 191, 193, 195, 198, 212, 218, 219, 224, 225, 232, 244, 245, 246, 247, 256, 257, 266, 268, 279, 281, 284, 285, 286, 288, 297, 305, 306, 307, 309, 315, 316, 318, 319, 327, 328, 332, 333, 339, 340, 347, 423, 427, 432.
Western Islands, the, 413.
Westfield, 211, 336.
West Indies, 113, 122, 264.
Wewenock, 242.
Wewonorawed, 408.
Whaleboat, service, the, 217, 218, 244, 275, 286, 301, 307, 309.
Whale fishery, the, 225, 347.
Wheelwright, Col. ——, 187, 189, 192, 225, 232, 233, 397, 426.
  John, letters of, 45, 151, 152.
  Capt. Samuel, letter of, 315, 316; mentioned, 310, 333, 334.
White Hills, the, 311.
White, Capt. ——, 271, 277, 318.
Whiting, Samuel, 269.
Whittemore, Mr. ——, 162.
Willard, Capt. ——, 271.
  the Rev. Joseph, killed, 175, 176.
  Josiah, letters of, 311, 312, 338, 347, 349, 350, 351, 381; mentioned, 134, 159, 211, 218, 287, 296, 349, 419, 428, 448.
Willet, Capt. Thomas, 75, 76.
William III, 8, 88, 89, 90, 92, 127, 131, 436, 438, 460.
Williams, Ensign ——, 313.
Wincittico Falls, 445.
Wind mills, 260.
Wines, 115, 158, 169, 170.
Wing, John, 11.
Winick's Neck, 193.

Winnebessehkick, 44.
Winnepesaukee, 204.
Winnett, ——, 219.
Winslow, Capt. ——, killed, 205, 206.
  Lieut. ——, 162.
  Mr. ——, 306.
Winsor, Court at, 326.
Winter Harbor, 232, 298, 305, 351, 416, 417, 418, 459; fort at, 50, 51, 108, 148, 449.
Winthrop, Gov. John, 53.
Witchcraft, 4, 5, 6, 7.
Woahaway, 375.
Wood Island, 46.
Woodman, John, 56.
Woods, Sergt. Nath., 269.
Woodside, Ensign ——, 255.
  Capt. James, 416, 418.
  the Rev. James, petition of, 163, 165.
  William, letter of, 373.
Woodstock, 63, 64, 68, 69.
Woolens, 111, 122, 123, 142, 261, 414.
Woweenocks, the, letter from the chief of, 400, 401; mentioned, 380, 405, 406, 410, 413.
Wowenog, 392, 405.
Wowerena, 356, 405.
Wright, Ensign ——, 192.

Wright, *continued.*
  Lieut. Benj., 312, 376, 378, 391, 392, 393.
Wummock, Aaron, 300.
Wyllys, Hez., letter of, 235, 237.
Wyman, Capt. ——, 318.
Wynongonet, 461.
Wyworney, 401.

X

XAVIER, FRANCIS, 396.
Xtian, 272.

Y

YA-HA-HAM-MA-WIT, 405.
York, 147, 152, 160, 183, 185, 187, 188, 189, 190, 191, 192, 194, 196, 197, 199, 232, 238, 274, 279, 283, 310, 311, 315, 316, 320, 321, 333, 335, 338, 339, 342; fort at, 186.
  Mr. ——, 202.
  Benjamin, 243, 421, 427.
  County, 52, 108, 191, 287, 292, 296, 354, 411, 431.
  Duke of, 29, 441; *see also* James II.
  John, 149.
  River, 190, 196.
Young, Mr. ——, 275.
  Joseph, 191.

www.ingramcontent.com/pod-product-compliance
Lightning Source LLC
Chambersburg PA
CBHW051332230426
43668CB00010B/1244